The Logical Problem
of Language Acquisition

MIT Press Series on Cognitive Theory and Mental Representation
Joan Bresnan, Lila Gleitman, Samuel Jay Keyser, editors

The Logical Problem of Language Acquisition, edited by C. L. Baker and John J. McCarthy, 1981

The Mental Representation of Grammatical Relations, edited by Joan Bresnan, 1982

The Logical Problem
of Language Acquisition

Edited by
C. L. Baker and
John J. McCarthy

The MIT Press
Cambridge, Massachusetts
London, England

This book was set in VIP Times Roman by Village Typographers, and printed and bound by Halliday Lithograph Corporation in the United States of America.

Library of Congress Cataloging in Publication Data

Main entry under title:

The Logical problem of language acquisition.
   (MIT Press series on cognitive theory and mental representation)
   Bibliography: p.
   Includes index.
   Contents: Learnability, restrictiveness, and the evaluation metric / Howard Lasnik—Some issues in the theory of learnability / Kenneth Wexler—A readjustment in the learnability assumptions / Edwin Williams—[etc.]
   1. Language acquisition—Congresses. 2. Grammar, Comparative and general—Congresses. 3. Language and logic—Congresses. I. Baker, C. L. (Carl Lee). II. McCarthy, John J., 1953–   III. Series.
P118.L64   401′.9   81–12351
ISBN 0–262–02159–5 AACR2

List of Contributors

C. L. Baker, University of Texas at Austin
Mark R. Baltin, New York University
Robert Bley-Vroman, University of Texas at Austin
Bezalel Elan Dresher, Brown University
Jane Grimshaw, Brandeis University
Per-Kristian Halvorsen, Massachusetts Institute of Technology
Jonathan Kaye, Université du Québec à Montréal
Howard Lasnik, University of Connecticut
David Lightfoot, Rijksuniversiteit, Utrecht
John J. McCarthy, University of Texas at Austin
Stanley Peters, University of Texas at Austin
Steven Pinker, Harvard University
Thomas Roeper, University of Massachusetts at Amherst
Susan F. Schmerling, University of Texas at Austin
Carlota S. Smith, University of Texas at Austin
Thomas Wasow, Stanford University
Kenneth Wexler, University of California at Irvine
Edwin Williams, University of Massachusetts at Amherst
Ellen Woolford, Massachusetts Institute of Technology

Contents

Series Foreword

The major focus of the series is on theories of mental representation of natural language. The editors hope to provide a forum for—and thereby to encourage—the exciting collaborative work now taking place among linguists, computer scientists, philosophers, and psycholinguists leading toward new cognitive theories of mental representation.

The series will publish original works of book and monograph length as well as unified collections of original articles which emerge from psycholinguistics. Special attention will be given to studies focusing on the formal aspects of mental representation.

Joan Bresnan
Lila Gleitman
Samuel Jay Keyser

Preface

In March 1980, a symposium entitled "The Logical Problem of Language Acquisition" was held under the auspices of the Cognitive Science Center of the University of Texas at Austin, with funds provided by a grant from the Alfred P. Sloan Foundation. This volume contains nine of the ten papers that were presented at the symposium, together with the accompanying discussions. In addition, it contains a paper by Mark Baltin which was presented in Austin during the same week. This paper appears in place of the paper Baltin discussed at the symposium, since that paper was withdrawn from the volume by its author.

The aim of the symposium was to bring together a number of people who had a shared interest in what has been called the projection problem, the learnability problem, or the logical problem of language acquisition. This last term, originally David Lightfoot's, was chosen for the symposium itself and ultimately for this volume. Whatever it is called, this problem is essentially that of determining the lawful relation between early linguistic experience for a human being and the mature unconscious knowledge that results from this experience. The scholars invited to this symposium all share a strongly nativist orientation, believing that human beings possess strong innate predispositions critical to bridging the gap between early experience and eventual knowledge. We felt that it would be more fruitful to choose a list of participants who shared at least this quite minimal common ground than to aim for a completely representative collection of speakers.

Although many people helped us in organizing the symposium and producing this volume, several deserve special thanks. First of all, we are grateful to Stan Peters and Phil Gough, Co-directors of the Cognitive Science Center of the University of Texas at Austin, for providing much encouragement and many helpful suggestions. We would also like to thank Judy Willcott for her invaluable assistance in organizing the symposium and Sondra Brady for her help in preparing the final manuscript. Finally, a special word of thanks to John McNutt of the Thompson Conference Center at the University of Texas; his help in the planning and his painstaking attention to logistical and nutritional matters of all kinds contributed enormously to the success of the symposium.

The Logical Problem
of Language Acquisition

Chapter 1

Learnability, Restrictiveness, and the Evaluation Metric

Howard Lasnik

At least in the last few decades considerations of learnability have played a guiding role in much linguistic research. In particular, there is fairly general agreement that restrictiveness is important. There is substantial controversy, however, over exactly what ought to be restricted and over the nature of the appropriate restrictions. I will explore the question of what has to be learned by the child and the implications for restrictiveness proposals, and I will discuss what I take to be the three major areas of concern: (1) properties of the evaluation metric; (2) restrictions on the class of grammars, particularly as they relate to the evaluation metric; and (3) restrictions limiting the type and amount of data required by the child.

Some Parameters of Restrictiveness

I will begin by examining a number of related proposals that appear in the literature, and I will argue that contrary to appearances certain of them do not in fact bear on learnability. Putnam (1961) presents one very precise and often repeated restriction: that a human language must be a recursive set of sentences. Section V of that article, entitled "The grammatical sentences of a language are a recursive set," includes one argument of particular relevance.

[A] consideration supporting the view that the classification of sentences into grammatical and ungrammatical is a machine-like affair is the teachability of grammar and the relative independence of intelligence level to this skill. Even a person of very low-grade intelligence normally learns both to speak his particular dialect grammatically and to recognize deviations from grammaticalness . . . But an ability of this kind . . . is almost certainly quasi-mechanical in nature. (p. 40)

Levelt (1974) has a more elaborate version.[1]

A non-decidable language is unlearnable, even if the learner benefits from an informant. In short this means that there is no algorithm by which an (observationally) adequate grammar can be derived from a sequence of strings marked "grammatical" and "ungrammatical." If there is no learnability in terms of an algorithm, there is certainly no learnability in terms of human cognitive capacities, given the finite character of the latter. The incontrovertible learnability of natural languages pleads that natural languages be considered as decidable sets. (vol. 2, p. 40)

Left unspecified in these two arguments is the nature of the special problem that would be created for the learner confronted with a non-recursive language.

It is important to note further that these arguments are at best indirect. Language acquisition involves arriving at a particular grammar. The properties of a particular language have no direct bearing on the selection of the appropriate grammar. Rather, it is properties of the class of (biologically) possible grammars that are most clearly relevant to acquisition. Perhaps an extreme case can help to clarify this point. Suppose the theory of grammar allowed exactly one grammar—that is, human biology did not admit of linguistic variation. Suppose further that a person acquired this grammar by exposure to one sentence of the generated language L. To use customary, though perhaps misleading, terminology, L is learnable under the stated conditions. Consider now the possibility that L is not a recursive set of sentences. This changes nothing in the example. Therefore, the logical possibility exists that a nonrecursive language could be learned, contrary to the assertions of Putnam and Levelt. As Hamburger and Wexler (1973, p. 153) point out, "the problem facing the learner is to select a language from a *class* of languages. If the class consists of a single language, then the learner can, trivially, succeed simply by guessing that language, even though the language itself is exceedingly complex."

It is important, then, to clarify what it means to learn a language, and also to specify the properties of the device doing the learning and the procedure it follows. The question then might arise whether the child acquiring a natural language is more like the language acquisition device of the extreme example above, in which case the problem of acquisition is potentially soluble, or more like a device that must search among all logically possible grammars for all logically possible sets. Although Levelt perhaps assumes the latter, linguistic research of the past two or three decades suggests that the former is the case—that is, that biology provides a rich system of principles that severely restrict the class of available grammars.

Interestingly, Gold (1967)—research that Levelt heavily relies upon in his discussions of learnability—admits of exactly this sort of possibility for the learning algorithms considered there. Investigating classes of languages in the Chomsky hierarchy, Gold concludes that "only the most trivial class of languages considered is learnable in the sense of identification in the limit from text" (i.e., from positive instances). Even accepting learnability in the limit as the appropriate model,[2] it does not follow that only a class of finite languages is text-learnable. As the first of three alternative possibilities, Gold suggests that "the class of possible natural languages is much smaller than we would expect from our present models of syntax. That is, even if English is context-sensitive, it is not true that any context-sensitive language can occur naturally. Equivalently, we may say that the child starts out with more information than that the language it will be presented is context-sensitive" (p. 453).

Failure to acknowledge such a possibility is presumably behind the claim in Levelt (1974, vol. 1, p. 123) that "it is impossible to 'learn' an infinite language only on the basis of text presentation." This claim can be construed two ways. If it is construed as a claim about any class of languages whatsoever including an infinite language, it is not correct. For certain trivial cases the incorrectness is immediate—if the theory of grammar allowed but one grammar, for example. The claim fails for more interesting cases as well. As Wexler pointed out to me, it is simple to construct a learnable infinite class of infinite languages. Consider the following class of infinite languages on a one-element vocabulary:

(1)
$L_0 = \{a, aa, aaa, \ldots\}$
$L_1 = \{aa, aaa, aaaa, \ldots\}$
$L_2 = \{aaa, aaaa, aaaaa, \ldots\}$

The following grammars generate the languages in (1), where

$L(G_i) = L_i$

(2)
$G_0 = S \rightarrow A, A \rightarrow aA, A \rightarrow a$
$G_1 = S \rightarrow aA, A \rightarrow aA, A \rightarrow a$
$G_2 = S \rightarrow aaA, A \rightarrow aA, A \rightarrow a$

In general,

(3)
$G_i = S \rightarrow a^iA, A \rightarrow aA, A \rightarrow a$

As shown in Culicover and Wexler (1977, p. 10), this represents a learnable class of grammars: "The function f that learns G simply selects the grammar that generates the smallest set of strings compatible with the data D. It does this by finding the shortest string in D and mapping D into the grammar which generates the language with that string as the shortest string."

If, on the other hand, Levelt's claim is construed as following from Gold's result that "any class of languages containing all finite languages and at least one infinite language [on a fixed alphabet] is not identifiable in the limit from a text" (p. 460), it is simply irrelevant to human language acquisition. Surely, the class of human languages includes no finite languages.

Restricting the Class of Grammars

Levelt (1974, p. 40) offers an additional argument for recursiveness that, unlike the first, apparently concerns the class of grammars: "There remains the methodological principle . . . that the strongest possible model must be chosen for a natural language. On the basis of this principle, the first step after the rejection of context-sensitive models is the decidable subset of type-0 languages." But this seems to deny that the precise nature of the restrictions is an empirical question. As Chomsky (1965, p. 62) points out, "one can construct hierarchies of grammatical theories in terms of weak and strong generative capacity, but it is important to bear in mind that these hierarchies do *not* necessarily correspond to what is probably the empirically most significant dimension of increasing power of linguistic theory."

In contrast, Levelt implies that a priori there is only one relevant parameter—that given by the Chomsky hierarchy. This hierarchy, while providing one interesting and useful metric for the power of a linguistic theory, clearly does not provide the only one. It seems that some researchers, unlike Gold, have drawn the incorrect conclusion that every logically possible theory of grammar must be representable as some concentric circle in the standard illustration (not necessarily a concentric circle already present).

(4)

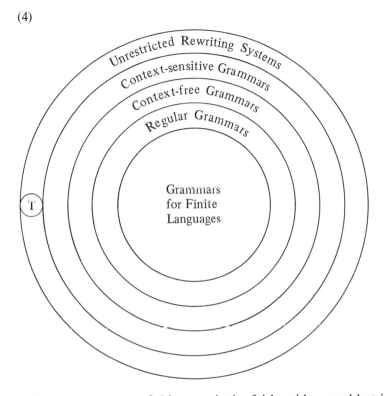

One consequence of this error is the fairly widespread but incorrect assumption that a theory of grammar allowing a nonrecursive recursively enumerable language allows *all* recursively enumerable languages. I will return to this point. Another consequence is the failure to recognize that there must be restrictions "from below" as well as "from above." For example, there are no finite human languages.[3] In the hierarchical model, we might choose to consider concentric doughnuts as the possibilities for the correct theory of grammar. But considerations of restrictiveness do not lead to such a conclusion. A theory not in the hierarchy at all, such as the one labeled T in the diagram, could be more restrictive than any of the others, in the empirically significant sense of restrictiveness. It might also be observed that even if one considered only the circle and doughnut possibilities, the outer circumference of the correct model could not be identical to the boundary of the recursive sets. This is so since there is no decision procedure for the recursive sets, or the nonfinite recursive sets, or the nonregular recursive sets, and so on. Surely, in this realm there is no reason to expect more of biology than of mathematics.

One question that might arise, in fact that has arisen, is whether all human languages are context-free (or context-sensitive, or regular, or something else).

I take it as established that not all context-free languages are possible human languages (presumably not even all infinite context-free languages). But suppose research were to establish that all human languages are context free, that is, that human languages are a proper subset of the context-free languages. Note that this leaves entirely open the question of what types of grammars should be allowed by universal grammar. Suppose that a good approximation is provided by, say, the transformational components of Lasnik and Kupin (1977) operating on $\overline{\text{X}}$ base components.[4] Must such a theory of grammar be given up in favor of a theory allowing only context-free grammars? Clearly not. A theory allowing *all* context-free grammars would be wildly incorrect. The context-free theory must then be restricted, and it is simply unknown whether natural restrictions can be stated such that the grammars permitted are equivalent to those permitted by the restricted transformational theory (and whether a suitable evaluation metric would exist for the set). A priori it would be surprising if that turned out to be the case.

In this regard, much (too much) has been made of the fact that the *Aspects* theory of grammar as formalized by Peters and Ritchie (1973) provides a grammar for every recursively enumerable set. Levelt (1974, vol. 2) concludes that this fact demonstrates the failure of the program defined by Chomsky: "The linguistic consequences of the overcapacity of transformational grammar are great" (p. 151); and "the main problems of linguistics are insolvable by the formal means of the *Aspects* type" (p. 154). This discussion continues: "The principle cause of the undecidability of *Aspects* type transformational grammars is the fact that there is no upper limit to the size of the deep structure of a given sentence . . . It was precisely the purpose of the principle of recoverability to avoid this . . . But on reflection, it is striking to notice how poorly the *Aspects* definition fulfills that original purpose" (p. 154).

An examination of the discussions of recoverability in Chomsky (1965) does not support this position. Especially relevant is the following:

Notice incidentally, that this identity condition [on deletion rules] need never be stated in the grammar, since it is a general condition on the functioning of grammars. This is important, since . . . the condition is not really identity of strings but rather total identity of structures, in all cases in which identity conditions appear in transformations. But to define identity of structures in terms of Analyzability it is necessary to use quantifiers; in fact, this may be the only case in which quantifiers must appear in the structural analyses that define transformations. Extracting the identity condition from grammars, we are therefore able to formulate the structural analyses that define transformations strictly as Boolean conditions on Analyzability, thus greatly restricting the power of the theory of transformational grammar. (p. 225, fn. 13)

The concern is with restricting the class of possible transformations and the proposal is successful, since clearly *Aspects* does not allow as a grammar every function whose range is some recursively enumerable set. Whether or not the grammars permitted by the restricted theory generate solely recursive languages is entirely orthogonal, since the grammar is what must be selected. The only suggestion in Chomsky (1965) that human languages are recursive sets of sentences is based explicitly on an empirical consideration.[5] "This possibility [that the theory of grammar is equivalent in generative capacity to the theory of Turing machines] *cannot be ruled out a priori,* but, in fact, it seems definitely not to be the case [emphasis added]. In particular, it seems that, when the theory of transformational grammar is properly formulated, any such grammar must meet formal conditions that restrict it to the enumeration of recursive sets" (p. 208, fn. 37). The claim about recursiveness thus is not fundamental to the theory but rather is an observation about the theory (as it happens, an incorrect observation, apparently). Nothing more is at stake here.

Peters and Ritchie (1973, p. 82) have made an observation similar to Chomsky's, again "based on empirical research in linguistics." They observe that the grammars that linguists have constructed have the interesting property that there is an exponential bound on the size of a deep structure as a function of the size of its generated sentence. Under this circumstance, the language of the given grammar is recursive. Note that this is not an argument that human languages must be recursive, but rather an argument that they are recursive.[6]

The goal of linguistic research presumably is not to limit the class of grammars to those generating recursive sets, then, but rather to limit the class of grammars to those that are biologically possible,[7] in order to account for the possibility of language acquisition. (See Chomsky, 1976, for elaboration.)

Wasow (1978a) presents a particularly clear explication of the alternative point of view. After observing that many proposed constraints on grammars don't affect the class of languages generated, Wasow advocates "seeking constraints on grammars which will have the effect of limiting the class of transformational languages. Such constraints narrow the notion 'possible human language,' thereby making claims about the limits of language acquisition, regardless of whether the grammars themselves have any psychological reality . . . [C]onstraints which limit the class of languages generable must restrict the class of hypotheses available to the language learner" (p. 85). Wasow contrasts this approach, the L-view, with the G-view, which seeks "limitations on the class of grammars, regardless of whether the limitations restrict the class of languages generated . . . Grammars are descriptions of languages; constraints on grammars which do not constrain the set of languages generable limit only the sorts of descriptions allowable" (p. 83).

If we regard a child who has learned a language as having arrived at a particular mental state characterized in terms of a grammar, restrictions on the class of grammars *are* of importance, in fact are crucial, regardless of the class of languages generated. The child must select the appropriate grammar relying on fixed data; hence, eliminating certain options in advance potentially simplifies the problem.

Although Wasow's discussion implies that languages are what really exist and that grammars are mere descriptions, I would maintain, on the contrary, that languages are essentially artifacts having no independent existence apart from the grammars that generate them. Restrictions on the class of grammars facilitate acquisition by making it possible for the evaluation metric to provide a clear decision. Suppose that many—even infinitely many—grammars are compatible with the data available to a child. The heavier the restrictions on what counts as a grammar, the fewer highly valued grammars will be compatible with the data, no matter how many compatible grammars might be available in total. Imagine, for example, that structural descriptions of transformations have a small upper bound on the number of their terms. Presumably, there could still be a very large number of such transformational components compatible with any given set of data. But these components might vary wildly in the number of transformations they require. This is just the sort of scattering that would facilitate acquisition.[8]

Note further that limitations on the class of languages need not perforce entail limitations on the class of grammars. Conditions on the application of transformations virtually by definition say nothing about the form of grammars but could well affect strong, or possibly even weak, generative capacity. Some of the constraints suggested by Wasow appear to be of this type. Presumably, if language is to be learnable, the class of grammars (biologically) given by the theory of grammar must be small, or there must be a powerful evaluation metric, or both. Further, except for a situation closely approaching the limiting case, the evaluation metric will be required. Thus, it is not even clear that the class of possible grammars must be small, assuming that the evaluation metric gives an ordering of the grammars compatible with a fixed set of data. Chomsky (1965, p. 61) discusses this point. "The problem is to impose sufficient structure on the schema that defines 'generative grammar' so that relatively few hypotheses will have to be tested by the evaluation measure, given primary linguistic data. We want the hypotheses compatible with fixed data to be 'scattered' in value, so that choice among them can be made relatively easily."

Later, Chomsky (1977a, p. 125) takes up this issue again. "Note that reduction of the class of grammars is not in itself an essential goal, nor is restriction of the class of generable languages; it is the class of 'available' grammars that is important. We might in principle achieve a very high degree of explanatory adequacy and a far-reaching psychological theory of language growth even with a theory that permitted a grammar for every recursively enumerable language." In this case, one could hope to achieve explanation of the acquisition of language even with a theory of grammar allowing grammars that could not be learned under normal circumstances. The acquisition of such a grammar might require more data than is available to the child, or might require a particular sort of exotic data; or the grammar might be so low on the evaluation metric that the child would never reach it.[9] Obviously, if all such grammars could be formally characterized in such a way that the theory of grammar itself rules them out, this would be an interesting positive result. The point Chomsky makes, I believe, is that there is no a priori necessity that the class of grammars have this formal property. The situation is reminiscent of the traditional discussion of center-embedded sentences. Transformational theory seems to provide no natural way to rule out all of the unacceptable instances. Rather than rejecting transformational grammar on this basis, linguists sought and discovered various independently plausible performance factors that might account for the facts. Similarly, the theory of grammar might provide no way to exclude all unavailable grammars. One might then seek various feasibility factors to account for the facts.[10]

I am now in a position to attempt a further answer to the initial question of this paper: What are the relevant parameters of restrictiveness? I have argued that constraints on the form of grammars are of central importance since they narrow the class of hypotheses that the child must consider. Even where the cardinality of the class is not reduced (i.e., when the class remains infinite), the density of grammars compatible with fixed data will in general be lowered, thus facilitating acquisition.

The Data Required and the Data Available

Constraints (whether on form or on application) that serve more directly to limit the range of data needed would further facilitate acquisition. For example the Binary principle of Wexler and Culicover (1980)—essentially Chomsky's Subjacency constraint—in effect guarantees that the learner will not require very complex sentences as data.

As discussed in Chomsky and Lasnik (1977) and in Baker (1979a), properties of the theory reducing or eliminating the learner's need for negative data (ungrammatical instances labeled as such) are of special significance. Baker (p. 536) points out that "recent studies of the child's language environment suggest that the abundant supply of information that he receives concerning which sequences of words are to be taken as well-formed sentences of his language is accompanied by little if any useful information on what sequences of words are *not* well-formed."

It is important to be clear about just what is at stake here. Even if it were to turn out that negative evidence is available to the child in some as yet undiscovered way, there would still be an acquisition problem. That is, the choice of grammar would still be drastically underdetermined by the available data. Thus the importance of the issue of negative evidence lies solely in what it can potentially tell us about the class of grammars and how they are evaluated. The apparent lack of such evidence[11] has provided motivation for a number of specific proposals for restricting the class. For example, a decision about whether a particular transformation is optional or obligatory would generally require both positive and negative instances. If all transformations are obligatory or all transformations are optional, no decision need be made. Hence a move in either direction reduces the cardinality of the class of grammars (or at least scatters the grammars more widely) and would be desirable for that reason alone. Additionally, a qualitative reduction is provided in the type of evidence the child requires. A similar line of reasoning holds with respect to extrinsic ordering. A theory allowing no extrinsic ordering has drastically fewer grammars than one requiring strict linear ordering of rules. A mixed theory allowing, but not requiring, ordering would again provide a great number of grammars, and certain of the learner's decisions might require negative instances. Consider the situation of a learner incorrectly hypothesizing that two particular transformations are freely ordered with respect to each other. To discover that he is wrong, he would need the information that one of the orders gives an ungrammatical output.

Chomsky and Lasnik (1977) suggest that obligatory transformations and extrinsic ordering can be dispensed with in favor of a theory of filters. But as observed there, and in Baker (1979a), the theory of filters potentially raises the same learnability problems that it seeks to eliminate. Certain of these problems can be dealt with by the evaluation metric, consideration of which I now turn to.

The Evaluation Metric

The gross properties of the evaluation metric are hinted at by Chomsky and Lasnik (1977, p 430): "We will assume that UG is not an 'undifferentiated' system but rather incorporates something analogous to a 'theory of markedness.' Specifically, there is a theory of core grammar with highly restricted options, limited expressive power, and a few parameters. Systems that fall within core grammar constitute 'the unmarked case;' we may think of them as optimal in terms of the evaluation metric."

It is important to note that although "evaluation" and "simplicity" are often used interchangeably in this context, the correct notion of simplicity is not given a priori but rather is entirely an empirical question. To take the standard example, there appears to be no computational sense, apart from the biologically given properties of the language faculty, in which structure-dependent transformations are simpler than string-dependent transformations. Along certain other dimensions intuitive simplicity does seem more or less correct. All other things equal, a grammar requiring fewer transformations would presumably be of higher value than a descriptively equivalent grammar requiring more transformations. What the trading relation should be, though, between a large number of simple transformations and a small number of complicated ones is not evident a priori. Certain aspects of this question are amenable to solution, as I will discuss.

Although in certain respects the evaluation metric favors the intuitively simple, there are complex properties that could well constitute the unmarked case. Filter (20) of Chomsky and Lasnik—(5) here—provides a clear example. In what follows, I will be concerned with the logic of the argument rather than with the correctness or incorrectness of the specific proposal.

Chomsky and Lasnik present some evidence for the existence of filter (5):

(5)
*[$_{NP}$NP Tns VP].

Given a rule of free deletion in Comp, as seems desirable on a number of grounds, some device is needed to exclude examples such as (6).

(6)
*[$_{NP}$The man [e met you]] is my friend.

Compare (6) with the grammatical (7).

(7)
[$_{NP}$The man [you met e]] is my friend.

Note that (5) gives the correct result here. Finite sentential subjects might be a further instance of the operation of the filter. Compare (8) and (9).

(8)
*He left is a surprise.

(9)
That he left is a surprise.

However, if (5) is simply a free option for the learner, there is no reason to believe it would ever be selected, since its postulation is based, it would seem, solely on negative evidence, that is, on ungrammatical sentences labeled as such. Such evidence is apparently not available to the learner. On this basis, if (5) is the correct explanation of the data, one would like to claim that it is the unmarked case.[12] Note that one cannot solve the learner's dilemma by claiming that (5) is universal, since in fact it is not. There are even dialects of English in which it doesn't obtain.

Is there any reason that (5) should be the unmarked case? In fact, (5) might be motivated by the fact that it supports a reasonable perceptual strategy such as (10)—(22) in Chomsky and Lasnik.

(10)
In analyzing a construction C, given a structure that can stand as an independent clause, take it to be a main clause of C.

Thus, in a sense, (10) is part of a functional explanation of (5). More precisely, (10) functionally explains that aspect of the evaluation metric that makes (5) the unmarked case. (See Chomsky and Lasnik, sec. 1.2, for further discussion of this important distinction.)

Frazier (1978) points out that Chomsky and Lasnik provide no functional explanation for (10) itself. That is, no reason is given for why a strategy such as (10) is favored instead of something like (11)—(iv) in Frazier, sec. 4.2.3.

(11)
In analyzing a construction C, given a structure that can stand as a dependent clause, take it to be a subordinate clause of C.

To quote Frazier, "by postulating principle P [the principle of UG that makes (5) the unmarked case], Chomsky and Lasnik were claiming that Universal Grammar was facilitating an arbitrary parsing strategy" (p. 200). However, Frazier argues, (10) is not arbitrary at all but rather follows immediately from Minimal Attachment, one of the two basic parsing principles Frazier postulates.

(12)
Minimal Attachment:
Attach incoming material into the phrase-marker being constructed using the fewest nodes consistent with the well-formedness rules of the language.

Frazier presents experimental evidence that (12) is involved in parsing. She found that sentences that are compatible on line with Minimal Attachment were substantially easier to parse than non-minimal attachment sentences. Example (13) is one of her sentence pairs, with the minimal sentence first.

(13)

a. Sally was relieved when she found out the answer to her physics problem.

b. Sally found out the answer to the physics problem was in the book.

Frazier (1978, p. 166) goes on to suggest that Minimal Attachment might be even more than a plausible motivated strategy. "Assuming that the parser is under considerable time pressure (i.e., is rigidly driven by the incoming lexical string), it would be reasonable for it to pursue the first legitimate analysis of incoming material which is available to it, viz. the minimal attachment analysis. If so, Minimal Attachment would not be a specific strategy which explicitly guides decisions at choice points in the sentence but would be a consequence of the organization of the parsing mechanism, together with general constraints on processing time."

Even under this interpretation of strategy (10), filter (5) does not follow immediately. It must still be stated that (5) is the unmarked case,[13] though now perhaps we have the beginnings of an (evolutionary) explanation of why this should be so.

In Chomsky and Lasnik we argue on other grounds that another class of filters constitute the unmarked case. We note that for a certain class of infinitival constructions considered, one might expect eight surface structures from each deep structure. In fact, only one of the resulting sentences is grammatical. Several of the impossible outputs are ruled out by language-specific filters, and we suggest that perhaps performance systems "prefer" a grammar in which the relation between deep and surface structure is as close as possible to biunique. We raise the possibility that the required filters, as a result, are the unmarked case.

Wexler (personal communication) carries this line of argument further. He notes that biuniqueness does not always hold and hence cannot be some sort of universal (transderivational) constraint on the application of rules. Instead, he argues that biuniqueness is itself part of the evaluation metric. That is, except in the face of evidence to the contrary, the child will assume that any particular deep structure gives rise to only one surface structure. Where alternative rule orderings or different application choices of already learned transformations would yield new sentences, the child takes the absence of these sentences in the data base as tentative negative evidence, in effect. Ideally, given a sufficiently restrictive theory of filters, either there would be no statable filter for the case at hand, in which case the relevant potential sentence would be assumed grammatical, or exactly one filter would be applicable. In the latter case, the filter would be assumed to hold unless violations of it occur in the child's data. Such an account would extend to filter (5) as well. This line of reasoning contrasts with the more simplistic approach in Chomsky and Lasnik in that no particular filters need be designated as the unmarked case.

I have discussed two ways in which nonuniversal "negative" devices—filters—could be part of the grammar acquired by a language learner, by virtue of properties of the evaluation metric. Those same properties could potentially allow the acquisition of a grammar with both optional and obligatory transformations. Another negative device, unaffected context terms in rules, is not amenable to exactly the same treatment, however. Biuniqueness would not invariably prefer a rule with a context over a rule without. The brute force alternative would require the postulation of specific context terms in particular rules as the unmarked case. Slightly less ad hoc would be a characterization of the unmarked case for any transformation as requiring a context. The child's special task would be to identify exactly what the context is. Only after exhausting all of the context possibilities provided by the theory of transformations would the child reluctantly conclude that his transformation applies unconditioned. Here the problem is twofold. First, the child's task seems very great. Second, it is not at all clear that context-dependent transformations should be the unmarked case.

Suppose, on the contrary, that unconditioned transformations constitute the unmarked case, as Chomsky has suggested in a number of articles. On the face of it, it would seem that no rule could then have a context, since only negative evidence could disconfirm the initial hypothesis. Interestingly, under certain very special circumstances, this line of reasoning breaks down. In Lasnik (1981) I present an analysis of the English auxiliary roughly along the lines of that in Jackendoff (1972) but within the restrictive transformational theory of Lasnik and Kupin (1977). The central properties of the system are: (1) the Aux consists of Tense and an optional aux verb; (2) this aux verb can in the base be filled by a modal or can be left empty; (3) if the position is left empty, it must eventually be filled by either a rule promoting *be* or *have* or a rule inserting *do*. One virtue of such a system is that the rule for *yes-no* questions can be simply permutation of NP and Aux. Further, no rule of *not* placement is required. As a first approximation, the relevant rules are stated as follows.[14]

(14)
Aux Verb Raising:

$$\begin{bmatrix} +v \\ -n \\ +aux \end{bmatrix} \quad \begin{bmatrix} +v \\ -n \\ +aux \end{bmatrix}$$ 2/1 (i.e., replace the first term by the second)

(15)
Do Support:

$$\begin{bmatrix} +v \\ -n \\ +aux \end{bmatrix}$$ *do*/1 (i.e., replace the first term by *do*)

Since the system I was assuming allows no ordering statements and no obligatory rules, potential inputs to (14), such as (16), would be susceptible to (15) as well.[15]

(16)

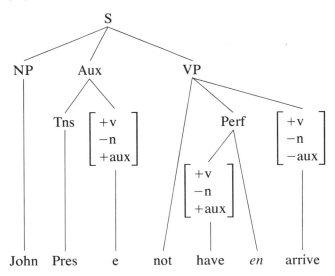

Thus, both (17) and (18) are potential outputs, yet (18) should not be.

(17)
John has not arrived.

(18)
*John does not have arrived.

I argued that ordered obligatory rules need not be reinstated to rule out (18). Rather, a general property of the relation between the two rules could be called upon, given a slight modification of the Elsewhere condition of Kiparsky (1973b).

(19)
Modified Elsewhere Condition:
If transformations T and T' are both applicable to a phrase-marker P, and if the set of potential structures meeting the requirements of T is a proper subset of the set of potential structures meeting the requirements of T', then T' may not apply to P.

A more specific rule is given absolute precedence over a more general rule.

So far, this is simply another example of complex properties of transformations replaced by a condition on application. Consideration of certain imperative sentences indicates that something a bit more interesting might be involved. One striking difference between imperatives and nonimperatives is that in the former, rule (14) apparently never applies whereas rule (15) is always applicable. Consider the following contrasts:

(20)
a.   John is not careless.   b. *John does not be careless.

(21)
a. *Be not careless.   b.   Do not be careless.

If transformation (14) can be blocked from applying in imperatives, condition (19) will not prevent transformation (15) from applying. I argue in Lasnik (1981) that imperative sentences have an affix but the affix is not Tense. The appropriate modification of (14) would then be as in (22).

(22)
Aux Verb Raising (revised):

$$\text{Tense} \quad \begin{bmatrix} +v \\ -n \\ +aux \end{bmatrix} \begin{bmatrix} +v \\ -n \\ +aux \end{bmatrix} \quad 3/2$$

Descriptively, this rule gives exactly the right results. But what of the child attempting to learn the English auxiliary system on the basis of positive instances alone? Recall that context terms in general raise the same problems as ordering, filters, and so on. Interestingly (22), the only rule in Lasnik (1981) requiring a context term, is the one rule for which positive evidence would suffice: the context term does not merely prevent the generation of the ungrammatical (21a); derivatively, the context term permits the generation of the grammatical (21b). By virtue of the Elsewhere condition, if (14) could apply so as to produce (21a), then (15) would be blocked from applying. The modification to (22) is thus motivated, for the linguist, by both (21a) and (21b); and for the child, at least by (21b).

Conclusion

I began with the question of what sorts of restrictions would be relevant to the projection problem. Restrictions on what counts as a grammar will be of central importance, particularly to the extent to which such restrictions scatter the grammars. Further, the issue is clearly an empirical one. No particular restrictions (for example, allowing only grammars generating recursive sets) have a logically privileged status, along the most significant dimension. Restrictions on the form of grammars may also, under certain circumstances, provide a qualitative and quantitative reduction in the data needed for acquisition. Further, certain constraints on the operation of transformations have this latter beneficial effect. All of this is significant to the extent that the learner's problem is the comparison and evaluation of grammars compatible with fixed data.

Certain aspects of language acquisition can perhaps be better described in terms of setting of parameters. Base word order comes immediately to mind. The evaluation metric apparently plays a role in other parameters. Luigi Rizzi (1977) has pointed out that Italian differs from English in allowing a relative pronoun to be extracted from an embedded question. This difference follows immediately under Chomsky's subjacency account of the *Wh*-Island condition if the bounding node is $\bar{S}$ in Italian but S in English. As Mona Anderson (personal communication) observes, the choice of S must be the unmarked case, since a child assuming $\bar{S}$ would never find evidence motivating a change. On the other hand, there are grammatical sentences in Italian indicating that S is the wrong choice in that language.

The child's task in learning a language can be construed as choosing one out of a class of competing grammars, as setting a number of parameters, or, the most likely, as a combination of the two. The difficulty of the task depends in large part on how scattered the grammars are that are compatible with reasonably limited data. Unless the theory of grammar is so restricted that it provides but one grammar under the normal situation of acquisition, the theory of markedness—that is, the evaluation metric—must play a central role.

Notes

The presentation of this material has benefited from the valuable suggestions of Robert Freidin.

1. The "incontrovertible learnability" mentioned by Levelt can, of course, only be construed as a remark about human learning. Although it is incontrovertible that human beings learn human languages, the question of whether the class of human languages is learnable in the technical sense of, for example, Gold (1967) has never even been formulated in a precise way, much less answered in the incontrovertible affirmative.

2. One possible objection to learnability in the limit as a model for human language acquisition is that it is a model of approach rather than of attainment. A limit model providing for sufficiently rapid convergence would perhaps mitigate this objection, however. Note in this regard that a theory guaranteeing convergence in principle for the entire class of grammars would be of little use as a model of the language learner. Far preferable might be a theory guaranteeing rapid convergence for highly valued grammars but offering no convergence guarantee for the entire class of allowable grammars.

3. Wasow (1978a) and Chomsky (1980c) make this point also.

4. Under such a theory there would be only a finite number of grammars. While these grammars might generate nonrecursive sets of sentences, most recursively enumerable sets would not be generated.

5. Chomsky (1964b) has the earliest argument for the principle of recoverability of deletion that I have been able to find. He claims that certain syntactic differences between relative clauses and *wh* questions can best be explained in terms of such a principle. Here too the argument is empirical.

6. Wasow (1978a) has an interesting additional argument of this general sort based on observed properties of the operation of certain deletion rules.

Wasow and many others have also presented a quasi-empirical argument for recursiveness. Following Putnam, Wasow indicates that speakers of a language have available a decision procedure for membership in the language. This point of view is presented particularly clearly in Levelt (1974). "Native speakers will in general be as capable of judging that a sentence belongs to their language as of judging that that is not the case. In other words, native speakers have an intuitive algorithm for the *recognition* of their language, and not only for accepting it" (vol. 2, p. 40).

Such arguments seem to confuse competence and performance. What are the facts about grammaticality judgments? There seem to be three possibilities: (a) People in fact have judgments for all sentences and nonsentences, and these judgments are accurate. (b) Same as (a) except that the judgments are not invariably accurate. (c) Judgments are not always available. If (a) held, one would conclude that the sentences of a natural language form a recursive set. Is there any reason to believe that (a) holds? In everyday experience it seems not to hold. Further, even if it appeared to hold in normal experience, as Peters and Ritchie (1973) observe, this would simply be evidence that "the set of sentences acceptable to a speaker under performance conditions is recursive rather than an argument about the set of sentences specified as grammatical by the speakers' competence" (p. 82). Grammaticality judgments are often incorrectly considered as direct reflections of competence. As Peters and Ritchie remark, responding to a grammaticality query is an instance of linguistic *performance*.

Levelt's elaboration of this argument is worth noting. He acknowledges that there are many unclear cases but dismisses their relevance: "If on the ground of this objection we drop the recursive enumerability of the complement of the language (the ungrammatical strings), on the ground of the same objection we must also drop the recursive enumerability, and therefore the type-O character, of the language itself" (p. 40). But no one would claim that the evidence of unclear cases *establishes* that human languages are nonrecursive, merely that the two situations are compatible, just as unclear cases would be compatible with recursiveness. Hence, the argument collapses. Note too that people have the ability to recognize a wide range of nontheorems of arithmetic. In fact, for all practical purposes, a statement of arithmetic can be just as easily judged a nontheorem as it can a theorem, even though the set of theorems of arithmetic is not recursive.

Finally, Levelt's claim that it is "more elegant" to ascribe the existence of unclear cases to "psychological circumstances" is without force in the absence of an argument.

Grammaticality judgments, then, provide no empirical basis for the claim that languages are recursive.

7. Or at least to limit the class of highly valued grammars.

8. Even if it turns out that all human languages are recursive, it might be that no formal constraint need stipulate this. Grammars for non-recursive languages might be ranked so low on the evaluation metric that the child would never entertain them as hypotheses. Whether this is so depends upon the correct formulation of the evaluation metric, which is clearly an empirical question.

9. As in the situation in fn. 8.

10. See Wexler and Culicover (1980, ch. 2) for useful discussion of this issue.

11. See Wexler and Culicover (1980) for an extensive survey of this question.

12. A modification of this account will be considered later.

13. This same observation pertains to many functional explanations in the literature. The additional statement is needed because the potential utility of a hypothesized grammatical principle does not guarantee its existence.

14. There are implied variables in all possible positions. Thus NP NP is to be construed as X_1 NP X_2 NP X_3, for example, where the X's are variables.

15. The structure is simplified for expository convenience. All category labels are to be taken as abbreviations for projections of feature bundles.

Chapter 1

Comments   Stanley Peters

Language Acquisition and Universal Grammar

Twenty years ago, in a paper called "Explanatory models in linguistics," Chomsky (1962) offered some programmatic speculations about how linguistic theory could help explain language acquisition. The most basic thing to be explained is why exposure to the particular linguistic experiences that a person has during the formative years leads to internalization of the particular linguistic system that the person does acquire and not of some other system. Of course this basic question has many important ramifications and elaborations that demand satisfactory answers. It would constitute very important progress, though, to achieve significant insight into just the basic question; so it has been the center of attention.

Chomsky suggested that linguistic theory would yield insight into language acquisition by specifying

1.
A class of grammars that are available to the would-be language learner, in effect constituting hypotheses the learner might tentatively adopt, assess, and then either reject or accept about the language he or she is experiencing a rather scattered sample of;

2.
A relation of compatibility between available grammars and samples of data such as a language learner might experience—compatibility of a grammar with given data being a necessary, but not sufficient, condition for that grammar to be acquired on the basis of those data; and[1]

3.
A measure that evaluates alternative available grammars compatible with given data to specify whether one is superior to the other and, if so, which is superior as a description of the language a person would learn on the basis of the given data.

The notion of superiority (sometimes termed "having a higher value" or "being simpler") is purely technical. It receives its principal, perhaps only, significance by virtue of how the three items are intended to function together in predicting what grammar any particular sample of data will lead a person to acquire. The operative principle is this:

(1)
Given data D a person will acquire an available grammar G which is (i) compatible with D and (ii) not inferior to (i.e., not less highly valued than) any available grammar that is compatible with D.

Thus the three parts of a linguistic theory can be taken to determine a mapping of data samples to grammars, which assigns to any sample D the grammar G_D that the theory predicts to be an adequate description of the language a person would acquire on the basis of D.[2] Accordingly, we assess the correctness of a theory in part by how well its predictions match the facts, as we are able to ascertain them, concerning what grammar a person actually would acquire on the basis of the various possible samples of linguistic data. (This much of the intended interpretation of a theory of language has not changed since Chomsky first introduced these concepts into the literature (1957).)

It would be enormously enlightening to have a clearly articulated theory whose predictions were a good match with the projection mapping—as the mapping from possible data samples to grammars that actually could be acquired on the basis of those samples is sometimes called. But however accurate a linguistic theory T might be at predicting what language will be acquired from arbitrary data, we would consider T to explain language acquisition only to the extent that we are able to elucidate connections between the content of T and the existence and nature of biological mechanisms through which a grammar emerges when linguistic data are presented. Such a connection is, of course, a matter of degree; one linguistic theory might exhibit widespread and detailed correspondences with biologically identifiable mechanisms, another only a very gross and highly abstract correspondence. In our present state of understanding we would, needless to say, be ecstatic to discover even the latter sort of theoretical explanation of language acquisition.

Perhaps the minimal connection with biological mechanisms of language acquisition needed for a linguistic theory to be considered as having any appreciable amount of explanatory adequacy is this: we must understand why the particular mapping of data D to grammar G_D which T determines is capable of being carried out or "computed" by a purely mechanistic biological computation. Maturation of a person's nervous system, and processing of information by the nervous system at any stage of its maturation, are mechanistic events that neither depend on conscious insight nor involve any magic in their operation. Thus whatever mapping of inputs to outputs they can be regarded as performing (e.g., mapping the data D of language acquisition to the full grammar G_D of the language learned) must be mechanically computable. In mathematical jargon, we assume that every mapping carried out by the nervous system is recursively computable. Much stronger assumptions are probably justifiable because of the tightly bounded computational capacity of the nervous system, but I will confine myself here to showing how difficult it is for a linguistic theory to pass even the test provided by this rather weak assumption. The crucial observation is that for a linguistic theory to be true (and thus to correspond fully to the biological mechanisms of language acquisition) it must certainly imply at a minimum that the processes involved in language acquisition are recursively computable.

Now, if it is correct to regard language acquisition as the process of computing grammar G_D from data D, the clear consequence is that the projection mapping of data to grammars, which is precisely the mapping determined by the true linguistic theory, is a recursive function. Perhaps this is the true state of affairs; maybe humans do in fact have a mechanical *discovery procedure* for arriving at the right grammar from any data. Some linguists and psychologists have believed that humans qua language learners possess such a discovery procedure, even though no human qua linguist or psychologist now possesses one—that is, none has a correct explicit description of one.

Another way exists to conceive of the acquisition process, however, a conception that does not entail that the projection mapping is a recursive function, despite the mechanistic nature of the acquisition process. Instead of regarding language acquisition as a process of going from presented data D to grammar G_D, one could think of it as a process of operating on D in a way that produces a succession $G_{D,1}$, $G_{D,2}$, $G_{D,3}$, . . . of grammars constituting successive refinements of the learner's knowledge of the language from which D is drawn. (The analogy with stages of language development is obvious.) The sequence $G_{D,1}$, $G_{D,2}$, $G_{D,3}$, . . . may eventually stabilize on a single grammar, which appears from a certain point ever onward in the sequence (i.e., no further refinement of the language learner's knowledge occurs after the point when stability is achieved). Presumably, in fact, such stabilization must virtually always occur eventually, the sequence converging to the grammar G_D which is internalized on the basis of data D.[3] If language is acquired through such a process, then the operative *convergence procedure* (as we might call it, on analogy with the term "discovery procedure") is recursively computable—by virtue of the fact that a biological process "computes" the sequence $G_{D,1}$, $G_{D,2}$, $G_{D,3}$, ... Our weak assumption about the mechanistic nature of biological processes implies that the mapping from D and any positive integer n to $G_{D,n}$ is a recursive function. This does not, however, imply that the projection mapping—a one-argument function that maps D to the grammar G_D on which the sequence $G_{D,1}$, $G_{D,2}$, $G_{D,3}$, . . . eventually stabilizes—is recursive, because it may not be possible to decide effectively when the sequence has reached stability so that it will never change afterward. In fact, Daniel Velleman (personal communication) has shown the assumption that a convergence procedure is recursive to be equivalent to the proposition that the projection mapping is in the class Σ_2 of the arithmetic hierarchy, two steps up from the class of recursive functions. (For a proof of this result, see the final section, "Velleman's Two Theorems about Convergence Procedures.")

Discovery Procedures and Convergence Procedures

When one attempts to demonstrate that a linguistic theory has explanatory value for language acquisition, it makes a great deal of difference whether one regards acquisition as a discovery procedure or a convergence procedure. Unfortunately, many linguists who claim that the theory of language which they advocate helps explain language acquisition show no awareness at all of the significance of this fundamental bifurcation of possibilities as to what sort of process acquisition is. Just what they are claiming is thus unclear, resulting in a loss of clarity about how the claim should be evaluated. One exceptional set of researchers who have been very explicit about their assumption that acquisition is a convergence procedure consists of those who work within the identifiability-in-the-limit paradigm—Gold, Wexler, Hamburger, and Culicover. These scholars have not investigated discovery procedures for theories of grammar, but they have carried out some detailed studies of the existence of convergence procedures.

On the other hand, Lasnik (like Chomsky in his many writings on the subject and like numerous other authors) leaves completely unclear whether he intends his theory to explain the existence of a discovery procedure or of a convergence procedure for language acquisition. Unfortunately, this degree of unclarity is typical of the approach taken in many linguistic papers to matters that are quite susceptible to treatment with mathematical precision. In fact, Lasnik's paper contains several examples of loose talk about precise concepts, talk that may be meaningless or false depending on how one construes it. For instance, he says that "*Aspects* does not allow as a grammar every function whose range is a recursively enumerable set." At first blush, the statement appears to be rendered meaningless by virtue of a category mistake; *Aspects* grammars are not functions of any kind. (One could interpret the remark as intending to treat both grammars and functions as formalized set-theoretically, and regard the sentence as trivially true on the grounds that an ordered triple—say, of semantic, syntactic, and phonological components—is not a set of ordered pairs and thus couldn't be a function.) But what Lasnik seems to mean, I think, is that not every recursively enumerable set is generated by an *Aspects* grammar, and this assertion is proved false in Peters and Ritchie (1971, 1973). Or perhaps he means that if one considers the transformational component of an *Aspects* grammar as defining a mapping of underlying to superficial structures (generally it will be many-valued, not a function at all), not every recursive function (let us read "recursively enumerable relation") is so definable—in which case his remark is true but insufficient to establish his point about the set of surface strings that have a deep structure underlying them.

A more damaging instance of confusion appears earlier in his discussion of the possible (ir)relevance of weak generative capacity to the explanation of language acquisition, where he seems to say that it is mathematically impossible for a linguistic theory to provide grammars for all and only recursive languages. In proving their Theorem 2, Janssen, Kok, and Meertens (1977) show how to construct a decidable class of transformational grammars generating all and only the recursive languages. They further show, in their Theorem 3, that no decidable (or even recursively enumerable) class of grammars exists which generates all and only the *infinite* recursive languages. Lasnik is unaware of the difference between the two cases, citing as the same imprecise and insufficient justification for both of his assertions something that I think may be an allusion to Rice's theorem (about bifurcating the class of recursively enumerable sets).

Janssen, Kok, and Meertens' article, incidentally, raises the very interesting possibility, missing from Lasnik's discussion, that there could be deep consequences for linguistic theory of the apparent fact that natural languages cannot be finite.

Lasnik's discussion of some proposals he endorses regarding evaluation measures is not a great deal better thought out. For example, he endorses Wexler's suggestion that an available grammar G is more highly valued than another one G' if the two grammars contain the same transformations (but not necessarily in the same order, nor need the grammars contain the same filters) and if, furthermore, deep structures are more nearly in a one-to-one correspondence with surface structures in G than in G'. From Lasnik's account it is impossible to tell with any certainty when the last condition holds and when it doesn't.

But imprecise formulation is not the only shortcoming in Lasnik's discussion of how an evaluation measure can help explain language acquisition. He makes one other affirmative proposal, which concerns the way a transformation's applicability may be restricted by an unaffected context term without necessitating an appeal to negative data. This proposal is clear enough that one can be rather confident about what its effects are. Nevertheless Lasnik's entire discussion of language acquisition in relation to evaluation measures contains not a single word directed at showing that a convergence procedure or a discovery procedure exists for the mapping of data to grammars defined by the complete linguistic theory he intends his evaluation measure to form a part of. I argued above that this implication for learnability of grammars as predicted by one's linguistic theory is the minimal connection with the biological mechanisms underlying language acquisition that should be demanded of an explanatory theory. Unless one can demonstrate that the implication holds, all one's rhetoric about explaining acquisition remains empty.

A second result of Daniel Velleman's (see next section) shows that providing such a demonstration is neither unimportant nor necessarily easy. The existence of a discovery procedure is a stronger condition than the existence of a convergence procedure. If a mechanical procedure exists for mapping any D to the corresponding G_D, then one can mechanically enumerate the sequence $G_{D,1}$ $(=G_D)$, $G_{D,2}$ $(=G_D)$, $G_{D,3}$ $(=G_D)$, . . . , which has G_D as each member and thus converges to G_D. This shows that a discovery procedure implies a convergence procedure; the falsity of the converse follows from the first result of Velleman's I cited. So the weakest implication for language acquisition which it is of interest to show is that one's theory of language implies the existence of a convergence procedure. Velleman's second theorem states that for certain rather constrained and well-behaved linguistic theories no convergence procedure exists.

Velleman's Two Theorems about Convergence Procedures[4]

From here on we need not concern ourselves with precisely what the class of available grammars is, nor the class of possible samples of data. We will simply assume that we have a Gödel numbering G_1, G_2, G_3, . . . of all available grammars and also a Gödel numbering D_1, D_2, D_3, . . . of all possible samples of data. Then any particular function of data to grammars can be represented as a function g from numbers to numbers, where $g(x)=y$ means that the data sample whose Gödel number is x is mapped to the grammar whose Gödel number is y. Thus a discovery procedure is simply a recursive function of one argument. Similarly a convergence procedure is a recursive function f of two arguments meeting the condition:

(2)
$\forall x \; \exists y \; \forall z[z \geqslant y \rightarrow f(x,z)=f(x,y)]$.

Regarding f's first argument as the Gödel number of a data sample and its second argument as position in the sequence, $f(x,0)$, $f(x,1)$, $f(x,2)$, . . . is simply the sequence of Gödel numbers of grammars that are recursively enumerated one after another for data D_x. Thus the condition (2) simply asserts that for any data, the sequence of enumerated grammars eventually stabilizes—it stays the same from position y onward.

   Now any two-argument function f on numbers, whether or not it is recursive, converges to a one-argument function on numbers if f meets condition (2). We will say f *converges to* g iff

(3)
$\forall x \; \exists y \; \forall z[z \geqslant y \rightarrow f(x,z)=g(x)]$;

that is, if $g(x)$ is the value that the sequence $f(x,0)$, $f(x,1)$, $f(x,2)$, . . . eventually stabilizes on.

Theorem 1: For any function $g(x)$ there is a recursive function $f(x,y)$ that converges to $g(x)$ iff g is Σ_2 (see, e.g., Rogers, 1965, ch. 8, for a definition of the hierarchy Σ_n).

Proof: ($\Rightarrow$) Suppose $f(x,y)$ is recursive and converges to $g(x)$. Then $g(x)=w$ iff $\exists y \; \forall z[z \geqslant y \rightarrow f(x,z)=w]$. Since the bracketed formula expresses a recursively decidable relation among w, x, y, and z, the quantified expression is Σ_2, and thus the function g is as well.

($\Leftarrow$) Conversely, suppose g is Σ_2 so that $g(x)=w$ iff $\exists y \; \forall z R(w,x,y,z)$—for some recursive R. Consider the following procedure for trying to compute $g(x)$:

Search through all pairs $\langle w,y \rangle$. For each pair examine all possible z's in increasing order, and for each one decide whether or not $R(w,x,y,z)$. As soon as you reach a z such that $\neg R(w,x,y,z)$, go on to the next pair $\langle w,y \rangle$.

If $g(x) \neq w$ then for any pair $\langle w,y \rangle$ we will sooner or later come to a z such that $\neg R(w,x,y,z)$, and thus will eventually go on to the next pair $\langle w,y \rangle$. Eventually the procedure must hit a pair $\langle w,y \rangle$ such that $\forall z R(w,x,y,z)$, and it can never go on to the next pair. Clearly the w of the pair $\langle w,y \rangle$ to which the procedure converges is $g(x)$.

   Now define $f(x,z)$ as follows: $f(x,z)$ equals the w of the pair $\langle w,y \rangle$ which is being considered after the procedure above has been carried out for z steps. Clearly $f(x,z)$ is recursive and converges to $g(x)$.   Q.E.D.

   We can treat the compatibility relation between grammars and data as a relation C on numbers such that $C(x,y)$ holds iff the grammar G_x is compatible with the data sample D_y. Similarly, we can use a relation S on numbers to let $S(x,y)$ represent the assertion that grammar G_x is more highly valued (simpler) than grammar G_y.

Theorem 2: There are a Π_1 relation C and a recursive relation S such that no Σ_2 function $g(x)$ satisfies

(4)
$$\forall x[C(g(x),x) \wedge \forall y[C(y,x) \rightarrow \neg S(y,g(x))]].$$

(Note: The condition (4) expresses the claim that for any data sample D_x the grammar $G_{g(x)}$ is compatible with D_x and no available grammar G_y is both compatible with D_x and simpler than $G_{g(x)}$.)

Proof: Let $f_n(x,y)$ be a recursive enumeration of all two-argument recursive functions (partial as well as total). The four-place relation $f_n(x,y)=z$ is recursively enumerable. Now define C and S by:

(5)
$$C(x,y) \leftrightarrow [\neg\exists z[f_y(y,z) = x] \vee x = 0].$$

(6)
$$S(x,y) \leftrightarrow [0<x<y \vee [x \neq 0 \wedge y = 0]].$$

(Note that grammar G_0 is consistent with all data samples, but every other grammar is simpler than G_0.)

Clearly S is recursive; C is Π_1 since it is the negation of a Σ_1 (i.e., recursively enumerable) relation. The unique function $g(x)$ which satisfies (4) for C and S is:

(7)
$$g(x) = \begin{cases} \text{the least } y>0 \text{ such that } C(y,x), \text{ if such a } y \text{ exists,} \\ 0 \text{ otherwise.} \end{cases}$$

By Theorem 1, g is Σ_2 iff some recursive $f(x,y)$ converges to it.

Suppose $f_n(x,y)$ converges to $g(x)$. Then the sequence $f_n(n,0)$, $f_n(n,1)$, $f_n(n,2)$, . . . eventually attains and remains constant at $g(n)$. Therefore there are infinitely many x such that $\neg\exists z[f_n(n,z)=x]$ and thus, by the definition of C, for infinitely many x $[C(x,n) \wedge x \neq 0]$. By the definition of g, $g(n)$ is the least such x. Therefore $[C(g(n),n) \wedge g(n) \neq 0]$, and hence $\neg\exists z[f_n(n,z)=g(n)]$. But this contradicts the assumption that f_n converges to g and, since every two-argument recursive function appears in the list f_0, f_1, f_2, . . . , f_n, . . . , no recursive function converges to g. Q.E.D.

Notes

1. The range of this relation, i.e., the set of possible data samples with which some available grammar is compatible, is seldom considered with any care outside of the technical literature on learnability (e.g., Gold, 1967; Wexler and Culicover, 1980). Unfortunately, very little is known about what collections of partial information about a language constitute a possible sample of data. The question of what kinds of partial information such a sample may contain has,

however, received some serious consideration (Baker, 1979a; Braine, 1971a; Brown, Cazden, and Bellugi, 1969; Brown and Hanlon, 1970).

2. The mapping of data samples to available grammars defined by "D maps to G iff (i) G is compatible with D and (ii) any available grammar G' more highly valued than G is not compatible with D" upon specification of a particular choice of 1, 2, and 3 need not be single-valued. Suppose a particular linguistic theory's choice of 1, 2, and 3 determines a many-valued mapping. How shall we interpret the fact that some D is accordingly mapped both to a G_1 and to a different G_2? Two options are open. One, which I think implausible and unlikely to lead to progress, is to interpret such a theory as predicting that a person whose data of language acquisition are D will internalize both G_1 and G_2. This would reflect what happens when, for instance, someone becomes fully bilingual in the course of "first language" acquisition. I believe it better to reject this option—and to regard such cases of bilingualism as resulting from contemporaneous exposure to intermingled data from different samples D_1 and D_2; it is even harder here than in the monolingual case for a language learner to categorize raw experience properly so as to extract linguistic data from it. The second option is to regard a many-valued mapping as reflecting a weakness in the specific linguistic theory's predictive power; if D is mapped both to G_1 and G_2, then the theory fails to predict which of the grammars will be acquired upon exposure to D. Adopting this second option necessitates seeking to keep such predictive weakness in one's theory of language to an irreducible minimum. It may be, of course, that some real indeterminacy exists in what grammar will be acquired on the basis of certain samples of data. We should be satisfied with a linguistic theory, however, only if for any data D and grammar G to which D is mapped, it would be possible for some person to learn G upon exposure to D. This will insure that whenever data are mapped to distinct grammars, which of the grammars a person will internalize either is a matter of random chance or—what amounts to nearly the same thing—is determined by some factor or factors that do not appear in the linguistic data.

3. Lasnik's remark in his note 2, contrasting approach with attainment, suggests that he misinterprets this conception of language acquisition as analogous to asymptotic convergence, in which a sequence might not stabilize on the grammar G_D but only draw ever nearer to it. That is definitely not the conception that is presented in the literature he refers to.

4. This section was contributed by Daniel Velleman.

Chapter 2

Some Issues in the Theory of Learnability

Kenneth Wexler

The solution to the problem of language learning is often cited as the major goal of linguistic theory, and the criterion of language learning is used to distinguish between linguistic theories. At the same time, the question of language learning is an important problem for psychology. Inasmuch as the study of learning can hardly proceed without some understanding of what is learned, the learnability of a linguistic theory (which characterizes what is to be learned) must be an important question for psychology as well. Thus from the standpoint of both linguistic and psychological theory, the learnability of a linguistic theory is a central question.

The question of how to create a theory of language learning does not admit of an obvious or easy answer. At every step in the construction of such a theory we face numerous choices. Our empirical knowledge vastly underdetermines a correct theory, and it is not at all obvious how to collect data to fill the empirical gaps. In such circumstances it is conceivable that theoretical analysis can play a useful role.

Given that the problem of language learnability is both central and difficult, it is perhaps not surprising that the criterion of learnability has been used to support quite different conclusions, even about fundamental issues of argumentation and methodology. It seems to me, however, that theoretical analysis can lead to some precise conclusions that should help pave the way for serious inquiry into the actual properties of language learning. I will discuss some of these issues and conclusions. In order to make the discussion more concrete, I will often refer to a theory of language learning that we can call the Degree-2 theory, for reasons that will become clear (Wexler and Culicover, 1980).

The Degree-2 Theory

The Degree-2 theory is just that—a theory. It is put forth tentatively, as is any theory, subject to empirical confirmation. On the other hand, a counterexample to any part of the theory does not count crucially against it, any more than does a counterexample to any theory. Counterexamples are useful, for the most part, to the extent that they lead to and are predicted from better alternative theories. Moreover, the Degree-2 theory attacks only part of the problem of language learning. Many important parts of linguistic competence are not touched by it (for example, phonology and the lexicon). The Degree-2 theory is mostly a theory of the learning of transformations. At various points assumptions have to be made about other linguistic components, such as the base grammar or semantic interpretation. But for the most part these assumptions are quite general, expressing only some large properties without detailed analysis. The situation is familiar from linguistic theory, where a theory may be developed in detail which discusses only part of linguistic competence but which nevertheless makes some general assumptions about how the detailed analysis connects with other aspects of linguistic competence. This was especially true in the earlier stages of modern linguistic theory. For example, in a syntactic theory assumptions may be made about which level of the theory interacts with semantic interpretation, but only the properties of the syntactic theory are formalized. Ultimately, of course, one would wish to formalize as much as possible. But it is probably impossible to proceed without this limitation of scope. The problem has to be broken down into subproblems, and these studied. If the assumptions about how the subproblems interact are very wrong, the analyses of the subproblems themselves may turn out to be wrong. This danger always exists. But for any serious subject of inquiry, it is difficult to see what alternative to follow. As analysis deepens, the interaction of the subproblems can be studied.

The Basic Problem

The Degree-2 theory approaches the learning of syntactic transformations in the following way. The problem is taken to be the learning of a finite set of transformations A. The descriptions of these transformations can be relatively rich, as in earlier versions of linguistic theory. Structural descriptions are sequences of categories and variables that fit a phrase-marker in the usual sense, and structural changes involve various operations on these phrase-markers.

The input data consist of (b,s) pairs, where b is a base phrase-marker and s is the surface sentence. This assumption is a formal assumption, made for the purposes of analysis. In a stricter sense neither b nor s is part of the environmental input. The question is whether it is plausible to formalize the problem in this way. I shall return to this question. For now, I will simply state the motivation for this assumption. The learner—the child—hears a sentence and thus s is available. At the same time, the child has a cognitive understanding of the intention of the speaker, given that he already knows the meaning of the words in the sentence and has cognitive abilities with respect to understanding situations. From these abilities and partial knowledge, together with a (strong but unspecified) theory of the relation between syntactic structure and logical form, the child can derive the deep structure of a sentence. This is b. The problem, then, is to learn the set of transformations that connect all possible deep structures b with their surface sentences s. Since a grammar generates an infinite number of such pairs, the problem is nontrivial.

The assumption that in many instances the child can construct the deep structure of sentences even when he doesn't know the transformations is a very strong assumption (which nevertheless may be correct). It is interesting, therefore, that in order to show that a set of transformations is learnable, it is still necessary to make many other assumptions, restricting the power of transformations (Wexler and Culicover, 1980, ch. 4). In fact, the object is to show more than that a set of transformations is learnable; it is to show that learnability can occur even when the input data are quite restricted. A sentence that contains no other sentences is said to be of degree 0. If a sentence contains one embedded sentence it is of degree 1. If a sentence contains a sentence that itself contains a sentence, it is of degree 2, and so on. The degree of a sentence is one measure of its complexity. Therefore, if one can show that transformations are learnable from sentences of low degree, one has shown that they are learnable from input of low complexity (according to one reasonable measure). The complexity of a sentence is measured by the degree of its base b. The fundamental result of learnability theory to date is that transformations are learnable from data of degree 2 or less. (The learned transformational component, of course, can generate sentences of arbitrary degree. The bound is only on the necessary input.) Thus we can take the input to the learning procedure to be (b,s) pairs of degree 2 or less. If the learner can use more complex input, he will still learn. The theoretical result implies the sufficiency of degree-2 data—it does not imply that higher degree data mean nonlearnability.

Error Detectability

The learning procedure operates by creating transformations based on the (b,s) pairs with which it is presented. In order to create a transformation (or reject one it has already created) the procedure must make a mistake on some datum. This means that the learner's transformational component, at the moment of mistake, must generate a pair (b,s'), where the presented pair (generated by the correct transformational component) is (b,s), $s \neq s'$. A child's grammar C makes a *detectable error* on a base phrase-marker b if the surface sentence surf($C(b)$) that C maps b into is different from the surface sentence surf($A(b)$) that the adult grammar A maps b into. (The surface sentence is the string of words, not the surface phrase-structure.) In other words a detectable error occurs on b when surf($C(b)$) $\neq$ surf($A(b)$). In order to show that a set of transformations is learnable from data of degree 2, it is necessary to show that if C makes a detectable error on some phrase-marker then it makes a detectable error on some phrase-marker of degree ≤ 2. This is called degree-2 error detectability.

The central theoretical task in this framework is to show that degree-2 error detectability holds. Without further constraints the property doesn't hold. I will give an example here that shows how these constraints are derived. A formal example is found which violates degree-2 error detectability. A new hypothesis is then made which does away with the counterexample. Ultimately, of course, more is needed than solutions to particular counterexamples. We need to know that no counterexamples are left. In chapter 4 of Wexler and Culicover (1980) we prove that, given the set of assumptions and constraints made there, the class of transformational grammars satisfies the property of degree-2 error detectability.

An Illustrative Failure of Error Detectability

The example I give here shows how one of the "learnability constraints" is hypothesized on the basis of the failure of degree-2 error detectability. The example is simplified from the actual theoretical development in Wexler and Culicover. In particular, some of the constraints on the system are not followed (for example, the Freezing

principle), and rules are stated informally. (The example closely follows an example in Wexler, 1980.) Despite these differences from the
formal development, the methodology should be clear.

(1)

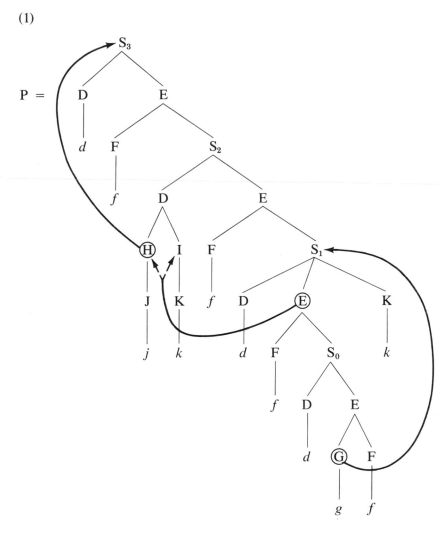

In (1), a base phrase-marker P is shown. The symbols are abstract,
not standing for any particular category, such as NP (noun phrase).
This idealization helps theoretical analysis to proceed but in some respects makes the job more difficult; more content might allow richer
restrictions to be stated. One exception is the symbol S, which stands

for sentence. The highest symbol is S_3, the inclusive sentence. S_3 contains an embedded sentence S_2, which in turn contains S_1, which contains S_0. By our definition, P is therefore of degree 3. The other symbols stand for any category except S. The arrows in (1) indicate transformational operations, in particular, movements of categories from one sentence to the next higher one. Thus, G is raised from S_0 to S_1, E is raised from S_1 to S_2, and H is raised from S_2 to S_3.

The assumption is that the child is caught at a moment when his grammar C has the following properties, with respect to the adult grammar A. Both the raising of G and the raising of H (the first and third raisings, respectively) proceed identically for child and adult (C and A). There is one difference—in how E is raised. Grammar A raises E so that it attaches under H, whereas grammar C raises E so that it attaches under I. This difference in A and C in the raising of E doesn't immediately cause a detectable error, however, because in either case E winds up in the same position in the surface sentence in S_2. There is a difference in structure, however, and thus an error has been created, although not a detectable error. Then an interesting thing happens. When grammar A raises H, E comes along, since H dominates E. But when grammar C raises H, E doesn't come along. Therefore, for the whole phrase-marker P, the derived surface sentence under A—surf(A(P))—starts with the words under H, namely *jfdf*, whereas under C, the sentence surf(C(P)) starts with *jd*, since E isn't raised with H. The surface structures and sentences are shown in (2) and (3). Therefore there is a detectable error on the degree-3 phrase-marker P. But there is no detectable error on the degree-2 phrase-marker P_2 formed by taking only the substructure dominated by S_2. In order to maintain degree-2 error detectability, we need to find a degree-2 phrase-marker on which a detectable error exists.

A natural way to find such a degree-2 phrase-marker is to drop the substructure dominated by S_0 from P. Given natural assumptions, this procedure will result in a degree-2 base phrase-marker P', shown in (4).

(2)

A(P) =

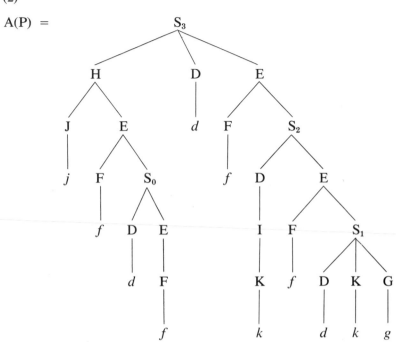

(3)

C(P) =

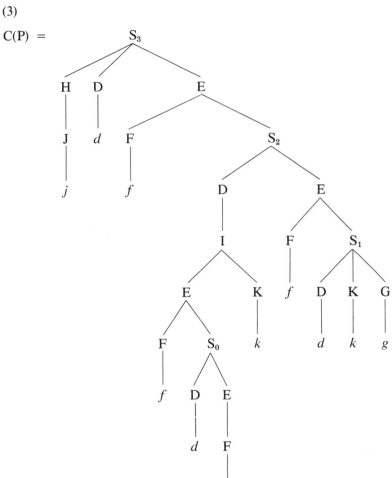

(4)

P′ =

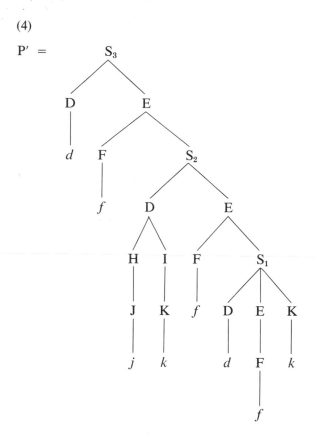

Since, in P′, E is raised, causing a (nondetectable) error, and then H is raised, causing a detectable error, (4) seems to be a degree-2 phrase-marker on which a detectable error exists, thus preserving degree-2 error detectability.

But this argument isn't necessarily correct. The role of the raised G in P has been ignored. Although G appears not to take part in the creation of the detectable error, because it isn't raised again, it may have a more subtle effect. Suppose that the presence of G is necessary to the raising of E. This effect of categories as necessary context if transformations are to apply is well known in many versions of transformational theory. Thus the assumption is that if G is not present (perhaps in a particular position) E cannot be raised. Therefore no error will be created, and when H is raised there will be no detectable error. The result of applying transformations to P′, then, is given in (5).

(5)

$$A(P') = C(P') =$$

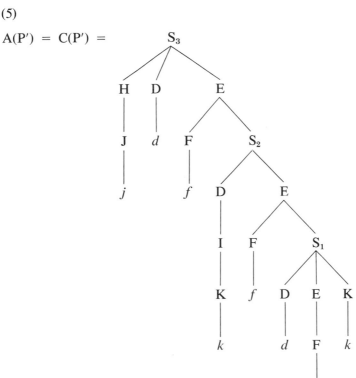

The lack of G in P' results in the failure to create a detectable error. Given appropriate assumptions, there will be no detectable error at all on degree-2 phrase-markers, and the property of degree-2 error detectability fails.

The No-Bottom-Context Principle

In order to maintain degree-2 error detectability a new assumption is added to the linguistic system. This is an example of a learnability constraint. The assumption is called the principle of No Bottom Context (NBC). According to NBC, a raising transformation (or any other transformation that involves a sentence and a lower, embedded sentence) may not involve any context of the lower sentence as part of the structural description that determines when the transformation can apply. In the present example, the raising of E involves the movement of a category from a lower sentence (S_1) to a higher sentence (S_2). Thus

NBC implies that no context from the lower sentence (S_1) may be used in determining whether E can be raised. In particular the presence of G (raised from S_0) cannot be required in order for E to be raised. Therefore, since E is raised in P, E will be raised in P', even though there is no G in P'. Therefore, an error, and then a detectable error, will be created on P', which is of degree 2. Invoking a learnability constraint, NBC, has preserved degree-2 error detectability.

The learnability constraints, derived from such analyses, become candidates for hypotheses as innate principles of mind, principles that have the functional role of allowing learnability. Note that the concept of functional explanation here must lie at the evolutionary not biological (or linguistic) level, as Chomsky and Lasnik (1977) have pointed out. That is, the learnability constraints (or other principles underlying them) must be part of the language learning mechanism with which the child is born. Following the learnability analyses, the child cannot develop the constraints from an unformed state. But the constraints might develop in evolutionary time, for the (functional) reason that without them language would not be learnable by the organism.

The learnability constraints are subject to empirical confirmation or disconfirmation by the usual linguistic methods. In the case of the present example, one can ask whether NBC is true of language. I know of no counterexamples in English. Even more strongly, some of the learnability constraints make predictions as to linguistic data. In Wexler and Culicover (1980, ch. 5) and other places (Culicover and Wexler, 1977) we study such predictions for a number of constraints. Interestingly, one of the constraints (the Binary principle), although introduced for learnability reasons of the kind described, is almost identical to Chomsky's independently introduced Subjacency condition, which was invoked for reasons of linguistic description. When two such different kinds of evidence favor a hypothesis, that is good reason to take the hypothesis seriously.

As to NBC, it is difficult to find positive evidence for it because in current versions of linguistic theory transformations do not have much in the way of context. For purposes of illustration, however, suppose that Passive is considered a transformation and (as in traditional analyses) the raised NP can only be one that follows a verb. That is, ...V NP... is part of the structural description of Passive. Then V is a context element, in the sense of NBC. If V is in an embedded sentence when the transformation is applying to a higher sentence, then NBC rules out application of the transformation. Given a structure like (6),

(6)

$[_{NP}$ e] expects $[_{\bar{S}}$ Bill to build the house],

the Passive transformation should apply to yield the ungrammatical (7):

(7)

*The house is expected Bill to build.

The ungrammaticality of (7) means that Passive didn't apply to (6), and this can be explained by NBC, since a context element, V, is in an embedded sentence in (6).

Of course, there may be other explanations for this fact, and many linguists wouldn't want to assume that V is part of the structural description of Passive. But even if all positive evidence for a learnability constraint is taken away, that is not evidence against the constraint. Rather, to give evidence against the constraint, one must show that it makes wrong predictions. In the case of NBC, one would have to show that there was a transformation that mentioned a context element, and that this transformation could apply to a structure with the context element fitting a node in an embedded sentence, and that the derived structure was grammatical. I know of no such evidence, but of course it is an empirical question.

In addition to empirical linguistic evidence, how else can one distinguish between various proposals each of which rules out a given counterexample? One way is to observe that a given constraint must not only deal with the counterexample, but must enter into the total theory in such a way that degree-2 error detectability can be proved. Furthermore, in some cases it is possible to obtain certain kinds of (relative) necessity results. That is, it can be shown that if a particular constraint is dropped out of the theory, degree-2 error detectability breaks down. Such a result holds, for example, for NBC (for the proof, see Wexler and Culicover, 1980, ch. 4).

Of course, neither of these methods, empirical linguistic or necessity results, guarantees a unique solution, that is, guarantees that there is exactly one set of learnability constraints that will satisfy empirical and theoretical requirements as stated so far. As in any serious science, there is almost always some open possibility, and the science advances by finding stronger and stronger theoretical and empirical evidence in an attempt to discover the true theory. That there is more than one theoretical possibility at any stage of the investigation should surprise no one.

Further Issues in Learnability

With the Degree-2 theory as background, I would like to discuss a number of issues that have arisen in the literature concerning learnability. A program of learnability theory, as realized for example in the Degree-2 theory, fits in squarely with Chomsky's (e.g., 1965) original formulation of the problems of explanatory adequacy and later formulations of the projection problem (e.g., Peters, 1972; Baker, 1979a). The problem is to discover how the child, while receiving only a relatively small and limited set of primary data, achieves an adult grammar that generates an infinite variety of data that go way beyond the primary data. As Chomsky (1980c) points out, the "argument from the poverty of the stimulus" implies that the learner must have a fairly richly structured initial state. The example of a Degree-2 argument given earlier is just such an argument. The stimulus is limited (degree-2) which implies that some property (hypothesized as NBC) must be part of the initial state of the organism.

Plausibility of the Input

How plausible is it to assume that the input to the learning procedure (with respect to the learning of transformations) is a sequence of (b,s) pairs? First, the claim is not that b is in any real sense "presented to" the learner. Rather, the learner constructs b from other abilities. Such construction is necessary even for more obvious kinds of input. Presumably it is less controversial that the learner is presented with the string of words s. But in many ways even s must be constructed, because the segmentation of the string into words is not given in any obvious way in the speech signal. How the child learns to segment it is a problem in itself. Moreover, the learning of phonetics and phonology is not discussed in the assumption that part of the input is a string of words s.

I see no way to get around such abstractions and idealizations. We have to break the problem of language learning into parts. We can study the learning of transformations, say, by assuming that the child can segment strings into words, even if we don't understand how he learned to do this segmentation. Of course, if it turns out that our idealizations are wrong, that we have missed crucial interactions, then we cannot arrive at the correct answers. For example, if it turned out that the learning of segmentation (of strings into words) strictly depended on the learning of transformations first, then we would have made the incorrect idealization, and we could not understand the learning of transformations by assuming that segmentation (or part of it) was available while the learner was learning transformations. But serious empirical inquiry cannot proceed without assumptions of this kind, even though the assumptions may later be questioned based on future evidence.

Therefore, the logical status of the assumption that b is constructed from other abilities is no different from the logical status of the assumption that other aspects of the input are constructed from other abilities. Since I don't formally analyze the abilities that underlie the construction of the (b,s) pairs, I might as well formally treat the pairs themselves as the input. This reduces the notational load, and is harmless, as long as the correct interpretation is kept in mind.

The question still remains: How plausible is the assumption that the child can construct the deep structure of a sentence before he knows transformations? Relatively little currently existing formal analysis is relevant here, and I can give, for the most part, only plausibility arguments. The notion is that in many simple cases the child can understand the context of an utterance well enough that, given a prior understanding of the words in a sentence, he can create an interpretation of the sentence even if he doesn't completely understand its (transformed) syntactic structure. For example, he sees Daddy hitting a ball and hears (8).

(8)
The ball was hit by Daddy.

Understanding the words in the sentence, the child creates the interpretation of (8) (based on other abilities) and from the interpretation creates the deep structure underlying (8) (based on innate and learned abilities that relate interpretation to deep structures).

Could this course of events occur? A serious answer would involve extensive investigations of such matters as the relations between argument structures in logical forms (or similar entities in other theories) and syntactic structures. What would be needed for a convincing plausibility argument would be a theory that severely restricted the relations possible in the mapping from logical form to syntactic structure. On the one hand, such a restriction would help to show how the child could easily (based on the strong restriction) learn to construct syntactic structures from logical forms. On the other hand, such a restriction would help to show how hearing a sentence, together with partial syntactic knowledge, would enable a learner to construct the correct logical form for a sentence. For some very tentative suggestions about part of this restriction, see chapter 7 of Wexler and Culicover (1980), but these suggestions don't touch on some of the most central and difficult problems (for example, quantification). Of course, it may be that quantification is not involved at certain levels of learning.

Conclusions here are vague. But it seems to me that restrictive theories of the relation between logical form and syntactic structure are beginning to emerge; we know less about how a child learns to represent a situation cognitively, or to translate between a visual representation and a cognitive representation or between a cognitive representation and a linguistic representation (e.g., logical form). But even if we don't understand how the child derives a linguistic representation from a situation, we can still make use of a theory of the linguistic representation that he derives in order to study language learning. Furthermore, the study of the linguistic levels should prove helpful in the study of the cognitive levels with which they interact.

What would *not* be an argument against the plausibility of (b,s) pairs as input would be the demonstration that a particular (situation, sentence) pair was such that there seems to be no reasonable way that a child could derive the deep structure of the sentence without knowing the grammar completely. Even the demonstration of a large set of such sentences would not be an argument against (b,s) plausibility. First, note that only sentences of degree 2 or less are needed as input, so the plausibility of deriving the deep structure of any more complicated sentence is not relevant. Thus the demonstration that understanding complex sentences would be difficult for a child without the complete grammar is not relevant. And, second, by no means are all possible sentences in the language of degree 2 or less needed as input. Given the assumptions of the theory, lexical items are irrelevant to the application of transformations. Suppose that we call a base phrase-marker without lexical items a nonlexical base phrase-marker. Then any nonlexical base phrase-marker corresponds to a very large number of lexical base phrase-markers (with lexical items). But the input set of (b,s) pairs need involve no more than one lexical base phrase-marker for each nonlexical base phrase-marker. This vastly reduces the number of (lexical) base phrase-markers needed. An argument against the plausibility of (b,s) pairs as input would have to show that there was a nonlexical base phrase-marker such that none of the lexical base phrase-markers related to it was such that it could be created by the child without the set of transformations.

So much is certain. But even this set of needed base phrase-markers may be quite a bit overestimated. There are many reasons in principle why certain base phrase-markers would not be needed as input. For example, a transformation might be learnable from quite a few different (nonlexical) base phrase-markers, so though a base phrase-marker might never be presented, the child would have no problem in learning the transformation.

Nor is the claim that a situation is related to a very large number, even an infinite number, of base phrase-markers a counterargument. The line of argument here is often based on notions like truth value or synonymy. The claim might be that another deep structure underlying (8) could be the deep structure of (9).

(9)
The ball was hit by Daddy and two plus two equals four.

I would expect the child to have a theory that would select the correct deep structure here. And in other cases it must be remembered that I assume that the child knows the meaning of (most or all) the words in the sentence, which eliminates other possibilities.

On the other hand, the Degree-2 theory allows no syntactic role to lexical items in the governing of transformations or with respect to the learning of subcategorization rules or lexical rules. In order for the child to learn these particular lexical properties the input of particular lexical base phrase-markers would be needed.

At the psychological level there is evidence that supports the plausibility of (b,s) pairs as input. Newport, Gleitman, and Gleitman (1977) argue from their data on maternal speech to children that, for the most part, the only purpose of special characteristics of this speech is to make its interpretation more intelligible to a child with limited linguistic abilities. A review of evidence on properties of "fine-tuning" of speech to children may be found in Wexler and Culicover (1980, ch. 2). Pinker (1979), in a section entitled "Possible solutions to the encoding problem," makes some suggestions concerning mechanisms that the child might use to create the appropriate representations. He also suggests that "the primary role in syntax learning of cognitive development, 'fine-tuning' of adult speech to children learning language, knowledge of the pragmatics of a situation, and perceptual strategies is to ensure that the child encodes a situation into the same representational struc-

ture that underlies the sentence that the adult is uttering concurrently"
(p. 275).

Cardinality of the Class of Grammars

Sometimes it is suggested that if there are only a finite number of
possible grammars (which knowledge the child starts with), then there
is no learnability problem. In one sense this is correct. If learnability
means only that there exists a function mapping from sets of primary
data into the grammar that generated the primary data, then, of course
learnability is guaranteed for a finite class of grammars.

But learnability must mean more than the existence of such a function. One criterion that has to be added is that learning can take place
from reasonably simple data. Suppose that there are only two possible
grammars. Then a procedure exists for selecting one of the grammars
based on finite data. But suppose that the simplest sentence on which
the two grammars disagree (i.e., make contrary predictions about
grammaticality or some other property available to the learner) is of
degree 1000 (or length 1000). Then one would not believe that an appropriate learnability function exists for this class of grammars, on the
assumption that both grammars are learnable. A property analogous to
degree-2 learnability must hold. A criterion including such notions has
been called *feasibility* by Chomsky (1965), who claims that feasibility is
the next level of adequacy after explanatory adequacy.

Thus finiteness of the class of grammars is not sufficient to guarantee
learnability in the appropriate sense. This is not to argue that finiteness
is wrong. Many current versions of linguistic theory make it look as if
there are only a finite number of possible grammars.

In fact, in the Degree-2 theory there are only a finite number of
possible grammars. The original theory was not stated in this way. But
as constraints were invoked which allowed degree-2 error detectability,
it turned out that one can establish that there are only a finite number of
possible grammars (transformational components).

The finiteness of the number of transformational components allowed in the Degree-2 theory can be established in the following way.
First, it can be shown that the number of different structures that allow
transformations to be defined on them is finite. For each of these
structures only a finite number of different structural analyses may be
defined. Therefore, only a finite number of structural analyses are possible. The theory does not allow copying, and morphological insertion
is strictly limited. No copying means that if a category is moved, it must

be deleted in place. Short of morphological insertion, which can be ignored, the length of a structural change must be no greater than the length of the associated structural analysis (because the prohibition against copying means that any element in the structural change must appear in the structural analysis). Therefore, the number of structural changes for each structural analysis is finite. It follows that the number of definable transformations is finite and therefore the number of transformational components is finite.

Even if one wanted to allow copying, the finite bound on the number of transformations could still be derived as long as there was a strict bound on copying. This seems plausible. Such a bound would imply that there was a fixed number such that no transformation could copy a particular element more than that fixed number of times. (That is, the structural change part of a transformation could not contain the same integer more than n times, if n is the bound, though the transformation itself could apply an indefinite (unbounded) number of times.)

The crucial properties that allow the derivation of the finiteness of the number of structural analyses are the Freezing principle, which forbids applications of transformations to nonbase parts of phrase-markers and the Binary principle, which allows transformations to apply only to a sentence and to the next sentence down in a phrase-marker. Other properties might be substitutable for these principles, allowing finiteness to be derivable. For example, one might limit the number of elements in a structural description. But what must be derived in the end is not finiteness of number of grammars but feasibility, learnability from relatively simple data—analogous to degree-2 error detectability.

Generative Capacity and Learnability
It is sometimes suggested that the generative hierarchy plays a crucial role in language learning. The suggestion is that restricting the class of grammars to a smaller class in the generative hierarchy is a major advance toward the solution of the learnability problem. In chapter 1, Lasnik has shown that the fallacy underlying this argument is the assumption of the doughnut model, where each possible class of grammars must contain or be contained in every other class. If the doughnut model doesn't hold, the actual class of grammars might cut across the classes in the generative hierarchy, including some context-free grammars but not all of them, some context-sensitive grammars but not all of them, and so on. Lasnik uses this argument to show that there is no a

priori learnability argument in favor of the notion that all natural languages must be recursive.

For some reason, the class of context-free languages seems to be often suggested by those who think that restricting grammars to membership in certain classes of the grammatical hierarchy will aid learnability. For example, Gazdar (1979, p. 1) writes that restricting grammars to be a subset of those that generate only context-free languages "would have two important metatheoretical consequences, one having to do with learnability . . . In the first place, we would be imposing a rather dramatic restriction on the class of grammars that the language acquisition device needs to consider as candidates for the language being learned." But the class of context-free languages is unlearnable, by any reasonable definition of learnable. On the other hand, suppose there were only two possible languages, neither of them context-free. This class would, very likely, be easily learnable (subject to the earlier qualification about feasibility).

A restriction in generative capacity simply doesn't seem to be what the problem of language learnability is about. The relevant property, rather, is that restricted data can nevertheless point to the correct grammar—Chomsky's (1965) "scattering" in value. One might speculate that weaker grammatical mechanisms might aid this scattering and help learnability, though I haven't seen any arguments. In fact, Berwick and Church (1979) have raised the interesting possibility that the Degree-2 theory, despite its transformational framework, allows only context-free languages to be (weakly) generated. They ask whether this context-free property might be related to the learnability results. There seems to be no reason even if the languages of the Degree-2 theory are all context-free, that this should have anything to do with the degree-2 error detectability result. Nevertheless, it might be of interest to see whether the suggestion is correct that the languages of the Degree-2 theory are context-free.

I can show that (up to an undesirable assumption) the Degree-2 theory can generate some context-sensitive languages. In particular I will generate $\{a^n b^n c^n\}$, a classic example of a non-context-free language. (The idea of how to generate this language arose during a discussion with Robbie Moll.) (Note that, as Noam Chomsky points out, such context-sensitive languages would be immediately derivable if the Degree-2 theory allowed copying. But it does not. Therefore other ways to generate these languages must be found.)

I assume the base grammar G has the following rules:

(10)
S → ASBC′
S → ABC′
C′ → C
A → a, B → b, C → c.

With terminal vocabulary $\{a,b,c\}$, G generates the (context-free) language $\{a^n(bc)^n \mid n \geq 1\}$. I now add one transformation T to the system. T raises C′ and sister-adjoins it to the right of C. We can write T: X-C′-Y-C-Z $\Rightarrow$ 1-$\emptyset$-3-4+2-5. Since transformations apply cyclically, T keeps reapplying. The effect is to move all the c's to the right, thus, for any n, transforming $a^n(bc)^n$ to $a^n b^n c^n$. As an example, the derivation of $a^3 b^3 c^3$ is shown in (11). Terminals are omitted.

(11)

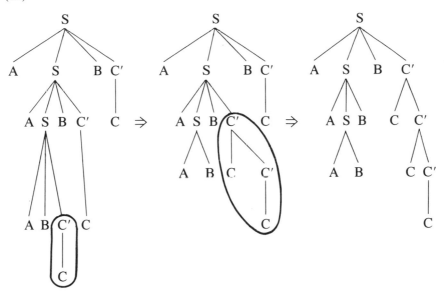

The Binary principle assures that C moves only one level at a time. All assumptions of the Degree-2 theory are met except one. Note that when C′ is raised, the higher C′ dominates the sequence CC′. Since C′ → CC′ is not a base rule, this higher C′ is frozen by the Freezing principle. The Freezing principle itself is not broken: it allows a frozen node to be analyzed by a transformation, though not a node dominated by a frozen node. In fact, the Freezing principle is used in the derivation, for it assures that at every cycle the raised node is the highest C′ in the embedded sentence (the lower C's are dominated by a frozen node and thus can't be explicitly raised).

Near the very end of the proof of degree-2 error detectability I found it necessary to add one assumption in order to make the proof go through. This is the assumption of Freezing Principle Strict Determinism, which says that if a transformation would apply, except that the Freezing principle rules it out, then the derivation is filtered. I don't think this assumption is necessary to the proof and I think it would be desirable to replace it. When I was doing the proof, however, I couldn't make it work without the assumption. An undesirable feature of the assumption is that it takes away most of the power of the Freezing principle (see Wexler and Culicover, 1980, ch. 4, for further discussion, where the undesirable nature of the assumption is pointed out).

So it may very well be possible to eliminate Freezing Principle Strict Determinism from the Degree-2 proof, in which case G will satisfy all the assumptions of the Degree-2 theory. Alternatively, G is only one possible example of a grammar that might generate context-sensitive languages. We might very well be able to come up with other grammars for the same language or other context-sensitive languages. Thus the most reasonable conclusion at the present time is that degree-2 error detectability can hold for a grammatical theory that can generate non-context-free languages. (It would be easy to demonstrate this for some artificial examples.) Since degree-2 learnability is quite a step in the direction of feasibility, one can conclude that restricting languages to being context-free is not a particularly useful step in the pursuit of explanatory adequacy, feasibility, and learnability.

Are All Possible Grammars Learnable?

By possible grammar I mean a grammar that meets the formal conditions that the organism, in its initial state, sets on grammars. The Degree-2 theory has been developed under the working hypothesis that all possible grammars are learnable. As Chomsky (1980c) has pointed out, this assumption might be false. Certain grammars might meet all the biologically specified formal conditions and yet not be learnable. One could in principle imagine many reasons for this state of affairs. There might be too many rules, or the time for learning would be too great, or degree-2 error detectability might not hold.

If it turns out that there are possible grammars that are not learnable, then the conclusions of the Degree-2 theory will have to be modified. If degree-2 error detectability does not hold for certain examples, the conclusion will be either that hypotheses have to be added that allow it to hold or that certain grammars are not learnable even though possible. In principle, experimental tests could determine which alternative held. The Degree-2 theory could be used as a theory (or part of a theory) that would allow us to derive as a prediction that certain possible grammars were not learnable.

According to this second view, the class of learnable grammars is a subset of the class of possible grammars. We discuss these possibilities in chapter 2 of Wexler and Culicover (1980), where possible grammars that can be learned are called attainable. Universals of grammar can then be divided into two kinds. *Innateness* universals hold for the class of possible grammars. *Attainability* universals hold for the class of attainable grammars. In principle, attainability universals can be calculated by the theorist from the innateness universals and the learning mechanism. Some scholars might be tempted to speculate that all universals could be attainability universals. In Wexler and Culicover (ch. 2) we argue that it is very unlikely that this is the case: if there were only very weak innateness universals, there is no way to see how descriptively adequate grammars could be attained.

Recent theories of grammar have suggested that there are only a small, finite number of possible grammars. To the extent that this is so, one might imagine that all possible grammars will be learnable. The possibility of unlearnable but possible grammar is more plausible when the number of possible grammars is large and they can vary in all sorts of ways.

It has been suggested in recent work that there is a special, very limited theory of core grammar, which admits of only a few parametric variations. In addition, there may be other grammatical possibilities which vary more widely. One possibility is that every instantiation of core grammar is learnable whereas only some of the possible noncore grammars are learnable. Determining whether this is so would require extensive investigation.

Is Learnability Theory a Theory of Learning?
Much of this question is notational. Learnability theory concentrates on the most solid facts about learning. Language is learned, and it is learned from fairly simple data. Other facts—say, about the course of learning—are much more variable and one can be much less confident about them. Thus learnability theory is a theory of learning that stresses certain facts.

It is perhaps an historical accident that learning theory has come to be identified with theories that concentrate on the notion of the time-to-time changes in learning and the notion of an "atom" of learning. The accident may be due to the historical fact that for the examples of learning that have been most studied there was no problem in principle about conceiving how learning could take place: for example, a rote list or a simple generalization over a small number of dimensions. Given the lack of challenge in the induction problem, it was natural that secondary properties of learning were studied, such as time-to-time changes, reaction times, and so on.

Sometimes it is argued that a true learning theory has to explain exactly how each act of learning takes place and that if the time course of learning is not accounted for, a theory of learning does not exist. Of course, no theory of learning attempts to account for the actual course of learning, in the most physical sense: psychological theories of learning involve hypothetical constructs not related in any understood fashion to the underlying physical events. This is not to argue that theories of learning should not be studied, but to point out that theories of learning in psychology have not achieved an ontological state to study that is in any sense central or unique. The account in psychological learning theory remains metaphorical with respect to the "actual course of learning," as does learnability theory. What is important is to see what crucial problems can be solved and what insight can be achieved.

Note

The research on which this paper is based was supported in part by a grant from the National Science Foundation. Some of the research was carried out while I was a Sloan Foundation Visiting Scientist in the Departments of Computer and Information Science and of Linguistics at the University of Massachusetts, Amherst. I wish to thank Noam Chomsky for useful comments on an earlier version.

Language learnability is a notoriously difficult subject. One should not be surprised at the confusion that pervades many discussions of it. Attempts at conceptual clarification therefore can only be welcomed, and Wexler's paper is a fine example. Though he devotes much of it to defending the assumptions underlying the Degree-2 theory that he has developed in conjunction with Henry Hamburger and Peter Culicover, the issues he raises are germane to the problem of explaining language acquisition in general. I find myself in agreement with most of Wexler's points, so my remarks will consist largely of elaborations of the paper's discussions. (Some points I raise are presented in more detail in Pinker, 1979, and Pinker, 1981.)

Learnability of Mathematically Well-Defined Classes of Languages

Wexler asks, as does Lasnik in chapter 1, whether restricting the class of human languages to certain mathematically tractable classes—specifically, the class of context-free languages and classes of languages known to be finite in number—would contribute significantly to an explanation of language acquisition. He concludes that it would not. As he points out, the context-free class of languages is so vast that learning one of its members does not present the learner with a significantly easier task than learning, say, an arbitrary primitive recursive language. Furthermore, concocting some set of circumstances that did allow the learning of context-free languages would at best be a Pyrrhic triumph, for surely no one wants to claim that a child can acquire just any context-free language (palindrome languages, IBM 360 Assembly Language, the Boston telephone directory) upon exposure to a set of its strings. Nor does making the class of languages finite render learnability a trivial problem, since ideally one should show (as Wexler, Hamburger, and Culicover do) that the learner can succeed with relatively simple data.

Nevertheless, I think that both the context-free conjecture and the finiteness conjecture[1] have grains of truth to them, if they are stated somewhat differently. Recall that Wexler's dismissals of these conjectures draw on Gold-type learning situations (Gold, 1967), in which a learner acquires and discards grammars in one piece. When what is at stake is the learnability or unlearnability of a class of languages, that is the most direct way to support a given claim. But nowadays most theorists agree that the germane issue is what Wexler calls feasibility (Wexler and Culicover, 1980) and what I have called the Time, Input, Developmental, and Cognitive conditions (Pinker, 1979), namely the ability of a theory to account for language acquisition in a manner that is faithful to the facts about children and their linguistic environments. As such, learning models should acquire grammars rule by rule, should converge in bounded time rather than in the limit, and should use a procedure that is a plausible description of how children process linguistic data. All of these considerations point to a learning model that processes each datum directly instead of spinning hypotheses in vacuo and testing them against the input in the manner of Gold's learner. Several chapters in this volume call for various sorts of parameter-setting models, whose learners are equipped with innate rule schemas containing parameters that can be fixed upon exposure to a relatively small set of sentences (see also Pinker, 1981). I will argue that when the learning mechanism is considered to be parameter setting rather than hypothesis testing, the context-free and finite class conjectures begin to look less misguided. It turns out that many of the features of grammars that ensure context-freeness and finiteness are just those that make a parameter-setting model attainable.

Consider first the context-freeness of rules. With strong innate constraints on the form of the base rules of a grammar, such as those in $\overline{X}$ theory (Chomsky, 1970a; Jackendoff, 1977), it is fairly straightforward to show how a learner who knows the categorization of lexical items can deduce a rich set of base rules on the basis of a small number of sentences (e.g., Berwick, 1980; Pinker, 1981). To take a simplified example, if the learner knew a priori that the rule expanding a verb phrase could be either $\overline{V} \rightarrow V \overline{\overline{N}}$ or $\overline{V} \rightarrow \overline{\overline{N}} V$, a simple sentence like *Abner ate oysters* would suffice to fix the order of symbols on the right-hand side of the rule (assuming that the learner had already mastered the equivalent of the $S \rightarrow NP\ VP$ rule). The $\overline{X}$ constraints uniquely determine the phrase structure tree that the learner can assign to the string, and the tree uniquely determines the corresponding rewrite rules, as in (1).[2]

But what if the rules could be context-sensitive, that is, of the form $A \rightarrow B / X \underline{\quad} Y$? Because rules could now admit context terms, the phrase structure tree would no longer determine the rewrite rules uniquely. As a result the learner could no longer fix the order parameter on the right-hand side of rules on the basis of a single sentence. In the current example, for all the learner knew, this particular VP expansion might apply only in the presence of a proper noun on the left or the absence of an adverb on the right. The problem becomes particularly acute if the grammar permits both context-free and context-sensitive rules (as Braine, 1971a, points out). Since children receive no feedback about the syntactic well-formedness of their utterances (Brown and Hanlon, 1970), the failure to hypothesize an obligatory context term would leave the child speaking ungrammatically for the rest of his life. On the other hand, a conservative learner, who always appended to his rules context terms corresponding to the constituent's neighbors in the input tree, would be unable to use the rule productively in new contexts if the rule happened to be

(1)

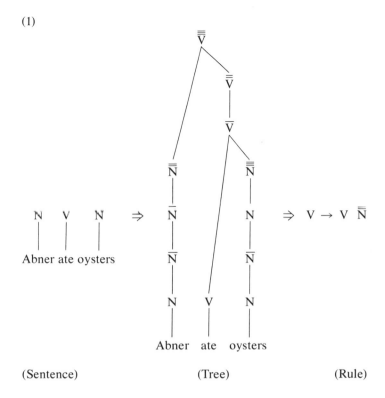

(Sentence)   (Tree)   (Rule)

context-free. The learner would also have to have some way of deciding which category node among those strung vertically along a neighboring branch was the correct context term. And if the rules expanding recursive nodes could also be context-sensitive, the bound on the degree of phrase-marker that the learner would have to see before acquiring the complete set of base rules could be very large.

Since context-sensitivity increases the learner's burden, it is not surprising that many of the simpleminded learning procedures that have been proposed in the mathematical and computer science literature work for only context-free languages (see Biermann and Feldman, 1972; Fu and Booth, 1975; Knobe and Knobe, 1977; see also J. R. Anderson, 1975). For the same reason it is not surprising that Wexler, Hamburger, and Culicover's constraints reduce the context-sensitivity of grammatical rules, perhaps, as Berwick and Church conjecture, to the point where context-free rules would be sufficiently (weakly) powerful.

In sum, context-free rules are more easily deducible from a phrase structure tree than context-sensitive rules, all other things being equal, so it is correspondingly easier to account for their acquisition by means of a data-driven or parameter-setting learning procedure. It is crucial to note, however, that this plausibility argument is a far cry from the hypothesis that context-free grammars in general are more easily learnable than context-sensitive grammars. The lack of context terms accompanying a nonterminal symbol on the left-hand side of a rewrite rule is a necessary and sufficient condition for a grammar to be context-free. But it is neither necessary nor sufficient for a grammar to be easily learnable in the sense just discussed. If the right-hand sides of rewrite rules in a class of grammars could be totally arbitrary (as they can in the context-free class), learnability would be impossible, never mind easy. Conversely, if the context-sensitivity allowed in a class were sharply constrained (e.g., if only certain categories could be context-sensitive, if only certain categories could serve as context terms, if only certain tree configurations could contain context nodes, and so on), the phrase structure rules might be trivially deducible from the phrase structure tree subtended by an input string. So the ceteris paribus condition in the beginning of this paragraph is big enough to drive a truck through. Context-freeness is useful, but it is not enough, and other constraints may be equally useful or more so.

Similar arguments can be made for trying to keep the class of grammars finite in cardinality. Recall that one of the subcriteria of easy learnability is learning in bounded time. The time needed to converge on a correct grammar is a joint function of the number of sentences that must be inspected and the amount of processing that must be done for each sentence. Wexler, Culicover, and Hamburger have succeeded in reducing the number of sentences needed by their learner, since a tiny subset of data (those of degree 2 or less) suffices to identify a correct grammar.[3] But this alone says nothing about how many operations the learner must perform on each datum. We know that hypothesis-testing learners like the one in Gold's model (1967) can take an unbounded amount of time between strings, because at any time, the first grammar the learner hypothesizes that is consistent with the observed data can be arbitrarily far down in its enumeration of grammars. We also know that computer implementations of hypothesis-testing learners consume vast amounts of time—on the order of minutes of IBM 370 time, using an optimally compiled version of an efficient grammar enumerator (see Biermann and Feldman, 1972; Wharton, 1977)—to acquire simple grammars even when less than a dozen strings are inspected. But if the number of possible grammars is finite, at the very least we know that the amount of time the learner spends enumerating grammars is bounded.

This result would seem to be true of the Degree-2 model as well. Since the (b,s) pairs needed for convergence are of bounded size, the time necessary to test the current transformational component against a datum and to verify that a hypothesized transformation (or the omission of an existing transformation) is capable of mapping the b onto the s, should also be bounded. Furthermore, Wexler's demonstration that the Degree-2 model allows only a finite number of possible transformations guarantees that the learner will not take an arbitrarily long time to draw up the hypothesization and rejection sets (see Hamburger and Wexler, 1975) before rolling the dice to decide how to change the grammar. Therefore, the time spent processing each input datum is bounded. Finally, since the number of possible inputs of degree 2 or less is finite, the total amount of time that will elapse until the learner converges (actually, reaches a given probability level of having converged) is also bounded.

Although it is better to have a bound than not to have a bound on the amount of time the learner spends processing each datum, it would be better still to know that the bound is reasonably small. By using parallel hardware, it is possible to make the bound close to zero. Imagine a learner composed of a large number of independent modules hardwired with different grammars, one module for each grammar. The modules simultaneously test a datum against their grammars, and any module that makes an error turns itself off permanently. The modules are wired together so that the lowest-numbered module that has not yet turned itself off announces its grammar as the learner's guess. This contraption will take no more time to guess a grammar than the longest time any of its modules needs to test the datum; furthermore, it needs no memory for past data and does not require that data be repeated. Similarly, the Degree-2 learner could contain modules hardwired with every possible transformation so that when it comes time to hypothesize a new transformation, all the models could test themselves at once (in conjunction with existing transformations) against the current (b,s) pair. The time–space tradeoff exemplified by this sort of learner would be impossible if the class of grammars were infinite, since a finite learner cannot have an infinite number of modules.

Returning now to Planet Earth, it is possible to show that finite classes of grammars allow more plausible advantages to a learner—again, not by virtue of finiteness per se but by virtue of the sorts of constraints on rules that guarantee finiteness. These constraints, like those that guarantee context-freeness, allow the learner to squeeze as much information as possible out of each datum by fitting a tree to the string and reading the corresponding rewrite rules off the tree. For example, the finiteness of the class of phrase structure rule components is ensured in part by the restriction of phrasal categories to no more than three levels of projections (bars in $\overline{X}$ notation) above the lexical category. Imagine a class of grammars whose cardinality was infinite by virtue of allowing an arbitrary number of category projections. A learner faced with this class could not use the tree-fitting procedure outlined here, because there would be an infinite number of ways to attach any word to the tree. The branch connecting the word could have an arbitrary number of nonbranching nodes along it, and it could be attached to a neighboring branch at one of an arbitrary number of different nodes along that branch.

Another restriction needed to prove the finiteness of possible base rules is on the number of permissible repetitions of a category symbol on the right-hand side of a rule—if an arbitrary number are permitted, an arbitrary number of rules is possible. One way to impose such a constraint is to pair the category symbols in the right-hand sides of rules with grammatical functions such as object and complement (e.g., Kaplan and Bresnan, in press; Pinker, 1981) and to stipulate that no category:function pair may appear more than once in a right-hand side.[4] (I assume that constraints to the same effect could be stated within a revised extended standard theory framework.) Category:function pairs that can occur any number of times in an expansion, such as prepositional phrase adjuncts, would be generated by rules using an asterisk notation symbolizing iteration (e.g., VP $\rightarrow$ V PP*). This finiteness constraint—that

predicate locative

a category:function pair can occur either once or an infinite number of times in an expansion—allows the learner to deduce that a category:function pair should be asterisked in a rule if and only if it appears more than once as a daughter of a given node in the tree. If a class of grammars violated this constraint by permitting a category:function pair to appear any particular number of times in a rule, including an infinite number of times, it would be unlearnable in principle (see Gold's proof about the unlearnability of the superfinite class of languages). And if the iterated case were ruled out, the class would be learnable but not with input of bounded complexity. So in this case, the constraint that makes the class finite assists the learner in deducing the correct rewrite rules on the basis of trees fit onto individual sentences.

The caveats concerning the advantages of context-freeness apply again here. Finiteness of the class of possible grammars is neither necessary nor sufficient for easy learnability. Finite classes with enormous bounds on rule length may be unlearnable within a human lifespan; classes admitting of an infinite number of members may be easily learnable if other constraints minimize the number of possible rules that may be inferred on the basis of a given input sentence. In both cases, the formal results (context-freeness or finiteness) are less important for easy learnability than the particular mechanisms that yield those results.[5]

Input to the Learner and the Biuniqueness Condition

Wexler asks whether we will ever understand how a child's internal representation of a situation can correspond to the linguistic representation underlying the adult's utterance, given the creative nature of language use. But difficult though the problem may be, it is a problem that every two-year-old solves: the child somehow infers what the adult is trying to communicate. (Alternatively, it is a problem that every parent solves: the parent somehow says what the child is thinking.) I think this is cause for guarded optimism. Language use in general may be entirely creative, but what we are dealing with is a certain type of discourse—parent–child interaction in the first few years—that would seem to be far more constrained and stereotyped than adult-to-adult conversation.

In any case, in discussing the plausibility of the (b,s) pairs that serve as the input to the Degree-2 learner, it is crucial to remember that the base structures (b's) function as a surrogate for information about nonsentences, at least as far as weak learnability is concerned.[6] Recall Gold's summary of the learnability problem with sentence-only samples: "If you guess too large a language, the sample will never tell you you're wrong." One way of informing the learner that he has guessed too large a language is to associate a unique number with each sentence in the target language according to some primitive recursive function and to present the learner with strings together with their numbers. If the learner's hypothesis grammar (considered here as a primitive recursive function that maps all and only the strings of a language onto numbers) generates nonsentences for certain numbers, the error will be detected when one of those numbers appears in the sample paired with the correct string. Naturally, there must be a one-to-one mapping between strings and numbers in both the target grammar and the learner's grammars. If many strings could be mapped onto a single number, the learner would have no way of knowing whether a discrepancy between the sample and his grammar indicated (a) that his grammar was incorrect or (b) that the target grammar associated several strings (including the one generated by his grammar) with the number. Once again, if the learner guessed too large a language, the sample would never tell him he was wrong.

Gold suggested that the integers in this "primitive recursive text" might be interpreted as the ordinal numbers of successive trials, but surely parents' speech is not uniquely determined by the number of sentences they have uttered to their children since learning started. J. R. Anderson (1975) has suggested instead that the integers be interpreted as referring to the meaning of the sentences, according to some Gödelization or enumeration of possible semantic structure as expressed in some formal notation. In fact, the integers could refer to anything that can both be inferred from the situation and uniquely paired with sentences. The plausibility of a learning model using (b,s) pairs as input thus depends on whether b, or some combination of b and additional information, can meet these two criteria. I think this condition is at the root of Baker's (1979a) concern about theories that allow both obligatory and optional transformations, since the latter allow two strings to correspond to a given base structure. The condition also seems related to Wexler's Biuniqueness condition (see chapter 1, by Lasnik), which favors grammars that map deep and surface structures in one-to-one fashion.[7] And the problem of meeting the condition is virtually identical to what I have called the encoding problem (Pinker, 1979).

I have no idea whether it will be possible to restrict the theory of grammar in such a way that at most one surface structure corresponds to each base structure, even as the unmarked case. But I would like to ease the burden on grammarians somewhat by pointing out that it is not a necessary condition for weak learnability even in the Degree-2 theory. All that is needed is a unique mapping from situations to strings, so as to signal the learner when a string generated by his grammar is ungrammatical. If a base structure is all that the learner extracts from the situation, then of course it must map uniquely onto a string. But it seems likely that the learner extracts more than just the base structure. Wexler points out that the learner could, for example, use the set of words in a string to help decide which of the base structures logically consistent with the situation is the one underlying the adult's sentence. Conceivably that information could also be used to decide whether an optional transformation had applied. For example, if the learner had at some point hypothesized a version of an optional Passive transformation, the presence of the word *by* in an input sentence that was paired with a base structure containing a single proposition could inform the learner that the Passive had been applied in the derivation of the sentence. This in turn would allow him to determine whether the rest of the hypothesized rule (say, the form of the participle) was correctly formulated.

Other extragrammatical principles might also reduce the uncertainty between situation and string left open by the grammar. Perhaps there are pragmatic constraints on gross word order, so that only one sentence among those sharing a base structure might be permissible within a given context of discourse. As an example of such a pragmatic principle, Strunk and White's (1972) Elementary Principle of Composition #18 seems as precise as any: "Place the emphatic words of a sentence at the end." Within a given context, this principle would dictate whether an active or passive sentence was called for; if the counterindicated sentence appeared instead, the learner could conclude that something in his grammar needed changing. For example, a child in a toy store might hear his father say to the owner: *For a bicycle, I could understand*. Then, on the basis of his grammar, social perceptiveness, and Elementary Principle of Composition #18, he might expect to hear: *But are you telling me that a hundred dollars is cost by this chintzy scooter?* When he hears the embedded sentence in the active voice instead, he could rightfully conclude that his grammar is in error and could add the feature [−passive] to the lexical entry for *cost* (thereby solving one of Baker's projection problems). For more careful treatments of principles with this effect, see Weiner and Labov (n.d.) and Ransom (n.d.).

Other principles come to mind. Presumably the child can use his incomplete grammar to analyze parts of novel sentences and use this partial parse to eliminate some of the surface strings that his grammar would otherwise allow in the situation. Or perhaps his parser assigns a processing complexity value to each transformation and rejects derivations whose total assigned complexity is above a certain bound, under the reasonable assumption that the adult is speaking so as to be easily understood. Or the child might exploit the correlations that Ross (n.d.) and Oehrle and Ross (n.d.) have observed between the brevity of constructions and their semantic immediacy (some combination of proximity, permanence, completeness, and the like). If enough of these extragrammatical uncertainty-reducing principles could be stated precisely and justified empirically, it would support the key assumption that there is a unique mapping between situations and strings, even if it should turn out that there is a one-to-many mapping between base structures and strings. The nondeterminacy of the grammar would be offset by the determinacy imposed by the extragrammatical principles. As such, these principles would preserve the reasonableness of the idealization that (b,s) pairs are the input to the learner.

The Instantaneous Acquisition Idealization

Linguistic research addressed toward language acquisition has assumed that acquisition can be idealized as an instantaneous process (Chomsky, 1965). In other words, the time dimension in an acquisition model can be collapsed or scrambled without altering any of the conclusions about the mental mechanisms that make learning possible. Since acquisition is not in fact instantaneous (children pass through well-defined, universal stages of partial knowledge on their way to adult competence: see Brown, 1973), the justification for the idealization must be that it makes the problem tractable in its early stages of investigation. The idealization would then be vindicated if a successful instantaneous model could be fleshed out to account for the highly lawful observed sequence of language development, and if none of the central features of the model would need to be discarded in doing so. The methodology, then, is exactly parallel to that in the study of grammar in general, whereby it is expected that one will be able to embed a descriptively adequate competence grammar in a production/comprehension model and account for psychological data without undoing any of the pure linguistic work.

Though the notion of instantaneity seems reasonably clear, it is not at all clear what one would do to an instantaneous model to make it consistent with the noninstantaneous child. Some linguists seem to harbor the suspicion that a noninstantaneous model addressed to both the child's success and his development would be such a Rube Goldberg device that it would illuminate neither phenomenon. An optimist might hope, on the other hand, that a maturationally driven change in a single parameter, like the size of working memory, would cause an otherwise instantaneous model to behave like a developing child. Perhaps it would be instructive to spell out the different ways in which a learning model could be noninstantaneous and what each type of noninstantaneity would mean for the study of language acquisition. I distinguish three types of noninstantaneity here: nonstationarity, order-sensitivity, and developmental sequencing.

I borrow the term *stationarity* from automata theory, where it refers to changes in the properties of the mechanisms of a device as opposed to a temporal change in the device's behavior with its mechanisms held constant (say, if the device entered a certain state at some point, never to leave it). What we call maturation is thus a form of nonstationarity. Nonstationarity is perhaps the most fearsome form of noninstantaneity, since if the learner were free to change its mechanisms in arbitrary ways over time (say, by dissolving one sort of representation or process and replacing it with another of a completely different nature) we would be at a loss to explain what was happening as we observed its behavior (cf. Pinker, 1978). It might also scuttle the hope that studies of adult competence will shed light on acquisition, inasmuch as similar-appearing parts of a grammatical component conceivably could have been acquired by completely unrelated mechanisms. Naturally, this is a possibility that no one would entertain seriously until forced to by repeated explanatory failures. But there are more innocuous forms of nonstationarity that would cause a learner's behavior to be sequenced in time without making him completely inscrutable. An increase in working memory or processing capacity would be one example (Pinker, 1978); another would be the gradual emergence of semantic or cognitive notions, each of which might necessarily predate the acquisition of its syntactic realization (see chapter 6, by Grimshaw; Pinker, 1979; Pinker, 1981).

A second form of noninstantaneity might be sensitivity to the order of presentation of the primary linguistic data. Learning models could be order-sensitive in three ways, which I will call strong, intermediate, and weak order-sensitivity. Strong order-sensitivity applies to learning models that succeed only if the inputs are ordered in a certain way (several mathematical models have this property; see Biermann and Feldman, 1972; Gold, 1967); intermediate order-sensitivity applies to learners whose grammars at convergence assume different forms depending on the input order; weak order-sensitivity applies to learning models that converge more or less rapidly depending on the input order. Although it might be possible to concoct input orders that could befuddle a child, it seems unlikely that the child is either strongly or intermediately order-sensitive in any interesting way (see Pinker, 1979). On the other hand, if the child's processing capacity or cognitive concerns changed as he matured, he might learn faster when the complexity and subject matter of the sentences addressed to him at a given stage were appropriate to those abilities. This is because a greater proportion of the data would pass through his attentional filters to be given an opportunity to inspire rule changes. Such might be the function of the special register parents use when speaking to children (as Wexler and Culicover, 1980, and Pinker, 1979, have suggested), though much more research would need to be done to substantiate that claim.

Finally, a learning model might exhibit an invariant sequence of stages of partial knowledge on its way to convergence, above and beyond any sequencing that might be entrained to the order of the input. Let us call this property developmental sequencing. A model might be developmentally sequenced if the acquisition of some parts of the grammar were contingent on the earlier acquisition of other parts. For example, the child might first use semantic correlates of syntactic structures to learn the rules generating them (e.g., he might use thinghood and actionhood to identify nouns and verbs on his way to fixing the order of symbols within phrase structure rules) and then might learn rules for structures lacking semantic correlates by observing their distribution within known constructions (see chapter 5, by Roeper; chapter 6, by Grimshaw; Pinker, 1981).

Is the Degree-2 model instantaneous according to these three criteria? Inasmuch as it is set to learn the base rules first and then the transformational component, it is nonstationary and hence noninstantaneous (the nonstationarity in this case entails order-sensitivity and developmental sequencing as well). But within the transformation acquisition phase, which is the theory's central concern, it seems to be instantaneous. Although the time domain exists in the sense that data are presented in discrete trials, the model would learn in exactly the same way if it had all the data in front of it to process in any order it pleased. In addition, the model's transformation acquisition mechanisms do not change at any point, and though there may be interdependencies in the learning of various rules, it is hard to think of any case in which a particular transformation *must* be acquired before another particular transformation.

It should be evident from the preceding discussions how little we really know about the mechanisms of language acquisition. But I hope it is also evident that only by raising issues of the sort that Wexler discusses here and elsewhere can we hope to make significant advances in the foreseeable future.

Notes

I am grateful to Jane Grimshaw, Bob Berwick, and Haj Ross for helpful discussions.

1. In this discussion I use the term *finite class of grammars* to refer to the cardinality of the grammars within the class and not the cardinality of the sentences within the languages generated by the grammars.

2. The tree does not uniquely determine the abbreviated rules in the base (e.g., of the form VP $\rightarrow$ V (NP) $\begin{Bmatrix} (S) \\ (NP) \end{Bmatrix}$ (PP*) and so on). These would have to be derived by collapsing several nonabbreviated rules acquired individually.

3. Because the Degree-2 model is stochastic, that subset may still be immense. The learner may have to come across many tokens of each nonlexical base phrase-marker upon which his grammar makes an error before he hits upon the appropriate change to make in his transformational component—i.e., whether to drop or add a transformation, and which transformation among the many possible should be dropped or added.

4. The constraint is stated in terms of category:function pairs instead of in terms of categories alone so as to allow rules that mention a category twice: e.g., VP $\rightarrow$ V (NP)   (NP)   generating sentences like *She called him a jerk.*
                                  object N-complement

5. In these discussions I have only mentioned the inference of phrase-structure rules from single inputs. I believe that a similar data-driven or parameter-setting procedure is applicable to the learning of other sorts of syntactic rules, possibly triggered by specific conditions defined jointly over the partial analysis of the input string and the semantic representation. See Pinker (1981) for some proposals along these lines.

6. Clearly base structures also provide the learner with information about how sentences map onto semantic representations and hence also play a role in strong learnability.

7. Incidentally, it is not at all clear that the relation need be *bi*unique. While it is imperative that no more than one string be derivable from a base structure, I can see no harm in allowing two or more base structures to be mapped onto a single string.

Chapter 3

A Readjustment in
the Learnability
Assumptions

Edwin Williams

This paper reports on an effort I have made to play the learnability game of Wexler and Culicover (1980). The goal of the enterprise is to prove that language is learnable from data of a certain maximum complexity (of degree ≤ 2, where *degree* refers to the number of embeddings). The game is won by finding a set of assumptions about language that allow the proof to go through. Wexler and Culicover propose and defend one such set. An important criterion of any such set, aside from logical independence, simplicity, and so on, is how well they fit the empirical facts of language and the goals of grammatical theorizing.

I will propose a set of assumptions different from those of Wexler and Culicover. It is my belief that this set is closer to being empirically true to language than theirs and that it will also support the degree-2 learnability proof. To the extent that this is true, I am playing their game, but with a different strategy.

I will assume a rough familiarity with their enterprise and with the particular set of assumptions they use for the proof. My set of assumptions can be characterized in terms of theirs in the following way: I have eliminated the Freezing principle, revised the Raising principle, and, along the way, eliminated the principle of Transparency of Untransformable Base Structures (TUBS). I also have a speculation about how the principle of Uniqueness of S-Essential Transformations (USET) might be eliminated.[1] I will present linguistic arguments against the Freezing principle, show how a revision of the Raising principle can supplant the Freezing principle, present linguistic arguments against the Raising principle, show how the Freezing principle can be reinterpreted in the context of a plausible model of syntax so as to evade these arguments, and, finally, show how a natural constraint on deletion can replace the part of TUBS that still remains even when the Freezing principle has been eliminated.

The "Relative" Necessity of the Freezing Principle

Wexler and Culicover (1980, p. 188 ff.) present only two types of cases
where the Freezing principle contributes to the learnability proof, despite the great linguistic defense of it in their chapter 5. It is not surprising that it plays such a slight role, since it does not specifically limit
intercyclic interactions, as the Raising and Binary principles do, and it
is the intercyclic interactions of rules that make degree-2 learnability
nontrivial. For example, if there were no S-essential applications of
transformations, degree-2 (or for that matter degree-1) learnability
would be trivially provable. Both examples involve non-structure-
preserving raisings, the first involves deletion, the second does not.

The first case is illustrated in (1)—Wexler and Culicover's (54).

(1)

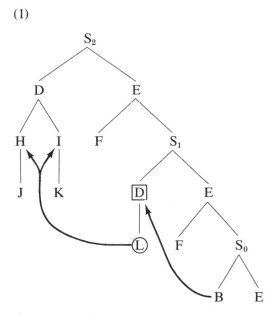

Suppose that the adult grammar has a rule that adjoins L to H but that
the child has postulated a rule that instead adjoins L to I. Then the child
will differ from the adult in the structure of (1) but not in the string.

Assuming that L B is not a base expansion of D, the raising of B to D
freezes D, preventing the non-detectable-error-producing raising of L
to D on S_2, by the Freezing principle. Without the Freezing principle, a
nondetectable error is created on S_2; furthermore, there is no smaller
phrase-marker on which the error will be created, since if S_0 is elimi-

nated, then a rule that deletes L when it immediately precedes F will bleed the error-producing raising transformation. Thus, S_2 is the smallest phrase-marker on which the error can be created and S_3 is the smallest on which it can be detected, and of course it is too large.

The second case involves not deletion but a peculiar use of boundary conditions. It is illustrated in (2)—Wexler and Culicover's (56).

(2)

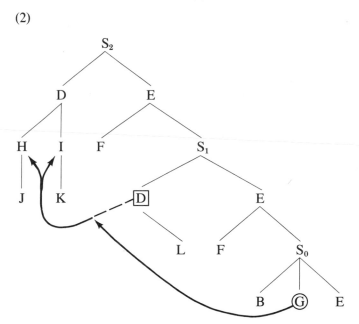

Here G is raised, creating an error on S_2, only when it immediately follows F; it can get to a position immediately following F only by being raised from a lower S; hence, the smallest phrase-marker on which the error can be created is degree 2 and the smallest on which it can be detected is degree 3. The Freezing principle would prevent the raising of G from under D, which creates the error, assuming that D is not rewritten as G L in the base. (If it did expand as G L in the base, there would be no need of S_0 to supply the G.)

Thus, in both these cases the Freezing principle prevents the derivation of a nondetectable error on a degree-2 phrase-marker.

Wexler and Culicover do not cite any further cases in which the Freezing principle does any work not done by the other principles. I will therefore assume that if these two cases can be taken care of, the Freezing principle can be dispensed with, although it is conceivable that there may be cases it is crucially involved in that neither they nor I have thought of.

Eliminating the Freezing Principle

The Freezing principle can be eliminated by strengthening the Raising principle—in the preceding two examples there was a non-structure-preserving raising. If this possibility is eliminated by requiring that all raising be structure-preserving, then these two cases are covered without the Freezing principle. I will leave till later the justification (linguistic) for this move. Note now that in (1) the structure-preserving requirement will prevent B from raising and so L will always delete; in (2) G in S_0 can never be raised to the position immediately following F. Thus in neither case can the error be created. I will tentatively say, then, that all raising is structure-preserving.

Linguistic Arguments against the Freezing Principle

The next problem is to counter Wexler and Culicover's arguments (1980, ch. 5, sec. 1) in favor of the Freezing principle. I will consider their arguments in the order in which they present them.

Dative
Because of the immobility of the first NP in a double object construction and the mobility of the second, Wexler and Culicover assign the following structure to that construction:

(3)

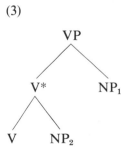

Given that V is not rewritten as 'V NP' by the base, this predicts that NP_2 is frozen by the Freezing principle but NP_1 is not; the evidence from the long-distance subjacency bound rules aligns with this prediction fairly well.

But for passive, the Freezing principle, in conjunction with the structure in (3), makes a doubly wrong prediction. It predicts that NP_2 should be passivizable, and it predicts that NP_1 is not passivizable. One solution to this problem proposed by Wexler and Culicover is untenable: that passive is lexical. If passive is lexical, then so is Dative Movement (cf. *Bill was given the book*) and all of the good predictions that follow from making Dative Movement a non-structure-preserving rule fall by the wayside. The solution in Wexler and Culicover that is not incoherent is ad hoc: the Freezing principle is not applicable to rules that fill empty nodes. Furthermore, no explanation is given for why NP_1 is not passivizable. Dative cannot count as evidence for the Freezing principle, for if the facts were reversed (that is, if NP_1 but not NP_2 were passivizable) they would be in fact more easily accommodated to the Freezing principle than they are as they are.

Gapping data are also adduced:

(4)
*John gave Bill a book and Sam Mary a record.

This sentence is bad, according to the Freezing principle, because the V is frozen and should not be deletable. But the true generalization seems to be that only one constituent can follow the verb after gapping, as the following attests:

(5)
a. *John put the pencil in the drawer, and Bill the crayon in the box.
b. *John considers Bill happy, and Mary Bob unhappy.

I have no doubt that the badness of these sentences is related to the fact that all constituents after gapping must be realized as focuses (see Bing, 1979). At any rate, these cases have no Dative Movement and yet seem as bad as the one that does, so the use of the Freezing principle here is suspect.

Pseudocleft
A very interesting fact about the pseudocleft construction, attributed to Culicover in Wexler and Culicover, is adduced in favor of the Freezing principle.

(6)
*Which theorem was what Susan did prove?

This example is extremely ill-formed. The idea is that the Pseudocleft transformation has moved the VP *prove which theorem* from the embedded S to the postcopular position; given that the postcopular position does not admit of VP in the base, this operation is structure-destroying and the Freezing principle should prevent further extraction, which it certainly does.

Two things are wrong with this argument. First, Higgins (1973) presented a strong case that the pseudocleft construction could not arise by way of a transformation of pseudoclefting, and in fact more arguments than he gave are possible (see Williams, forthcoming b). Second, even if VP is not possible in postcopular position, other categories are, in particular, NP, PP, and AP; if pseudoclefting moves any of these, the operation is structure-preserving and extraction should be possible. But it is not:

(7)
a. *Who is what John is proud of?   (AP)
b. *Who is what John took a picture of?   (NP)

Clearly, something more general is going on. In fact, there is a general prohibition against extracting from (or extracting) the focus of a specificational pseudocleft, as discussed in Higgins (1973) and Williams (forthcoming b). The case where the VP is the focus is merely a special case of the specificational pseudocleft.

Heavy NP Shift and the Freezing Principle
One of the most interesting cases in which the Freezing principle is invoked is the following:

(8)
*What kind of frogs did John send to Horace a book about?

Here, Heavy NP Shift has moved an NP to a non-structure-preserving position, given that VP does not rewrite as V PP NP, predicting, according to the Freezing principle, that extraction is impossible.

One can imagine several alternatives to the Freezing principle. One is without much interest, since it grants the Freezing principle: nothing can be moved from a moved constituent, a proposal in Higgins (1973) and G. Williams (1972). The Freezing principle is a special case of this principle.

Another possibility is suggested by recent work by Hornstein and Weinberg (1978). Their theory of preposition stranding includes a rule of reanalysis that groups together under a V node everything from the V of a VP up to the *wh* word; then *wh*-movement applies. If this rule applied to the deep structure of example (8), we would have:

(9)
*What kind of frogs did John [send a book about] t to Horace?

Now, if Heavy NP Shift is a postcyclic transformation, it will not be able to apply to such a structure, because transformations cannot refer to sublexical material, by all reasonable accounts. Thus, although interesting, this example is not necessarily support for the Freezing principle.

Conjoined Structure Reduction and the Freezing Principle
Conjoined Structure Reduction (CSR) provides two types of counter-examples to the Freezing principle. The first is that when a VP has undergone Dative Movement, its V can still be deleted by CSR, despite the Freezing principle:

(10)
John gave Mary a book and Susan a magazine.

Wexler and Culicover propose that CSR leaves a trace in place of the deleted V, and thus the Freezing principle is not applicable. But according to current theory, all movement rules leave a trace; hence the Freezing principle should not be applicable to them either. Unless something is done to distinguish the CSR trace from the other traces, this proposal will not do.

The second problem is that the deletion of a V by CSR does not inhibit extraction, even though VP should be frozen:

(11)
Who did John give a book to and a magazine to?

Again it is claimed that the deleted V is replaced by a trace; if this is so, then the structure is not deformed and no counterexample results. This avoidance of counterexamples seems reasonable.

In sum, it appears that while the extraction from VPs with missing Vs is accounted for (though consider *Who is John happy about*), the deletability of Vs from frozen VPs is not sufficiently accounted for.

Rather weak support is adduced for the Freezing principle from Right Node Raising (RNR) as well. It is claimed that the correct analysis of RNR is as a deletion rule not a movement rule. This does not follow from the Freezing principle in any strict sense. Rather, the Freezing principle would be incompatible with a movement analysis of RNR (given that the movement is not structure-preserving) and with the fact that extraction from constituents to which RNR has applied is possible. Without the Freezing principle both the movement and the deletion analyses are possible. Thus although the support given for the deletion analysis by Wexler and Culicover is extremely interesting, it could be correct and the Freezing principle still wrong.

The upshot of this discussion, if it is all correct, is that no support remains for the Freezing principle. If it is reasonable to suppose that all raising is structure preserving, then the Freezing principle is entirely dispensable, from both the linguistic point of view and the learnability point of view.

Is it reasonable to think that all raising is structure-preserving? The NP raising cases (as with *seems* and the passive *believed to be*) certainly are—they move NPs into subject position. If Tough Movement is a movement rule, it is certainly structure-preserving as well. *Wh*-movement remains a problem—is it structure-preserving? It must be, because given the Binary principle, which forces successive cyclic movements for long-distance *wh*-movement, *wh*-words would be frozen in the first Comp they moved into by the Freezing principle if *wh*-movement were not structure-preserving. So, despite the oddness of saying that *wh*-movement is structure-preserving, we must do so whether there is a Freezing principle or not and whether we accept the original or the amended Raising principle. Thus no reason remains for retaining the Freezing principle.

The Elimination of TUBS

The elimination of the Freezing principle puts within reach the opportunity to eliminate TUBS, a welcome result, as the following remarks are intended to indicate.

TUBS has no motivation other than its contribution to the learning theorem—no linguistic facts are predicted by it. TUBS says that if there is a partially expanded phrase structure tree to which no transformation is applicable, then there is a way to expand it so that still no transformation will apply. Note that there will be no particular sentence that will tell a child that the grammar he has constructed is not in accord with TUBS, and the property that a grammar must have in order to meet TUBS is not located in any rule, pair of rules, or even triple of rules. The entire grammar must be inspected in order to determine whether TUBS holds. Furthermore, I can think of no simpler algorithm for determining that TUBS holds than an inspection of every partial expansion of degree ≤ 2 and every transformation of each partial expansion. TUBS is thus a quite bizarre and arbitrary condition to place on grammars.

But one important function of this principle is to solve a problem created by the Freezing principle. Suppose that on some phrase-marker of degree 3, a G raised from S_0 causes some of S_1 to freeze, and this freezing prevents a transformation T from applying, where T would apply in such a way as to block an error-producing transformation from applying. Then an error would be produced on S_2 and detected on S_3. Now, suppose that in forming P', the S_0 is dropped; the raising of G is then impossible, nothing is frozen in S_1, and T can apply; thus the error-producing transformation is blocked, so there is no error, detectable or otherwise, on S_2, and learnability in degree 2 is impossible. TUBS prevents this situation. It says that there must be some expansion of S_1, after the dropping of frozen nodes (and S_0), to which transformations—in particular, T—are inapplicable. If T is inapplicable in at least one P', then in that P' the error-producing transformation will not be blocked and the error will be produced.

The whole problem is caused by the Freezing principle. If the raising of G does not freeze anything in S_1, then T will apply always and there will never be an opportunity for the error-producing transformation to apply.

In a way, I have already made this example irrelevant, since I have proposed a strengthening of the raising condition (to: raising is always structure-preserving) in such a way that the problem does not arise—the example crucially depends on freezing by a non-structure-preserving raising (at least, Wexler and Culicover's (41) does). I believe, though, that it is possible to create a situation in which the freezing rule is not a raising. Suppose that G is not raised but is moved—a non-structure-preserving movement (within S_1)—in such a way as to freeze material relevant to the application of T; suppose further that this movement of G was sensitive to something on the right or left periphery of S_0. I believe the same need for TUBS can be shown to hold in this case. But of course, if we have no Freezing principle, we have no need for TUBS anyway.

The other case that TUBS covers has to do with deletion. Suppose that E is deleted in the environment of some base G but not in the environment of some raised G. This situation could arise if the deletion rule were sensitive to something dominated by G—this something would be inaccessible in a raised G, by the Raising principle, but would be accessible in a base G. Now, suppose that E is raised, producing an error on S_2, and this error is detected on S_3. In forming the degree-2 P', G is stripped of its daughters and assigned a zero expansion. Suppose every zero expansion of G permits the deletion of E. Then the error-producing transformation that raises E will never apply in P'. TUBS avoids this problem by stipulating that there always be a zero extension to which transformations, in particular, the one deleting E, do not apply.

The problem is that E can be deleted in S_1 on the basis of a context in S_1 (the unraised G). Suppose that this kind of deletion were prevented; suppose that all deletion had to be S-essential. By this, the deletion of E in S_1 would have to involve material in S_2—but this means that S_0 is irrelevant to the deletion, since by the Binary principle S_0 cannot affect context located in S_2. This S-essential deletion principle says, in conjunction with NBC (No Bottom Context), that the context provided by S_1 can never be relevant to the deletion of any material in S_1; this is because NBC requires that there be no context in the lower clause (here, S_1). Thus the kind of example considered here cannot arise. Either E is deleted from S_1 in P on the basis solely of context in S_2, in which case it would be deleted in P' as well, or there is no deletion in either.

With this principle, that all deletion is S-essential, we have no use for TUBS. But the empirical status of the principle must be considered. It appears to be the case that all deletion under identity is S-essential: consider gapping, VP deletion, comparative deletion, coordinate structure reduction, and so on. In addition to deletions under identity, deletions of specified material must be considered, if there are any such rules. We might suppose that deletion of specified material is limited to the deletion of grammatical formatives. One could then restrict raising to major categories (not including grammatical formatives), thereby guaranteeing that raisable material can be deleted only under identity (and thus, S-essentially).

In sum, by eliminating the Freezing principle and adding the linguistically quite reasonable restriction that all deletion be S-essential, I have accounted for the cases that TUBS was needed for. Wexler and

Culicover give only these two examples in support of TUBS—the implication is that these are the only two kinds of cases that TUBS is useful for. But, again, there may be other cases that both they and I have overlooked. If not, TUBS can be eliminated without loss of the degree-2 theorem.

The Raising Principle

The Raising principle, which says that raised nodes are frozen, is one of the two powerful limitations on intercyclic interactions in Wexler and Culicover's set of assumptions. In conjunction with NBC it prevents the situation where an error is preserved through several (crucial) raisings, until it is finally exposed. I do not foresee eliminating the Raising principle; in fact, I have already added a further condition on raising—that it be structure-preserving.

However, there are apparently some linguistic problems with the Raising principle, which I will consider. I will then consider a revision of the Raising principle that avoids these problems.

Counterexamples
Ross (1967) showed that Extraposition from NP was postcyclic (he also showed that *it*-S was postcyclic, but his argument would not be accepted today). The examples involve extrapositions from *wh*-headed NPs that have been fronted:

(12)
Which packages will you say that John mailed tomorrow which haven't been sealed yet?

The fact that the extraposed relative appears after *tomorrow,* a matrix adverb, shows that the relative is in the matrix; it could be there only if it were extraposed after *wh*-movement, because Extraposition is rightward bounded (Ross, 1967); therefore Extraposition follows *wh*-movement, at least in this derivation (or, as Ross showed, in all derivations). But the application of *wh*-movement in this example is S-essential; that is, it is an act of raising, and Extraposition should then be impossible, by the Raising principle.

A similar example can be constructed with PP extraposition and NP (*seems*) raising:

(13)
A new book seems to have appeared by John.

If the extraposed PP is in the matrix, then the extraposition must have occurred after the raising of *a new book by John,* again counter to the Raising principle.

It will not do to respond thus: "Since *wh*-movement and these extrapositions are universal, they pose no learning problem." It is never a raising that creates an error (or is in error); rather, raisings have the potential to conceal, for several cycles, errors created by other rules. It is quite possible that an error could be wedged into a PP on a lower cycle, the PP could then be extraposed (again by a universal rule), and finally the error could be exposed, but on no phrase-marker of degree less than some arbitrarily large number.

Solution

What the Raising principle is meant to do is limit intercyclic interactions. But the rules of PP extraposition and of Extraposition from NP do not give rise to intercyclic interactions. For example, they cannot be iterated (and this has been an embarrassment to the theory of subjacency)—a PP cannot be moved to the right, by successive cyclic application, to arbitrarily high positions (as a *wh*-phrase can to the left). Also, nothing can be removed from the moved constituents—an extraposed relative clause is nevertheless an island, as Ross showed. Thus it appears that the rules that give rise to counterexamples to the Raising principle are in fact innocuous with respect to the intent of that principle, because they don't give rise to cyclic interactions of the kind that such rules as *wh*-movement and raising do.

Suppose the Raising principle is restricted to cyclic rules such as *wh*-movement and raising. Suppose further that such rules as Extraposition from NP and PP extraposition are identified as stylistic rules, where the notion "stylistic rule" has the following content: stylistic rules are rightward bounded (by subjacency, or the Binary principle), they apply after all cyclic rules have applied, and they apply "simultaneously."

If the stylistic rules apply after all cyclic rules, there will be no cyclic interaction of the kind where a stylistic rule precedes a cyclic rule. Also, if the stylistic rules apply "simultaneously," they cannot interact among themselves; in particular, they will not be able to effect apparent long-distance movement by successive cyclic application, and in general the effect of a stylistic rule will be always limited to adjacent cycles. It seems reasonable to think that this limitation of simultaneous application will make up for the fact that the Raising principle does not apply to cyclic rules; it is still possible for a cyclically raised item to have something it dominates undergo one further raising (by a stylistic rule), but no further rules could apply after that to expose any error. It might be possible to construct cases where the stylistic raising exposed an error and did it only on a degree-3 phrase-marker, but I have been unable to construct such cases.

It remains, of course, to explicate the notion "simultaneous application"; the principle of subjacency would seem to make this a trivial exercise (without subjacency, where a PP_1 could be extraposed out of a NP contained in a PP_2, the output might be indeterminate).

One final nagging problem about the Raising principle. In English, extraction by *wh*-movement from a NP-raised NP is prohibited:

(14)
*Who do pictures of t seem t to bother Fred?

This is as predicted by the Raising principle, since NP raising freezes the subject, making *wh*-extraction impossible, since *wh*-movement is one of the cyclic rules. But, of course, this is ruled out in English quite independently of the Raising principle: no subject can be extracted from, whether raised or not:

(15)
*Who did pictures of upset Bill?

But I wonder whether extraction from NP-raised subjects will be allowed in a language where extraction from subjects is permitted (speaking in terms of subjacency theory, say a language—like Italian—where $\bar{S}$, not S, is the subjacency node). I strongly suspect that it will. If so, the Raising principle is invalid—it cannot be maintained even for the cyclic rules. I do not at present have any suggestion about what it could be replaced with should this turn out to be the case.

USET

The most aggravatingly inextirpable constraint remains—the Uniqueness of S-Essential Transformations (USET). This constraint says that at most one thing can be extracted from an S. It is a theorem of nearly every model of grammar that two things (and, in the best models, at most two things) can be extracted from an S. When both NP raising and *wh*-movement apply, we get the most commonplace violations of USET:

(16)

the man *who Bill* seems t to like t.

Here, both of the italicized NPs have been removed from the embedded S.

The reason USET is needed is as follows: In S_0 a constituent could be mistakenly attached to one of two adjacent NPs instead of the other; if both of these NPs are raised several cycles and are adjacent again in later cycles, the mistake is preserved for those cycles, forestalling detection. USET could be replaced by a principle that says that two raised items cannot ever be adjacent (Wexler and Culicover make such a suggestion), but this principle as well is falsified by the example just given. It is not even possible to revise this principle to apply only to NPs that were adjacent on the lower cycle:

(17)

the books that Bill seems to have been given t t.

The universality of *wh*-movement and NP raising does not solve the problem, because, universal though they are, they can still conspire to hide errors, in the manner described, by a nonuniversal rule improperly formulated. Furthermore, no strengthening of the Raising principle will replace USET, as Wexler and Culicover have shown.

Unfortunately, I have no suggestion about how to get rid of USET, except perhaps by the strengthening of NBC.

Conclusion

The outcome: The Freezing principle is eliminated, raising is structure-preserving, the Raising principle is maintained but applies only to cyclic nonstylistic transformations, the stylistic transformations apply simultaneously, TUBS is eliminated, and deletions under identity are all S-essential. These revisions are, I hope, all in the direction of linguistic accuracy. I also hope, and believe but cannot prove, that they are sufficient for the Degree-2 learnability theorem.

A line of attack not pursued here, but one that would seem to hold some promise of simplifying the overall set of assumptions, would be to strengthen NBC so as to reduce even further the ability to specify the content in a lower clause. At present, it remains possible to refer to the periphery of a clause by referring to material adjacent to the clause in a higher S. In effect, then, one can require in a structural description that some term be initial or final in an embedded clause. If this residue of the ability to refer to context in lower clauses were eliminated, I believe that a good deal of simplifying could be done, including the elimination of USET, but I have not worked out the details.

It seems to me that it would be useful to have the proof made from a number of different sets of assumptions, with "relative necessity" relations well worked out. If this were done, it is certainly possible that the learning theorem could become a tool for syntacticians.

Note

1. The *Freezing principle* says that if a phrase is moved to a non-structure-preserving position, no proper subpart of that phrase may be extracted from that phrase. The *Raising principle* says that if a phrase has been removed from an S, no proper subpart of that phrase may be removed from that phrase. An application of a transformation is *S-essential* if more than a single S is spanned by its SD, disregarding end variables. USET says that for any pair of Ss in a tree, only one transformation may apply S-essentially to them. TUBS says that if no transformations are applicable to some partially expanded phrase-marker, there must be a full expansion of that phrase-marker to which no transformations are applicable. These definitions are rough paraphrases of the definitions given in Wexler and Culicover (1980).

Chapter 3

Comments   Per-Kristian Halvorsen

I shall begin with a brief review of the assumptions and intent of the research in learnability theory to which Williams's paper is a contribution. I will then look at his proposals in the light of these assumptions and goals. Finally, I shall consider the impact of the paper, given certain adjustments in the background assumptions suggested by an approach to syntax that relies more heavily on base generation.

Assumptions of the Degree-2 Theory of Learnability

The child's task, according to the Degree-2 version of the learning game, is to discover the set of transformational rules required to accomplish the mapping from base phrase-markers to surface structures. For any sentence, it is assumed that the child knows (a) what its base phrase-marker is and (b) what the surface sequence of lexical items in the sentence is. Information about the surface sequence is derivable from the sentences the child is presented with in the course of the learning process. The corresponding base phrase-marker is assumed to be available to the child by force of the fact that she understands the sentence.

In order to explain how the leap from understanding a sentence to recovering its base phrase-marker takes place, it is necessary to assume that the child is able to recover the semantic representation of the sentence once it is understood. It must also be assumed that there is a tightly constrained, and thus easily learnable, mapping from the semantic representation to the base phrase-marker. This mapping entails the adoption of semantic representations that are isomorphic, or near isomorphic, with the syntactic deep structure.[1] In short, it is the assumption of the Degree-2 theory of learnability that a child who understands the sentence has automatic access to its semantic representation, and once the semantic representation is recovered the base phrase-marker is essentially also reconstructed.

It should be noted, however, that the task of understanding a sentence and the task of recovering a semantic representation for it are not necessarily identical. Textual and contextual information may provide sufficient clues to secure the understanding of (1) and (2), even if the lexical information indicating the complex sentence structure of (2) is masked by noise.

(1)
John hasn't brought in the apples.

(2)
It isn't the case that John has brought in the apples.

Examples (1) and (2) are synonymous. In a noisy situation, the internal state of the language user after having understood one of these sentences is presumably identical to the internal state of the language user after having understood the other. However, if the mapping from the semantic representation of the sentence to its base phrase-marker is to be an isomorphism, or at least transparent, it cannot be the case that the two sentences have identical semantic representations, since (1) is a simple clause whereas (2) is a complex clause.

The acquisition of the transformational component is assumed to proceed in the following manner: The child checks each sentence for compatibility with the grammar she has hypothesized. Each time an error is detected, the grammar is revised. Step by step the child's transformational component approaches that of the adult. But for the learning process to succeed—that is, for the child to arrive at a transformational component that is identical to the adult transformational component, the child has to encounter all possible errors in a finite amount of time. This can be guaranteed if all possible errors will show up on phrase-markers with a limited degree of embedding. The goal thus becomes to constrain the transformations in such a fashion that if two transformational components differ in the way they apply to any phrase-marker at all, this difference will be discoverable by examination of their application on phrase-markers with a limited amount of embedding as well. Wexler's learnability proof for transformational grammars (Wexler and Culicover, 1980), shows that, given the constraints he proposes, it is only necessary to examine phrase-markers with two or fewer levels of embeddings. Williams proposes a revision of certain of these principles in the direction of principles with independent linguistic evidence in their favor.[2]

The Freezing Principle versus the Revised Raising Principle

Theoretical Considerations
The first constraint on the application of transformations to come under attack by Williams is the Freezing principle. He points out that its original motivation was derived from two sources (see Wexler, Culicover, and Hamburger, 1974): it served a function in the proof of degree-2 learnability; it was also claimed to account for linguistic phenomena not covered by already existing linguistic principles. Williams observes that the Freezing principle performs a crucial job for the learnability proof only insofar as it freezes non-base-generated structures that result from the raising of material from an embedded clause. Consequently, if we want only to assure the existence of a learnability proof, we may want to replace the Freezing principle by a principle like the revised Raising principle, which specifically freezes these raised structures while it leaves any derived constituent arising from the application of simplex sentence transformations open to fit the structural description of subsequent transfor-

mations, regardless of whether they are base structures.[3] We may, however, decide not to limit our interest simply to the *existence* of a learnability proof. The speed with which a transformational component may be learned should also be of concern.

The Freezing principle contributes more to the transparency of surface structures than the revised Raising principle because it keeps all nonbase structures, simple and complex, from being further transformed. One aspect of the learning task consists of acquiring the transformations that apply in simplex sentences. Furthermore, it is presumably simpler for the child to deduce the correct set of simplex sentence transformations if the relation between base structures and surface structures is maximally transparent. Consequently, it is possible that a grammar where the Freezing principle holds may be more quickly learnable than one where the Freezing principle has been replaced by the revised Raising principle.

The general point I wish to make is that principles that guarantee the efficiency of the learning procedure may in reality, that is, in a world where natural time constraints on the learning process are operative, be as important as principles that guarantee the logical possibility of a child's acquisition of a transformational component.

Linguistic Arguments
Williams also launches an attack on the Freezing principle based on the weakness of the linguistic motivation of the principle. Even though there are problems with its linguistic predictions, I do believe it fares somewhat better under linguistic scrutiny than Williams's discussion suggests.

Phenomena connected with Pseudoclefting, Right Node Raising, Complex NP Shift, Gapping, Dative, and long-distance movement rules have previously been cited in favor of the Freezing principle. For all of these cases Williams either contests the claim that the construction provides evidence in support of the Freezing principle, or proposes alternative explanations for the facts which do not rely on the Freezing principle.

With respect to pseudocleft sentences Williams correctly points out that the restrictions on extraction from them cannot be explained by reference to the Freezing principle if one assumes that this construction is base generated. I shall not disagree with him on the issue of base generation of pseudoclefts, since I have argued in favor of the same position in Halvorsen (1977). It also appears to be correct that no conclusive evidence in favor of the Freezing principle can be found in Right Node Raising cases.

The evidence in support of the Freezing principle derived from facts concerning Complex NP Shift relates to sentences like (3) and (4). The Freezing principle predicts that the entire VP in which Complex NP Shift has occurred is frozen. Examples (3) and (4) seem to confirm this prediction.[4]

(3)
*What did you sell to Fred a beautiful and expensive painting of $\emptyset$?

(4)
*Who did you sell to $\emptyset$ a beautiful and expensive painting?

Since Williams has set out to abolish the Freezing principle, he appeals to Hornstein and Weinberg's (1978) theory of preposition stranding to account for the data in (3) and (4). But (6) shows that it is not just objects of prepositions (as in (3)–(4)) that are inextractible after the application of Complex NP Shift.

(5)
Why did you discourage from visiting France the young soldier who had a short leave?

(6)
*Which place did you discourage from visiting ∅ the young soldier who had a short leave?

Example (6) is as ungrammatical as (4). But (5) and (6) fall outside the domain of the theory of preposition stranding, and their status would be left unexplained under Williams's account. If we instead maintain the Freezing principle, we will have a unitary account of the ungrammaticality of (3), (4), and (6), since the Freezing principle freezes the entire VP, not just the objects of prepositions, after the application of Complex NP Shift.

The Gapping facts are not so clearly in the Freezing principle's disfavor either. Williams's claim is that (7) and (8)—his (4) and (5)—are both bad. I have quizzed approximately fifteen speakers on their reactions to these sentences, and they uniformly agree that the sentence exhibiting both Gapping and Dative Movement, (7), is ungrammatical, whereas (8) is acceptable.

(7)
*John gave Bill a book and Sam Mary a record.

(8)
John put the pencil in the drawer, and Bill the crayon in the box.

Given these facts the Freezing principle appears to have an edge on the suggested alternative explanation, which claims that the correct generalization governing the ungrammaticality of (8) is that only one constituent can follow the verb after Gapping.[5] In any case, the statement concerning the number of admissible constituents after Gapping would remain an isolated fact, since the general principle it is related to—that all constituents after Gapping are realized as focuses (Bing, 1979)—is invalid. This can be seen from the sentences in (9)–(11). It is customary to claim that the postcopular position in clefts and pseudoclefts is the focus of the sentence, but in these constructions, as well as in gapping constructions, it is possible to limit the focus to a subpart of the so-called focus constituent by means of contrastive stress.

(9)
It was **John's** dog that ate the cake.

(10)
What Mary wants is a **tiny** dog.

(11)
John put the **yellow** crayon in the drawer, and Bill the **blue** crayon in the box.

The status of the comparison between the Freezing principle and the proposed replacements is thus that the Freezing principle handles the Complex NP Shift cases and the data relating to Gapping better than the alternative, whereas the Pseudocleft and Right Node Raising phenomena neither support nor contradict it. The long-distance movement cases remain to be considered.

The Freezing principle nicely accounts for the restrictions on application of long-distance rules to the dative-moved object, illustrated by the examples in (12)–(15).

(12)
What did John give to Bill?

(13)
Who did John give a book to?

(14)
What did John give Bill?

(15)
*Who did John give ∅ a book?

But the freezing effect of Dative is nevertheless the subject of the severest of Williams's criticisms, because the behavior of Passive directly contradicts the prediction that the Dative-moved object is frozen.

(16)
Mary was given a book by John.

(17)
*A book was given Mary by John.

It is this observation, and the fact that intrasentential freezing is not essential for the degree-2 learnability proof to go through, that leads Williams to scrap the Freezing principle and introduce in its place the revised Raising principle (RRP).

The revised Raising principle forces upon us the assumption that the transformational rules fall into two groups: cyclic long-distance rules (wh-movement, raising, etc.), and rightward bounded stylistic rules. But one could have chosen a different tack. Where the Freezing principle runs into serious trouble is with respect to Passive in sentences where Dative Movement has applied. Its predictions concerning the application of long-distance rules show a good record. We could, therefore, assume a grammar with a different split between the rules than the one Williams has suggested. One group would consist of strictly local rules, like Passive and Dative, that apply within simplex sentences. These would cause freezing if they are not structure-preserving, but they can themselves melt frozen structures.[6] The other group would consist of intersentential rules, which operate in questions and relative clauses, raising constructions, extraposed sentences, and so on. These may themselves cause freezing, just as the local rules do, but they cannot analyze frozen structures.

What does this different split buy us? Two things: (1) We can maintain a single principle, the Freezing principle, to account for the Complex NP Shift evidence, the long-distance movement and Dative evidence, the Gapping evidence, and the Right Node Raising evidence. (2) We are able to constrain the application of the essentially nonlocal rules even when they operate on simplex sentences, as in (12)–(15).

It should be noted that the revised Raising principle itself has no linguistic motivation. It serves only the function of insuring learnability from degree-2 data. (It makes predictions about the result of certain rule applications, but these predictions are, as Williams points out, duplicated by the predictions of independently needed, and more widely applicable, principles such as the Fixed Subject constraint.) Indeed, it seems as if the only constraint with linguistic motivation is the Freezing principle. The Binary principle is claimed to have linguistic motivation by force of the fact that it is essentially identical to the linguistically motivated principle of Subjacency.[7] This convergence of linguistic evidence and the principles dictated by learnability considerations is at first blush both amazing and compelling. But it must be remembered that the Binary principle is not necessarily a requirement for learnability per se. It is only a requirement for the proof of degree-2 learnability. There is no hard evidence to indicate that humans do not make use of data with more than 2 degrees of embedding in the acquisition process. Wexler and his colleagues might therefore have set out to prove degree-3 or degree-4 learnability. Wexler (personal communication) informs me that a principle comparable in its function to the Binary principle is likely to be required even in this case, but there is no reason to believe that this principle would be identical to the linguistically motivated principle of Subjacency.[8]

Conclusions

My suggestions have been focused on ways to save the Freezing principle. The reason is not that I believe in its linguistic infallibility. Rather, I want to emphasize the usefulness of constraints that enhance the transparency of surface structures, and possibly the efficiency of the learning process, even though they do not make a crucial contribution to the existence of a learnability proof. Another reason is that it seems to be the *only* principle in the Degree-2 theory with the beginnings of a linguistic motivation.

A number of interesting and controversial assumptions of the Degree-2 theory of learnability fall outside the scope of Williams's investigation, but they nevertheless deserve attention in view of their potential impact on important questions in linguistic theory.

The Degree-2 theory assumes that the child is able to recover the semantic representation of a sentence once it is understood. I have pointed out that for the crucial assumption that there is a simple mapping from this semantic representation to the base phrase-marker to go through, the semantic representation will have to have traits determined by the structure of the sentence which are irrelevant to its meaning. If learnability is to be provable, what are the exact properties one has to assign to the semantic representations that the child recovers? What is the evidence that the child is able to recover representations with these properties and not just to understand the sentences uttered? The attempts to limit the complexity of the transformational mapping squeeze together the space that separates semantic representations and surface structures. In the limit these efforts lead to a base-generation approach to syntax. Obviously, there would still be something left for the child to learn, according to this model, even though there is no transformational component. How can one describe what the learning task would be in this case, maintaining the admirable level of explicitness that characterizes the Degree-2 theory of learnability?

Notes

1. The invariance principle governs the mapping between semantic representations and syntactic deep structures. See Wexler and Culicover (1974).

2. Culicover and Wexler (1977) present the following definitions which are relevant to the discussion in the next sections: *Frozen Node:* If the immediate structure of a node in a derived phrase-marker is non-base, then that node is frozen. *Freezing principle:* If a node X of a phrase-marker is frozen, then no node which X dominates may be analyzed by a transformation.

3. Williams's revised Raising principle requires that all raising be structure-preserving.

4. Examples (3)–(6) are from Culicover and Wexler (1977).

5. There are obviously restrictions on the application of Gapping which cannot be subsumed under the Freezing principle. One example from Williams's paper is *John considers Bill happy and Mary unhappy*. The point I want to make here is that the Freezing principle does not fare any worse than any proposed alternatives when matched with the gapping facts.

6. This of course weakens the argument made in the previous section in favor of the Freezing principle, which was based on the contribution it made to the preservation of transparency of simplex sentences.

7. "The Binary Principle says that when a transformation T applies to a cyclic node the structural description of T may not apply (except for variables) to any node in the phrase marker not in the cycle at which T is applying or a cycle immediately below that one" (Culicover and Wexler, 1977, p. 14).

8. I find the arguments Williams presents for the elimination of the principle of Transparency of Untransformable Base Structures (TUBS) convincing, and I have nothing further to add to his discussion of it, nor to his comments concerning the principle of Uniqueness of S-Essential Transformations (USET).

Chapter 4

<table>
<tr><td>The History of
Noun Phrase Movement</td><td>David Lightfoot</td></tr>
</table>

Explaining Historical Change

I view the theory of grammar as an attempt to define one part of
our mental capacity, an innate biological endowment common to the
human species. A child is exposed to some particular linguistic
environment consisting of a fairly haphazard set of sentences and
pseudosentences uttered in an appropriate context. That environment
normally suffices to trigger the emergence of a mature system of
knowledge that goes far beyond the triggering experience: one comes
to know without instruction that certain sentences are ambiguous,
others are paraphrases of each other, others are ungrammatical—that
is, absent from one's experience for principled reasons and not as a
matter of accident. A particular grammar characterizes the mature linguistic knowledge of some individual who has been exposed to some
linguistic environment in this way, and that grammar falls within the
limits given by the theory of grammar.

Taking this perspective, one can view a theory of grammar as specifying a set of choices to be made on exposure to a linguistic environment. For example, it is plausible to claim that the theory of grammar
specifies that a noun phrase will consist minimally of a Specifier and a
$\overline{N}$, with the order to be fixed for an individual's grammar by his experience. In turn, $\overline{N}$ will consist of a noun (N or $\overline{N}$) and (optionally) a
prepositional phrase, noun phrase, or subordinate clause, again with
the order to be determined on exposure to relevant data. These two
choices can be made for an English-speaker's grammar on the basis of a
few phrases like *the house that Jack built* (assuming some preliminary
analysis of words, category membership, etc.). Given such a theory of
grammar—often called universal grammar (UG)—exposure to such
phrases will suffice to trigger the phrase structure rules of (1).

(1)

$$\overline{\overline{N}} \rightarrow \text{Specifier } \overline{N}$$

$$\overline{N} \rightarrow \left\{ \begin{array}{c} N \\ \overline{N} \end{array} \right\} (\left\{ \begin{array}{c} \overline{\overline{S}} \\ \overline{\overline{P}} \\ \overline{\overline{N}} \end{array} \right\})$$

These phrase structure (PS) rules will interact with other rules of grammar (attained in a similar way, by fixing parameters left open by UG) and entail automatically that certain "sentences" will never occur, that an indefinite number of sentences never encountered in actual experience may in fact be uttered, that other sentences are ambiguous or paraphrases, and so on. (For details of the noun phrase structure example, see Hornstein and Lightfoot, 1981, Intro.) Chomsky (1981) takes a similar line in arguing that a theory of grammar specifies that S or $\overline{S}$ can be cyclic nodes. Many speakers of English take S as cyclic, whereas Italian speakers opt for $\overline{S}$. Chomsky discusses how these choices are made under normal childhood experiences and the consequences of each choice for the quite different mature linguistic knowledge of English and Italian speakers.

Under a restrictive theory of grammar, fixing a parameter of grammar some particular way may have elaborate consequences for the form of a person's knowledge; researchers try to define those consequences as accurately as possible, in this way narrowing the set of choices to be made by a child developing a particular grammar. For each choice, one wants to specify what kind of linguistic experience or data would be needed, being concerned to appeal only to experience that can plausibly be assumed to be available to the normal child. One would want to say that the Italian child can determine that $\overline{S}$ is cyclic when exposed to some simple sentences of Italian and that that decision in turn determines various aspects of his eventual knowledge for which there is no evidence in the haphazard set of sentences he happens to experience in childhood.

The aim, then, is to specify the choices to be made by children as their particular grammars emerge, and to specify them in such a way that the choice can be made on the basis of readily available data. The choice so made should predict aspects of the child's knowledge for which there is no evidence in the environmental data.[1] I shall therefore be particularly interested in those instances where differences in two (or more) grammars can be traced to some parameter of UG that was fixed differently—for example, the choice of S or $\overline{S}$ as cyclic nodes, which entails several differences between English and Italian. This is where data from language change become relevant.

A language may change historically in a variety of ways: Speakers may introduce a new set of sentence types in imitation of another language with which they have regular contact or in order to achieve stylistic or expressive force through a novel and unusual construction. But changes often take place in clusters, apparently unrelated changes taking place simultaneously or in fairly rapid sequence. So Old English developed a new stress pattern, lost much of its case system, and acquired new patterns of word order. Linguists have been puzzled by the relation between these particular changes and have sometimes claimed that one change was foreshadowed or even determined by another. Under the view of grammar just outlined, such clusters of changes are of particular interest because apparently unrelated simultaneous changes may manifest one parameter of UG that has been fixed differently. If so, a change can be "explained" by showing that it is related to some other novel aspect of the grammar. The relation may be quite surprising. A simple illustration is appropriate.

In earlier English, the verbs *like, ail, repent,* and several others, used to occur in the environment [object ___ subject], and exactly these verbs have undergone a reversal in their meaning. At the earliest stage sentences like (2a) were construed as object-verb-subject and could be glossed as 'pears pleased the king,' with *like* meaning 'to cause pleasure for'; one also finds sentences like (2b), where the plural verb form shows that it is the postverbal noun which acts as the subject; (2d) did not occur. In Modern English (2c) and (2d) are equally unambiguous in having a subject-verb-object analysis and (2a) and (2b) do not occur. But in an intermediate stage (2c) could be treated as object-verb-subject with *like* meaning 'to cause pleasure for' or as subject-verb-object with *like* meaning 'to derive pleasure from.'

(2)
a. Þam cynge licodon peran.
b. The king like pears.
c. The king liked pears.
d. The king likes pears.

The subject-verb-object analysis came to prevail: (2c), formerly construed as object-verb-subject, became analyzable only as subject-verb-object, with a concomitant change in the meaning of *like* (see Lightfoot, 1977 or 1979b, for evidence of the reanalysis). This change occurred hard on the heels of a change in the underlying word order and can be explained by that change, if one assumes a certain theory of grammar.

When English was underlyingly subject-object-verb, a sentence like (2b) was derived as in (3a), from an initial *pears the king like* by a movement rule. However, as the language became underlyingly subject-verb-object, (2b) would have to be derived as in (3b). But this derivation is unavailable if one assumes that movement rules leave traces and that traces can be erased only by a designated morpheme and not by a random $\bar{\bar{N}}$. (My trees omit much structure.)

(3)

a.   b.

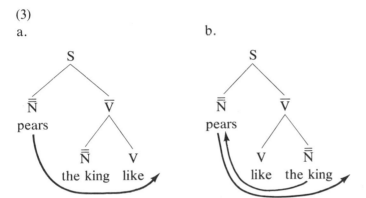

This assumption was motivated by Dresher and Hornstein (1979) and exploited by Freidin (1978), who labeled it the Trace Erasure principle. These writers argue that English sentences with the expletives *there* or *it* involve rightward movement, as indicated in (4), and that the trace of the moved element is covered by a designated morpheme, *there* in (4a) and *it* in (4b).

(4)

a. t was [$_{\bar{\bar{N}}}$ a student] arrested

b. t was obvious [$_{\bar{S}}$ that Harry left]

These are legitimate derivations, but Dresher and Hornstein argue that passive sentences should not be derived by successive postposing of the agent $\bar{\bar{N}}$ and preposing of the object, as is often supposed. They give reasons to prohibit such a derivation and effect the exclusion by the Trace Erasure principle: again, a trace would be erased by a random $\bar{\bar{N}}$ (here by *a student*).

(5)

t was arrested [$_{\bar{\bar{N}}}$ a student] by [$_{\bar{\bar{N}}}$ the police]

The Trace Erasure principle is a plausible proposal because it guarantees that precisely one lexical item will be associated with each deep structure $\bar{\bar{N}}$ position, and that no second $\bar{\bar{N}}$ can be moved through a position vacated by another $\bar{\bar{N}}$. If it is correct, it guarantees that the derivation of (3b) could not occur in Middle English or any other grammar.

The Trace Erasure principle entails that when a child develops the new subject-verb-object PS rules, (2a,b) will no longer be generated and (2c) will no longer be construed as object-verb-subject. Such a sentence would no longer exist in its original analysis—unless, of course, there were a further change of some kind in the grammar. A child with subject-verb-object PS rules hearing a sentence *The king liked pears* would assign it the only available structural analysis: subject-verb-object. If the child also realized the intended meaning of the sentence, namely that pears pleased the king, he would infer that *like* meant 'to derive pleasure from.' The child might also hear a relic form like (2b), which is incompatible with the new grammar. But these forms were presumably not robust enough to trigger a special rule interchanging subject and object; these forms were therefore ignored and, in fact, dropped out of the language. The change in meaning of *like* and the change in the functioning of the grammar are fully explained on the assumptions that the child comes upon sufficient evidence to fix a PS rule $\bar{V} \rightarrow V\,\bar{\bar{N}}$ (for discussion of how that evidence arose see Lightfoot, 1981) and that the theory of grammar is structured in such a way as to preclude the erasure of traces by random $\bar{\bar{N}}$s. The nature of this change suggests that there is something correct about a theory of grammar along these lines.[2]

This, then, is the kind of explanation that I seek for historical changes. Any given change will be explained if one demonstrates two things: (a) that the linguistic environment has changed in such a way that some parameter of UG is fixed differently (e.g., that a PS rule $\bar{V} \rightarrow \bar{\bar{N}}\,V$ is replaced by $\bar{V} \rightarrow V\,\bar{\bar{N}}$); and (b) that the new phenomenon (e.g., the modern meaning of *like*) must be the way that it is, given some general principle(s) of grammar and the new property of the particular grammar (assuming, of course, other relevant aspects of the child's experience: absence of morphological case, a basically configurational syntax, etc.). Therefore, given the new PS rule $\bar{V} \rightarrow V\,\bar{\bar{N}}$, it follows that *like* must come to mean 'derive pleasure from' if one assumes that UG contains the Trace Erasure principle; it also follows that subordinate clauses will have verb-object word order if one assumes that UG subsumes the structure-preservation principle of Emonds (1976). Principles of UG therefore play a crucial role in explaining historical change.

To make the same point backwards, a restrictive theory of grammar containing principles like the Trace Erasure principle and structure-preservation will lead to certain expectations about the clustering of historical changes: given a change in some parameter, certain phenomena must follow. By observing the kinds of clusterings that take place and comparing them with the predictions derived from specific theories of UG, we can presumably revise and refine our theories of grammar. In general, the particular perspective offered by language change is that historical texts sometimes provide a fairly continuous record of the changing linguistic environment; we can therefore see fairly accurately when a parameter is fixed differently and when the linguistic environment became such as to provoke that new fixing. In this paper I shall argue that by refining slightly some recent ideas about a theory of "government" and abstract cases, it is possible to attain impressive levels of explanation for several changes in the history of English.

A brief comment is in order on the scope of explanation to be aimed for. One cannot predict the future development of English short of showing which foreign influences will be successful and which novel expressions will be developed in the constant quest for unusual forms. However, with a good theory of grammar one can show how slightly different environments will fix the parameters left open by UG—this is the crucial element of my perspective. Fixing a parameter differently may entail different properties elsewhere in the grammar, as with the meaning of *like*. These changes, therefore, will arise for reasons of necessity and not be chance; in short, they will be explained.

One can visualize alternative formulations of the theory of UG. They may differ in terms of which historical changes they explain (by attributing them to properties of grammar) and which changes they attribute to chance innovations on the part of adult speakers. There must be a role for chance, since languages diverge and pursue different courses of development. Since chance changes and necessary changes do not come labeled as such, alternative versions of UG may vary in the range of historical phenomena they explain. It seems legitimate to suppose that changes involving the *loss* of certain constructions demand explanation and cannot be attributed to chance factors of foreign influence or stylistic force, but there are few other guidelines. This lack of guidelines would entail a problem of indeterminacy if grammatical theories were responsible only for explaining historical phenomena or if historical developments were explained by a "theory of change." In fact, the theory of grammar must meet many other demands (see the papers in Hornstein and Lightfoot, 1981), and at this stage of research it is difficult to imagine a real problem of indeterminacy. By studying language change in the context of a psychological view of grammar and by placing the explanatory burden for historical change on the theory of grammar (i.e., a theory of this mental capacity), one avoids or at least postpones any problem of indeterminacy. Historical analyses can also be used to illuminate the proper form of the theory of grammar, as I show in the next section.

An Inadequate Account of NP Movement

Universal grammar makes available for particular grammars various classes of rules: PS rules, lexical redundancy rules, transformations, rules of interpretation, and so on. Each class of rules has distinct formal properties, given by UG. There is now an extensive literature about restrictions on the expressive power of transformations and I assume in particular that transformations are insensitive to grammatical relations, cannot be annotated for optional versus obligatory application, and can mention at most two syntactic categories and an intervening variable but not quantificational statements, dominance relations, semantic features, or the other items familiar from introductory textbooks on generative grammar; it is also impossible to state lexical exceptions to these rules. So one can have a transformation like (6), which simply moves a $\bar{\bar{N}}$. Application of this rule is constrained by general conditions provided by UG and must contribute to a surface structure that can receive a phonological and a semantic interpretation.

(6)
Move $\bar{\bar{N}}$.

Lexical redundancy rules, however, have quite a different shape and relate subcategorization frames in the lexicon. Redundancy rules therefore apply only to base-generated structures and affect particular lexical items (not necessarily *all* words of a given syntactic category). Since subcategorization frames are local (Chomsky, 1965) and refer

only to adjacent categories, redundancy rules operate on very restricted domains, but they are able to mention various categories, relating a noun to an adjective, and so on.

A distinction along these lines between transformations and lexical
redundancy rules seems entirely plausible. Wasow (1977) accepted
such a distinction in UG and argued that the grammar of Modern English had both a lexical rule and a transformation for passive sentences.
So (7a) was derived from (7b) by a movement transformation; it could
not be related to an active *Somebody expected* [$_{\bar{s}}$ *John to win*] via a
lexical rule because the strict subcategorization frame of *expect,* being
local, specifies only that *expect* is followed by $\bar{S}$ and it does not specify
the subject $\bar{\bar{N}}$ of the lower clause.

(7)
a. John was expected [$_{\bar{s}}$ t to win]
b. $\bar{\bar{N}}$ was expected [$_{\bar{s}}$ John to win]

A simple passive like *John was arrested* might be base generated and
related to the corresponding active by a lexical rule. Wasow does not
state the lexical rule that he has in mind, but presumably it is along the
lines of (8).

(8)
$$
\begin{bmatrix}
V \\
\bar{\bar{N}}_i \underline{\quad} \bar{\bar{N}}_j \\
\text{object}
\end{bmatrix}
\leftrightarrow
\begin{bmatrix}
[_{Adj} \ V+en] \\
\bar{\bar{N}}_j \ \text{be} \underline{\quad} \\
\text{STATIVE}
\end{bmatrix}
$$

This says that there is a one-to-one relation (subject to lexical exceptions) between verbs that have direct objects and verbs that have participial forms that are adjectives and have a stative semantics; an $\bar{\bar{N}}$ that
can occur as the direct object of the active verb can occur as the subject
of the adjectival form, and vice versa.

I have noted that some passives, for example, (7a), cannot be base
generated and then related to the corresponding active by a lexical rule.
But why not the reverse? Why not derive all passives by movement and
dispense with the lexical rule (8)? Wasow's answer is that the lexical
rule stipulates that the passive participle is an adjective and conveys
stative force; not all participles have these two properties and consequently they are not related to the active by the lexical rule. There
are three problems with this account.

Problem 1. The lexical rule (8), stipulating a semantic feature and a
case relation in addition to the subcategorization frame, has great ex-

pressive power. This power may turn out to be necessary in order to achieve descriptive adequacy, and lexical rules of this type may turn out to be attainable by a child under normal circumstances. But a priori the rule looks suspect.

Problem 2. The distinction between adjectival and nonadjectival passive participles is by no means clear. Wasow offers four criteria for adjectivehood: ability to occur after *very,* after the *un-* prefix, as a predicate to verbs like *seem, act, sound,* and in prenominal position. None of these criteria is very persuasive in isolation and in combination they do not define the correct set of participles.

Several simple passives with stative semantics cannot occur after *very:*

(9)
*The door was very closed.
*The house is very owned by Max.
*John was very arrested.

Ability to occur with *un-* is not a good diagnostic for adjectivehood because many clear examples of adjectives do not take *un-: *unangry,* *untall,* *unfat.* Therefore, one is not surprised that not only transformational passives but also several lexical (i.e., adjectival) passives do not occur with *un-: *The book was ungiven to Mary, *Fred was unirritated at John.* In many dialects clear cases of nonlexical passives occur with verbs like *seem: John seems expected to win.* Finally, the fact that *expected to win* cannot occur prenominally does not make *expected* a nonadjective; an alternative explanation for the nonoccurrence of *the expected to win athlete* lies in the requirement that prenominal adjectival phrases in English must be "light"—hence the unacceptability of *the obvious to everybody solution, *the interested in genetics linguists* (this requirement probably extends to all prenominal items: *the man who I met yesterday's mother*). In any case, lexical passives like *surprised at Fred* also do not occur prenominally—presumably because they too are too "heavy."

Independently of these criteria, Wasow (1977, p. 341) argues that to take *given, considered,* and so forth, as base-generated adjectives would entail an otherwise unnecessary PS rule, $\overline{\text{Adj}} \rightarrow \text{Adj} (\overline{\overline{\text{N}}})$, for passives like *John was given a book, considered a fool.* I have argued (Lightfoot, 1979a,b) that these forms should be treated as lexical, therefore adjectival passives if one invokes Wasow's criteria. Moreover, they can be treated adjectivally without complicating the grammar. The allegedly unnecessary PS rule is needed for phrases like *worth a dime, near the house* (where *near* is probably an adjective, if only because it has comparative and superlative forms). This is not surprising if one assumes a strong version of the $\overline{\overline{X}}$ conventions. If all lexical categories are subject to the same geometrical constraints, the fact that $\overline{V}$ can be expanded as V ($\left\{\begin{array}{c} \overline{\overline{\overline{N}}} \\ \overline{\overline{P}} \\ \overline{S} \end{array}\right\}$) suggests that $\overline{N}$, $\overline{P}$, $\overline{Adj}$ can have a similar complement structure; it would therefore follow that, like a V, an Adj could be followed by a noun phrase. Such a strong version of $\overline{\overline{X}}$ conventions seems quite plausible.[3]

Problem 3. If Wasow is correct to postulate two rules for passive constructions, there will be massive indeterminacy in the grammar in that a simple passive like *John was arrested* may be related to the corresponding active by the lexical rule or by the movement rule. The only empirical claim here is that it will have a stative meaning when base generated and a dynamic meaning when movement is involved. But if problem 2 is not resolved and if there is no reason to distinguish adjectival and nonadjectival participles, then there is no reason to adopt two *syntactic* analyses. At a more speculative level, if passives have two quite different analyses, one wonders why they look so similar at surface structure.

In Lightfoot (1979a) I adopted Wasow's essential framework, ignoring problems 1 and 3 and amending the framework to avoid some aspects of problem 2. I then argued that the transformationally derived passive did not exist in the grammar of Old English and was introduced at the end of Middle English. In (1979b) I went further and argued that rule (6)—that is, a more general rule than just a passive transformation (one affecting other construction types)—was introduced. I took the passive transformation to be involved in the derivation of (10) (but, unlike Wasow, not in the derivation of *John was considered a fool*) and argued that there was no motivation for such a rule before late Middle English.[4]

(10)
a. John was expected [$_{\bar{S}}$ t to win].
b. John was given t a book.
c. John was taken advantage of t.
d. The bed was slept in t.

Also occurring for the first time in late Middle English were sentences like (11), where movement takes place over an active intransitive verb and an adjective.

(11)
a. John seems [$_{\bar{S}}$ t to be happy].
b. John is certain [$_{\bar{S}}$ t to win].

To say that the rule Move $\bar{\bar{N}}$ was introduced in late Middle English accounts for the introduction of sentences like (10) and (11), but this analysis is inadequate for two reasons. First, if transformations must be stated in as general a form as (6) and therefore do not hold of specific construction types, it is implausible (but not impossible) to claim that Old English lacked the rule, because it had fairly free word order and therefore presumably movement rules were operative—although deeper analysis may show that the movement was stylistic and therefore not part of core grammar. (The occurrence of objective genitives, *Rome's destruction*,[5] does not constitute evidence for movement because the potential source, *the destruction (of) Rome*, seems not to have occurred in the very earliest texts; the usual alternant was *destruction Rome's*, which could be related to *Rome's destruction* by a stylistic permutation. I am grateful to Anthony Warner for that point.)

Second, even if the description is correct, no explanation is offered for why Move $\bar{\bar{N}}$ should be introduced; one would want to know how the linguistic environment had changed such that a grammar with (6) became most highly valued. Of course, not all historical changes must be explained in this way. But it is not plausible to attribute a set of simultaneous innovations like (10) and (11)—and some others yet to be discussed—to a chance factor having to do with foreign influence and the stylistic force stemming from a novel expression.

The two inadequacies of the historical account and the three problems with the synchronic framework on which it was based suggest that it may be possible to formulate something better. Wasow (1978b) has sought to do this by discarding the movement analysis altogether and handling all passives with two kinds of lexical rule. He assumes the "realistic" framework of Bresnan (1978), and extends the definition of lexical rules so that one type can apply nonlocally and does not refer to thematic relations. One can now subsume (10a) under this new kind of nonlocal lexical rule for verbal passives, but there is a high price: for example, Wasow (1977) used the essential localness of lexical rules to explain the nonoccurrence of **John's inexperience showed to be a* *problem* (cf. *John's inexperience showed* and *Mary showed John's inexperience to be a problem*); now it would have to be attributed to the formulation of the Middle Voice rule in English, which happens to be local, that is, to refer only to the thematic relations of such verbs as *show*. One wonders how this knowledge could be attained by a child without access to ungrammaticality judgments, inasmuch as the rule might have been nonlocal (i.e., the theory of lexical rules is loose enough for a nonlocal Middle Voice rule to be available). One is again left with no explanation for why the nonlocal lexical passive rule was introduced in Middle English. Furthermore, lexical rules would now need to be subject to something along the lines of the Tensed S constraint in order to avoid **John was expected would win.*[6]

Lieber (1979) offers an interesting critique and, again, focuses on the lexical rule, extending its scope so that it relates the base-generated *John was given the book* to the active (unlike Wasow, 1977, and Lightfoot, 1979a,b, who invoke movement for such sentences). Lieber argues that the lexical passive rule was as in (8) throughout the history of English, crucially applying only to an 'objective' $\bar{\bar{N}}$. In Old and early Middle English *John* would have dative case in *I gave John the book* and therefore could not be related to *John was given the book* by (8). As the dative case is lost, so *John* in such constructions becomes subsumed under 'objective' and is liable to be affected by (8). There is something attractive about this notion and, I think, something correct, in that Lieber relates the emergence of *John was given a book* to a morphological change. Nonetheless, a fundamental flaw is that she assumes a movement analysis for sentences like (10a,c,d) and (11a,b) and gives no reason for why the Old English movement rule does not apply to *John* in $\bar{\bar{N}}$ *was given John the book* to yield the nonoccurring *John was given the book*. She is also open to the objections concerning Wasow's (1977) dual analysis of passives: the lack of reasons to distinguish adjectival and nonadjectival participles, and the resulting indeterminate analyses for simple passives like *John was arrested*. Finally, Lieber deals only with part of the problem and ignores the other innovative forms.[7]

The moves of Wasow (1978b) and Lieber strike me as retrogressive. The essential problem is the dual analysis of passives. What is common to their analyses is a permissive definition of lexical rules. In contrast, I shall investigate eliminating altogether the lexical rule that relates actives and passives, postulating instead a movement analysis for all passives. In doing this, I do not deny the distinction between lexical and transformational rules outlined earlier (i.e., the distinction assumed in Wasow, 1977, and Lightfoot, 1979a,b, not in Wasow, 1978b). That distinction strikes me as plausible but I no longer think that it is relevant for passives.

I shall argue that rule (6) Move $\overline{\overline{\overline{N}}}$ has always been part of English grammars and that the lexical rule (8) has never played a role. In that case, one will want to know why (6) did not yield the sentences of (10) and (11), which did not occur before late Middle English. I shall preserve the attractive aspect of Lieber's analysis by relating the innovation to the change in the morphological case system.

A Theory of Abstract Case

I shall work within the general framework of Rouveret and Vergnaud (1980) and Chomsky (1980a,b, forthcoming), introducing some small amendments. What is common to these publications is the aim of unifying various conditions of UG via some notion of abstract case.

Differing from Chomsky's recent work but taking up an idea of Kayne (1979), I assume that UG makes available two kinds of case: those assigned at surface structure and those assigned in the base. Surface cases are assigned to $\overline{\overline{\overline{N}}}$s on the basis only of the structural notion of "government":

(12)
Government:
Where α is a lexical category or Tense, α governs β iff the first branching node over α dominates β (where α does not dominate β) and there is no lexical category γ intervening between that branching node and β.

(13)
Surface Case:
a. $\overline{\overline{\overline{N}}} \rightarrow$ Nominative iff governed by Tense.
b. $\overline{\overline{\overline{N}}} \rightarrow$ Objective iff governed by V.

Cases will be assigned to the surface structures (14) and (15) as follows. In (14), [$_{\overline{\overline{N}}}$ John] is governed by Tense but not by V and is therefore Nominative. [$_{\overline{\overline{N}}}$ Mary] is governed by V and not by Tense and therefore is Objective (Tense does not govern [$_{\overline{\overline{N}}}$ Mary] because a verb phrase node ($=\gamma$) intervenes between the first branching node over Tense (S) and [$_{\overline{\overline{N}}}$ Mary]). In (15), [$_{\overline{\overline{N}}}$ John] becomes Nominative and [$_{\overline{\overline{N}}}$ t] becomes

Objective in the same way as in (14); *who* has moved to the Comp position and does not receive any case by these rules.

(14)

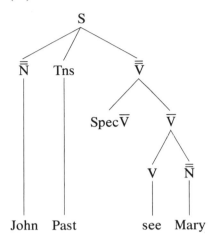

John   Past   see   Mary

(15)

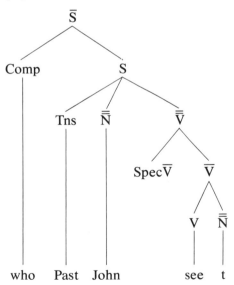

who   Past   John   see   t

I assume that the definition of (12) and the rules of (13) are given in UG. If this assumption is correct, all individual grammars will distinguish Nominative and Objective cases. The rules of (13) are minimal in that all grammars so distinguish Nominative and Objective, but any particular grammar may extend these rules such that Objective will be assigned to a $\bar{\bar{N}}$ governed by a verb or by a preposition; the extension to P as a governor taking Objective case would have to be motivated in the child on exposure to relevant evidence. I shall return to this.

Any other case will be assigned in the base and will often depend on notions other than government. For example, in languages like Latin and Old English, where particular verbs may subcategorize a dative or ablative object, these cases would be assigned in the base. Some grammars, like that of French, may treat prepositions as assigning a nonobjective (call it Oblique) case; if so, UG would demand that it be assigned in the base.

In addition, UG imposes the requirements of (16).

(16)
a. A rule of interpretation always inserts a variable into a position containing a case-marked trace (e.g., 15), but never into any other position.
b. In logical form there must be a one-to-one relation between quantifiers and variables.
c. In surface structure, all lexical Ns except those in Comp (which are quantifiers) have exactly one case.

The Case Theory Applied

Given such a theory of case in UG, particular grammars may vary according to whether they have Oblique and other base-assigned cases and whether prepositions may assign case in surface structure by an extension to (13b). Other variations may be possible but that will depend on an examination of a wider range of languages than I consider here: for example, it might prove necessary to allow Adj or even N to assign Objective case to the $\bar{\bar{N}}$s they govern if a language has expressions like (17), as, apparently, in Vietnamese (Howard Lasnik, personal communication).

(17)
a. It is obvious John that Fred went.
b. Who is it obvious that Fred went?
c. The destruction Rome bothered Fred.
d. What did the destruction bother Fred?

However this may turn out, we have the makings here of a successful theory of case, which allows good descriptions for several languages.

Consider first a grammar that assigns surface case by the rules of (13), not extended to designate prepositions as assigning Objective— for example, French as outlined by Kayne (1979). For French one can assume that prepositions assign Oblique case, which must therefore be assigned in the base. I follow Kayne in assuming that a *wh*-word when moved takes along any base-assigned case; this differs from Chomsky (1980a). So an initial (18a) would become (18b) by *wh*-movement, with the trace non-case-marked. In surface structure, t is not assigned any surface case by (13) because French prepositions do not assign surface case. Since $[_{\bar{\bar{N}}}$ t] has no case, it receives no variable; hence the structure is ill-formed, having a quantifier $[_{Comp}$ qui] but no variable (see 16b).

(18)

a. Comp vous Pres parler à $\begin{bmatrix} \text{qui} \\ _{\bar{\bar{N}}} \ \text{Obl} \end{bmatrix}$

b. $\begin{bmatrix} \quad \text{qui} \\ _{Comp} \ \text{Obl} \end{bmatrix}$ vous Pres parler à $[_{\bar{\bar{N}}}$ t]

Kayne points out that it therefore follows from general principles of case assignment and logical form that a preposition assigning Oblique cannot be stranded by *wh*-movement. There is no need for Weinberg and Hornstein's (1981) filter singling out Oblique traces; instead, the special status of Oblique stems from the fact that it is assigned in deep structure.

In a language allowing preposition stranding, prepositions are not limited to assigning Oblique in the base; they may assign both Oblique in the base and surface case by an extension to (13b) or only surface case. So, Modern English allows not only verbs but also prepositions to assign Objective case in surface structure; here prepositions assign no base case. Thus an initial (19a) has no cases assigned. The result of *wh*-movement is (19b), and (13) assigns Nominative to *you* and Objective to $[_{\bar{\bar{N}}}$ t], yielding (19c). Since the trace is now case-marked, a variable must be inserted, yielding a proper quantificational reading: for which *x*, you spoke to *x*.

(19)

a. Comp you Past speak to who

b. $[_{Comp}$ who] Past you speak to $[_{\bar{\bar{N}}}$ t]

c. $[_{Comp}$ who] Past $\begin{bmatrix} \text{you} \\ \text{Nom} \end{bmatrix}$ speak to $\begin{bmatrix} \quad \text{t} \\ _{\bar{\bar{N}}} \ \text{Obj} \end{bmatrix}$

So those languages that do not allow preposition stranding by *wh*-movement have prepositions that assign only Oblique; those that allow preposition stranding have prepositions that assign surface case. This difference in prepositional case assignment also plays a crucial role in the possibility of preposition stranding in passives. Here there are two necessary ingredients: (i) no basic case assignment to nouns governed by a preposition, (ii) presence of an optional reanalysis rule converting a structure like $[_{Adj}$ speak$+en]$ $[_{\bar{\bar{P}}}$ about $\bar{\bar{N}}]$ into $[_{Adj}$ speak$+en$ about] $\bar{\bar{N}}$, as advocated by Weinberg and Hornstein (1981). Weinberg and Hornstein assume that English has such a reanalysis rule, but not French or the other Romance languages. Kayne (1979) reports that Pollock has argued that French has such a rule, but I shall show that I capture the preposition stranding facts just on the basis of the case theory, regardless of whether French has reanalysis.

Turning first to English, consider an initial (20a). If reanalysis takes place, subsequent movement to subject position yields (20b); the trace has no case (it is governed by neither Tense, V, nor P) and therefore receives no variable. *John* is assigned Nominative by (13a) and a non-quantificational reading is derived. Correct result. If reanalysis does not take place, the result of $\bar{\bar{N}}$ movement is (20c), where the trace will receive Objective and therefore a variable in logical form. Now there is a variable but no quantifier, an impossible result by (16b).

(20)
a. $\bar{\bar{N}}$ Past be $[_{Adj}$ speak$+en]$ $[_{\bar{\bar{P}}}$ about $[_{\bar{\bar{N}}}$ John]]
b. John Past be $[_{Adj}$ speak$+en$ about] $[_{\bar{\bar{N}}}$ t]
c. John Past be $[_{Adj}$ speak$+en]$ $[_{\bar{\bar{P}}}$ about $[_{\bar{\bar{N}}}$ t]]

French prepositions, however, assign only Oblique in the base. Therefore, in an initial (21a) *Jean* receives Oblique (base case assignment must precede reanalysis). Now whether or not reanalysis applies, *Jean* can be moved to subject position and receive Nominative by (13a) in surface structure. *Jean* now has two cases and is therefore ill-formed by (16c).

(21)
a. $\bar{\bar{N}}$ Past être $[_{Adj}$ parlé] $\left[_{\bar{\bar{P}}}\ \text{avec} \left[_{\bar{\bar{N}}}\ \begin{array}{c}\text{Jean]} \\ \text{Obl}\end{array}\right]\right]$

b. $\left[_{\bar{\bar{N}}}\ \begin{array}{c}\text{Jean} \\ \text{Obl} \\ \text{Nom}\end{array}\right]$ Past être $[_{Adj}$ parlé] $[_{\bar{\bar{P}}}$ avec $[_{\bar{\bar{N}}}$ t]]

Notice that $[_{\bar{\bar{N}}}$ t] cannot receive surface case in (21b) or the reanalyzed equivalent because in neither instance would it be governed by Tense or V. It therefore cannot receive any variable and there is no problem on that score.

The different passivizing possibilities of English and French, like the different possibilities for preposition stranding by *wh*-movement, stem from a difference in the abstract case systems, particularly about whether a $\bar{\bar{N}}$ governed by a preposition is assigned a case before or after movement. It is obviously crucial to this account that items can move transformationally both to Comp and to another base-generated $\bar{\bar{N}}$ position.

The History of NP Movement

I now return to the history of NP movement. I shall argue that English grammars have always had a rule Move $\bar{\bar{N}}$, but that prepositions used to assign Oblique in the base and now assign Objective case in surface structure. This, then, is the parameter of grammar that changed in Middle English. In fact, for the purposes of case assignment, the grammars of Old and early Middle English were like that of modern French.

Given the theory of case I have outlined, movement of a $\bar{\bar{N}}$ to another $\bar{\bar{N}}$ position will take place only from a non-case-marked position; if the $\bar{\bar{N}}$ is a *wh* element moving to Comp (i.e., a quantifier), it moves only from a case-marked position, which will contain the variable in logical form.

Consider first the complement to a N. Assuming the strong version of

$\bar{X}$ conventions, the relevant PS rule is $\bar{N} \to N\ (\left\{\begin{array}{c}\bar{\bar{N}}\\\bar{P}\\\bar{S}\end{array}\right\})$. This will allow

the structures of (22).

(22)
a. SpecN̄ $[_{\bar{N}}\ [_N$ portrait] $[_{\bar{\bar{N}}}$ Saskia]]
b. SpecN̄ $[_{\bar{N}}\ [_N$ portrait] $[_{\bar{P}}$ of $[_{\bar{\bar{N}}}$ Saskia]]]

In (22a) *Saskia* is not case-marked and the structure is ill-formed by (16c); in (22b) *Saskia* receives case: Objective in Modern English, Oblique in early Middle English. Since *Saskia* in (22a) has no case, it may move to another $\bar{\bar{N}}$ position, giving the objective genitive, *Saskia's portrait;* the residual trace has no case, therefore no variable, therefore no quantificational reading.[8] If instead of *Saskia* we had *who*, when *who* moved to Comp its trace would receive no variable and so no quantificational reading would be possible: **Who did you see the portrait?*

Turning now to (22b), movement of *Saskia* to the Specifier position would leave a trace, which would receive case in Modern English and therefore a variable; since there is no quantifier binding the variable, the structure is ill-formed by (16b): **Saskia's portrait of*. Such structures were also ill-formed in early Middle English but for a different reason: *Saskia* would receive Oblique case in the base and then Possessive case in surface structure through being in a Specifier slot (cf. *John's hat*)—hence violating (16c). Suppose now that we replace *Saskia* by *who* and move it to Comp. In early Middle English *who* receives Oblique in the base and takes it along to Comp; the trace has no case, hence the quantifier binds no variable and is ill-formed. In Modern English, however, *Who did you see a portrait of* is well-formed: *who* receives no case in the base, but after movement its trace becomes Objective and acquires a variable. Therefore, for all stages of English this case theory yields correct results for movement from a nominal complement to $\overline{\overline{N}}$ and Comp positions.

Continuing with a strong version of $\overline{\overline{X}}$ conventions, I assume that $\overline{Adj}$ is expanded with the same complement structure as other lexical categories, $\overline{Adj} \rightarrow Adj \left(\left\{ \begin{matrix} \overline{\overline{N}} \\ \overline{\overline{P}} \\ \overline{\overline{S}} \end{matrix} \right\} \right)$, and that Adj does not assign case to its complement $\overline{\overline{N}}$ (with the exception of *near, worth,* which do assign case). Now, the discussions of Wasow (1977) and Lightfoot (1979a,b) conflated two separate questions. For any passive construction: (i) Should it be related to the active lexically or transformationally? (ii) Is the passive participle adjectival or not? Both Wasow and I assumed that lexical but not transformational passives were adjectival. As noted earlier, the criteria for distinguishing adjectival and nonadjectival participles were not good. Robert May (personal communication) has convinced me that for English there is no reason not to treat all passive participles as members of the same syntactic category; that category can be Adjective. In which case, the initial structure for *The bread was stolen* would be (23). I shall assume here that Adj is the right category label, but this is not crucial. Whether or not [steal$_v$ + *en*] is labeled Adj, the internal V does not govern the complement $\overline{\overline{N}}$, which therefore cannot receive case in surface structure by rule (13b) (see Rouveret and

Vergnaud, 1980; perfect participles need a different internal structure because of the grammatical . . . *has stolen the bread*).

(23)
$\overline{\overline{N}}$ Past be [$_{\overline{Adj}}$ [$_{Adj}$ [$_V$ steal] + *en*] [$_{\overline{\overline{N}}}$ the bread]]

Therefore, if [$_{\overline{\overline{N}}}$ the bread] does not move, it will receive no case. If it moves to a $\overline{\overline{N}}$ position as in (24), it receives Nominative in surface structure; again, the trace receives no case and cannot be a variable. This is a good result and one is not surprised that such passives occur at all stages of English.

(24)
[$_{\overline{\overline{N}}}$ the bread] Past be [$_{\overline{Adj}}$ [$_{Adj}$ [$_V$ steal] + *en*] [$_{\overline{\overline{N}}}$ t]]

In Old and early Middle English, however, some verbs assigned dative case to their object $\overline{\overline{N}}$. Such a case, being neither Nominative nor Objective, cannot be assigned in surface structure and therefore will be insensitive to government. A dative object cannot become the subject of a passive verb, and this follows from the theory. In an initial (25), *him* receives Oblique (= dative) case (and *ðæs inganges* gets Inherent case in surface structure, as the second of two objects); if it subsequently moves to subject position, it receives Nominative in surface structure, hence violating (16c).[9] (Here I ignore the underlying object-verb order of Old English.)

(25)
$\overline{\overline{N}}$ Past be [$_{\overline{Adj}}$ [$_{Adj}$ [$_V$ forwyrn-] + *en*] [$_{\overline{\overline{N}}}$ him] [$_{\overline{\overline{N}}}$ ðæs inganges]]

For the same reason *John was given the book* did not occur in Old English. Assuming an initial (26), in Old English *John* would receive Oblique in the base and therefore subsequent movement to subject position would result in case conflict. Modern English has no Oblique case, therefore *John* receives no case in the base; subsequent movement to subject yields a well-formed structure where *John* has Nominative case and the trace is caseless (and therefore not a variable). So the introduction of *John was given the book* can be viewed as a function of the loss of the base-assigned Oblique case.[10]

(26)
$\overline{\overline{N}}$ Past be [$_{\overline{Adj}}$ [$_{Adj}$ [$_V$ give] + *en*] [$_{\overline{\overline{N}}}$ John] [$_{\overline{\overline{N}}}$ the book]]

Under this theory, predicative passives like *John was considered a genius* would be expected to occur at all stages of the language. In an initial (27) *John* would receive no base case whether the grammar had Oblique case or not. In surface structure, after movement to subject, *John* would be Nominative and the trace caseless.

(27)

$\overline{\overline{N}}$ Past be [$_{\overline{\overline{Adj}}}$ [$_{Adj}$ [$_V$ consider] + *en*] [$_{\overline{N}}$ John] [$_{\overline{\overline{N}}}$ a genius]]

Consider now some further consequences of this theory, which make it an improvement over Lieber (1979). The passives *The bed was slept in* and *John was taken advantage of* did not occur in Old English. One might have the base forms (28), where *the bed/John* would receive Oblique. Regardless of whether or not reanalysis now applies to build [$_{Adj}$ sleep+*en* in] [$_{Adj}$ take+*en* advantage of] (as in French, if reanalysis applies, it does so after base case assignment), subsequent movement of *the bed* or *John* to subject position will yield a case conflict, as is now familiar. In Modern English, however, with no Oblique case assigned in the base, the result of reanalysis and movement to subject position is a well-formed structure. Therefore the introduction of these passives is also explained by the loss of the Oblique case.

(28)

a. $\overline{\overline{N}}$ Past be [$_{\overline{\overline{Adj}}}$ [$_{Adj}$ [$_V$ sleep] + *en*] [$_{\overline{P}}$ in [$_{\overline{N}}$ the bed]]]

b. $\overline{\overline{N}}$ Past be [$_{\overline{\overline{Adj}}}$ [$_{Adj}$ [$_V$ take] + *en*] advantage [$_{\overline{P}}$ of [$_{\overline{N}}$ John]]]

As prepositional passives developed, so did the possibility of preposition stranding with *wh*-movement. This can also be related to the loss of Oblique case. Consider first the straightforward instance of *wh*-movement (29).[11]

(29)

a. [$_{Comp}$ who] [$_S$ [$_{\overline{N}}$ t] Past [$_{\overline{V}}$ see John]]

b. [$_{Comp}$ who] [$_S$ [$_{\overline{N}}$ John] Past [$_{\overline{V}}$ [$_V$ see] [$_{\overline{N}}$ t]]]

In neither instance would *who* receive a base-assigned case at any stage of history. In (29a) the trace receives Nominative in surface structure and therefore becomes a variable; in (29b) the trace receives Objective and also becomes a variable. In Modern English, *Who did you speak to?* would be derived as in (19): the trace after the preposition would receive Objective and would become a variable. In Old English, prepositions assign Oblique in the base; in surface structure a trace after a preposition would have no case, therefore no variable.

So far I have not discussed passives like (10a) *John was expected to win,* but I have outlined a theory that accounts for the continuous existence of forms like *The bread was stolen, John was considered a genius,* and *Saskia's portrait,* and that accounts for the new passives of (10b,c,d)—*John was given a book, John was taken advantage of,* and *The bed was slept in*—and for the new possibilities for preposition stranding with *wh*-movement (*Who did you speak to?*). All these innovations are attributed to the loss of base-assigned Oblique case.

I have spoken here only of abstract cases but the loss of Oblique coincides in the history of English with the loss of the morphological dative case. It is tempting to postulate a relation between abstract and morphological case systems. The temptation is heightened by the observation that French has a three-way morphological distinction (manifested in the pronoun system: *il, le, lui*) and has Nominative/ Objective/Oblique at the abstract level. This parallelism suggests that grammars will have symmetry between morphological and abstract case systems; children may postulate three abstract cases if there is a three-way morphological distinction, two abstract cases if there is a two-way morphological distinction (ignoring Possessive and Inherent). This statement may hold as an absolute restriction on grammars or it may reflect the unmarked situation. Which alternative is true can be determined only by investigating other grammars; languages where the morphological case system is undergoing a change would be of particular interest.[12]

Whether the symmetry between morphological and abstract case holds absolutely or at the level of markedness, one can relate the syntactic changes in English discussed here to the loss of the dative case in Middle English. The changes are therefore explained by the theory of grammar I have outlined and by the fact that English lost its dative case. Given that the linguistic environment at some point ceased to distinguish accusative and dative, the changes discussed here follow as a natural consequence.[13]

Of course, there is no reason to stop here. One could ask why the dative case was lost, perhaps relating the loss to phonological changes involving word stress, reduction of vowels in final syllables. But that is another story.

S̄ Deletion

One other novel passive form is discussed in Lightfoot (1979a,b) and not explained so far here: *John was expected to win,* where the surface subject of the passive verb must be understood as the subject of the subordinate infinitive. Presumably *John* is moved from the lower clause, in which case the surface structure will be (30). Since English infinitives are always tenseless, the trace has no case; it is governed by neither Tense, verb, nor preposition.

(30)
John Past be $[_{\overline{Adj}}$ $[_{Adj}$ $[_V$ expect$]$ + *en*$]$ $[_{\overline{s}}$ $[_S$ $[_{\overline{N}}$ t$]$ $[_{\overline{V}}$ to win$]]]]$

But the trace would be caseless at all stages of the language, so we have no explanation for why such structures did not occur in Old and early Middle English. Certainly the theory of case as developed so far here plays no relevant role.

Alongside *John was expected to win,* other Middle English innovations that are relevant include (31). For documentation of (31a,b) see Traugott (1972, p. 152 f.), Kageyama (1975), and Lightfoot (1979b, sec. 6.2); on (31c,d) see Lightfoot (1979b, sec. 4.2).

(31)
a. John seems to be happy.
b. John is certain to win.
c. You expect John to win.
d. Who do you expect to win?

In contrast, *You expect to win, You try to win* occur from earliest times. I shall pursue the possibility of a unified account for these facts.

Notice in particular that sentences like (31c) did not occur in Old and early Middle English. Visser (1973, p. 2235 ff.) points to the rarity before late Middle English of verbs followed by $\overline{\overline{N}}$ *to* V . . . , where the $\overline{\overline{N}}$ is the subject of the infinitive. One finds verbs like *persuade* and *prevent* in such environments, but with these verbs the following $\overline{\overline{N}}$ is a direct object and not the subject of the infinitive, for familiar reasons. Visser (p. 2298–99) cites the first attestations of V $\overline{\overline{N}}$ *to* V . . . , where $\overline{\overline{N}}$ is the subject of the infinitive, as in (31c). Some verbs that are familiar in this environment in Modern English began to occur there only quite recently: Visser's first citation for *expect* is 1805, *intend* 1874, *mean* 1860, *want* 1670, *hate* 1847, *like* 1591, and *prefer* 1887.

I could subsume these facts under my case theory: in Modern English *John* receives Objective in (31c), because *expect* governs *John* (cf. *You expect him to win*); but perhaps in Old English, Objective could not be assigned to this position. Chomsky (1980b) takes $\overline{S}$ to be a barrier to government (given by UG) and assumes that particular grammars may have a rule deleting $\overline{S}$ when it contains only S, that is, when Comp is null. Hence an initial (32a), where *John* can have no surface case because it is not governed by Tense or verb, would become (32b), where *John* receives Objective.

(32)
a. You Pres [$_\bar{V}$ expect [$_\bar{S}$ Comp [$_S$ John to win]]]
b. You Pres [$_\bar{V}$ expect [$_S$ John to win]]

If there were a trace in the position of *John,* it would also not receive Objective unless $\bar{S}$ were deleted. So if and only if $\bar{S}$ were deleted, could a variable be inserted. Therefore to say that the rule deleting $\bar{S}$ became available only in Middle English would account for the introduction then of (31c,d).

So far I have conflated surface case assignment and government, saying in (13b) that a $\bar{\bar{N}}$ will be Objective if governed by V (or by P in Modern English). But these are distinct notions. A $\bar{\bar{N}}$ may be governed, even governed by a verb, but still not have case—presumably only transitive verbs assign Objective case to the $\bar{\bar{N}}$s that they govern. Traces may or may not have case, but every trace considered so far has been governed. In a well-formed structure, traces of *wh*-movement are case-marked, therefore governed; traces of $\bar{\bar{N}}$ movement to a non-Comp position never have case but are always governed. In (33) the traces are governed respectively by [$_N$ destruction], the adjectives [[$_V$ arrest]+*en*] and [[$_V$ sleep]+*en* in] (but not by the verbs *arrest* or *sleep*). Since nouns and adjectives do not assign case, the traces remain caseless.

(33)
a. Saskia's [$_{\bar{N}}$ [$_N$ portrait] [$_{\bar{N}}$ t]]
b. John Past be [$_{\overline{Adj}}$ [$_{Adj}$ [$_V$ arrest] + *en*] [$_{\bar{N}}$ t]]
c. The bed Past be [$_{\overline{Adj}}$ [$_{Adj}$ [$_V$ sleep] + *en* in] [$_{\bar{N}}$ t]]

Rather than viewing the governed nature of traces as an accident, one could structure one's theory of UG in such a way as to require that traces be governed. In fact Chomsky (1980b) attempts to derive as a theorem the requirement that the trace of $\bar{\bar{N}}$ movement is always bound in its governing category (i.e., the minimal S or $\bar{\bar{N}}$ domain within which something governs it). If this is correct, the innovative *John was expected to win, is certain to win,* and *seems to be happy* can also be attributed to the availability from Middle English of a rule deleting $\bar{S}$. Assuming such a rule, the surface structures would be (34), where the traces are governed by [$_{Adj}$ [$_V$ expect]+*en*], [$_{Adj}$ certain], and the intransitive verb *seems*. The traces remain caseless because neither adjectives nor intransitive verbs assign case. Therefore they mark positions from which items may move to $\bar{\bar{N}}$ but not to Comp.

(34)

a. John Pres be [$_{\overline{\overline{Adj}}}$ [$_{Adj}$ [$_V$ expect] + *en*] [$_S$ [$_{\bar{N}}$ t] to win]]
b. John Pres be [$_{\overline{\overline{Adj}}}$ [$_{Adj}$ certain] [$_S$ [$_{\bar{N}}$ t] to win]]
c. John Pres [$_{\bar{V}}$ [$_V$ seem] [$_S$ [$_{\bar{N}}$ t] to win]]

The subject of an infinitive, then, cannot receive case or be governed from across a $\bar{S}$ node. If there were no $\bar{S}$ deletion, as in Old and early Middle English, the traces would not be governed and the structures would be ill-formed. In that event, the subject of the infinitive would be neither governed nor case-marked; therefore there could be no lexical $\bar{\bar{N}}$ in this position, no *wh*-movement from it to Comp, *and* no $\bar{\bar{N}}$ movement to another $\bar{\bar{N}}$ position—because the trace would not be governed, and therefore would have no governing category, in the terminology of Chomsky (1980b). These are the conditions under which Pro occurs, that is, an empty $\bar{\bar{N}}$ that is interpreted as an anaphor and from which there is no movement, as in *John tried $\bar{\bar{N}}$ to win, John expected $\bar{\bar{N}}$ to win*. Such sentences occur from the earliest times and do not depend on deletion of $\bar{S}$; rather, they are conditional on the empty $\bar{\bar{N}}$'s not being governed.

There is considerable evidence for the view that infinitival subjects became governable only in Middle English. In Lightfoot (1979b, sec. 4.2) I documented the fact that when *to* infinitives arose in early Middle English, their subject was always empty and was never the source of movement to Comp or another $\bar{\bar{N}}$, that is, the subject was Pro. Regardless of the construction type, lexical nouns did not occur in this position until much later. In (35) I reproduce a list of constructions without a lexical subject (data mostly drawn from Visser, vol. 2). All these constructions are now obsolete (except for (35d), which survives in Ozark English and some rural dialects of England), but the dates cited record the first (column A) and last (column B) attested examples of the type. In (36) I list corresponding constructions that have lexical subjects. The striking fact is that, although several infinitival clause types are represented (subject complements, extraposed subjects, object complements, adjectivals, *fear* constructions, comparatives, purpose clauses, etc.), the subject construction appears consistently about two hundred years later than the corresponding subjectless form. The constructions in (36) survive until the present day; I cite the date of the first recorded example of the type. To facilitate comparison, under column C in (35) I give the first date of the corresponding subject form (i.e., the corresponding form in (36)). Thus the *(for) to* V construction in a subject complement (35a) occurs first in 1205, last in 1590; while the *for* $\bar{\bar{N}}$ *to* V construction in a subject complement (36a) occurs first in 1567, which I enter also in column C in (35). The earliest infinitival form varied between *to* V and *for to* V (often written as one word: *forto*). As discussed in Lightfoot (1979b, sec. 4.2), the constituent structure for the *for to* form would be either $[_{\bar{\bar{N}}}$ for to go], where *for to* is regarded by traditional grammarians as a reinforced version of *to,* or $[_{\bar{P}}$ $[_{P}$ for] $[_{\bar{\bar{N}}}$ to go]]. In neither case would the PS rules allow a $\bar{\bar{N}}$ to intervene between *for* and *to*.

(35)

	A	B	C
a. (For) to go is necessary.	1205	1590	1567
b. It is good (for) to go.	1300	1590	1534
c. . . . that stood in aunter (for) to die.	1205	1623	1391
d. The king did it (for) to have sibbe.	1100	dial.	1422
e. This is a fouler theft than (for) to breke a chirche.	1205	1601	1534
f. He taketh of nought else kepe, but (for) to fill his bagges.	1385	1405	1568
g. (For) to say the sothe, ye have done marvellously.	1300	1583	1673

(36)

a. For us to go is necessary.	1567
b. This would make it imprudent for him to . . .	1534
c. I'm afraid for them to see it.	1391
d. He brought it with him for us to see.	1422
e. What would be better than for you to go.	1534
f. There is nothing to do but for him to marry Amanda.	1568
g. For this low son of a shoemaker to talk of families . . .	1673

In Lightfoot (1979b) I argue that *to* infinitives were originally nominals (like their inflected ancestors, *þincan,* etc.), later being reanalyzed as verbs and losing their nominal properties. What is crucial here is that when they first developed, they had no lexical subject. If, instead, one views this not as a category change but as a change in the possibilities for government, the changes of (35) and (36) can be related to the innovations of (31) and to *John was expected to win:* infinitives were always verbs but their subjects could never be governed, so they were always Pro. As infinitive subjects became governable, (35) became obsolete and (36) and (31) started to appear. The introduction of $\bar{S}$ deletion relates all of these Middle English novelties.

A rule deleting $\bar{S}$ may look somewhat ad hoc, but this device makes good sense under the biological approach to grammar I outlined at the beginning. Given the restrictive theory of abstract case I have developed, the rule would be trivially learnable; it would be triggered on exposure to a simple sentence like *John expected Mary to win.* Given a genetic endowment subsuming this case theory, some device making infinitival subjects governable would be needed in order to square such a sentence with one's preprogrammed expectations.

Deletion of $\bar{S}$ is presumably a lexical property, holding in Modern English for *expect* but not for *try,* although subject to structural factors—that is, that $\bar{S}$ contain a lexically null Comp and a tenseless (infinitival) S. If these structural conditions are met and if the verb is one that may undergo the rule (a verb that can occur in the environment: ＿＿ $\bar{\bar{N}}$ *to* V . . . , where $\bar{\bar{N}}$ is lexical), the rule applies optionally, like all other such rules. That is, most verbs either never govern the lower subject (*try, persuade*) or do so optionally (*want, expect*). However, some problematic verbs never allow Pro but do allow a lexical subject for the lower infinitive: *believe, acknowledge, assume, certify, declare, feel, guess, hold, imagine, judge, know, note, proclaim, reckon, recognize, reveal, report, rule, suppose, take, understand* (and some others have different meanings according to whether there is a Pro or a lexical subject: *presume, remember*).

To say that $\bar{S}$ deletion is obligatory for these verbs raises problems of attainability: the trigger experience for the obligatoriness of $\bar{S}$ deletion cannot appeal to knowledge that *I believe to win* is ungrammatical in English, because children do not have systematic access to this kind of information. This fact suggests that one may need a sophisticated markedness convention or need to claim that for each verb taking an infinitival complement children have to learn, on the basis of experience, whether the infinitive may have a lexical or a Pro subject; the option of having both types (*want, expect,* etc.) would also have to be triggered by relevant experience.

If one ignores this kind of lexical variation, postulating the introduction of $\bar{S}$ deletion in Middle English yields a good description, making it possible to account for a wide range of changes. But I do not have an explanation of the type obtained for the change in the meaning of *like* and for the innovations discussed in connection with the rule Move $\bar{\bar{N}}$. The question arises: why was this rule introduced?

Given the case theory I have outlined, a rule of $\bar{S}$ deletion (or some other device permitting government of infinitival subjects) is a natural, perhaps inevitable, response to sentences like *John expected Mary to win*. If such sentences were introduced for some chance reason like foreign borrowing or, more likely, as a result of translating Latin accusative + infinitive constructions, and then became part of the linguistic environment, the rule would follow as a natural consequence. Once the rule was available, novelties like (31) and (36) would emerge. If correct, this explanation involves a chance factor unlike the explanations offered earlier. This, of course, does not make it wrong or inadequate, since chance factors must play some role in the history of languages.

In the earlier account I attributed some Middle English changes in passive sentences to the development of one rule, Move $\bar{\bar{N}}$. Here I have invoked two changes, a change in case assignment and in the possibility of deleting $\bar{S}$. The temptation arises to try to relate the introduction of $\bar{S}$ deletion to the loss of Oblique case, and thus to subsume the changes discussed in this section under the same explanation offered in the preceding section. That temptation should probably be resisted. One can imagine grammars without Oblique case, that is, with only a two-way Nominative/Objective distinction, and without a rule deleting $\bar{S}$. Therefore, it is likely that the simultaneity of the historical changes in Middle English is accidental. Certainly the kind of lexical variability in the government of infinitival subjects seems to be quite different from that in the inventory of abstract cases. However, the possibility of governing an infinitival subject emerged at about the same time as the first instances of preposition stranding and indirect passives.

Since writing the first version of this paper, I have seen two quite different attempts to relate the two clusters of properties; both dispense with the device of $\bar{S}$ deletion. Hornstein and Weinberg (1980) do so in the context of the thematic indices of Rouveret and Vergnaud (1980), arguing that *Harry* inherits the thematic index of the verb in *I talked about Harry;* particular grammars may relax the locality condition on government by a degree of 1, so that in a configuration like (37) B may govern not only C but also E, where E is the object of a preposition or the subject of a lower infinitive.

(37)

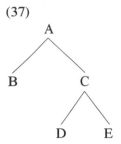

Kayne (1980) treats a null complementizer under verbs like *believe* as prepositional and, like *for,* as a surface case assigner for *John* in . . . believe[∅[John to be happy]]; equivalent prepositions in French and Old English are not surface case assigners, whether they occur in Comp or not.

I have been less ambitious than these writers and I have invoked two, so far independent, changes. The possibility of relating these two changes remains open and will depend on establishing the correct conditions under which an infinitival subject may be governed. In the meantime, I have related a wide range of phenomena, both synchronic and diachronic, and offered an explanation for the changes.

Notes

An earlier version of this paper appeared in T. Hoekstra et al., eds., *Lexical Grammar,* Foris Publications, Dordrecht (1980). I am grateful for helpful comments on that version from Richie Kayne, Jean-Roger Vergnaud, Anthony Warner, and the members of my Utrecht syntax seminar. Since this paper is largely a reconsideration of earlier analyses, I have not burdened the reader with much Old and Middle English data. The relevant documentation may be found in the references cited.

1. It is crucial to this research program that one distinguish between the sparse and haphazard data available to the child and which trigger the emergence of his grammar, and the data available to the linguist. The linguist has access to data about ambiguity, paraphrase, unacceptability, complex sentences in English and many other languages, all of which are unavailable to the child.

2. For the Trace Erasure principle to function at all, it is important that there be rules that may move items to $\overline{\overline{N}}$ positions. This account is therefore not immediately compatible with the approach of Bresnan (1978) and Koster (1978b). Also, the explanation offered here differs from that offered in Lightfoot (1979b, sec. 5.1), where the innovation was attributed to what I called a Transparency principle. Rather than being an independent principle of grammar, this was a more or less intuitive idea about the work load that could be borne by transformations. I claimed that work on syntactic change could be expected to sharpen this idea, enabling us to make more accurate claims about the evaluation metric. As discussed on p. 137, I couched things in terms of a Transparency "principle" for ease of exposition, but this was probably misleading. The Trace Erasure principle is a much more accurate claim about the theory of grammar.

3. So the PS rules allow transitive and intransitive verbs and adjectives. For any particular verb or adjective the strict subcategorization frame will specify whether it is transitive or not. In English, transitive verbs are common and transitive adjectives are rare; van Riemsdijk (1980) proposes a system of markedness conventions to express such discrepancies and to derive a rich set of further predictions. Here I exploit the fact that transitive adjectives do exist and so avoid Wasow's complications.

4. Also relevant to this claim were some issues relating to stative/dynamic interpretations and the fact that early passives marked the agent $\overline{\overline{N}}$ with a wide range of prepositions, whereas in Modern English *by* is fairly standard.

5. Here I accept Jack's (1978) correction to my earlier claim about the history of these expressions. However, it does not follow from the occurrence of objective genitives that there must have been a movement rule in the core grammar of OE.

6. It is sometimes claimed that such a view of lexical rules receives support from facts about language processing (e.g., Bresnan, 1978; Wasow, 1978b). These claims strike me as highly implausible, but I shall not examine them here; see Weinberg (1980) for some good discussion.

7. In Lightfoot (1979a,b) I note a small number of OE sentences like *She was seen to shine,* which Lieber (1979, p. 671) takes as a basis for denying that (10a) represented a ME innovation (but see note 12). She

also denies that passives of complex verbs (10c) and prepositional (pseudo) passives (10d) were ME innovations because there were a few example in OE texts and "it is possible that . . . the gradual increase does not reflect the fact that the construction was actually used more frequently in the spoken language, but rather means that it merely occurred in manuscripts more frequently . . . If it is the case . . . that occurrence in manuscripts cannot be directly correlated with occurrence in the language, then even a single example from the thirteenth century of a construction such as the pseudo-passive is significant and cannot be discounted [footnote omitted]. There is therefore little basis for the claim that the prepositional passive is a fifteenth-sixteenth century innovation" p. 672. Lieber describes this as "an important methodological point."

In studying syntactic change, one is bound to one's texts for data about early stages of some language; one should never discount data, but one must interpret the texts with some philological skill. Taking "a single example from the thirteenth century" as evidence that such sentences were grammatical for all speakers of the language may allow one to suppose that there was no change in grammars and therefore nothing to explain, but this does not strike me as sensible. If there is a significant increase in certain sentence types in fifteenth-century texts (which Lieber concedes), it is reasonable to suppose that there was a change in many individual grammars, i.e., that many individuals began to fix some parameter of UG differently from many of their forebears. One would therefore want to explain why that parameter was fixed differently and precisely what the parameter was. That is the approach I take. I do not suppose that there was an entity "the grammar of Middle English," which changed uniformly and simultaneously for all speakers of English, although it is often useful to abstract away from the kind of variation that Lieber emphasizes.

8. Under this account *Saskia* could also move to the subject of a passive verb: *Saskia$_i$ was seen [$_{\bar{\bar{N}}}$ a [$_{\bar{N}}$ portrait t$_i$]]. The ungrammaticality of this is due to the binding theory, which requires an anaphor (here t$_i$) to have a coindexed antecedent within its governing category (here $\bar{\bar{N}}$) (see Chomsky, 1980b).

As noted earlier, structures like (22b) seem not to occur in the earliest texts; the chronology of these forms needs to be checked. At this earliest stage *Saskia* would occur in the genitive instead of with *of*.

However, I assume that there was an intermediate stage where these structures did occur and where the grammar still had the Oblique case.

9. In ME most verbs taking a dative object may also take an accusative, as has often been noted. Given the accusative option one would expect these verbs to occur in the passive. See Lieber (p. 679–686) for several examples and good discussion.

In OE–ME and other languages where verbs may take dative, genitive, ablative, etc., objects, these objects can usually move to Comp: Latin *cui credis?* 'Whom do you trust?' or Greek *tínos deîtai* 'What does he need?' This fact suggests that a variable can be inserted into the object position and therefore that a trace in this position can receive Objective case in accordance with (13) regardless of what happened in initial structure.

10. So *give* is subcategorized to occur with either ___ $\overline{\overline{\text{N}}}$ ($\overline{\overline{\text{P}}}$), as in *give $5 (to John)*, where the postverbal $\overline{\overline{\text{N}}}$ denotes the item given, or ___ $\overline{\overline{\text{N}}}$ $\overline{\overline{\text{N}}}$ (*give John the book*), where the postverbal noun denotes the recipient. Only the immediately postverbal noun can become the subject of a passive: *$5 was given (to John), John was given $5.* So in *John was given, John* cannot be interpreted as a recipient. The movement analysis leads to good results in this regard and there is no need to invoke a lexical/transformational distinction, pace Wasow (1977, p. 341).

Some dialects allow both *It was given him* and *I gave it him*. Here *give* is subcategorized to occur also in an initial frame ___ $\overline{\overline{\text{N}}}$ $\overline{\overline{\text{N}}}$, where the postverbal $\overline{\overline{\text{N}}}$ denotes the item given (and is usually a pronoun) and the second $\overline{\overline{\text{N}}}$ the recipient. Again, only the immediately postverbal $\overline{\overline{\text{N}}}$ can become the subject of a passive. Notice that Inherent case is assigned in surface structure but does not depend on being governed by the verb: *the book* must be case-marked in *John$_i$ was given t_i the book*.

11. Allen (1977, sec. 6.1) shows that the first sporadic examples of preposition stranding occurred in the thirteenth century and developed simultaneously with *wh*-questions, relative clauses, passives, and topicalized constructions. Preposition stranding became more common in the fourteenth and fifteenth centuries and again affected all the relevant construction types uniformly. *R*-pronouns—forms with nonhuman reference appearing as objects of prepositions—are an exception to the general prohibition on preposition stranding, and in this respect the OE facts parallel those of modern Dutch. I shall not discuss the *r*-pronouns in terms of the theory presupposed in this paper, but see Vat (1978) for

some good discussion; see Horst (1980) for an account in these terms of preposition stranding in Dutch.

12. Dutch is a language where a dative case has been lost fairly recently and changes seem to be taking place in permissible passive forms. See den Besten (1980) for some discussion. Den Besten shares the view adopted here that a trace left by movement into Comp must bear Case, but he also assumes that a trace left by movement into another $\overline{\overline{N}}$ position may bear Case, and he invokes a surface filter. He argues that Dutch and German distinguish verbal and adjectival passive, but it seems to me that several of the complications he notes fall away under the theory adopted here. Apart from the status of Oblique Case in Dutch, there are some interesting questions about the role of $\overline{S}$ deletion (to be discussed in the next section in the context of OE); for example, it is intriguing that the first passive verbs to occur in the frame [$\overline{\overline{N}}$ _____ infinitive] in OE were verbs of perception (see note 7); the same class of verbs occur regularly in this frame in Modern Dutch, and there is some evidence that the frame is now being extended to other verbs such as causatives and some epistemics: jij wordt niet geacht [$_s$ t dat te weten]. If one adopts the analysis of Akmajian (1977), there is no reason to suppose that passive perceptual verbs involve $\overline{S}$ deletion.

13. There is certainly more to be said about this treatment of movement. The theory says nothing about distinctions like *Mary is regarded/ *struck by John as tall, Mary was persuaded/*promised to leave*, but Williams (1980a) offers a plausible account that is consistent with the claims here. Second, notice that I treat the strandability of prepositions that dangle from S somewhat differently from the way Weinberg and Hornstein (1981) do. For them, movement from a sentential PP to subject position would be impossible because the reanalysis rule affects only daughters of $\overline{V}$, hence (i) *The syntax class was slept during*. But nothing prevents movement to Comp if sentential prepositions assign Objective case in the normal way: (ii) *What did he sleep during?* — though not perfectly natural—is far better than the ungrammatical movement to $\overline{\overline{N}}$ in (i).

There may be a problem for the fundamental idea that grammars may differ in the level at which they assign cases, although that idea has served us well so far. The subject of an infinitive in French generally does not get case, presumably because it is not governed in surface structure by a case assigner: *Je crois [Jean être intelligent]. Therefore, something else is needed to block *Je crois [Jean être parlé à t_i], which is well-formed under this analysis: t has no case in surface structure, and *Jean* has just its base-assigned Oblique (recall that **Jean est parlé à* t was blocked by virtue of *Jean*'s having Oblique and Nominative cases in surface structure).

Chapter 4

Comments   Susan F. Schmerling

I will begin by outlining my own perspective on the contribution historical linguistics makes to this conference. In my view the fundamental contribution of empirical studies of linguistic change is to indicate that we cannot expect to fully predict the grammar that a child with a given linguistic experience will acquire, this being a probabilistic matter. The significance of this point for linguistics is that the burden of explaining language acquisition is borne by the theory of universal grammar just to the extent that it is a theory of grammars. My position is, I believe, quite close to that expressed by Grimshaw in chapter 6.

To appreciate my assertion about the significance of linguistic change, it is important to bear in mind that the field of historical linguistics is traditionally the study of linguistic populations; it is essentially sociolinguistic. What are observed—or reconstructed—in historical studies are grammatical innovations in subparts of larger populations. (It is precisely this that makes so-called genetic reconstruction possible.) In some cases we have evidence of a particular geographical spread of an innovation over time. When we speak of the English language as having changed in some way, we are speaking of an innovation that has spread throughout the entire population of what we designate as English-speakers. Now, some observed innovations can be attributed with more or less confidence to influence from other languages, and one can indeed document expressive creations by adults.[1] But it is essential to recall that such adult innovations are not the typical case. Innovations occur continually in monolingual populations, and it is a by-now traditional assumption (and one that is difficult to dispute) that most linguistic change is to be explained by the nature of first-language acquisition—that is, as resulting from what is often called imperfect learning.

Consider what the traditional notion of innovation in historical linguistics means in grossly idealized terms. A generation of speakers share a language. In the succeeding generation, a subgroup of speakers has acquired the same language and another subgroup has acquired a different language. By definition, the grammars acquired by the members of the two subgroups differ. The conclusion seems inescapable that a child with a given linguistic experience must select a particular grammar from among several possibilities available to him (I return at the end of my comments to the question of why this might be a reasonable state of affairs). A somewhat more refined model of change might hypothesize that each child tentatively selects a grammar from among the available possibilities and retains it if a sufficient number of his peers happen to have selected grammars with the same output; accounting for the latter aspect of a change (what many would call the implementation of a change) is a task for sociolinguistic theory rather than the theory of universal grammar.

From the perspective I have just outlined, linguistic changes do not in general appear to be explainable in the sense that we can show that their adoption by a population is inevitable. What we can often do is argue plausibly that some observed change is in fact just one aspect of a more general change; in a different sense of explanation, we can say that the change from /p/ to /f/ in Germanic is explained as part of the more general phenomenon of Grimm's Law. It is this latter kind of explanation that Lightfoot really seems to me to be attempting. Thus in Lightfoot's analysis the appearance of novel types of passive sentences is a manifestation of two changes in the grammar of English, namely, a change in the case system and the addition of a rule of $\overline{S}$ deletion. These changes were themselves presumably not inevitable, just likely to some degree. I think that an assumption that is consistent with the usual practice of historical linguists is that we explain the likelihood or naturalness of a change to the extent that we succeed in demonstrating that the innovating speakers have acquired a grammar that universal grammar should in fact make available to them on the basis of their linguistic experience, which is to say that the innovative grammar must overlap in output with the grammar of the older generation to some significant degree. What this degree is, is then an empirical question.

Lightfoot's example of the meaning change in verbs like *like* illustrates the pitfalls inherent in trying to show the inevitability of some change. Let us assume for the sake of argument (though the assumption is not uncontroversial) that the base constituent order changed in English as Lightfoot supposes. As far as I can see, the theory of universal grammar that he has adopted predicts any of a number of outcomes with regard to *like*. This fact does not constitute an argument against that theory, precisely because the change in question was so clearly not inevitable. This is clear because not all the "verbs like *like*" underwent the same reanalysis; *like* and *please,* in fact, constitute a minimal pair in this respect.[2]

Ignoring for the moment the question of lexical variability in the meaning change Lightfoot discusses, the fundamental difficulty with his approach becomes evident when one recalls that the theory of universal grammar he has adopted makes no predictions about any sentence's being unacceptable to English-speakers; it simply rules out certain sentences as sentences of core grammar. My purpose in noting this point is not to question the validity of Chomsky's core/periphery distinction but simply to point out what it entails, and no Trace Erasure principle entails that a sentence derived in violation of it cannot figure in a speaker's actual linguistic performance.

Moreover, nothing entails that *The king like pears* must be derived by structure-preserving NP movement. In fact, an analysis of such sentences embodying Lightfoot's stated assumptions about Old English verb position must presumably specify main-clause word order by root transformations. Under Lightfoot's assumed derivation for the Old English version, it is indeed possible to postpose *pears*—but if this is structure-preserving movement,[3] then by Lightfoot's other assumptions *pears* is not easily assigned Nominative case. Even if this turns out not to be a real problem, we must still contend with the subject's trace, which will be assigned Nominative case and will thus correspond to a free variable in logical form. The hypothesis of structure-preserving movement thus seems disconfirmed for Old English as well as for Middle English; I see no obvious alternative in Lightfoot's framework to saying that it was a marked construction that was lost with the Middle English verb reanalyses. But it is not clear that one would be justified in invoking the marked nature of a construction as the reason for its loss. The question of whether marked constructions are readily lost is an empirical one, the answer crucially depending on what constructions the theory designates as marked.

A more traditional approach to *like* relates its change in meaning not to a change in base constituent order but to a change in the rigidity of constituent order. The traditional way of thinking is that subjects came to be marked as such by sentence-initial position rather than by morphological case; in this view *The king like pears* would violate a maximally general agreement rule. As far as I can see, the traditional notion of a change in the formal marking of subjects ought to be reconstructable in any theory of universal grammar that permits both Old English and Modern English as possible languages. This kind of approach would then explain the likelihood or naturalness of the change in *like* as a reflection of a language-learning strategy that resulted in speakers' positing an agreement rule that was too general from the point of view of the older generation. This point should hold regardless of what kind of rule one takes agreement to be. There is, in fact, some evidence for a stage of English where NP position rather than morphological case is clearly the concomitant of being an agreement trigger. Examples (1)–(3), which contain verbs that agree with nonnominative NPs, are taken from Butler (1977), who got them from Visser (1963–1973):

(1)
Me seem my head doth swim.   (1571)

(2)
Me think it not necessary to do so.   (1475)

(3)
Sum men þat han suche likynge wondren what hem ailen. 'Some men that have such pleasures wonder what ails them.'   (c. 1450)

This kind of example is of very great interest in indicating that innovating speakers have acquired a rule that is actually counterexemplified in the speech of the older generation. To put it differently, the innovative agreement rule could in principle have been disconfirmed by data actually available to the innovators. A second point that these examples illustrate, of course, is the variability in the means of eliminating the anomalous impersonal constructions: *seem* and *ail* do not exhibit the same reanalysis as *think* and *like* in contemporary dialects.

The kind of perspective I have been taking here suggests a problem in Lightfoot's discussion of the introduction of S̄ deletion as well. There is clearly another option speakers could have taken on encountering *I expect John to go* (apart from that of assuming that it was just ungrammatical): they could have decided that *expect* shared a subcategorization with *persuade*. A priori, one might expect the latter analysis to have been preferable; intuitively, the addition of a new subcategorization frame for a verb already in one's lexicon is a far less drastic innovation than the addition of a new syntactic rule. I suspect, in fact, that this alternative is exactly what happened, because as far as I know the types of sentences that argue against an Equi analysis of so-called subject-raising verbs are attested only in the last century.[4] One might then suppose that a new rule was innovated only after a new lexical redundancy was well established. Was a new syntactic rule in fact innovated? The answer to this question is precisely the answer to the theoretical question of how the phenomenon of subject raising is to be reconstructed in a theory. S̄ deletion is one possibility, but it should be borne in mind that this rule is no less open to criticism on learnability grounds than a traditional raising transformation. Lightfoot essentially acknowledges this difficulty, though he seems not really to appreciate the fact that the theory of universal grammar he purports to assume in the paper simply does not permit rules like S̄ deletion that have lexical exceptions.[5]

Assuming that innovative passives like *John was expected to go* can be traced to changes in the lexical properties of the relevant verbs, one must now ask whether Lightfoot succeeds in demonstrating that the remaining innovative passive types result from a single change in the grammar, namely, the loss of an abstract oblique case inspired by the loss of a morphologically distinct dative case. I see a number of problems with his account.

Lightfoot rejects the arguments given in Wasow (1977) for distinguishing lexical passives (involving stative adjectives) from syntactically derived passives and concludes that there is no need to assume a lexical passive rule for any stage of English. It is crucial to his account, however, that passive participles not belong to the same category as perfect participles (else they would assign case), and since for every transitive verb in the language there is a passive participle with exactly the same form as the perfect participle, his framework presumably requires a lexical redundancy rule for Wasow's syntactically derived passives! (One would then say that the NP complements of these passive participles must undergo movement to be assigned case.) This poses a learning question of the sort raised by Wasow in his comments on chapter 10, namely, the question of why there are no exceptions to the redundancy I have just cited; the redundancy becomes especially striking when one observes relic adjectives like *blessèd* and *molten* that diverge in form from the productive participles of Modern English.

There are other reasons to be troubled by a requirement that passive participles not be verbs. I believe that Lightfoot has been rather hasty in dismissing Wasow's arguments that productive passive participles are not adjectives. Wasow's diagnostics for adjectivehood are no less valid for involving necessary rather than sufficient conditions.[6] One can, of course, always say that passive participles are neither adjectives nor verbs, but the theory of categories embodied in $\overline{X}$ theory has as a consequence that they must then be prepositions (which they clearly cannot be if failure to assign case is a valid reason for not regarding them as verbs), or nouns, or elements of some mystery category. It seems to me that restrictive theories are useless if one does not take them seriously; perhaps the theory is trying to tell us that passives are not derived by NP movement. (I take up a related problem later.)

The crucial feature of Lightfoot's account of NP movement in Old English is his adoption of Kayne's suggestion (1979) that the impossibility of stranding prepositions in French results from the prepositions' assigning oblique case in the base. Whatever the merits of Kayne's proposal for French,[7] it cannot be a correct description of Old English for the simple reason that Old English is not like French with respect to preposition stranding. (Lightfoot's note 11 is an implicit acknowledgment of this fact.) Whether or not a preposition could be stranded in Old English depended not on the case assigned a prepositional object but rather on the construction in which the preposition appeared, and it is the question of fleshing out this latter notion that has been the focus of a recent transatlantic debate in *Linguistic Inquiry*. Much of what has in fact been at issue can, I think, be fairly characterized as the question of the extent to which Old English is like Dutch; in note 11, Lightfoot appears to side with his colleagues in Amsterdam (Vat, 1978) in this regard. Cynthia Allen, who has studied Old English data most extensively (1977, 1980), holds that there are crucial differences.

The linguistic issue with regard to Old English preposition stranding is a real one precisely because Old English did not have an across-the-board constraint against preposition stranding; it appears, rather, that some difference in syntactic relations between prepositions and their objects was crucial to strandability. For Vat, the crucial difference is in the nature of the NP functioning as prepositional object: stranding is seen as resulting from the movement of a special pronoun from an "escape-hatch" position. The alternative view, championed by Grimshaw (1975), Bresnan (1976), Maling (1978), and Allen, is that the crucial difference lies not in the nature of the prepositional object but in the nature of the process potentially separating an NP from its governing preposition. This view is incompatible with the theory of Chomsky (1977a) and Chomsky and Lasnik (1977) because both the process(es) permitting preposition stranding and those not permitting stranding appear to have been subject to island constraints, and in the revised extended standard theory these constructions must therefore be derived by one and the same process.[8] Allen (1980) argues that Vat's alternative, proposed in Chomsky and Lasnik's framework, is false to the Old English facts.

The treatment of unbounded dependencies is very much up in the air these days, and it is unlikely that Old English preposition stranding is going to be any more decisive a factor in linguists' acceptance or rejection of a given framework than Modern English *to* contraction has been. What is beyond dispute is that some preposition stranding was possible with Oblique NPs in Old English. Oblique case is sufficient neither to rule out strandability nor to ensure it.

The change in late Middle English preposition stranding thus seems to have to do not with case but with a change in precisely that aspect of the Old English phenomenon that did not pertain to case. It does not, of course, follow that the appearance of pseudopassives is not related to the new possibilities for stranding prepositions elsewhere;[9] what does follow is that any changes in English passives that are related to changes in the case system do manifest a distinct change in the grammar. For this reason, I do not believe that Lightfoot can relate pseudopassives to the novel passive datives, at least if he, Lieber (1979), and many a traditional grammarian are correct in holding the loss of a distinct dative case responsible for the passive datives. This result does not necessarily strike me as bad; the available evidence suggests that English-speakers have been waffling on passive datives since the loss of dative case. The fact that we find not only the innovative *John was given a book* but also the archaic *A book was given John* suggests that the loss of a distinctive dative case paved the way for rival analyses of the double object construction. The innovative passive was clearly not a necessary consequence of the loss of dative case, inasmuch as the archaic passive is perfectly compatible with Lightfoot's Objective/Inherent case distinction. Once again, however, it is a natural consequence if taken to reflect a new general rule for the identification of direct objects (however this notion is to be reconstructed in a theory) as being NPs immediately following the verb.

The traditional view of the loss of a distinct dative case permitting a syntactic reanalysis does not in itself require the assumption of anything other than morphological case, and it seems to me that Lightfoot's own proposals about case raise serious learnability questions. If one takes the elements of $\overline{X}$ theory seriously, then a rule saying that verbs and adjectives assign Objective case is more general than a rule saying that verbs assign Objective case. Yet it is crucial to Lightfoot's account that virtually every adjective taking an NP complement not assign any case at all. One must then contrive a solution saying that the child assumes an adjective not to assign case unless there is positive evidence to the contrary. But it is then unclear to me how the child ever learns whether *worth* and *near* assign Objective or Inherent case. Here, at least, the choice appears to have no empirical consequences; a different problem arises when one asks how the child can learn that the second object of a double object passive participle is assigned case. (This problem is especially acute because the assignment of Inherent case in this context does not really fit into Lightfoot's case theory, as he seems to acknowledge in his note 10.) A speaker who rejects *A book was given John* presumably does so on the basis of the grammar he has already constructed, and the latter was presumably not constructed with any preexisting knowledge that such passives are ill-formed. What is missing from Lightfoot's account is precisely any reconstruction of the notion of direct object and the notion of some expectation on the part of the language learner that there is at most one direct-object complement per verb.[10]

To summarize my discussion of the innovations in English passives, I agree with Lightfoot that each of the innovations he observes can probably be related to other innovations in English; I disagree that the addition of pseudopassives and the addition of the innovative passive datives manifest the same change in English grammar. I have also suggested that if $\overline{S}$ deletion is a rule of contemporary English, its addition is much more recent than Lightfoot suggests. I have dwelt on the notion that it is unlikely that observed changes can ever be fully explained in the sense of being shown to have been inevitable, suggesting instead that universal grammar guides change by making only certain grammars available to language learners. The point I would emphasize is that observed changes would not have been possible if every sentence a child heard could potentially be taken as a crushing counterexample to a tentatively adopted grammar; a child's incipient theory of his language must itself direct him to ignore certain data. This seems to me to be a very reasonable language-learning strategy if one recalls the point emphasized by Chomsky and reiterated by Lightfoot that the data the language learner hears are imperfect. A child who is in some sense aware of speech errors and dialect variability can expect his grammar not to account for all the utterances he hears.[11]

My conclusion is thus that a theory of language acquisition must include a theory of what data children decide to pay attention to (including a theory of what speakers they take as linguistic models). The theory of universal grammar is just one component (crucial though it is) of a theory of acquisition; it is the total acquisition theory that must be invoked to account for linguistic change.

Notes

I am most grateful to Chad Butler and Ellen Woolford for very helpful discussion during the preparation of these comments; they are not to be held responsible for anything I say here.

1. The latter are generally of very minor importance; such changes are most successful when they are most trivial, like the addition of individual lexical items or minor derivational processes like -*wise* suffixation. Foreign influence has been most persuasively argued for in bilingual populations; uncontroversial examples, especially in syntax, are hard to come by. (Especially persuasive are so-called area phenomena like the loss of infinitives in languages of the Balkan peninsula.)

2. In his presentation at the conference, Lightfoot suggested that in "emphasizing variability" I am refusing to make the sorts of idealizations one makes in synchronic linguistics. But the counterfactual assumption of lack of variability in a class of verbs that one is trying to argue must have undergone a particular change is an illegitimate idealization, for obvious reasons.

3. If Old English was actually verb-final in base structures, the relevant movement could not have been structure-preserving, by definition.

4. Visser's earliest citation containing a "raised" dummy NP is from 1968.

5. The facts concerning the traditional raising constructions are quite different from the fact about the possibility of expressed subjects in *for* clauses, where Lightfoot makes a convincing case for a general syntactic change; in his terms, this change is presumably case assigning capability for *for*. It is quite traditional to assume that this change was inspired by the existence of the preposition *for*

and the much discussed possibility of reanalyzing a sentence like (ia) as in (ib):

(i)

a. It is good [$_{PP}$ for linguists] [$_{\bar{S}}$ to read Jespersen].
b. It is good [$_{\bar{S}}$ for linguists to read Jespersen].

I see no reason, however, to assume that this change has anything to do with changes in the lexical properties of verbs like *expect* (and what is relevant about *expect* is at bottom its lexical properties, in anyone's analysis). The notion of an NP's becoming governable independently of the contexts in which it occurs makes no sense to me (I assume that Lightfoot is not assuming that universal grammar changed in the sixteenth century).

6. The analysis of sentences like *The door was closed* as involving an ambiguity not shared by *The door was opened* seems unavoidable, and Lightfoot's worry that a lexical rule of the sort suggested by Wasow is possible only in an overly permissive theory of lexical relations strikes me as unfounded. It is reasonably uncontroversial, for example, that English has a lexical rule deriving adjectives in *-able* from transitive verbs; a rule like this has exactly the properties Lightfoot finds "suspect" in Wasow's rule.

7. I see a problem with Kayne's account (I do not know whether it is addressed in his paper, which I have not had access to). Since no prepositions can be stranded in French, Kayne's approach precludes the possibility of analyzing any preposition as transformationally inserted. One might want to do precisely this, given the motivation Chomsky has discussed (1980) for inserting *of* transformationally and the completely parallel motivation for so analyzing French *de*. Chomsky's motivation, of course, is to preserve a maximally simple $\bar{X}$ theory of the base, and it seems to me that this motivation is not lightly dismissed: as far as I can see, it is the motivation for the entire apparatus of the government-binding framework.

8. At least this seems to be assumed. I am not sure that Chomsky's conception of core grammar rules out a system of constraints for peripheral grammar that happens to mimic the core system, though this does not strike me as a position one would want to have to defend.

9. It is not clear to me, however, that sentences like *This bed was slept in* indicate a transformational derivation, since a strong case can be made for the relevant reanalysis being lexical itself (compare *This bed was slept beside*). This possibility raises the question of why Old English could not in principle have had such lexical reanalyses, with the derived verbs assigning objective case.

10. A small point to note is that Lightfoot's approach would seem to predict that the second object of a double object verb in Old English could never be the subject of a passive (since its trace would be assigned Inherent case). I believe this prediction is false, because of the archaic passive datives I have alluded to. It may be that Lightfoot does not intend his characterization of his example (25) to cover all double object verbs.

11. For this reason it is not sufficient, in attempting to account for the acquisition of a particular rule, to assert that simple exposure to the relevant utterance type will trigger the formulation of the rule. Lightfoot's appeal to this kind of account ignores his own warning about the nature of the data the child is exposed to.

Chapter 5

On the Deductive Model and the Acquisition of Productive Morphology

Thomas Roeper

Linguistic theory is a first step in a biological theory of language ability. A successful theory of language acquisition is one of the biological criteria of the success of linguistic theory. Therefore, one goal of linguistic theory has been to provide a sufficiently rich account of universal grammar to explain a child's acquisition of language. A linguistic explanation is achieved if, given exposure to a representative set of sentences, a child equipped with universal grammar can induce the particular grammar of his community. A linguistic explanation, however, may permit a number of biological instantiations. Therefore a linguistic explanation must be embedded within a restrictive biological theory before we have a full explanation of language acquisition.

This essay has two goals. The primary goal is to provide a demonstration of the claim that universal grammar can be enriched to the point where an explicit deductive acquisition procedure can be provided for an important domain of grammar: morphology. The procedure relies only upon knowledge of universal principles and input sentence data. In particular I shall explain how a child determines the syntactic implications of productive morphology. For instance, a child can know, without instruction, that *I reput the ball in the closet is ungrammatical and I redirected Bill to the airport is grammatical. Furthermore, the child knows that the latter does not presuppose that Bill was directed to the airport initially. These are subtle facts. I believe that it is subtle facts that point most clearly to the necessary role of abstract formal principles in acquisition.

The second goal is to place the linguistic logic of acquisition in perspective. I shall sketch a theory of genetically programmed "triggers" for linguistic knowledge that are not in principle (nor in fact) limited to linguistic information. This theory may, moreover, complicate or supplement the linguistic logic of acquisition based on fixed universals (i.e., the instantaneous model) in ways that are significant for our view of human cognition (Chomsky, 1976, 120–123).

Lexical Rules and the Projection Problem

Transformational grammar has seen a transfer of expressive power from the syntax to the lexicon in order to make certain syntactic rules sensitive to lexical information (Bresnan, 1978; Baker, 1979a; Roeper and Siegel, 1978). One virtue of this transfer is that it invites a plausible theory of acquisition (Roeper et al., in press). The classic example is dative:

(1)
a.   John told Bill a story.
b.   John told a story to Bill.
c.   *John said Bill the answer.
d.   John said the answer to Bill.

The relation between the double object construction and the prepositional construction can be expressed as a transformation. The transformational notation however cannot express the fact that the relation holds for some verbs (*tell*) but not others (*say*). Therefore the relation between (1a) and (1b) must be captured through lexical rules or alternative subcategorizations.

Baker (1979a) has argued that a theory of acquisition must succeed with positive evidence alone. That is, one cannot assume that a child is instructed that (1c) is ungrammatical. The theory of positive evidence fits the lexical approach. We must argue that a child will use the double object construction only when he hears a particular verb with that construction. Therefore he will not generalize the fact that he hears *tell John a story* to the verb *report,* producing the ungrammatical **report John a story.* Syntactic rules are stated in a notation that is insensitive to lexical differences. Therefore the rule of question formation (*What did John report?*) generalizes to (almost) all transitive verbs. The lexical approach works if the child has a means to distinguish the rules that are lexical from those that are syntactic. One natural proposal (Roeper et al., to appear) is that a child knows that only sisters of the verb are governed by the verb. This in turn leads to the true prediction that lexical government involves no long-distance rules.

The Problem of Productivity

This explanation marks a step forward, but it is insufficient to explain the syntactic properties of productive morphological rules. The generation of new words poses the same problem as the generation of new sentences. How does a child use positive evidence to determine the subcategorization for possible words?

Consider a concrete example: How does a child know what happens when he adds *over-?* The first answer might be that he assumes a principle of inheritance:

(2)
Inheritance:
A derived word has the same subcategorization as the base word.

It would be easy to specify a mechanism that simply copies subcategorization frames onto a new word. Inheritance seems to work for examples like (3).

(3)
a. John reacted to Bill.
b. John overreacted to Bill.

However a closer look reveals some problems:

(4)
a. John reacted strangely to Bill.
b. *John overreacted strangely to Bill.

Similarly the double object construction does not generalize:

(5)
a.   I allowed John a deduction.
b. *I disallowed John a deduction.
c.   I heated John the meat.
d. ?*I preheated John the meat.
e.   He overthrew second base.
f. *He overthrew Bill second base. (Compare: threw Bill the ball)
g.   I thrust him a note.
h. *I rethrust him a note.

Traditionally there have been proposals (Fraser, 1974) that seek to account for these facts in semantic terms or in ad hoc terms with respect to particular prefixes. These proposals, as I shall show, remain both programmatic and without any account of the evidence needed for language acquisition. If one takes a larger perspective one can see (a) that an independent restriction on morphological rules is needed and (b) that such a restriction leads to a clear definition of the evidence a child uses to know the syntactic limitations on productive morphology. (The argument and much of the discussion is drawn from Carlson and Roeper, 1980, where further details can be found and a connection to case grammar is made.)

A Large Domain of Relevant Data

I provide here an overview of the domain of evidence needed to solve this problem. A wide variety of subcategorized phrases are permitted by simple verbs (those without affixes):

(6)

∅ (intransitive)	John ran.
NP (transitive)	John saw Bill.
∅ (null direct object)	Bob read.
NP PP	John put the book on the shelf.
NP NP	John gave Harry a headache.
to VP	John tried to leave.
NP *to* VP	John forced Harry to leave.
that S	John thinks that the earth is flat.
NP *that* S	John told Bill that dogs bark.
PP *that* S	John remarked to Bill that the food was good.
Adj	John looks tired.
PP	John laughed at Harold.
Particle	Bob got up.
NP Part	Bob called Betty up.
NP VP	Bob saw Alice swim to the boat.
Adv	He stepped lightly.
NP Adv	This job paid us well.
NP Adj	They called her lazy.
for NP *to* VP	He asked for there to be less noise.
PP *to* VP	They pleaded with him to leave.
Question	He wondered whether she would see him again.

This variety is not surprising. All of these words are listed in the lexicon and therefore are learned by direct positive evidence. They permit whatever diverse subcategorizations are congenial to their meanings.

The verbs that involve productive morphology show heavy restrictions.

(7)

that complements	a.	Bob miscalculated the time of our arrival. *that we would be late.
	b.	John re-proved the theorem. *that the moon was round.
Particle	c.	Dennis rewrote the proposal. *the proposal up.
	d.	John unfolded the paper. *the paper out.
	e.	John fought Bill down.
	f.	John outfought Bill. *Bill down.
Adv	g.	John overstepped his bounds. *lightly.
	h.	John thought quickly.
	i.	*John rethought quickly.
Adj	j.	John remade the bed. *good.
	k.	John set him free.
	l.	*John misset him free.
	m.	John misset the clock.
PP	n.	He rethought the problem. *about the problem.
	o.	It repierced the wood. *through the wood.
Question	p.	John re-asked the question. *whether it rained.
	q.	John reprobed the jury. *(into) where the money had gone.
NP Inf	r.	John underestimated our expenses. *Fred to be a good player.
	s.	He disbelieves our warnings. *John to be our best bet.

Inf   t.   He mismanaged   the situation.
                                                   *to get another ticket.
                             u.   He restarted   the car.
                                                   *to go outside.
                             v.   He rearranged   the room.
                                                   *to go outside.

The same kind of generalization holds for suffixes:

(8)
He glamorized   Bob.
                *Bill Bob.
                *to become president.
                *that the world is good.
                *us to win.
                *beautiful.
                *into the night.

The same holds for *sensationalize* (the news), *scandalize* (the town), *modernize* (your room), *vocalize* (complaints). The other productive suffix is *-en*, which also typically allows one complement (*lengthen the rope*, *lengthen that you will be on vacation*).

    The same generalization holds for compound verbs:

(9)
a. John badmouthed   Bill.
                     *Bill his lines. (Compare: mouthed Bill his lines.)
                     *that Bill likes rock.
                     *us to be good children.
                     *deep.

b. Bill air-conditioned   the room.
                          *John the room.
                          *that it is cool.
                          *cool.

c. grandstand, backpedal, hogtie, windowshop, deep-fry, handpaint

The compound verbs are either transitive or intransitive.

A Morphological Universal
The grammatical examples in these data share one characteristic: they all take a simple direct object or no object. They are either transitive or intransitive. (The intransitive cases are relatively few: *reappear, re-*

occur, overeat, etc. In addition, particles sometimes detransitivize: *hammer away, get up, show up, give up.*)

This leads to the following universal claim about such morphologically complex forms, which I shall call complex verbs:

(10)
a. Productive rules create complex verbs.
b. Complex verbs have the unmarked form of transitive or intransitive.

The affixes in question are not many: *mis-, dis-, re-, pre-, over-, under-, out-, super-,* and *de-,* as well as *-ize* and *-en.*[1]

There is evidence that the direct object of the complex verb is not inherited from the base word but is itself created. Examples like (11) suggest no source for an inherited direct object:

(11)
a. I thought about the problem.
b. I rethought the problem.
c. John out-Kennedyed Kennedy.

The prefix *out-* converts nouns, which have no objects, to verbs with direct objects and nothing else.

The rules for complex verbs stand in stark contrast to other morphological rules, which do not create new subcategorization frames and do permit inheritance:

(12)
a. his sureness that John would win
b. He was sure that John would win.
c. He was happy that Mary came.
d. He was unhappy that Mary came.

It is not an accident that new subcategorizations are created only for verbs. It is related to the fact that verbs take case and play a central role in both the lexicon and syntax. (See Carlson and Roeper, 1980, for an extension of the notion of complex verb to syntax. See also Bach, 1979; Rouveret and Vergnaud, 1980; Vergnaud and Roeper, forthcoming; and Hornstein and Weinberg, 1980.)

Counterexamples and Counterproposals
My theory includes the possibility that any form may be listed. Consequently an unmarked lexical rule can tolerate more exceptions than an unmarked syntactic rule. It could be the case that half of the known

examples are exceptions; they may be known or listed because they have exceptional properties. Thus we find forms like the following:

(13)

a. theorize that John was here
b. the theory that John was here

(14)

a. babysit the kids
b. babysit with the kids
c. sit with the kids
d. *sit the kids

Example (13a) is derived from (13b). We find both (14a) and (14b), predictably, but no source (14d) to produce (14a). It is with respect to the potentially infinite set of unknown forms that the universal (10) is proposed. The goal, once again, is not to account for the contents of the current fixed lexicon but to state the principles that a child uses in projecting new forms.

Each example in list (7) could be extended into an area of intuitional uncertainty. One can imagine a situation in which one would say *I sent you the card and then when it came back I re-sent you the card*. In fact such examples occur in response to the exigencies of conversation. Nevertheless, upon reflection most people will say that they seem undesirable. Furthermore, whenever one explores the domain in depth one finds that most examples of complex verbs fail: *I called him a fool*, **I re-called him a fool*. (See Koster, 1978b, for an analogous argument with respect to violations of structure-preservingness.)

In addition a kind of local analogy allows an extension of the double object form to new examples. Thus we find *Radio him a message, Wire him the news, Cable me some money;* it would therefore not be surprising to find *Let's telex him the news*. Likewise we find *make you a copy* and *xerox you a copy*. Again these forms do not generalize very well. (See Carlson and Roeper, 1980, for a discussion of why denominal verbs are not complex verbs.) We do not find **table you the discussion, *carpet you the room, *eye me the cake, ?*pool us our resources*.

Consider another set of examples that deal with writing:

(15)

a.   I wrote you a letter.
b.   I lettered you a card.
c. ?*I calligraphed you a card.

These become grammatical through a local analogy based on meaning. Thus I would argue that some examples are ruled in by the pragmatics rather than ruled out. They remain ungrammatical within the theory.

Semantic arguments. The literature contains a number of arguments about the semantics of prefixes (Fraser, 1976; Green, 1974). They include references to perfectivity, stativity, extensionality, Anglo-Saxon origins. Each is limited in its domain, hampered by vagueness, and remote from explanatory power with respect to acquisition. (See Carlson and Roeper, 1980, for discussion.) The interactive effects of these factors may, however, contribute to intuitional instability and the impression of gradation.

Consider *perfectiveness*. The prefix *re-* imposes perfectiveness in certain instances:

(16)
a. They played the game until six o'clock.
b. They replayed the game until six o'clock. (From Carlson and Roeper, 1980.)

Example (16b) (suggested by S. J. Keyser) implies that the game was played over and over again. However, this implication does not hold for all cases: *John rethought Republicanism until the beginning of the convention*. Nor does it hold for other prefixes: *John disconnected the phone for fifteen minutes*.[2]

The semantic content of prefixes can influence the complements that words accept, but again there is a lack of uniformity. For instance, *over-* occurs with intransitives (*John overate*), transitives (*John overthrew second base*), and idiosyncratic cases (*John overreacted to Bill*) where inheritance is involved. The semantic content of *over-* interacts with the verb in each case to produce a certain output. There are no instances of novel verbs where the subcategorizations are not inherited and not transitive or intransitive: **John overate fat*. A pattern of forms of this kind would constitute the only kind of true counterevidence to the proposal in Carlson and Roeper (1980).[3]

In general I think two points are central: (1) Intuitional uncertainty can itself be an indication that an abstract principle is at work but obscured by local pragmatic and semantic factors; and (2) if one can provide a procedure demonstrating learnability, then it can substitute for arguments from intuitions of ungrammaticality. Thus one can argue that complex verbs that fail to conform to principle (10) are ungrammatical in theory even if acceptable in practice. In all cases where a semantic or pragmatic factor does not allow its usage, the child will know that complex verbs that deviate from the unmarked form are ungrammatical.

Marked Complex Verbs and Positive Evidence

The systematic exceptions to the unmarked subcategorization for complex verbs provide an interesting challenge to an acquisition theory because of their subtlety. First note that the principle (10) accounts for the ungrammaticality of the following examples:

(17)
a. *John reput the dog in the kennel.
b. *Bill relet the dog in the house.
c. *We reconfined Billy to his room.

However, there is a set of exceptions:

(18)
a. We redirected John to the airport.
b. We readvertised the position in the *Sun*.
c. We reread a book to Bill.
d. We resituated Bill in the front room.

Some speakers find expressions such as in (18) ungrammatical. Nevertheless we must account for their general acceptability. It is clear that the prepositional phrases have been inherited from the base word (e.g., *direct John to the airport*). It can nevertheless be argued that the direct objects are not inherited. Notice the contrast between:

(19)
a. *We situated John.
b. We resituated John.
c. We situated John in the front room.
d. We resituated John in the front room.

Only the prefixed form allows the object by itself. The inherited PPs must be attached to the VP (following familiar tests like the *do so* test) but they are generally predictable through redundancy rules. Nevertheless they constitute the marked cases in this system.

How does the child know the difference between (17) and (18)? The first thing to observe is an interesting presuppositional difference between them. In (17a) the presupposition is that the dog was put in the kennel the first time, but in (18a) one need not suppose that John was directed to the airport the first time. (One must however presuppose that it was John who was directed the first time: *Bill directed Fred to the airport and then he redirected John to the airport. However: Bill directed John to the station and then he redirected him to the airport.) This difference leads to the following principle:

(20)
Only those subcategorizations can be inherited that are not arguments of the verb.

I now have a distinction between what a verb subcategorizes and what its arguments are. I shall not pursue a definition of *argument* but simply define it operationally to mean that which is presupposable. (See Bresnan, 1980, for an interesting discussion of subtleties in how PPs relate to argument structure. Also see Hornstein and Weinberg, 1980.) Thus *put* does not allow the inheritance of *in the kennel* because it would be presupposed, hence an argument of the verb. On the other hand *direct* allows the inheritance of *to the airport* because it is not presupposed.

The indirect object case is parallel: *reread the book to Bill* does not entail that Bill heard it the first time, whereas *reread Bill the book* does invite the presupposition that Bill heard it the first time, which makes it ungrammatical. These arguments hold for adjective and adverb cases as well. We find *John reappeared lame,* which does not imply that he appeared lame the first time, and *John retrained himself quickly,* which does not imply that he trained himself quickly the first time. These cases contrast with *John remade good* and *Bill restepped back* where the adjective and adverb are presupposed (*make good* and *step back*). In general those added frames produced by redundancy rules, which are marked in the theory, are not necessarily marked in our intuitions of grammaticality.

How can the child acquire this knowledge? The goal is to stipulate positive evidence from simple sentences that will allow the child to determine the grammaticality of novel morphological forms. There is no reliable meaning difference between (17) and (18) because, for instance, nothing requires that Bill not be directed to the airport both times. Therefore it is very difficult to see what inferences from contextual meaning could reliably trigger the correct decisions.[4]

The crucial distinction between *put* and *direct* is that for *put* the subcategorizations are obligatory, for *direct* they are optional. This leads to making a connection between optionality and arguments of the verb:

(21)
Only optional subcategorizations are not arguments of the verb. (Or: All obligatory subcategorizations are arguments of the verb.)

Now I have reduced the acquisition problem to the determination of whether a subcategorization frame is optional or obligatory. Everything else follows automatically. In order to provide a basis for determining whether the subcategorizations for *put* are obligatory or not, I must introduce an assumption about acquisition:

(22)
Acquisition Principle:
All subcategorizations are obligatory until positive evidence shows that they are optional.

The child will always hear *I put the dog in the kennel* but never **I put the dog*. However, he will hear *I directed John* or *I read the book*. These sentences indicate to the child that the other subcategorizations are optional. It follows, using these principles (10, 20, 21, 22), that a child can know that **I reput the dog in the kennel* is ungrammatical without ever having heard it and that *I redirected John to the station* is grammatical without ever having used *re-* with *direct*. He will also know that the sentence does not imply that John had been directed to the station before.

Apparent Exceptions
There are examples where the PP is optional but apparently presupposed:

(23)
John reintroduced Mary to Bill.

A pragmatic factor limits the meaning of this expression to the interpretation that John introduced Mary to Bill twice. If we explore other possibilities, it is clear the presupposition is not necessary. Consider: *First I introduced him to all the people in one room and then I had to reintroduce him to all the people in the other room.* In the general case the PP is not presupposed and the special cases are forced by pragmatics. The argument is parallel to arguments about anaphora. We argue that *he* is free in reference in the following discourse although it can refer to John: *John likes girls. And he knows it.*

Uniqueness Principle

This system has an implication for the representation of subcategorization frames. I have argued that only obligatory frames are arguments of the verb and that the marked case allows, in addition to one direct object, other nonargument subcategorizations. This means that in order to rule out **John reread Bill the book* I must claim that *Bill* is an obligatory subcategorization. (A marginal reading of this sentence is possible with stress on *Bill*.) Now, the subcategorizations of *read* can be represented as follows:

(24)

a. *read:* (NP) NP (PP)

The indirect object would then be optional and hence inheritable. The normal assumptions about the construction of subcategorization frames and the conditions under which they should be collapsed would lead to this assumption.

Is there a way to argue that the indirect object NP should be obligatory? If one wrote the subcategorization possibilities in two lines, as in (24b), this result could be achieved.

(24)

b. *read:* NP (PP)

NP_2 NP_1

This double set of subcategorizations can be justified as a marked construction by invoking the Uniqueness principle proposed by Wexler. Wexler has argued (personal communication) that in the unmarked case every deep form has a single surface structure in syntax. Only with positive evidence do we allow a marked second surface form. If this approach is transposed to the lexicon, one can argue that in the unmarked case each functional structure has a single subcategorization structure. If there is more than one subcategorization for a function (say, indirect object), then it is marked and written on a separate line of subcategorizations. (See Roeper et al., to appear.) This argument for an obligatory NP_2 NP_1 sequence provides support from unsuspected quarters for the Uniqueness principle.

Phonological Trigger

We now have a statement of the positive evidence needed to establish that certain frames are obligatory and others optional. We do not have a trigger whereby a child can determine when complex verbs exist. I am unsure of the answer to this question, but I can make a suggestion.

What distinguishes complex verbs is that they involve a productive affix or a compound. They can therefore be loosely identified with words that contain a word-boundary on the inside. Thus the difference between *return* (re+turn) and *rewrite* (re#write) can be represented in the kind of boundary they take and consequently their phonology. *Return* allows a schwa in *re-* whereas *rewrite* does not. This phonological difference is part of the evidence available to the child and therefore could trigger knowledge of the word-boundary difference, which in turn triggers the sequence of principles I have outlined.

Thus a piece of phonological evidence could set in motion a series of syntactic decisions. This is therefore an example of how a system of *triggers* can operate across levels in grammar.

An Experiment

My colleagues and I have not made more than a cursory exploration of other languages. Informal examination indicates that a wide variety of languages (German, ergative languages) are consistent with the claims in Carlson and Roeper. If so, a child should apply the unmarked complex verb principle automatically. We have, moreover, performed a small pilot experiment (designed and carried out by Lee Seraydarian) whose results are compatible with our predictions.

Six five-year-olds were given a series of ten stories like the following one. Their task was to fill in the last part of the unfinished sentence:
(25)
Mary was heating up some soup for lunch but the doorbell rang, so she turned off the stove and went to answer the door. When she got back to the kitchen, the soup was cold so she $\begin{Bmatrix} \text{heated} \\ \text{reheated} \end{Bmatrix}$ ———.

In 11 instances children completed the *heated* version with *the soup up again*. There were no cases of their adding *up* when the verb was *reheated*. Thus they knew that the prefix prohibited the particle. Of interest is the fact that only one of the children, when asked, appeared to understand the meaning of *re-*. They interpreted it as negative or said they just did not know. Nevertheless they were apparently able to comprehend the fact that *re-* made the verb complex and therefore limited its subcategorizational possibilities.

Summary
It is perhaps useful to summarize the principles under discussion:

(26)
a. Unmarked Case:
   All complex verbs are transitive or intransitive (i.e., take an NP or nothing).
b. Marked Case:
   Subcategorizations may be inherited that are not arguments of the verb.
c. Subcategorization System:
   Obligatory subcategorizations are arguments of the verb. Optional subcategorizations are not arguments of the original verb.
d. Acquisition Principle:
   All subcategorizations are obligatory unless there is positive evidence that they are optional.
e. Suggested Trigger:
   Complex verb = verb with internal boundary indicated by phonological differences.

There are points at which one can offer alternatives to every argument in linguistics. The fact that this set of proposals provides a sequence of steps from data to a correct grammar should function not only as an argument in its own behalf but in behalf of the linguistic argumentation behind it. Not every descriptively adequate proposal in linguistics can be associated with an explicit theory of acquisition. It is worth noting, finally, that the emphasis in these proposals has been upon how the rules are restricted. The special characteristics of the acquisition mechanism, from this perspective, are not complex.

A Larger Theory of Triggers

A theory of triggers is an extension of the theory of parameters. Chomsky (1980a) has argued for a parameterized version of acquisition. A series of implicational universals can be expressed as a series of choice points for an acquisitional mechanism (Williams, forthcoming a). The initial stage of the device reflects the set of unmarked universals that do not presuppose prior language-particular decisions.

Evidence moves the mechanism down a path toward a grammar marked in certain ways. Acquisition is thus a process of *instantiation* with a set of particular parameters that respond to a small amount of data.

The concept of triggers should be distinguished from the general properties of experience and good health, which are also needed for successful acquisition. I shall argue that the linguistically defined triggers (parameters) may be augmented by language-specific triggers which are defined in nonlinguistic terms. It is, of course, possible that there are no language-specific triggers defined in nonlinguistic terms. Acquisition could be a result of the interaction between linguistic triggers and general maturational phenomena. It is important to observe however that it is perfectly plausible for there to be nonlinguistic triggers that have specific linguistic functions.

The notion of a trigger can be construed in four ways: (1) a deductive trigger, (2) a hardwired trigger, (3) a cognitive trigger, and (4) a neurological trigger. Acquisition may consist of a biologically specified interaction between them all.

A Deductive Trigger
A deductive relation exists when universals and language-particular facts interact. For instance, we assume that a child knows the A-over-A principle. Then he learns the phrase structure rules NP $\Rightarrow$ PP and PP $\Rightarrow$ P NP. The A-over-A principle is triggered when *wh*-movement applies, preventing the extraction of NPs in PPs under NPs (see Otsu, 1981; Roeper, to appear).

A Hardwire Trigger
The relation between a phonological boundary and syntactic subcategorizations can be regarded as a hardwire trigger. There is no logical relation, necessarily, between these domains. The relation is stipulated in universal grammar. Its function lies in providing an elementary discovery procedure for a child. Unlike a theory of evaluation metrics defined over the complexity of a notation, these triggers operate without cost over different domains.

The deductive and hardwired triggers are both in principle discoverable by examining adult languages. It remains possible, however, that the adult language is too rich in connections; therefore a number of paths, or trigger sequences, are conceivable. If this notion is true, then the possibility of acquisition can be guaranteed, but crucial questions about realistic acquisition will remain underdetermined.

A Cognitive Trigger

I can give an example of an alternative between a purely linguistic trigger and a nonlinguistic trigger. How does a child identify the abstract categories NP and VP? Under $\overline{X}$ theory a deductive trigger is constructible. Suppose the child has knowledge that both NP and VP are composed of Specifier X Complement with order undetermined. Let us assume that the child has a rough distinction between content words and function words but nothing more. Now, crucially, he may also know that noun phrases require a preposition between the head and the complement in the unmarked case; thus he could distinguish between *John rejects the offer* and *John's rejection of the offer* (*John's rejection the offer* is ungrammatical). If he guesses that the function word *of* is the preposition he seeks, the whole structural distinction between NP and VP follows. He can infer that articles specify nouns and modals specify verbs. This in turn leads to the conclusion that *prove* is a verb in *can prove* and *proof* is a noun in *the proof*.[5] This explanation has the virtue that it is entirely formal (beyond a rudimentary knowledge of words) and it makes no incorrect claims about correlates of nouns and verbs in the world. In particular it does not operate with the assumption that a noun (like *the dancing*) is a person, place, or a thing.

The same conclusion can be obtained with a nonlinguistic cognitive trigger. The organism can begin with the counterfactual assumption: noun = person, place, or thing. This definition would allow the child to isolate a number of single words as nouns. These noun-words in turn have two consequences: they trigger recognition of specifier articles *the, a,* and they trigger dissolution of the earlier cognitive trigger. In other words, the trigger system shifts from a cognitive to a formal definition of a noun. This system would allow a child to fix aspects of noun phrases long before he considered Specifier-Noun-Complement sequences. Evidence from acquisition suggests that children do correctly connect articles to nouns before they learn complements. That is, they say *the dancing* long before they say *the dancing of the foxtrot*.

This system has the effect of requiring that all languages have a grammatical category that refers to person, place, or thing among other possible referents. This is not a heavy constraint on universal grammar. Nevertheless since nouns are explicitly not limited to person, place, or thing, it is not perspicuous within universal grammar itself but, rather, obscured. In effect the logic of triggers entails the possibility that later triggers obscure the role of earlier triggers.[6]

If a later trigger obscures the role of an earlier trigger, the result is a form of reanalysis. From the perspective of an instantaneous model, acquisition begins at this point and the earlier stages do not exist (Chomsky, 1976, 120–123; personal communication). Reanalysis will produce the adult grammar. One consequence of reanalysis, however, may be that it is no longer possible to state the relation between primary data and the final grammar because the primary data for the final grammar are not a series of sentences but a primitive grammar. An attempt to build a deductive model is, in effect, an hypothesis that reanalysis will not distort the relation between primary data and the final grammar.

A Neurological Trigger

This is a possibility for which I have no concrete suggestions. It is possible that a system of neurological triggers could make the final grammar opaque. If such were the case, it would be difficult to make any deductive arguments on linguistic grounds alone. Therefore it seems unlikely that changes in neurological status (that is, maturation) have a substantial impact on acquisition. Nevertheless the possibility should not be ruled out a priori.

The claim that acquisition follows triggers contrasts with the claim that the child uses an evaluation metric. One can state the evaluation metric in such a fashion that it mimics a system of triggers. However, several natural interpretations of evaluation metrics are ruled out, interpretations that, significantly, have little support in empirical data for acquisition of syntax[7] (e.g., that a child moves through a series of non-English grammars). The fact is that children appear to learn or follow the major principles of grammar and the particular principles of their own languages directly without extensive use of radically non-English grammars. Most rules appear to have the correct form upon first appearance: tag-formation, conjunction reduction, wh-movement, NP preposing, relative clause formation. All of these particular rules favor the parameterized or trigger theory.

A Micro-Trigger

I have said that a deductive logic derived from linguistic theory can both provide an explanation for language acquisition and leave open a variety of possible instantiations. Let us consider a case where the linguistic logic is fairly clear. In current versions of case grammar (Chomsky, 1980) it has been argued that the structure *for to* in infinitives is a marked structure. It is not the unmarked universal form and it is acceptable in English only with a lexical NP. Thus we can say *I hope for Bill to win* but not *I hope for to win*. All *for to* constructions are marked and the restriction against the latter form is particular to some dialects of English.

How does a child learn these exceptional structures? The logic of linguistics suggests that the child would first establish the presence of the unmarked form: *I hope to win*. Evidence gathered by M. Phinney (in preparation; 1979) supports this prediction. Next a sentence with an infinitival subject would be registered by the child: *I want for John to win*. The child knows that the subject must be case-marked and therefore immediately understands that the function of the preposition *for* is to give case to *John*. Finally the incorrect form *I want for to win* would be excluded by the Uniqueness principle, since it does not differ from *I want to win* in deep structure (unless a child were in a dialect group where he heard exemplars).

This logic is appealing because it makes universal claims that apply directly to the surface of the language. Nevertheless, there is room for different routes to that knowledge. First, it may not be accidental that the case-marking preposition *for* also functions in regular PPs. Otherwise one might expect a preposition whose unique function was to introduce infinitival subjects. Because the *for* preposition occurs independently in phrases like *I did it for you*, the child does not need to infer directly that the *for John* phrase is a case-marked infinitival subject. A prior step—realization that *for* is a preposition—in turn triggers the knowledge of infinitival subjects. In fact, children do acquire the *for* prepositional phrase first.

The following quotations from a two-year-old suggest a further trigger, which might be called a micro-trigger: *Let's get the bench for to jump in* (repeated three times) and *These are matches for make a fire*. All the first uses of *for to* constructions are notable for the semantic role of the preposition *for*. It has a purposive role in the quotations just as it does in the phrase *I got the present for you*. This reading is not present in the sentence *I hate for Bill to win*. It is possible that the presence of a purposive use of *for* in sentences with infinitival subjects is a necessary trigger that must be used before the child can advance to understanding *I hate for you to win*. It is also possible that it is unnecessary.

The logic of linguistics does not give an answer to this question. The answer is important because it says something about what kinds of operations and minioperations are involved in the induction of grammars. In sum, though one might see a trigger relation between any forms X and Y, a series of intermediary triggers remain a possibility. Empirical research in acquisition should answer some of these questions (but there is no guarantee).

The theory of triggers makes a strong innatist claim. Each trigger is a stipulated relation between data and a feature of language structure. It makes no difference whether the trigger is linguistic or nonlinguistic. In particular, the concept noun = person, place, or thing is not itself a part of knowledge of the world but rather a stipulated relation between a grammatical concept and knowledge of the world. Such a relation is, in part, less formal but not less abstract than the $\overline{X}$ trigger for NPs.

The theory of triggers, which claims a tight relation between evidence and grammar, does not claim that the trigger and its output belong to the same domains. At the moment, nothing constrains the possible relations between triggers and grammars. What a full theory of acquisition requires, then, is a restrictive biological theory of triggers together with a restrictive linguistic theory.

Notes

I would like to thank Greg Carlson, Lyn Frazier, Janet Randall, Muffy Siegel, and Ken Wexler for discussions of the ideas herein. This work was partially supported by a grant from the A. P. Sloan Foundation.

1. A number of potential prefixes are excluded because they are unproductive or very weakly productive: *inter-*, *counter-*, *anti-*. The prefix *counter-* is proposed by Smith in the commentary, but it has little generality: **countersuggest*, **counterpush*, **countermake*, **counterelect*. The example *counterpropose that he is here* seems to be a marginal result of backformation from *counterproposal*. The prefix *counter-* is quite productive with nouns: *counterpart*, *counterpoint*, *counterintelligence*, *counteragent*, *counterforce*, etc.

2. Smith pursues this line of reasoning in her commentary where she claims that the nonstative form *restate that Bill is here* is acceptable, but the stative **rethink that Bill is here* is not. This provides no

explanation for why other nonstative forms are ungrammatical or questionable:

(i)
*re-prove that Bill died
*resay that Bill lied
*rewrote that Bill was here
*reclaimed that John was a liar

Nor does she have any explanation for why we can say *think republican* but not *rethink republican* though it is possible to say *rethink republicanism*. It appears that re- can impose nonstativity in some but not all instances. If it can impose nonstativity on *rethink democracy,* why does it fail to do so with *rethink that democracy is right?* It appears that the semantics of these words involves a very subtle interaction between the meaning of the prefix and the meaning of the word. This interaction offers no explanation for why *think* takes the preposition *about* but *rethink* does not.

Smith points out that semantic factors may rule out simple NP objects as well: *re-finish the marriage ceremony* but *finish the marriage ceremony.* This is further evidence that the semantic principles are orthogonal to the principles I have proposed, rather than alternative to them.

In addition there is a notable lack of suggestion about what evidence a child would use to learn these rules (see section on "An Experiment" for evidence that children do not use semantics). For instance, if negative prefixes do not take sentential complements, how does a child know that it is just *mis-* and *un-* that prohibit them whereas *dis-* allows them?

3. Smith correctly notes that *dis-* appears to create a non-direct-object form: *dislodge from* but **lodge from.* These I assume are listed and nonproductive instances of *dis-,* much like *dispute* or the nonproductive use of *re-* in *return.* Again the phenomenon does not generalize. **Disenchanted from, *disinterested from, *disagree from, *disprove from, *disallow from, *disfame from, *disregard from, *disrespect from,* all take either the same preposition as their base word (*agree with* and *disagree with*) or a simple direct object: *disprove the theorem.*

4. A small class of double object constructions occur: *rename Bill Fred, reelect John president, ?redesignate Bob manager.* The class is small enough that it could be learned and listed on an individual basis. Note

that the second noun is never presupposed: *I repainted the barn a nice color* does not imply that it was a nice color before.

5. A number of cases could, in principle, confuse an acquisition device. For instance, verbs that take prepositions (*John looked at Bill, Bill talked of love,* etc.). In addition noun/verb doublets like *the love, to love* could complicate the misanalysis. These could be considered further reasons that a deduction from $\overline{X}$ theory is inappropriate. I do not think the confusion is serious, however. If *John looked at Bill* were briefly considered an NP, it would be ruled out later by a more fine-grained morphological analysis.

In general one must suppose that the acquisition device searches for clear cases and avoids all others. It has a kind of input filter. This perspective allows us to rule out problems that have sometimes been assumed to be quite serious. For instance, one might assume that an acquisition device must segment a phonetic stream without knowledge of what individual words are. Most of the sentences we hear have no clear phonetic or intonational boundary between words. Segmenting them will require a very powerful device because it must simultaneously attempt to identify words as it identifies possible segmentations. If both words and segmentations are unknown, the set of possibilities increases geometrically. It is, however, a fact that sometimes words are clearly separated intonationally from other words or appear in isolation. This may be true only one percent of the time, but given a child's exposure to hundreds of utterances every day, it should suffice. Therefore the acquisition device could begin with the counterfactual assumption that a word is an intonational unit. Once a set of words has been identified, the child can seek to identify known items in the intonational string. The requirement of adult grammars is that they *must* allow the expression of some single words as intonational units. This kind of provision, though crucial to acquisition, would presumably not be stated as a part of the grammar.

6. My position is very close to the proposal made by Jane Grimshaw in chapter 6. I do not believe there is any role for the canonical status of nouns as objects in the adult grammar. Therefore it is more accurate to label the relation as a trigger with no further functions.

7. I take no position with respect to phonology.

Chapter 5

Comments   Carlota S. Smith

One of the important questions raised by Roeper's stimulating paper concerns the relation between language acquisition and language development. I will comment on this thorny topic and then present a critique and an alternative to the proposal of learnable rules for complex verbs.

The notion that children's initial hypotheses about language are somehow available from the study of language development is appealing. It suggests that by studying the early stages of child language, we can arrive at the entirely general initial hypotheses of the theory of language acquisition. But I think this view cannot be maintained. Take as an example the evolution of rules for anaphora.[1] Young children have a pronoun rule that allows only for forward pronominalization; they also have reciprocals but without the clause-mate condition. They change these hypotheses considerably, arriving at something like the standard adult system by roughly six years. Now this is just the point at which subordinate clauses begin to make their appearance in children's language.[2] Subordinate clauses are essential to the adult rules for backward pronominalization and reciprocals, so it is hardly surprising that these rules do not develop before the system of subordination is well under way.

At this point we must ask what this account can tell us about children's initial hypotheses; and I think the answer is, quite clearly, very little. What it brings out is the dependence of early hypotheses on nonlinguistic factors of development. Children's early rules for anaphora are constrained partly by the fact that they lack the capacities (computational, memory, and perhaps intellectual) that underlie the subsystem of subordination. At what stage, then, should we look for initial hypotheses? I would argue that there is, in principle, no such stage in children's language: language development has its own constraints. Early linguistic hypotheses are intertwined with nonlinguistic factors.Therefore an enterprise that seeks to uncover initial assumptions about language by studying language development faces enormous difficulties. But such an enterprise is also ill conceived.

There is no state of linguistic innocence when a child uses only the general rules that constitute initial hypotheses about language. By the time that children's early grammars have developed they are already talking and hearing a given language. At such a time they are not linguistically innocent but, rather, fatally marked by the particular language to which they have been exposed.

This means that one cannot look to language development for direct evidence about initial hypotheses. (I assume a distinction between language development, which occurs in real time and in different stages, and language acquisition, an idealization that telescopes these stages.)

Obtaining indirect evidence from language development for language acquisition, on the other hand, is extraordinarily difficult in practice, and problematic in principle. The practical difficulties are well known, though perhaps not always given sufficient attention in actual studies. Nonlinguistic factors affect and in some areas may determine the course of language development. An investigator must be scrupulously careful to investigate other possibilities before explaining a result on linguistic grounds. But there is also a problem of principle.[3] Even if one were reasonably successful in identifying a phenomenon as linguistic, one could not be sure of its status in the fully developed linguistic system of the adult. Although genuinely important in the child's grammar, the phenomenon might not (although of course it might) figure in the target grammar that is the object of the study of language acquisition. Grammars not only grow but change, as the children using them develop their various capacities. The relation between stages is neither inevitable nor clear; one cannot assume that the same principles organize early and later stages.

Data from language development studies is sometimes interpreted as providing indirect evidence to support a particular linguistic theory. I am skeptical about this use of the data as well. Such studies can be extremely interesting for their bearing on stages and patterns of language development. The work on the complement system cited in Roeper's paper shows that children control important aspects of the system very early. I cannot agree with Roeper, however, in his interpretation of the data as providing evidence for the acquisition of a particular type of grammar. The data show that the children are learning English, and they would accord with any descriptively adequate account of the English complement system. They no more constitute evidence for case marking or filters than for the *Aspects* model of grammar or for a base-generated model such as that recently proposed by Bresnan. I do not mean to dismiss the possibility of experiments that bear on linguistic theory; but I want to emphasize that evidence of knowledge of the structures of a language is not the kind of evidence that can decide in favor of a particular theory.

Considerations of learnability must inform work in language acquisition; they have led recently to an emphasis on deductive structures. The search for rich deductive structures is carried in Roeper's paper to the relatively uncharted area of productive rules of the lexicon. Roeper claims that the requirements of learnability and the facts of English converge on certain generalizations about complex verbs; his attempt to work out the details of a deductive account is both interesting and provocative. I will argue for an entirely different statement of the facts and for a different approach to the requirements of learnability and the lexicon. It seems desirable and perhaps necessary to develop alternatives to the paradigm case of a learnable generalization, one couched in negative terms (with exceptions learnable from positive evidence). The following discussion is intended as a contribution to the development of such alternatives.

Roeper's Proposal

Roeper proposes that complex verbs do not inherit the obligatory subcategorization of their ancestor verbs, except for ∅ and NP objects. So, for example, although we have *think about NP* and *think that S* the complex verb *rethink* has only the subcategorization NP object: *rethink the problem* but not **rethink that S*. Some complex verbs have complements other than NP, as in (1):

(1)
We redirected John to the airport.

Roeper points out that in this sentence the PP complement need not be taken as part of the original situation, that is, John may not initially have been directed to the airport but to a different place. To account for this interpretation of a sentence like (1), Roeper makes a distinction between optional and obligatory complements to a verb. Optional complements (such as the PP with *direct*) have a different status from obligatory complements (such as the PP that accompanies *put*): only obligatory complements are arguments to the verb and as such presupposed. Only optional complements may be inherited, as in (1).

This account is consonant with certain requirements of learnability. Learners will be able to find out that *direct* has an optional PP complement because they can hear sentences with only an NP complement, such as (2):

(2)
We directed John.

In other words, the cases of optional subcategorization are available to the learner through positive evidence. There are counterexamples to the generalization that complements are not inherited, it is conceded (and even expected, since the lexicon is the repository of the idiosyncratic). But counterexamples are not problematic for this approach: complex verbs that inherit subcategorization can be learned case by case, from positive evidence.

In discussing this proposal I will consider only one type of complex verb, that formed with prefixes such as *re-, mis-, dis-, counter-, pre-*.[4] I believe that my arguments extend to other types of complex verbs, although there will surely be differences of detail.

Counterexamples. There are a large number of counterexamples to this proposal. I cannot present long lists, but it will be useful to give some examples before discussing the adequacy of the proposal. I find many examples of complex verbs with inherited subcategorization other than object NP.[5] (In some cases I disagree with the judgments in Roeper's paper; the judgments given here were initially my own but have been checked with other native speakers of English.)

(3)
Complex verbs inheriting NP PP:

reconfine NP to	prewarn NP of	reinsert NP into
reread NP to	reintroduce NP to	preinform NP of
readjust NP to	reconfine NP to	misrepresent NP as
reassure NP of	preassign NP to	reinsure NP against

(4)

Complex verbs inheriting PP:

readvertise for	reenter into	reimpose on
prewarn of	overreact to	reapply to

(5)

Complex verbs inheriting *that* S:

presuppose that	rehypothesize that	rediscover that
counterclaim that	reestablish that	dislike it that
reassert that	preconvince that	overemphasize that
restate that	countercharge that	preguarantee that

Contrary to Roeper's claim, I do not find that NP objects are privileged in regard to inheritance with complex verbs, and know of no reason why they should be so privileged. The examples of (3) show that complex verbs with NP PP complements often have an interpretation in which the complement is taken as a unit with the ancestor verb (as in the second interpretation of sentence (1), in which John has been previously directed to the airport).

Note that some of these examples are novel rather than well-entrenched words. Such cases present insuperable problems for an analysis that blocks inherited subcategorization unless there are positive instances of exceptions. Novel coinages are just that: they go beyond the stock of words of a language and are in principle not available from positive evidence.

It seems to me that the evidence against the claim about inherited subcategorization is at least as good as the evidence presented for it. A serious examination of large numbers of candidate words—in and out of the dictionary, since we are dealing with a productive rule—might answer the question of whether the claim about the general pattern of complex verbs is correct. However, it would be preferable to settle the question on principled grounds; this is especially true in view of the large number of counterexamples. I will consider two rather different types of arguments: the linguistic account of complex verbs and subcategorization, and the requirements of learnability, crude as our notions of it may be.

Discussion. There are serious difficulties with Roeper's analysis of inherited subcategorization. It is based on a distinction between optional and obligatory complements as arguments and nonarguments to a verb, but this distinction is itself dubious. No account is given of a complement that is not an argument to the verb, nor of how it is to be interpreted. In his brief discussion of sentences like (1) it seems to me that Roeper does in fact interpret the relations of verb and complement in the standard manner for a verb and its arguments. The notion that an optional complement is not an argument to the verb is difficult to extend to counterexamples: are they cases where an obligatory complement is not an argument to the verb, or where an argument to the verb may be inherited, contrary to the usual pattern?

To make a different kind of objection, I find rather implausible the suggestion that, to form a complex verb, the learner must know that it can appear without certain complements. It would seem that if learners know, for example, the verb *direct* and the rule for prefixation, they would be able to produce *redirect*—even if they had never heard anyone use the verb *direct* without a PP complement. But on the proposed account, learners cannot form complex verbs with optional complements unless and until they have heard a verb used without its optional complement. This requirement follows from the claim that optionality is learnable through positive evidence.

The matter of exceptions is problematic also, as already noted in connection with the counterexamples in (3), (4), and (5). Roeper correctly notes that his theory is undisturbed by exceptions, since they can be learned through positive evidence. However, novel cases that run counter to a generalization are a serious problem because there is no way they could be exemplified. Yet it is easy to construct novel cases that would be blocked by Roeper's generalization. For example, (6) has a complex verb that is novel and retains the subcategorization of the ancestor verb. On the other hand, the complex verb of (7) is bad; an adequate account of complex verbs should be able to predict this difference:

(6)
A: I propose that we go to the movies.
B: And I counterpropose that we play a game of backgammon.

(7)
A: I think that we should go to the movies.
B: *And I counterthink that we should play a game of backgammon.[6]

The fact that the complex verb of (6) is good is a serious problem for Roeper's theory. Such a theory can tolerate any number of counterexamples of words that are well entrenched in the language, but it cannot tolerate counterexamples of novel words, because no positive evidence for them could be available to the learner.

The theory is attractive because it allows for learnable exceptions. However, it does not allow for novel exceptions, and this is a serious defect in the face of the evidence. Since the logic of the problem is of importance far beyond this one case, it is worth considering with care the problem of learnable generalizations. The requirements of positive evidence dictate a generalization couched in negative terms, such as: Complex verbs do not inherit subcategorization. This ensures that exceptions will be modeled to the learner. But novel exceptions make this generalization untenable, since in principle the learner could not learn them. On the other hand, a generalization couched in positive terms is untenable because—clinging to the need for positive evidence—there is no way at all that exceptions could be learned. What we seem to have here is a *deductio ad absurdum*. I will argue for another approach to the problem that allows for a more satisfying and more plausible analysis.

Another Approach

We appear to have reached an impasse: global statements about complex verbs and inherited subcategorizations are inadequate, whether couched in negative or positive terms. I suggest that the attempt to frame a global statement be abandoned in favor of an approach that seeks smaller regularities and looks at information other than complement type. There is evidence that stativity, and some aspects of functional structure, are also relevant for the formation of verbs with prefixes. I will demonstrate the importance of these factors in accounting for the formation of such verbs (following Roeper, I will refer to them as complex verbs). I will then argue that an account allowing for positive evidence can be constructed along lines rather different from those he has suggested.

Consider first the relation between verb, complement, and prefix. Roeper's account takes the unit for prefixation as the verb alone, and prefix + verb as the unit for determining subcategorization. This approach makes the assumption implicitly that the acceptance of a prefix is independent of the complement of a verb. Such an assumption has great simplifying power. We can ignore everything but the syntactic question of whether a given complement is appropriate for a given prefix + verb by using it. Unfortunately, framing the question this way oversimplifies to a degree that makes it impossible to uncover the regularities of the language.

The simplifying assumption that prefixation is independent of verb complement cannot be maintained, because more than one type of dependency obtains in English between prefix, verb, and complement. In some cases prefix and complement form a unit, in other cases verb and complement. In fact, all three possible dependencies—represented schematically in (8)—can be found in English.

(8)
Dependencies between prefix, verb, and complement:
a. (prefix + verb) complement
b. (prefix + complement) verb
c. prefix (verb + complement)

Schema (a) represents cases of the type discussed by Roeper, where the unit is prefix + verb. The (b) schema represents dependency between prefix and complement. An example of such a dependency would be a case where a complex verb has a complement that does not appear with the verb alone. The prefix *dis-* and its associated complement *from* NP is of this type, as the examples in (9) indicate:

(9)

disqualify NP from	*qualify NP from
dislodge NP from	*lodge NP from
disentangle NP from	*entangle NP from

The third type of dependency holds between prefixes and verbs subcategorized for sentential complements and double objects, as I shall show.

I present a series of small-scale generalizations about verb prefixation in English. The material is organized by complement type, although not all types could be dealt with in this preliminary inquiry.[7] Rather than assuming a particular relation between prefix, verb, and complement, I have looked at their interaction separately for each type, and have considered well-entrenched and novel words for each type.

All complement types have cases where the complex verb retains the subcategorization of the simple verb—in Roeper's terms, inherits subcategorization.[8] But for some types there are restrictions on the formation of complex verbs, and these restrictions make a global statement impossible. The pattern of restrictions also makes it impossible to deal with prefixation in terms of the type (a) dependency (prefix + verb).

Intransitive verbs remain intransitive with prefixes, for example:

(10)
reawaken
reopen
reappear
oversleep

Verbs subcategorized for NP PP, including those where NP or PP is optional, have the same complement types with prefixes, as shown in the examples of (3) as well as here:

(11)
Mary reread the story to the children.
They reattributed the plays to Bacon.
The company had prelocated a representative at the airport.
The clerk had precorrelated the applications with the test reports.

Depending on the prefix and lexical items, sentences of this type may have two interpretations. So in the first example, either Mary has read the story to the children previously, or on a previous reading did not include the children. The first interpretation, which is consistently present in such cases, indicates that verb + complement is the unit for interpretation.[9]

Some cases may require special treatment: verbs that allow object deletion in simple form change subcategorization possibilities with certain prefixes, for instance:

(12)

eat (NP)	John ate (bananas).
overeat $\emptyset$	*John overate bananas.

(13)

a. read (NP)	She read (the article).
reread NP	She reread the article.
	*She reread.
b. serve (NP)	Mary served (the first course).[10]
pre-serve	Mary pre-served the first course.
	*Mary pre-served.

Eat, read, and *serve* are transitive verbs that allow object deletion. With prefixes, however, they change: *eat* becomes intransitive with prefix *over-* and the other two require objects with *re-*. How general this type of pattern may be remains to be seen.

Verbs subcategorized for PP have the same complement type with prefixes, as shown in (2) as well as in the additional examples in (14):

(14)
a. He reapplied for the job.
b. She readjusted to the job.
c. He prearranged for the party favors.
d. They had pretrained for the assignment.

Verb + Particle. No verbs have both a prefix and a particle, as has often been observed. But this is a fact about the makeup of the complex verbs rather than about subcategorization. Both prefix and particle form a syntactic unit with the verb;[11] both have the semantic value of perfectivity. They can be said, in fact, to alternate with each other, as in the following examples:

(15)
 think about the problem
 rethink the problem
*rethink about the problem

(16)
 wash down the car
 rewash the car
*rewash down the car

These examples show not only an alternation between particle and prefix, but also that direct objects are undisturbed by the alternation. Treating the particle as a complement would obscure this fact and suggest a spurious regularity. Grammarians have often noticed the close relation between particles and prefixes. Bolinger (1971) notes that at an earlier stage of the language the same word could appear in both roles, that is, as either particle or prefix as in *upset, wash up; backfire, fire back*. Such forms are now fossilized with unpredictable meanings, whereas the meanings of regular coinages such as the ones under consideration here are quite predictable.

This analysis is based on a distinction between particles such as *in, up, out, about, down,* and prepositions *for, to, of, into*. Particles are part of the verb, prepositions have objects associated with them syntactically; particles are mutually exclusive with prefixes, prepositions are not. I will assume that a principled distinction can be made, perhaps along the lines suggested in Bolinger (1971).

Verbs subcategorized for NP Adj allow prefixes regularly, as indicated by the following examples:[12]

(17)
a. He prehammered the metal flat.
b. They repainted the house purple.
c. The maid had prefolded the sheets smooth.
d. The teacher retwirled the ballerina dizzy.[13]

These sentences with *re-* have two interpretations, consistent with other examples such as those of (11).

Verbs with sentential complements appear often with prefixes, as shown in the examples of (5). These, together with the sentences below, show that prefixation should not be blocked globally. Especially compelling are cases of newly coined words such as *remotivate,* which cannot be treated as exceptions perpetuated on the basis of positive evidence.

(18)
a. He prestated that he was opposed to the motion.
b. The scientist retrained the rat to run sideways.
c. This will remotivate John to try for the classics prize.
d. Let me reemphasize that I take this problem seriously.
e. The office had preinstructed the contestants to arrive at noon.
f. The challenger counterattacked that the incumbent had been disingenuous.

I believe that a coherent statement of the way these verbs work will depend on a semantic account of both prefixes and sentential complements. It is clear that subcategorization information alone fails to predict (much less explain) which forms are good and which are bad. There are some subregularities, which indicate that semantic considerations are essential in this area of the grammar. I discuss four of these subregularities briefly.

1. Aspectual verbs do not appear with prefixes, nor do verbs such as *manage* and *try,* as these examples show:

(19)
a. start the car   restart the car
   finish the table   refinish the table
   try the door   retry the door

b. start to run   *restart to run
   finish sanding the table   *re-finish sanding the table
   try to win the race   *retry to win the race

The example of sanding the table is striking because it shows that the relation between verb and complement is crucial, rather than the form of the complement. (I have not been able, in this preliminary study, to deal with the interaction between prefixes and gerundives.)

The semantic relation that is crucial here does not pattern neatly with complement type. Some sentences of the same pattern have a different analysis and accept prefixes: for example, (18b,c,e). In these sentences the subject and complement have grammatical relations with the verb, which is not the case with aspectuals and not the case for the complements of *manage* and *try.*

I would suggest tentatively that the grammatical subject of a sentence must be an agent for prefixation to be possible; this is not a generalization that holds for all verbs. I suppose that the reason for this restriction involves the semantics of the prefixes, and the relation of sentential complement to verb.

2. Perfective prefixes do not appear with stative verbs. I will illustrate this point with *re-,* which is strongly perfective. Consider these examples:

(20)
Stative verbs:
| think that | *rethink that |
| believe that | *rebelieve that |

(21)
Nonstative verbs:
| state that | restate that |
| assert that | reassert that |

The stative forms do not allow prefixes with *re-,* whereas the nonstatives do. The incompatibility of perfectivity and statives is predictable semantically (for discussion see Smith, 1980).

Prefixes on statives cannot be blocked according to complement type, as the examples show: some verbs with sentential complements are stative and others are not. On the other hand, in order to determine whether a verb is stative, both verb and complement must be considered: *think over* NP is nonstative; *think that* S is stative.

3. Certain negative prefixes do not allow sentential complements. *Mis-* and *un-* are of this type (but not *dis-:* cf. *I dislike it that he wears orange socks, What I dislike is that he wears orange socks*). I know of no sentences with a negative prefix and a sentential complement; the following exemplifies the situation.

(22)
a. understand the situation   misunderstand the situation
   understand Mary   misunderstand Mary
b. understand that S   *misunderstand that S

Although I have no detailed proposal to make, it seems likely that the combination of prefix and sentential complement constitutes a contradiction and is therefore unacceptable.

4. Manner-of-speaking verbs, such as *mutter, scream, whisper,* do not take prefixes. As noted in Zwicky (1971), these verbs are exceptional in a number of ways and therefore must be identified in a grammar of English.

It is evident from this discussion of prefixes and sentential complements that the relevant generalizations cannot be stated at the level of subcategorization. It is also evident that a sentential complement must be considered as a unit with a verb for one to determine what sort of verb it is. This second point is hardly uncommon in the literature; it has often been observed that, for example, *thinking that* is different from *thinking about*.

Verbs subcategorized for NP PP—double object verbs. The facts here appear to be chaotic, if reference is made only to the double object subcategorization. However, with additional information the situation becomes relatively orderly. Consider these examples of complex verbs with double objects:

(23)
We renominated John secretary.
They reelected her president.

(24)
*Sue reconsidered him a fool.
*They prebelieved John a sage.

(25)
I reforwarded them the package.
Mary reread John the story.

(26)
*Mary reheated John the soup.
*Susan replayed Paul the sonata.

The sentences of (24) are bad for the same reason that *rethink* is bad: the verbs are stative and cannot have a perfective prefix. Presumably the same restriction that blocks stative verbs with sentential complements can apply here.[14]

The difference between (25) and (26) is that of type of dative. In the double object construction, *to*-datives but not *for*-datives allow prefixes (that is, datives that appear with these prepositions in the associated NP PP construction).[15] Both types of dative allow prefixes in the full form:

(27)
I reforwarded the package to them.
Mary reread the story to John.

(28)
Mary reheated the soup for John.
Susan replayed the sonata for Paul.

The difference between types of dative holds for novel forms as well: consider the behavior of a verb that is new to English, *to microdot* or *to micro*. The verb accepts the prefix *re-* in both *to* and *for* dative constructions, and also in the double object construction:

(29)
We remicroed the documents to Mary.
We remicroed the documents for Mary.

(30)
We remicroed Mary the documents.

Note that in (30) only the *to*-dative interpretation is possible.

The double object construction is notorious for its irregularity and its resistance to analysis. Why *to*-datives and not *for*-datives should allow prefixes in this construction is unclear to me.[16] It is also unclear how the appropriate information is to be represented. In a grammar where the double object construction is derived transformationally from the full form, it would be possible (although inelegant at best) to block the transformation from applying to prefixed *for*-datives. In a lexically based grammar this kind of information might not be readily available, except as a kind of transderivational constraint: if the verb has a NP PP form with *for,* block prefixation for the NP NP form. Another approach, slightly more appealing, would put the burden on an interpretive mechanism, allowing only the *to*-dative interpretation for double object prefixed verbs and throwing out, as unintelligible, sentences for which no such interpretation was available. An even more appealing possibility would be to allow the rule for prefixation to have access to functional structure, of the type set out in Bresnan (1978). The different types of datives would presumably be distinguished in functional structure.

In summary, two categories of verbs have been established: one generally allows prefixes; the other blocks prefixes for certain subclasses that are not identifiable at the level of subcategorization. The members of the categories are listed in terms of complement type:

(31)

Verb Category	Complement
I Generally allows prefixes	∅, PP, NP PP, NP Adj
II Allows prefixes with limitations	NP NP, *that* S, Inf S

These categories are not exhaustive, since not all complement types were investigated for this paper. Verbs with particles are analyzed as complex verbs; already complex in the relevant sense, they do not accept prefixes.

I would suggest tentatively that the level of functional structure is appropriate for dealing with the limitations on prefixes for members of category II. Information about functional structure could reasonably be expected to be available for verbs, again following Bresnan (1978). At the level of functional structure, aspectual verbs and verbs such as *manage* and *try*, datives of different types, and perhaps manner-of-speaking verbs could be identified. Stativity is not part of functional structure but would have to be available, in any event, for word formation rules.

These categories give necessary but not sufficient conditions for the formation of complex verbs. Whether a given verb actually accepts a given prefix is a question that is beyond the scope of this type of analysis; certain combinations are ill-formed, regardless of complement type. There is a good deal of variation—why is *restate that* so much better than *resay that?*—which is due to subtle semantic differences, to be elucidated one hopes by semantic study of the prefixes.

I have stated some positive generalizations about prefixation and complement type, statable partly in terms of subcategorization and partly at a more semantic level. I must now ask whether an account of the type adumbrated here might be accessible to the learner.

It might seem that this sort of account is not consonant with the requirements of learnability because it does not consist of a generalization couched in negative terms. I have argued that such an approach cannot deal adequately with this particular set of facts. What is needed is an approach to generalization that allows for learning from positive as well as negative cases. There is such an approach: I would suggest that a generalization may be learnable from positive exemplars of a category, where the domain of the generalization (that is, the category) is known to the learner on independent grounds. The idea is that the learner could discover from positive exemplars that a rule applies generally to members of the class from which the exemplars were drawn. Never hearing exemplars from other classes (aspectuals, for instance), the learner would not attempt to construct them. It is important to note that this approach to learnability is not quite induction, inasmuch as the classes are known in advance. It is essential that they be available to the learner independently. In the case of prefixes, the relevant classes are all independently required in a grammar of English and therefore (I will assume) available to the learner.

The positive generalizations could be learned, I claim, on the basis of exemplars of independently known classes. The approach allows for exceptions to the negative generalizations, and these exceptions would be learnable from positive evidence. Novel forms are predicted to conform to the generalizations, however.

The rule for prefixation itself must somehow allow for a good deal of variation. The analysis given here deals with necessary but not sufficient conditions for prefixation. I assume that sufficient conditions would have to do with the semantics of the prefix and types of verbs with which it could combine.

I have not assumed any particular formulation of the lexical rule that forms verbs with prefixes from simple verbs. The interactions explored here in a preliminary way should be clearly understood, I think, before one attempts such a formulation. However, I would like to note that lexical rules of the type presented by Dowty (1978) allow word formation in such a manner as to include complements of verbs; the results of my inquiry suggest strongly that such an approach is desirable for dealing with verb prefixation.

Notes

1. The examples were chosen to accord with the version of the paper presented by Roeper at the conference. Their relevance to the questions at issue remains, however.

2. See Ferreiro (1971), Flores d'Arcais (1978), Smith (1979) for discussion.

3. I would like to thank Edwin Williams for an interesting challenge on this point.

4. The full list may include several other prefixes; *counter-* is not listed in Roeper's paper and there are other candidate prefixes such as *out-*, *over-*.

5. Although other types of complex verbs are beyond the scope of these remarks, I would like to note that there are many counterexamples to Roeper's claim about verbs with suffixes, for example: *theorize that, reradicalize, Glamorize up your room! Hooverize out the dust!*

6. The difference between the complement of *propose* (untensed) and that of *think* is irrelevant for the present discussion. See section on "Verbs with Sentential Complements" for an account that will cover these cases.

7. The inquiry is also limited to certain prefixes, those covered by Roeper for the most part; other prefixes with the (b) pattern have not been included here.

8. I will avoid this term in the following discussion, since it assumes a particular relation between prefix, verb, and complement.

9. How interpretations are assigned to complex verbs is of course beyond the scope of this paper, but it should be part of any full theory of the lexicon.

10. This example is adapted from Dowty (1978).

11. See Fraser (1976) for discussion of verbs with particles; Bolinger (1971) and Green (1974), among others, have noticed the alternation.

12. Carlson and Roeper (1980) note the existence of sentences like this. In their system, the verbs are formed by a lexical rule and such verbs are not limited in the way that, e.g., verbs with sentential complements are limited. Therefore the examples here are not counterexamples to their negative generalization about prefixes and complements.

13. Two of these examples are adapted from Randall (1979).

14. The stativity of such sentences and their relation to similar sentences with a *to be* sentential complement suggest that a semantic equivalent of *to be* deletion, now largely discredited as a transformation, might be useful in the grammar.

15. Carlson and Roeper (1980) note that a distinction between types of dative must be made and that cases that have a *for*-dative form are not good as double object verbs with prefixes. They make no proposal as to how such information would be available to a prefixation rule.

16. In localist theory (Anderson, 1971) *to* is the basic dative; *for* is less concrete and more marked. This distinction apparently holds for many languages.

Chapter 6

Form, Function, and the Language Acquisition Device

Jane Grimshaw

The "Logical Problem" of Language Acquisition

I take the logical problem of language acquisition to be the problem of achieving explanatory adequacy, in the sense established by Chomsky (e.g., 1965, 1970b). The task is to predict what grammar a learner will internalize as a function of the data available. The depth and complexity of the problem are well established (e.g., Peters, 1972; Baker, 1979a).

The set of data available to the learner is highly limited in character; its single most problematic property is the absence of negative evidence—evidence that certain sentences are ill-formed. Given this, the theory of acquisition must guarantee that the language acquisition device (LAD) will either be right every time or will be wrong in such a way that positive evidence (plus whatever negative information is accessible) will suffice to justify the appropriate changes in the grammar.

By and large, the burden of providing this characterization of the acquisition process has been assumed by linguists to fall squarely on universal grammar, which consists of a *theory of grammatical representation* (TGR) plus an *evaluation metric* (EM). The working hypothesis of researchers has been that the logical problem of acquisition is reducible to the problem of constructing the right theory of universal grammar (UG). This gives rise to the familiar model of LAD in (1).[1]

(1)

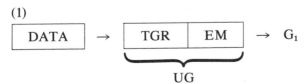

So if only we knew what UG in (1) stands for, we would know what LAD looks like.

I want to address two particular questions concerning (1). First, what is the nature of the evaluation metric? Is selection among grammars accomplished on purely formal grounds (e.g., by symbol counting) or do substantive criteria play a role? A hypothetical example may clarify the kind of evaluation metric I have in mind. Chomsky and Lasnik (1977) and Baker (1979a) have noted that obligatory rules pose a problem for language learning. If linguistic theory permits a given rule to be either optional or obligatory, LAD needs evidence to decide between the two for each rule. But to learn that a rule is obligatory, it is necessary to have access to negative evidence—to know that sentences in which the rule does not apply are ungrammatical. The evaluation metric does not seem to determine the choice. In sum, LAD could never learn that a rule was obligatory. Therefore, grammars that include both obligatory and optional rules are unlearnable.

The suggested remedy is this: linguistic theory must be restricted to disallow obligatory rules. (Of course the same result would be obtained if optional rules were disallowed.) This conclusion is, in my opinion, correct. However, it is not the only one possible. Suppose that LAD made the assumption that a rule is obligatory unless there were evidence for its optionality. Then LAD could learn the offending grammars with only positive evidence. If LAD heard a sentence in which a rule could have applied but didn't, the first hypothesis would be discarded, giving the rule optional status. Otherwise the rule would remain obligatory.

In this hypothetical case, the theory of grammatical representation simply says that rules can be optional or obligatory, but the evaluation metric assigns them a ranking in which obligatoriness has prior status. In effect, the fact that LAD exploits the proposed evaluation metric makes it possible for LAD to learn the grammars that are permitted by the theory of grammatical representation, on the basis of the available evidence.

This leads to the second issue raised by (1). If the construction or evaluation of grammars is partly dependent upon substantive criteria, are the criteria always a matter of UG, or do nonlinguistic criteria play a significant role? The projection problem cannot be solved without the right theory of UG, but is UG sufficient? In formulating and evaluating grammars LAD may make use of a set of principles that pertain not to the theory of grammatical representation or an evaluation metric, but to the wider cognitive domain. In this case, the choice of hypotheses would not be linguistically determined but would be a function of UG plus properties of the child's general cognitive capacity. LAD equipped with linguistic theory, even the best linguistic theory, may be a failure at language acquisition.

If this is true, (1) must be revised to include reference to the child's cognitive capacity (CC), giving the model portrayed roughly in (2).

(2)

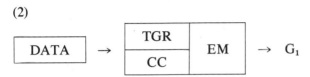

The model in (2) is of course the model assumed in studies of language development (as opposed to learnability). To explain how child language changes over time it is clearly necessary to understand the child's developing cognitive abilities. The issue is whether resolution of the projection problem, which abstracts away from developmental data, also depends on the interaction of LAD's cognitive and linguistic capacities.

I want to take a particular aspect of UG, which I think is correct at least in essentials, and explore its implications for these two questions. The property of UG that I will focus on is the autonomy of syntax (Chomsky, 1975). The linguistic motivation for the autonomy thesis is beyond the scope of this paper, but in the next section I will provide evidence from learnability which supports the theory.

I will argue that LAD can acquire grammars only by making use of a substantive evaluation metric relating form and function, and only by drawing on prelinguistic cognitive categorizations of the data. This study thus motivates the model in (2).

The Autonomy of Syntax and the Acquisition of Contextual Restrictions

It is a consequence of the autonomy of syntax that syntactic form and semantic type will not be in one-to-one correspondence in any principled way. A given syntactic form, such as NP or S, may correspond to a range of semantic types, and a given semantic type may have a number of alternative grammatical realizations. The implication for the acquisition of language is clear: UG does not permit deduction of a syntactic analysis from an analysis of the semantics of a phrase, and of course the same point holds for categorization of words. Thus the child must learn the two kinds of information separately; he must figure out what a word or phrase means, and what its syntax is.

Let me start by giving an illustration of how an autonomous system can be acquired. In the theory of contextual restrictions proposed in Grimshaw (1977, 1979), requirements imposed by predicates on their complements are expressed in terms of autonomous syntactic and semantic contextual restrictions. Predicates are subcategorized for the syntactic category—NP, $\bar{\text{S}}$, etc.—of their complements in the normal fashion. They select for the semantic type of their complements. Selection for indirect questions is represented by $\langle$ _____ Q$\rangle$, for exclamatory complements by $\langle$ _____ E$\rangle$, and for *that* complements by $\langle$ _____ P$\rangle$ (P for "proposition"). Subcategorization is checked over syntactic representation, selection over semantic representation.

How is a lexical entry learned? Consider, for example, the entry for *know* given in (3). *Know* is subcategorized for NP and $\bar{\text{S}}$, and it selects P, Q, and E.

(3)

$$know: [\ \underline{\quad} \left\{ \begin{matrix} \bar{\text{S}} \\ \text{NP} \end{matrix} \right\}], \langle\ \underline{\quad} \left\{ \begin{matrix} \text{P} \\ \text{Q} \\ \text{E} \end{matrix} \right\} \rangle$$

To learn this entry, five pieces of information are required. Does it take NP, $\bar{\text{S}}$, P, Q, E? Three sentences will suffice:

(4)
a. I know the answer. $[\ \underline{\quad}$ NP], $\langle\ \underline{\quad}$ Q$\rangle$
b. I know what a fool he is. $[\ \underline{\quad}\ \bar{\text{S}}$], $\langle\ \underline{\quad}$ E$\rangle$
c. I know that he is here. $[\ \underline{\quad}\ \bar{\text{S}}$], $\langle\ \underline{\quad}$ P$\rangle$

This contrasts with the situation under a nonautonomous representation, where the syntactic form and the semantic type of a complement are encoded in a single representation. The entry for *know* in this theory would be something like (5):

(5)

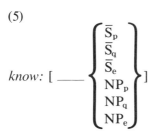

$$know: [\underline{\quad} \left\{ \begin{array}{l} \bar{S}_p \\ \bar{S}_q \\ \bar{S}_e \\ NP_p \\ NP_q \\ NP_e \end{array} \right\}]$$

Clearly the examples in (4) are insufficient for the acquisition of this entry (as is any other triple of sentences). From (4) LAD could deduce [$\underline{\quad}$ NP$_q$], [$\underline{\quad}$ $\bar{S}_e$], and [$\underline{\quad}$ $\bar{S}_p$], but three additional cases are needed for completion of the entry.

When one considers also the possibility of Null Complement Anaphora—whether the complements of the verb are syntactically omissible or not—a similar point emerges. Given the autonomous representation, any one example of Null Complement Anaphora will motivate parentheses around $\bar{S}$ (or, equivalently, around NP or around both).[2,3]

(6)
Did he leave?   I don't know.

(7)
$$know: [\underline{\quad} \left\{ \begin{array}{l} (\bar{S}) \\ NP \end{array} \right\}]$$

In the nonautonomous theory, this example will motivate parentheses around $\bar{S}_q$ but not around $\bar{S}_p$ or $\bar{S}_e$. Two further examples are required:

(8)
a. What a fool he is!   I know.
b. He left.   I know.

The key difference is that in the autonomous representation LAD has to learn only once that a predicate takes NP, that it takes Q, and so on. The combinatorial possibilities are a consequence of the representation and need not be learned at all. In the nonautonomous representation, LAD has to learn each possibility separately.

In general if there are n bits of syntactic information to be acquired, and m bits of semantic information, $n + m$ bits of evidence are needed for learning in the autonomous theory, nm in the nonautonomous theory.[4] In the case under discussion, $n = 3$ (does the predicate take NP, does it take $\bar{S}$, and are they optional?), and $m = 3$ (does it take P, Q,

E?). So it takes 6 bits of evidence to learn the entry for *know* given autonomy, 9 bits otherwise.

Thus the autonomy of syntax makes language learning easier, not harder. This is, of course, a paradigm case of the consequences of UG for learnability.

Form and Function

So it follows from the theory of grammatical representation that form and function (or type) cannot be expected to correspond in any pre-determinable or principled way. Nevertheless, I think there is reason to believe that LAD may rank grammars with a form–function correspondence over grammars that do not display one. I will discuss two cases where this seems to be true: with an evaluation metric to this effect, LAD will construct the correct grammar on the basis of the accessible data; without the evaluation metric the correct grammar is unlearnable, or at least no more highly valued than a number of incorrect alternatives.

Syntactic Rules
Consider the plight of LAD attempting to learn the grammar of matrix exclamations and nonecho *wh* questions.

(9)
a. How tall has he grown?
b. *Has he grown how tall?
c. *How tall he has grown?

(10)
a. How tall he has grown!
b. *Has he grown how tall!
c. *How tall has he grown!

LAD must learn that the (b) and (c) examples are ill-formed. This amounts to learning that *wh*-fronting must apply in both questions and exclamations, and that subject-auxiliary inversion must apply in questions and cannot apply in exclamations. The only evidence LAD has access to is that (9a) is a well-formed question, and that (10a) is a well-formed exclamation. Let us call the grammar that has (9) and (10) as consequences the "target grammar."

The question is, can LAD deduce the target grammar from UG plus the data? UG makes two relevant statements:

(11)

(i). All rules are optional.[5]

(ii). Form and function are independent.

Given this knowledge, LAD apparently has no reason to choose the target grammar over alternatives that would generate the (b) and (c) sentences.

Would a formal evaluation metric enable LAD to select the target grammar? Presumably it would, if the interpretation rules in the target grammar were simpler (or more highly valued in some way) than the interpretation rules in the alternative. There are two possibilities. First, the syntactic configurations in (b) and (c) simply might not be interpreted at all by the best set of projection and composition rules. But this is obviously not true—all the starred configurations in (9) and (10) correspond to grammatical, interpretable sentences. (9c) and (10c) are the same in form as (10a) and (9a) respectively, and the (b) cases are well-formed echo questions. So the projection rules will automatically interpret all the configurations.[6]

The second possibility is that rules which assign functions (like question, exclamation, declarative) to syntactic forms might be simpler in the target grammar than in the others. Suppose, for example, that the rules for the target grammar are those in (12):[7]

(12)

Wh Aux NP X = Q

Wh NP Aux X = E

Would these rules be selected by the evaluation metric over all other possibilities? The answer appears to be in the negative, since at least one alternative analysis is simpler than (12), namely, (13), which is equally compatible with the positive evidence.

(13)

$$Wh\ X = \begin{Bmatrix} Q \\ E \end{Bmatrix}$$

Thus a formal evaluation metric would never select the target grammar over grammar (13), and (13) predicts that (9c) and (10c) are well-formed.

So in this case, the theory of grammatical representation plus a formal evaluation metric is inadequate for the selection of the grammar. There is a plausible solution to the problem. The child hears only (9a) with an interrogative function, and (10a) with an exclamatory function. Suppose then that LAD incorporates a substantive evaluation metric which gives priority to a grammar with a one-to-one correspondence between form and function. The initial hypothesis will then be that (9a) is the only way of forming a *wh* question, and that (10a) is the only way of forming a *wh* exclamation. The rules in (12), those of the target grammar, will then be hypothesized rather than the formally simpler but incorrect (13).[8]

For the present example, there is never any need to revise the initial hypothesis. What of cases where form and function are not in one-to-one correspondence? Positive evidence will serve to trigger a change in hypothesis. Suppose LAD hears (14a) and hypothesizes the rule in (14b):

(14)
a. Is he (ever) wrong?
b. Aux NP X = Q

When (15a) enters the data base—same form, different function—(14b) will simply be revised to (15b):

(15)
a. Is he (ever) wrong!

b. Aux NP X = $\left\{ \begin{matrix} Q \\ E \end{matrix} \right\}$

So LAD will acquire the correct grammar when form and function do not correspond, as well as when they do.

What is the status of LAD's assumption that form and function correspond one-to-one? The theory of grammatical representation simply says that form and function *may* correspond, but there is no principled reason why they should. It certainly assigns no priority to correspondence over noncorrespondence: quite the reverse, since correspondence is accidental, and noncorrespondence is principled. It would obviously be unjustifiable to revise our theory of grammar to say that form and function do correspond—this would incorrectly predict that pairs like (14a) and (15a) could not exist. So here we have evidence for a substantive evaluation metric.

Syntactic Categories
It is universally agreed by linguists that the syntactic categories of a language are defined in structural not semantic terms. Syntactic cate-

gorization is autonomous, since syntactic category membership is not reducible to meaning.

How are syntactic categories identified? The problem falls into two parts: LAD must group words and phrases together into classes, and must assign the appropriate labels to those classes. UG simplifies the task considerably: if LAD can analyze words correctly, $\overline{X}$ theory will project the categorization of phrases from the lexical categorization (see Williams, forthcoming b). But UG does not provide a universal structural definition for lexical categories.

Some developmental psycholinguists (e.g., Maratsos and Chalkey, forthcoming) have argued that LAD can successfully determine category membership on the basis of purely distributional evidence. However, there seem to be a number of rather serious problems with this view, some of which are discussed in Pinker (1979).

Pinker points out that distributional analysis requires extremely large numbers of minimal pairs and that many errors will be made even if such pairs are provided: *Hottentots must fish* and *Hottentots eat fish* (from Pinker, 1979) can only mislead LAD. Pinker also argues that the notion of "context," crucial for this account, is suspect: "Given n words in a sentence other than the item of interest, there are $2^n - 1$ different ways of defining "context" for that item—it could be the word on the immediate right, the two words on the immediate left, the two flanking words, and so on" (p. 240).

This does not exhaust the difficulties: the distributional evidence for assigning words to categories rests on facts like cooccurrence with determiners, case-marking, agreement, complement type, word order, and so on. The particular factors, of course, vary from language to language. The difficulty is that many of these diagnostics depend on prior analysis of complex domains of grammar such as inflection. Many of these domains seem to be mastered quite late, well after the child starts to produce two- and three-word sentences that show evidence of grammatical categorization. Function words and morphemes are notoriously absent from children's "telegraphic" speech. Yet these are the very foundations of category learning, according to the distributional theory. Surely it is most unlikely that the child can use, and combine freely, words whose syntactic categories have not yet been ascertained.

Even if a purely distributional analysis could result in successful division of words into grammatical classes, it is not at all clear that the classes would be labeled appropriately. It is one thing to know that words fall into three major (open) categories, quite another to discover which class is the class of nouns, which the class of verbs, and so forth. What then prevents LAD from constructing a grammar like the one that generates (16)?

(16)

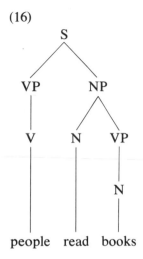

people   read   books

Note that (16) is entirely consistent with $\overline{X}$ theory. One might wonder whether it would matter if LAD did hypothesize (16). The answer is surely that it would be a disaster, given that universal constraints (such as Subjacency: Chomsky, 1977a) make reference to categorial information. Given these problems, a purely distributional theory of category learning does not seem very promising.[9]

The issue can be resolved by a further hypothesis about the nature of LAD. There is plenty of evidence that at an early stage of linguistic development, children have ready command of semantico-cognitive categories like "object" and "action." Suppose then that LAD uses these categories as the basis for assigning syntactic categories to words. If a word is the name of an object, it is assigned the category N. If it describes an action, it is assigned the category V.[10] Thus certain cognitive categories have what I will call a Canonical Structural Realization (CSR): CSR (object) = N, CSR (action) = V. LAD employs a CSR principle: a word belongs to its CSR, unless there is evidence to the contrary.

Of course the data will include many examples that cannot be analyzed this way, but they are likely to occur in relatively complex sentences that probably do not form part of the real data base at this point. In any event, should a sentence like NP *belongs to* NP occur, it will just have to be ignored.

LAD can construct phrase structure rules for NP and VP, by drawing on example sentences whose lexical items can be assigned category labels by the CSR principle. In so doing, LAD will in effect be establishing a set of structural generalizations governing the distribution of N, V, and so on. These can be used as evidence for the analysis of any new categories (such as Det, Modal) for which no CSR is defined. The rules will also make it possible to assign category labels to words like *belong: belong* is a verb because it behaves like one with respect to the phrase structure rules. As for cases that would presumably be misanalyzed by the CSR principle, such as *destruction,* LAD will receive positive evidence about their categorization.[11]

Universal grammar does not predict any particular relation between the meaning of a word and its syntactic category. LAD, however, uses a principle that expresses a dependency between syntactic and semantico-cognitive categories. What is the status of this dependency? The CSR principle could be viewed either as a matter of the theory of grammatical representation, or as a consequence of a substantive evaluation metric. For example, the theory of grammatical representation could be revised as follows:

(17)
(i).
Syntax is autonomous.
(ii).
Certain perceptual/cognitive/semantic categories have corresponding syntactic categories in the unmarked case.

However, I think there is good reason to consider the CSR principle to be external to UG.

First, the joint effect of (i) and (ii) is odd: syntax is autonomous except when it isn't. Second, the CSR principle makes use of notions like "object" and "action," which are general cognitive notions and not specific to language. CSR itself thus expresses a relation between linguistic and nonlinguistic constructs. There is no independent evidence that UG makes reference to any of these concepts.

Note a trade-off between UG and LAD here. If the theory of LAD is enriched to subsume principles like that of CSR, which relate cognitive capacity and UG, the simple form of UG can be maintained, together with the strongest version of the autonomy thesis. This in turn makes the potentially interesting prediction that systematic violations of autonomy (as opposed to accidental one-to-one correspondence) will be explicable in terms of the theory of acquisition.

Empirical Consequences of the Structure of LAD

The argument so far rests solely on the projection problem—without the suggested principles the grammars of natural languages could not be learned. But clearly the proposal made here makes extremely strong predictions about the course of linguistic development. Although it is hard to disentangle the effects of cognitive development from the effects of these principles, the available evidence is at the very least consistent with the theory.

Consequences for the Course of Acquisition

The first words a child analyzes should be those that are categorized by the CSR principle: action verbs, names of objects, and so on. Some caution is in order here, because certain fixed expressions (*thank you, gimme,* and so on) may be learned but not analyzed syntactically at this point. So the prediction is that the words that are used productively, in accord with a set of phrase structure rules, will be of the appropriate type. It is quite well established that this is the case. (See the discussion in Brown, 1957, 1973, for a summary of some relevant material.)

Brown (1957) and Katz, Baker, and MacNamara (1974) report experiments that support the basic point that children assume a systematic correlation between syntactic categories and categories like "object" and "action." The evidence suggests that children use syntactic cues to help them identify word meanings. If, for example, a nonsense word is used in a verbal context, it is taken to describe an action. If it is used as a noun, it is taken to refer to an object. Here the converse of the CSR principle is apparently being invoked.

More generally, the first grammar LAD constructs is one in which there is a one-to-one mapping between syntactic category or form and semantic or cognitive function. From the linguistic output of a child producing two- or three-word sentences it will be extremely difficult to determine whether the child's grammar is stated in terms of syntactic or semantic rules and categories. A brief glance at almost any of the literature on early acquisition will testify to the accuracy of this prediction.

Consequences for Language

The preceding cases suggest that learnability is not simply a function of data + UG, but of Data + UG + cognitive capacity. This has further consequences. It might explain how a grammar can be learned. It may also be the explanation for some linguistic universals.

Clearly not all language universals follow from UG. For example, morphological irregularity is generally confined to common words. Surely UG does not include a statement to this effect. Rather, the mere fact that irregular forms must be learned case by case, and therefore must be heard to be learned, is an adequate explanation. If an extremely uncommon verb had an irregular past tense, it would not stay irregular for very long.

Suppose then that LAD uses the CSR principle. This would suggest an explanation for the fact that languages do in fact display non-autonomy in just this way. Names of objects are typically nouns, names of actions typically verbs (or deverbal nouns). It is not at all clear that UG could be revised to express these tendencies in any illuminating fashion, and the purely distributional theory of category acquisition certainly offers no explanation. The CSR principle does illuminate this correlation: learning (and therefore evidence) is required for the words where the correlation does not hold; no learning (and no evidence) is needed for words that conform to the principle.

A less obvious example arises in the theory of complement selection, already discussed. The evidence for the claim that subcategorization and selection are autonomous seems to be extremely strong; nevertheless there is a class of generalizations that cannot be explained by the theory. If subcategorization and selection are independent, all possible combinations of the two should be realized in lexical entries. Although we do find predicates that take only *wh* questions and predicates that take both *wh* and NP questions, we do not find the third possibility—predicates that take NP questions but not *wh* questions. A predicate of this third type could be described simply by the theory of complement selection, as one that subcategorized NP (but not $\bar{S}$), and selected Q. (The same point holds, mutatis mutandis, for predicates taking E and P.)

(18)
Predicate [___ NP], ⟨ ___ Q⟩

Thus in fact the set of predicates that take NP question complements is a (proper) subset of the predicates that take *wh* forms, but this is not explained by the theory.

A parallel problem is found with Null Complement Anaphora; why are there no predicates taking only null complements? Such predicates would be subcategorized for no complements, and would select P, Q, or E. In fact the Null Complement Anaphora predicates are again a (proper) subset of the predicates that take realized complements.

It is conceivable that these gaps in the lexicon are accidental, that predicates of the relevant type could exist, and might be discovered in, or introduced into, English at any time. However it is much more likely that the subset relation between these predicates represents a real generalization about the lexicon, which must have an explanation.

What then are the options? Abandoning the hypothesis that selection and subcategorization are autonomous might make it possible to solve these problems, but then there would be no explanation for the generalizations that motivate the autonomy thesis to begin with. If the autonomy hypothesis is correct, apparently the only option is to build into UG constraints that would rule out the impossible cases. For example one could add the statement: If a predicate selects P, Q, or E, then it must be subcategorized for $\overline{S}$. This is hardly illuminating. Why should there be relations of this kind between subcategorization and selection? Why should the subset relation expressed by this condition hold equally for P, Q, and E? After all, the stipulation could just as well mention P and Q only, or Q and E only. Similarly, why $\overline{S}$? Why shouldn't the requirement be that a predicate that selects P, Q, or E must be subcategorized for AP, or NP?

It appears then that there is no interesting way of capturing relations between selection and subcategorization within the formal model of grammar. What I want to suggest is that the explanation for the subset relation may not be a matter of grammar at all; that it is not a problem for which linguistic theory should provide a solution. It can instead be viewed as a consequence of learning: a language that did not demonstrate the subset relation would be *representable,* but not *learnable*.

The notion of canonical structural realization can illuminate this problem. It seems extremely plausible that expressions of the semantic types P, Q, and E also have CSRs and that the correct CSR for all three is $\overline{S}$. Suppose then that there is a principle to this effect: If a predicate selects a semantic type, it is subcategorized for the CSR of that type. I will call this the Context principle. This principle can be viewed as an absolute requirement, or it can be interpreted as determining the un-marked case. The marked case would be unlearnable, because it would require negative evidence, so either formulation correctly predicts that the subset relation will hold absolutely.

The principle can be illustrated in the case where LAD receives evidence that a predicate takes NP questions but no evidence that it takes *wh* questions: (19) but not (20) is in the data base.

(19)
I askcd John the time.

(20)
I asked John what the time was.

Clearly LAD can posit [_____ NP] on the basis of (19). If *the time* is assigned the appropriate semantic representation, ⟨ _____ Q⟩ can also be associated with *ask,* giving the lexical entry in (21). But LAD also knows that the CSR(Q) is $\bar{S}$. Thus, by the Context principle, LAD adds [_____ $\bar{S}$] to the entry, giving (22).

(21)
ask: [_____ NPJ, ⟨ _____ Q⟩

(22)
ask: [_____ $\begin{bmatrix} NP \\ \bar{S} \end{bmatrix}$], ⟨ _____ Q⟩

Of course if LAD's data had consisted of (20) and not (19), only [_____ $\bar{S}$] and ⟨ _____ Q⟩ could be posited. There would be no evidence for [_____ NP], because NP is not the CSR of Q. Thus predicates that take *wh* questions and not NP questions should be possible, as of course they are.

The same result is obtained for Null Complement Anaphora. If LAD has the data in (23), (24) will be an impossible entry:

(23)
John left. I know.

(24)
know: [_____], ⟨ _____ P⟩

The Context principle will force the addition of $\bar{S}$ to the entry, so on the basis of (23) the entry in (25) will be constructed:

(25)

know: [_____ (S̄)], ⟨ _____ P⟩

Could the Context principle be a principle of UG? I have discussed this issue in connection with category acquisition; similar reasoning would lead to the same conclusion here. The notion of CSR plays no discernible role in linguistic theory, but it does appear to play a significant role in acquisition.

I have argued that in order to solve the logical problem of language acquisition we may have to enrich the theory of LAD in two ways. First, some of the choices that must be made between competing grammatical hypotheses depend on substantive evaluation metrics, like the one relating form and function. Second, acquisition draws on a conceptual characterization of the data, which feeds the theory of grammar. I have tried to show that this view has interesting consequences for the projection problem, for certain linguistic problems, and for language development. Principles like those proposed here may also form the basis for a theory of markedness in language.

If this line of reasoning is correct, solving the projection problem may depend not just on formulating the correct theory of universal grammar but also on a more general theory of the acquisition device.

Notes

1. "G_1" in (1) and (2) stands for the grammar (or perhaps more realistically the set of grammars) selected by the evaluation metric.

2. Presumably a subcategorized phrase is assumed to be obligatory unless evidence for its optionality is received.

3. Note that in fact (6) would also suffice to motivate ⟨ _____ P⟩, so (4a) and (4b) plus (6) would together provide all the evidence necessary for the complete lexical entry. Similar remarks hold, mutatis mutandis, for the nonautonomous theory.

4. For this formulation, thanks are due to Steve Pinker.

5. Jackendoff (1972), Williams (1980b), and Grimshaw (1977, 1979) give evidence for analyzing subject-auxiliary inversion and *wh*-fronting as optional. This analysis predicts that a matrix clause containing a *wh*-phrase can in principle have four possible realizations:

(i)

What has he done?   (+SAI, +*wh*-fronting)

(ii)

What a fool he has become!   (−SAI, +*wh*-fronting)

(iii)

He has done what?   (−SAI, −*wh*-fronting)

(iv)

Has he done what?   (+SAI, −*wh*-fronting)

All four possibilities are realized, (iii) and (iv) as echo questions.

6. It is of course quite likely that when LAD is learning the grammar of matrix questions and exclamations, echo questions are not part of the data base. If so, the simplest set of projection rules at this point would not in fact interpret (9b) and (10b), and the simplest grammar would not generate them. Although this may be true, it does not solve the problem of how the child knows that (9b) and (10b) are ill-formed. As soon as echo questions are analyzed, the simplest set of projection rules will interpret (9b) and (10b), so the problem simply reappears at a later point in time.

7. These rules are based on the analysis given in Williams (forthcoming a).

8. In fact, *wh* questions without subject-auxiliary inversion are generally produced before the adult forms, even though inversion is used in yes-no questions. This should probably be attributed to a complexity limitation on performance, rather than to an error of grammatical analysis.

9. It might seem that rather than trying to identify nouns and verbs and then projecting NP, VP, etc., from the lexical analysis, LAD could proceed by identifying NP, VP, and then deduce the lexical category from this. Would this make phrase structure learning easier? A phrase could perhaps be analyzed as an NP if it acted as a grammatical subject. But how would the subject be identified? Again, UG gives no universal definition of subject. What evidence there is suggests that grammatical relations are acquired via thematic relations—subject is initially identified with the agent, for example (see Pinker, 1981). Apparently any theory of category acquisition must rely on some principle that relates grammatical category or function with nonsyntactic concepts.

10. This solution is proposed in MacNamara (forthcoming). Braine (1971) questions its validity. He taught his daughter the words *niss* and *seb,* with no syntactic context. *Niss* was said while pointing at an object, *seb* while performing an action. He reports that most of the time *niss* was used as a noun, *seb* as a verb, as one would predict. However, his daughter also produced *more seb,* and *bit more seb,* from which Braine concludes that she had a dual noun/verb categorization for *seb.* However, this argument depends on the assumption that the child's analysis of *more* is essentially the same as an adult's: it precedes nouns but not verbs. Given the frequency of utterances like *more tickle* in child language corpuses, it seems to me very likely that *more* is used indiscriminately before nouns and verbs and cannot be used as a test of categorization. However, I refer the reader to Braine's article for further details.

11. If LAD misanalyzes a word, evidence will eventually emerge to show that the word belongs to another category. The difficulty is this: since the child would never receive evidence against the initial hypothesis, and since categorial ambiguity is not excluded by UG, why should the word not be treated as bicategorial? It appears that a mistake resulting from the CSR principle is irretrievable without negative evidence. If this were true, then there would of course be no cases of the crucial kind in any language. Any word that named an object would be a noun, whether or not it also belonged to another category. Note that the same issue arises in a distributional theory of category acquisition and that the problem seems similar to that posed by overregulation: how does the learner find out that *goed* does not exist? Baker (1979a) suggests a solution based on frequency for the overregulation case, which could perhaps be extended to categorial learning. Some kind of uniqueness principle might provide an alternative account: assume that *go* + Past has only one realization and that a word belongs to only one category unless there is direct and incontrovertible evidence to the contrary.

Ellen Woolford

Grimshaw presents an interesting model of semantic complement selection that is independent of, but interacts with, syntactic subcategorization. The basic model is quite elegant and well motivated and I have no criticism of it. Instead, I would like to question the need to propose a specific principle of language acquisition (the Context principle) to account for the combinations of selection and subcategorization that are predicted to occur but that are never actually realized in lexical entries.

Grimshaw's model predicts that all possible combinations of semantic selectional possibilities (P,Q,E) and syntactic subcategorizational possibilities (NP,$\overline{S}$,$\emptyset$) should occur. As she points out, many of these predicted combinations do not occur (21 out of 49, to be exact). These empirical gaps in the model's predictions can be characterized by a simple implicational generalization: If a verb selects for P, Q, or E, it must also be subcategorized to take $\overline{S}$ complements. Nevertheless, if this stipulation were added to the grammar, it would violate a basic assumption of this model and of most work in this framework—the autonomy of syntax. Abandoning the autonomy hypothesis would create more problems than it would solve in this case because, as Grimshaw demonstrates, a nonautonomous model predicts a far greater number of lexical entries that never occur. Moreover, it would greatly increase the number of bits of information that a child would need to learn lexical entries. Rather than altering the grammar, Grimshaw's solution is to propose a language acquisition principle, the Context principle, to explain these empirical gaps. I agree with Grimshaw that something in the acquisition process prevents these 21 types of lexical entries from being realized, but I will argue that the Context principle is unnecessary. The nonoccurring combinations of selection and subcategorization can be shown to be simply unlearnable.

The Context principle is a specific case of a more general acquisition principle, the Canonical Structural Realization (CSR) principle, for which Grimshaw provides independent motivation. It is defined as follows:

(1)
Context Principle:
Evidence that a semantic type is a possible complement to a predicate constitutes evidence that the CSR of the type is a possible complement.

With this principle and the assumption that the CSR of expressions of the semantic types P, Q, and E is $\bar{S}$, the correct predictions result. If a child learns that a verb selects for P, Q, or E, he will automatically conclude that the verb is subcategorized to take $\bar{S}$ complements, even if he has learned the semantic type of the verb from a concealed (NP) form or from a null complement form.

Underlying this line of thought is the assumption that a child actually can learn the semantic selection of a verb from a concealed (NP) form or a null complement form. Without this assumption, there would be no need to appeal to the Context principle at all. There would already be a simple explanation of the empirical gaps based on the acquisition process. If the child is unable to learn that a predicate selects for a particular semantic type on the basis of concealed forms or null complement forms, but only on the basis of hearing the full $\bar{S}$ form, then it is acquisitionally impossible for a verb that is not subcategorized to take $\bar{S}$ complements to select for P, Q, or E.

Grimshaw presents no evidence in support of this underlying assumption that a child can learn semantic selection on the basis of data from concealed or null complement forms. I will argue that these forms do not provide sufficient information for the child to determine which semantic type (if any) a predicate selects for.

Let us first consider the case of null complement anaphora.

(2)
Billy broke the vase.

(3)
a. Martha told me.
b. I'm not surprised.
c. Don't let his father find out.
d. You raised him.
e. His mother will faint.
f. Double his dose of Ritalin.

Listed in (3) are six possible responses to the utterance in (2). The first three involve null complement anaphora; the last three do not. According to Grimshaw (1979, p. 293) sentences such as (3a,b,c) are interpreted by a Null Complement rule, which copies the representation of sentence (2) into the complement position of the verbs in (3a,b,c). However, the Null Complement rule can apply only after the rules of sentence grammar have determined that there is an empty complement position to be interpreted (by checking the lexical entry of the verb involved to see whether it is subcategorized to take a complement). Otherwise the rule would apply to responses such as (3d,e,f), which have no null complements to interpret.

The Null Complement rule is a rule of semantic interpretation which identifies the semantic type of the missing complement. After its application, the adult matches the semantic type of the missing complement with the types that the verb selects for to determine whether the result is well-formed (Grimshaw, 1979). The child, not knowing what semantic type the verb selects for, will assume that the result is well-formed and learn that the verb selects for the type exemplified by the missing complement. Because of the nature of this inter-

pretation process, it will be impossible for the child to interpret a null complement and to learn that the verb selects for P, Q, or E unless he already knows
that the verb is subcategorized to take a complement. This explains why there
are no verbs that select for P, Q, or E that are not also subcategorized to take
complements.

This leaves the question of why no predicates that select for P, Q, or E are
subcategorized to take concealed (NP) complements but not $\bar{S}$ complements. It
can be shown by an argument similar to the one given for null complement
anaphora that these nonoccurring combinations are also unlearnable because of
the nature of the interpretation process.

If a predicate could be subcategorized for just NP and not $\bar{S}$ complements,
while selecting for P, Q, or E, then it would have to be possible for a child to
learn the semantic type that a predicate selects for on the basis of hearing only
the concealed form of that semantic type. It would also have to be possible for a
child to distinguish predicates that do take concealed forms—as in (4)—from
predicates that are also subcategorized for NP complements but do not select
for P, Q, or E—as in (5).

(4)
a. I asked John the time.   (Q)
b. Pat couldn't believe the money they spent.   (E)
c. Betty told me the answer.   (Q)

(5)
a. He gave me a headache.
b. Jeff will repay the money they stole.
c. Jill recited the poem.

As in the case of null complements, there are special rules for interpreting
concealed questions and concealed exclamations (Grimshaw, 1979, p. 305).
"The Concealed Question Rule interprets noun phrases as interrogative—it
assigns to them representations of the same form as those assigned to wh-ques-
tions. The Concealed Exclamation Rule interprets noun phrases as exclama-
tive" (p. 300). These rules of interpretation are free to apply to any noun phrase
(p. 305). Adults compare the semantic type resulting from the interpretation of
the complement to the semantic frame of the predicate. If there is a match, the
utterance and its interpretation are judged to be well-formed.

Since the child does not know the semantic frame of the predicate, he must
assume that what he hears is well-formed and learn that the predicate selects
for the semantic type that the complement has been interpreted to be an instance of. This would have the undesirable result that the child would learn that
all the verbs in both (4) and (5) select for both Q and E, and that each utterance
in (4) and (5) has three possible interpretations—a concealed question, a concealed exclamation, and an ordinary object. Since this does not occur, it is
likely that the child does not even attempt to use such data, because he cannot reliably deduce the proper selection frame of a predicate from hearing
only the concealed form. In fact, he is able to interpret concealed forms only
after he has learned the selection frame of the predicate from hearing the full $\bar{S}$
form. He can then cull out the incorrect applications of the Concealed Question

rule and the Concealed Exclamation rule by matching the results with the semantic frame of the predicate, as the adult does. If this is so, then we have the explanation for why there are no predicates that select for P, Q, or E[1] that are not also subcategorized to take $\bar{S}$ complements.

The learnability explanation that I have sketched for the empirical gaps in the predictions of Grimshaw's hypothesis is the simplest one possible. It does not require the postulation of any acquisition principles such as the Context principle,[2] since it follows directly from the interaction of the acquisition process with the rules of semantic interpretation in Grimshaw's model. This result makes Grimshaw's basic model of autonomous selection and subcategorization all the more attractive.

Notes

1. Concealed propositions are not discussed here because no concealed proposition rule is discussed in Grimshaw (1979). However, in her presentation at this conference, she mentioned the interpretation of sentential pronouns such as *that* as propositions.

(i)
John has left.

(ii)
I could have told you *that*.

Note, however, that such sentential pronouns can occur with predicates that are not subcategorized to take NP complements, and thus they cannot be concealed propositions under this model.

(iii)
He claimed that the earth is flat.

(iv)
He claimed *that* yesterday.

(v)
*He claimed a flat earth.

Nevertheless, there do appear to be good candidates for NPs that are interpreted as concealed propositions.

(vi)
I regret my promise.

(vii)
I regret that I made that promise.

(viii)
He denied his crime.

(ix)
He denied that he committed the crime.

If there are concealed propositions, the same argument will hold for them as for other concealed forms. The sentences in (4) and (5) would each have four possible interpretations instead of three, thus strengthening the argument that it is impossible for the child to learn anything about semantic selection from concealed forms alone.

2. One cannot conclude from this that special acquisition principles are never needed. Grimshaw's discussion of the Canonical Structural Realization principle in connection with the learning of the categories noun and verb seems quite reasonable.

Chapter 7

On the Learnability of Abstract Phonology

Bezalel Elan Dresher

The question of learnability is central to linguistic theory, and much work in phonology since Chomsky and Halle's *Sound Pattern of English* (1968) has, quite appropriately, been motivated by a concern with how the rather complex phonological systems proposed there could be acquired. Various constraints on phonological theory have been proposed with the aim of ruling out grammars deemed to be difficult or impossible to learn. On the negative side, this concern with learnability has for the most part been misdirected, for it has been guided by an a prioristic view of the nature of the language faculty. Clearly, any consideration of learnability must take into account what is actually learned—if there is evidence that knowledge of a certain type is attained, it follows that such knowledge must be attainable. Just as obviously, arguments from learnability must be backed up by an empirically supported theory of learnability if they are to have any force. Frequently, however, these two basic prerequisites are not met; rather, language acquisition is taken to conform to some plausible principle, as an axiom, and then constraints are placed on phonological representations to insure conformity with the principle.

In particular, it has been a common assumption of many discussions of learnability in phonology that abstract underlying forms of the *Sound Pattern of English* type are difficult, perhaps impossible to learn.[1] I will argue that in certain cases the abstract analysis is the easiest analysis to learn, given certain assumptions about the acquisition device. I will explore this question with respect to a portion of the phonology of Old English. First, though, I would like to consider the problem on a smaller scale. Although many theories have been considered to posit unlearnable representations, very few analyses in the literature can safely be said to be unlearnable in any obvious way. One such example is provided by Saporta (1965); consideration of his proposals might serve to illustrate some of the points I will be pursuing in more detail.

Learnable and Unlearnable Phonologies

Saporta (1965) discusses singular and plural forms in three Spanish dialects, represented in (1).

(1)
Spanish Dialects:

Castilian	Latin American	South Chile	
lúnes	lúnes	lúnes	'Monday'
lúnes	lúnes	lúnes	'Mondays'
lápiθ	lápis	lápis	'pencil'
lápiθes	lápises	lápis	'pencils'

In the most conservative dialect, Castilian, plurals are formed by adding -s after unstressed vowels and stressed é, -∅ after unstressed vowels followed by s, and -es elsewhere; Saporta formulates the rule as (2).

(2)
Spanish Plural Rule:

$$\text{pl} \rightarrow \begin{cases} \text{s} / \begin{Bmatrix} \breve{V} \\ é \end{Bmatrix} \underline{\quad\quad} \\ \emptyset / \breve{V}\text{s} \underline{\quad\quad} \\ \text{es} / \end{cases}$$

A sample grammar for the Castilian forms is given in (3).

(3)
Castilian:

Underlying	/lúnes+pl/	/lápiθ+pl/
Plural (2)	lúnes+∅	lápiθ+es
Surface	lúnes	lápiθes

This analysis is quite straightforward and, given standard assumptions, poses no special learning difficulties.

In Latin American Spanish a change took place whereby all θ became s. Now *lápises* looks like an exception to the old plural rule, which otherwise operates as before. Saporta proposes to keep the plural rule (2) and underlying /θ/ in words like *lápiθ* and to add another rule of Absolute Neutralization, as in (4).

(4)
Absolute Neutralization (AN):
θ → s

Sample derivations are given in (5):

(5)
Latin American:

Underlying	/lúnes+pl/	/lápiθ+pl/
Plural (2)	lúnes+∅	lápiθ+es
AN (4)	—	lápis+es
Surface	lúnes	lápises

In this case, the question of learnability is not so straightforward. But before discussing this example further let us consider the South Chile dialect. In this dialect, which represents a more innovative stage of Latin American, it appears that the old plural rule (2) is still working as before, with *lápis* now acting as a regular word that ends in *s*. One might suppose, then, that words such as *lápis* have been restructured in this dialect, yielding the grammar of (6a).

(6)
a. South Chile:

Underlying	/lúnes+pl/	/lápis+pl/
Plural (2)	lúnes+∅	lápis+∅
Surface	lúnes	lápis

Although Saporta considers this solution, he proposes instead to keep underlying /θ/ in *lápis* and to reorder the rules of Plural (2) and Absolute Neutralization (4), as in (6b).

(6)
b. South Chile:

Underlying	/lúnes+pl/	/lápiθ+pl/
AN (4)	—	lápis+pl
Plural (2)	lúnes+∅	lápis+∅
Surface	lúnes	lápis

Saporta argues that (6b) is to be preferred over (6a) because there is independent evidence for underlying /θ/ in other words in this dialect, and because representing *lápis* with underlying /s/ would obscure the relation between this dialect and closely related dialects.

From the point of view of learnability, however, these considerations are irrelevant. For even though other forms in this dialect can be shown to have underlying /θ/ and even though other dialects may have it in this form, one must ask how a child learning South Chilean Spanish could come to know that *lápis* ends in /θ/ but *lúnes* ends in /s/ in underlying form. Since the two words presumably behave identically in all relevant respects, someone ignorant of the history of Spanish or of distant dialects could have no way of distinguishing the two cases. Further, the requisite knowledge could hardly be innate, given standard assumptions; as there is now no possible source for the acquisition of the grammar of (6b), one can conclude that it is unlearnable. Moreover, in this instance there exists a much simpler analysis (6a), which generates the same forms without requiring special assumptions.

Having seen an example of a genuinely unlearnable phonology, let us return to Saporta's analysis of the Latin American dialect (5), and ask whether it requires similar untenable assumptions. Notice that in this dialect there is a difference in outward patterning between *lúnes* and *lápis,* so speakers must make some distinction in their representations in the grammar. Although it does not follow that the distinction is captured in the way Saporta proposes as opposed to some other way, this fact is enough to distinguish this case rather sharply from the South Chile situation.

Two separate questions arise: First, can evidence be produced in favor of abstract phonologies like (5)? Second, is it possible to construct a theory that could account for the acquisition of such phonologies? These are two separate issues, although they are related in obvious ways. Thus, if evidence can be provided in support of such phonologies, it follows that it must be possible to acquire them. Or if it can be shown that certain phonologies cannot be acquired, one would not expect to find any good evidence for them. Much of the abstractness controversy has been overtly concerned with the first question—whether there is evidence in favor of abstract grammars—but learnability considerations have played an important, sometimes overriding role.[2]

For example, Hooper (1976, p. 13) claims that Saporta's analysis of Latin American is not learnable. With respect to rules containing /θ/ she contends that "looking at the rule from the speaker's point of view, we find that such a rule would be impossible to learn because part of its structural description (SD) does not exist on the surface in Latin American Spanish." But no empirical finding is presented to support this assertion. The assumption that a rule cannot be learned unless its entire SD exists on the surface indeed has the effect of ruling out

Saporta's analysis; but it is possible to make other, quite minimal, assumptions that lead to different results.

Suppose, for example, we assume the following:

(7)
i. Segments are analyzed as complexes of features.
ii. A learner adopts the most highly valued rules (i.e., rules requiring the fewest features) consistent with, and sometimes even overriding, the available data.[3]
iii. Rules formulated in terms of phonetic feature specifications are preferred to rules containing nonphonetic features.

Now we observe that words ending in s are of two types—one type forms its plural in -$\emptyset$, the other in -es, like words that end in other consonants. In terms of features, s is distinguished from other Spanish consonants by the features [+strident, +coronal]; the s in *lápis,* however, acts as if it were not so specified. The smallest change that can be made in the feature specification of s to bring it in line with its behavior in pluralization is to change the value of [strident], keeping all else constant. This nonstrident s is just θ. Now a rule of $\theta \rightarrow s$ is needed to derive the surface forms. A more concrete alternative such as simply marking words like *lápis* as exceptions to the regular plural rule would be less highly valued, by (7.iii), and so rejected. Abstract alternatives, involving other possible underlying segments, would also be less highly valued, by assumption (7.ii), because the required rules would utilize more features.

It should be emphasized that none of this is offered as support for Saporta's analysis; more evidence is needed to decide that. Rather, this discussion is concerned with the issue of learnability and is intended to demonstrate that it is not difficult to construct a model of acquisition that leads to the acquisition of abstract segments and rules. Moreover, this model rests on assumptions that are fairly well supported on independent grounds. Hardly anyone would deny (7.i); (7.ii) and (7.iii) remain standard assumptions and often are implicit in the work even of those who explicitly deny them—which is not surprising, inasmuch as no cogent alternatives have been presented, to my knowledge.

In what follows I will explore how the principles in (7), supplemented by some others, could lead to the acquisition of a fairly abstract phonology of Old English. I will argue that such a phonology not only can be acquired, given (7), but will be preferred to more concrete alternatives; further, I will argue that a learner would be able to converge on these rules starting from different parts of the grammar. I will then present some historical evidence that supports the analysis.

Hidden *i* in Old English

Many generative analyses of Old English have posited the existence of an underlying /i/ that plays an important role in the phonological and morphological system, even though this /i/ never appears as such on the surface.[4] For example, it can be argued that the underlying morphology of the Class I Weak verbs is /stem+i+inflection/. The *i*-extension, however, is never observed in the surface forms of these verbs, as is evident from the sample paradigms of *ġefremman* 'complete' and *ġehēran* 'hear,' given in (8).

(8)

Class I Weak Verbs:

Infin.	-fremman		-hēran	
	Present	Preterite	Present	Preterite
Indic.				
1sing.	fremmu	fremede	hēru	hērde
2sing.	fremes	fremedes	hēres	hērdes
3sing.	fremeð	fremede	hēreð	hērdes
pl.	fremmað	fremedun	hērað	hērdun
Subj.				
sing.	fremme	fremede	hēre	hērde
pl.	fremmen	fremeden	hēren	hērden
Imper.				
sing.	freme		hēr	
pl.	fremmað		hērað	
Part.	fremmende	fremed	hērende	hēred

Evidence for the underlying *i*-extension exists, though it is not immediately obvious from these forms. However, a language learner following principles (7.i)–(7.iii) would be led rather quickly to posit an underlying /i/ in these forms, even though it does not occur on the surface.

The first bit of evidence involves the imperative singulars, where we find *freme* but *hēr*. Similarly, the preterite forms of *fremman* have an *e* between the stem and the preterite formative *-d-* whereas the preterite forms of *hēran* do not, except in the form *hēred*.[5] The pattern: an *e* follows a light stem, but not syllable-finally after a heavy stem. One might conclude that the stem extension was not *i* but *e*, and that this *e* is deleted by a rule that operates in the environment: heavy syllable ____ (CVX)#. Yet, there is much evidence from other forms that *e* does not in general delete in this environment—cf. *worde* in (9). Therefore, either the *e*'s that delete have to be specially marked—a possible though not highly valued solution—or the deleting *e* has a different underlying origin from the nondeleting *e*. As a solution of this nature would lead to a more highly valued grammar than one in which a morphological or arbitrary specification was placed on certain *e*'s, I assume that a language learner would pursue it.

The number of possible solutions of this type is large but, even at this point, partially ordered by the evaluation measure. Thus, since a rule changing one feature is more highly valued than a rule changing two features, the first set of candidates for a segment that becomes *e* would consist of those segments that differ from *e* by only one feature—e.g., *æ, i, o, ē*. I assume, then, that a language learner would consider these possibilities as favored. Next would come segments that differ from *e* by two features, then by three, and so on, down to the exceedingly unlikely candidates, such as *k* and *t*. So while it is no doubt an error to think of a child as diligently and systematically going about testing these various segments in order, the evaluation measure can be thought of as creating a structured solution space that predisposes the learner toward certain hypotheses.

To sum up the problem to here, I have arrived at the following hypotheses:

Hypothesis 1:

The stem extension in the Weak Class I verbs deletes in the environment: heavy syllable ____ (CVX)#.

Hypothesis 2:

This stem extension is a segment that is as close to *e* (not excluding *e* itself) in terms of features as possible.

Consider now the neuter *a*-nouns *sċip* 'ship' and *word* 'word':[6]

(9)

Neuter *a*-Nouns:

	Singular	Plural	Singular	Plural
Nom.	sċip	sċipu	word	word
Acc.	sċip	sċipu	word	word
Gen.	sċipes	sċipa	wordes	worda
Dat.	sċipe	sċipum	worde	wordum

The two nouns decline identically except in the nominative and accusative plurals, where we find *scipu* next to *word*. This pattern indicates a rule deleting *u* word-finally after a heavy stem. That this rule applies more generally, at the end of syllables, is shown by comparing the singulars of the neuter *a*-nouns *hēafud* 'head' and *weorud* 'troop':

(10)
Disyllabic Neuter *a*-Nouns:

		Singular
Nom.	hēafud	weorud
Acc.	hēafud	weorud
Gen.	hēafdes	weorudes
Dat.	hēafde	weorude

These facts can be described by a rule such as (11).

(11)
u-Deletion:

$$\begin{bmatrix} +\text{syll} \\ +\text{high} \\ +\text{back} \end{bmatrix} \rightarrow \emptyset \: / \: \text{Heavy syllable} \: \underline{} \: (CVX)\#$$

Rule (11), though operating in the familiar environment, would be of little use to a language learner with respect to the Class I Weak verbs. No rule changing *u* to *e* can be formulated on the basis of these facts, and as we have already noted, *worde, hēre,* etc., show that *e* does not generally drop in the environment of (11), precluding any generalization of the rule to *e*.

Rule (11), however, is not the most general rule of deletion that can be devised, given the data to here. The specification [+high] in the target of the rule cannot be deleted, because the *a* of *worda* does not delete; but the specification [+back] has not been needed yet. Thus, rule (12) will account for the same data as rule (11).

(12)
High Vowel Deletion (HVD):

$$\begin{bmatrix} +\text{syll} \\ +\text{high} \end{bmatrix} \rightarrow \emptyset \: / \: \text{Heavy syllable} \: \underline{} \: (CVX)\#$$

Since rule (12) has fewer features than rule (11), it is a more highly valued rule, by the hypothesized evaluation measure. So, by hypothesis, a language learner would posit rule (12) rather than rule (11) in the

interest of arriving at the most highly valued grammar. Now, rule (12), considered in the light of Hypothesis 1, yields Hypothesis 3.
Hypothesis 3:
The Weak Class I stem extension is a high vowel.

As the high vowel that is closest to *e* is *i*, Hypothesis 2 together with Hypothesis 3 yields:
Hypothesis 4:
The Weak Class I stem extension is *i*.

Hypothesis 4 entails the existence of a rule that lowers *i* to *e* in certain environments. Is there any other evidence for such a rule? Again, there is, albeit not in the form of a surface alternation between *i* and *e*.

Consider the paradigms of the masculine nouns *bearu* 'grove' and *here* 'army':

(13)
Masculine Nouns with Stem-final Glides:

	Singular	Plural	Singular	Plural
Nom.	bearu	here	bearwas	herġas
Acc.	bearu	here	bearwas	herġas
Gen.	bearwes	herġes	bearwa	herġa
Dat.	bearwe	herġe	bearwum	herġum

There is an asymmetry between the *u* ~ *w* alternation in *bearu* and the *e* ~ *ġ* alternation in *here;* for supposed underlying stems /bearw-/, /herġ-/, the most straightforward vocalization rule would be (14).

(14)
Vocalization:
$[-\text{cons}] \rightarrow [+\text{syll}] / \ldots \underline{\quad} \#$

Although (14) would correctly convert /bearw/ to *bearu*, it would change /herġ/ to *heri*, not *here*. These data lend support to the positing of a rule lowering *i* to *e*, for only by positing such a rule can a general vocalization rule be maintained.

Sample derivations are given in (15).

(15)
Sample Derivations:

Underlying	/frem+i/	/hēr+i/	/herġ/	/word+u/
Vocaliz. (14)	—	—	heri	—
HVD (12)	—	hēr	—	word
i-Lowering	frem+e	—	here	—
Surface	freme	hēr	here	word

Further Evidence for Hidden *i*

I have argued that a language learner guided by principles (7.i)–(7.iii) will be led, on the basis of relatively few forms, to the positing of an underlying *i*-extension in the Class I Weak verbs. I will now show that starting from an entirely different set of forms and following a further principle, one would arrive at exactly the same analysis.

The principle involved is not entirely new, but is an extension of principle (7.iii), which states that rules formulated in terms of phonetic feature specifications are preferred to rules containing nonphonetic features. This condition can be stated in a more general form, to require that all aspects of phonetic organization be highly valued throughout the phonology. This property follows from what Postal (1968, pp. 55 ff.) has called the Naturalness condition, the hypothesis that underlying systematic phonemic (often called morphophonemic) representations are organized in terms of phonetic principles rather than in terms of some other set of principles, as held for example by Lamb (1966), Fudge (1967), and Foley (1977), as well as advocates of most versions of Natural Phonology. In the generalized interpretation of the Naturalness condition, rules that are highly valued at the phonetic level (phonetically natural rules) will also be highly valued at other levels of phonological representation and so will be preferred by language learners attempting to construct highly valued grammars.

For example, it is true in general that the most common phonetic rules involve the assimilation of one feature to a feature in its environment, that is, a rule of the form (16).

(16)
Basic Template for Assimilation:

$$\begin{bmatrix} a_1 F_1 \\ a_2 F_2 \\ \cdot \\ \cdot \\ \cdot \\ a_n F_n \end{bmatrix} \rightarrow [a_j F_j] \Big/ \begin{matrix} \underline{\quad} X [a_j F_j] \\ \text{or} \\ [a_j F_j] X \underline{\quad} \end{matrix}$$

One can imagine several ways of incorporating this statement into the theory. Any such formulation would, moreover, undoubtedly involve a refinement of (16), specifying different values of X for different values of F_j, as well as the effect of contextual features. Whatever the final form of the principle, its incorporation as a principle available to the

language acquisition device has some interesting and surprising consequences, to which I now return.

Consider the present tense paradigm of the Old English verb *eotan*
'eat'.

(17)
Class V Strong Verbs—Present:

	Indic.	Subj.	Imper.	Infin.
1sing.	eotu	ete		eotan
2sing.	ites	ete	et	
3sing.	iteð	ete		
pl.	eotað	eten	eotað	

The stem vowel *e* alternates with *eo* when a back vowel follows. In the
2sing. and 3sing. forms only, the stem vowel appears as *i*. In both cases
an *e* follows in the next syllable; but *e* also follows an *e*, as in *ete*, so no
surface phonetic generalization about the distribution is immediately
apparent.

Given only these data, the theory leads to the following hypotheses:
assuming that /e/ becomes *i*, a rule such as (18) can be formulated,
where [+R] is a diacritic placed on *e*'s that cause raising:

(18)
Raising:

$$V \rightarrow [+high] / \underline{\quad} C_0 \; e_{[+R]} \; (= / \underline{\quad} C_0 \begin{bmatrix} +syll \\ -back \\ -high \\ -low \\ +R \end{bmatrix})$$

An alternative analysis, supposing that /i/ is lowered to *e* except
before *e*~[+R]~ is not as highly valued because the required rule would be
more complex at this stage.

The theory prefers solutions in which rules operate on features specified in terms of phonetic categories over such arbitrary features as
[+R] (the Naturalness conditon). Can one distinguish between *e*~[-R]~ and
e~[+R]~ in purely phonological terms?

Suppose the language learner wishes to maximize the value of the
Raising rule. This could be done by making it conform to a rule of type
(16), as in (19):

(19)
Most Highly Valued Raising:

$$V \rightarrow [+\text{high}] / \underline{\quad} X \begin{bmatrix} \vdots \\ +\text{high} \\ \vdots \end{bmatrix} Y$$

Fitting (18) to (19) produces (20):

(20)
Hypothesized Raising:

$$V \rightarrow [+\text{high}] / \underline{\quad} C_0 \begin{bmatrix} +\text{syll} \\ -\text{back} \\ +\text{high} \end{bmatrix} (= / \underline{\quad} C_0 \ i)$$

On the basis of very little data, a language learner following the theory sketched here would quickly be led in the direction of rule (20), which requires abstract underlying forms /et+is/, /et+ið/; this hypothesis in turn calls for a rule of *i*-Lowering ordered after Raising, to convert *it+is, it+ið*, into *ites, iteð*. This analysis converges with that based on the Class I weak verbs, which also led to the positing of abstract suffixal *i* and the same rule of *i*-Lowering.

There is more evidence for this analysis. The strong verb *eotan* forms its preterite by changing the stem vowel. The pattern is displayed in (21), where characteristic forms stand for the whole paradigm:

(21)
Class V Strong Verbs—Principal Parts:

Present	Preterite 1	Preterite 2	Participle
e(o)	e	ē	e
eotan	et	ēton	eten

There is a group of verbs which form their preterites according to (21), but their presents look like Weak Class I forms. An example is *sittan* 'sit,' which has the principal parts given in (22); the present forms are given in (23):

(22)
Class V Strong Verbs with Weak Presents:

Present	Preterite 1	Preterite 2	Participle
sittan	set	sēton	seten

(23)
Present Forms of *sittan:*

	Indic.	Subj.	Imper.	Infin.
1sing.	sittu	sitte		sittan
2sing.	sites	sitte	site	
3sing.	siteð	sitte		
pl.	sittað	sitten	sittað	

Note the Imperative singular *site,* as opposed to *et,* suggesting that the present forms of *sittan* are formed by adding an extension that surfaces as *e*. The stem vowel in these forms is *i;* yet, in the other Class V verbs it is *e*. The statement of the rules of Preterite formation would be simpler if all Class V verbs had the same stem vowel. Moreover, the appearance of *i* for *e* is predictable: it occurs before the extension *-e-*, which can be identified with $e_{[+R]}$ —which has been identified as /i/. In this way, one again arrives at the conclusion that the Weak Class I stem extension is derived from /i/.

The assumption that rules of the form (16) are valued highly by language learners supports the present analysis in yet another way, once it is joined with a principle that penalizes certain "unnatural" uses of the alpha-variable notation. The case in question bears on the rule of *i*-Lowering and concerns a rule of vowel epenthesis.

Apparent disyllabic stems such as *weter* 'water' and *fugul* 'bird' appear as monosyllabic stems in inflected forms: *wetres, wetre,* etc., and *fugles, fugle,* etc. As there is no general deletion rule in the relevant environment, such forms can be derived from monosyllabic stems /wetr/, /fugl/ by epenthesis. The epenthesized vowel is predictable: it matches the stem vowel in backness, and appears as *u* if back and *e* if front. The Epenthesis rule can be formulated as in (24):

(24)
Epenthesis:

$$\emptyset \rightarrow \begin{bmatrix} +\text{syll} \\ \alpha\text{back} \\ \alpha\text{high} \\ -\text{low} \end{bmatrix} / \begin{bmatrix} +\text{syll} \\ \alpha\text{back} \end{bmatrix} C_0 \, [-\text{voc}] \underline{\qquad} \begin{bmatrix} -\text{syll} \\ +\text{cons} \\ +\text{son} \end{bmatrix} (\text{CVX})\#$$

There is a difference between the two occurrences of the variable in the specification of the epenthesized vowel. In the alpha notation, [αback] expresses the fact that the backness of the epenthetic vowel matches that of the vowel in its environment, a desirable feature, and expected in the light of (16). On the other hand, the correlation between backness and height expressed by [αhigh] is not significant in the same way. The asymmetry between *e* and *u* does not follow from universal principles. If the theory were made to discriminate between these two uses of the alpha notation, another analysis of epenthesis would become more highly valued—namely, specifying the epenthetic vowel as [+syll, αback, +high], and having a separate rule of *i*-Lowering:

(25)
i-Lowering:

$$\begin{bmatrix} +\text{syll} \\ -\text{back} \end{bmatrix} \rightarrow [-\text{high}] / \underset{[-\text{stress}]}{\underline{\qquad}}$$

But (25) is just the rule of *i*-Lowering required by the various other considerations discussed. Thus, a language learner suitably endowed would converge on this rule from different parts of the grammar.

External Evidence for Hidden *i*

I have been arguing that, given certain fairly standard assumptions, it is possible to construct a model of acquisition that leads to the acquisition of a grammar of Old English that contains abstract rules and representations. I have posited underlying *i*'s that never appear at the surface; these *i*'s appear in the rules of *i*-Lowering and *e*-Raising. The interaction of these two rules leads to a surprising consequence of the extended Naturalness condition, according to which assimilation rules are highly valued at every level of the phonology. The result of following this principle in /et+is/ is that once *i*-Lowering has applied, we obtain a surface form *ites,* which manifests a phonetic dissimilation of vowel height. This example illustrates how the Naturalness condition, when viewed as a cognitive principle of phonological organization, can lead to phonologies that are quite abstract and phonetically unnatural.

I have mentioned two separate issues that need to be addressed in discussions of the learnability of abstract phonological systems. The preceding sections were aimed at the second of these issues: namely, whether it is possible to construct a theory that can lead to the acquisition of such systems. It remains to consider the first question: Is there, in the case being examined here, any evidence that my analysis is actually correct? Fortunately the dialect of Old English with which I am dealing—the Mercian dialect—can be traced through several historical periods, and the patterns of analogical change that are found do provide evidence for an analysis of the type proposed.[7]

It should be stressed, before embarking on an account of the diachronic developments, that the fact that it was possible to construct an elegant internally consistent analysis, which expresses observed generalizations and which is supported by several independent lines of evidence, all in accord with a set of plausible general principles, is itself prima facie evidence for the analysis. Lacking persuasive evidence to the contrary, one would prefer an analysis that best captured observed generalizations, and the burden of proof is on the proponents of "concrete" theories of phonology to construct an analysis without underlying *i*'s that is as well supported synchronically. Of course, it is always possible that the synchronic patterns are somehow misleading: for example, certain generalizations may be only artifacts of historical chance, without significance to phonological theory and, hence, to the language learner.[8] Again, the usual strategy is to assume that observed patterns in data are significant until it is shown that they are not, especially if they can be accounted for by a theory. But we need not stand only with the synchronic data in this case.

The historical evidence involves developments in the rule of High Vowel Deletion (HVD), rule (12), which deletes a syllable-final high vowel that follows a heavy (H) syllable. In early Old English, HVD operated also in a second environment: when the syllable-final high vowel followed two light (L) syllables (cf. Campbell, 1959, p. 345; Kiparsky and O'Neil, 1976; Keyser and O'Neil, 1980). The early version of this rule is represented schematically as (26):

(26)
Early Old English Vowel Deletion:

$$\begin{bmatrix} -\text{cons} \\ +\text{high} \\ -\text{stress} \end{bmatrix} \rightarrow \emptyset \ / \ \begin{Bmatrix} \text{H} \\ \text{LL} \end{Bmatrix} \underline{\quad} (CVX)\#$$

This rule is responsible for the alternations found in the nominative sing. *hēafud* versus genitive sing. *hēafdes,* nominative pl. *hēaf(u)du;* but nominative sing. *werud* versus genitive sing. *werudes,* nominative pl. *werud* (from /werud+u/). There is little doubt that the environments collapsed by braces originally formed a unified rule.[9]

Later, this rule was made opaque by the introduction of the rule of Epenthesis (24), which made underlying monosyllabic stems like

/waetr/ 'water' and /wundr/ 'wonder' look like disyllables on the surface. Because Epenthesis was ordered after Vowel Deletion, the derived disyllabic stems did not display the regular pattern of deleted vowels:

(27)

Underlying	/wundr+es/	/wundr+u/	/waetr+es/	/waetr+u/
Vowel Deletion	—	wundr	—	waetr
Epenthesis	—	wundur	—	waetir
Phonetic form	wundres	wundur	waetres	waetir

(28)
Inflectional Patterns (underlying and derived disyllables):

Stem	Nominative sing.	Genitive sing.	Nominative pl.
/hēafud/	hēafud	hēafdes	hēaf(u)du
/werud/	werud	werudes	werud
/wundr/	wundur	wundres	wundur
/waetr/	waetir	waetres	waetir

Words like *hēafud* and *wundur* would have looked the same throughout their paradigms, except for the nominative pl., where forms like *wundur* made Vowel Deletion opaque, since it appears from the surface that a final high vowel was incorrectly deleted following HL. Given also that—except again for the nominative pl.—many words like *wundur* could have been analyzed either as /wundr/ or /wundur/, the HL environment of Vowel Deletion must have become quite hard to learn correctly. By contrast, the alternation exemplified by *werudes* and *waetres* occurred in all inflected forms of such words (except nominative pl.). (In some dialects additional phonological evidence enabled language learners to distinguish the two types of forms.) Although there was some confusion as to which words declined like *werud* and which declined like *waetir,* as is attested by the fact that words changed from one type to the other, the alternation did not seem to create difficulties for the Vowel Deletion rule.

One result of these developments can be seen in the Mercian dialect represented in the *Vespasian Psalter.* After a single stressed syllable, the pattern is as would be expected from rule (26): high vowels drop after a heavy syllable and are retained after a light syllable. After two syllables, however, a fair amount of variation occurs, across stems and even within one stem. Thus, we find the expected *hēafudu* twice, but also *hēafud* five times; the expected *micel* 'much' derived from

/micl+u/ (originally /micil+u/, a form that should also yield *micel*) occurs four times, but the totally unexpected *micelu* occurs eight times.
Similarly, the accusative pl. of 'calf' occurs as both *calferu* and *calfur;*
the nominative pl. of 'lamb' occurs as *lomberu* as well as *lombur; īdel*
occurs with *īdelu;* and so on. (See Dresher, 1978, for details.)

It appears, then, that the original rule of Vowel Deletion (26) has, in
the *Vespasian Psalter* dialect, been split into two rules: a rule that
applies regularly after H, and another, irregular, rule that applies to the
left environment V́ . . . V . . . ____.

Now one can construct an argument bearing on the abstractness
question. To do this, I must consider a bit more closely the environment immediately after a stressed heavy syllable. In the *Vespasian
Psalter* dialect, Vowel Deletion occurs exceptionlessly. But this does
not mean that the rule in this environment is totally transparent; on the
contrary, there occur many apparent exceptions on the surface. Examples are *wītu* 'punishments,' *ermðu* 'misery,' *ældu* 'old age,' and many
similar forms, all with a final *u* immediately following a heavy syllable,
in apparent violation of (26).

In a concrete theory along the lines of Hooper (1976), these surface
violations would be sufficient grounds for ruling out the phonetic formulation of Vowel Deletion after H, as well as after V́ . . . V. In such a
theory, these two environments would be accorded the same phonological status: since both parts of the rule are opaque (i.e., not surface
true), they must both be recast as morphological rules. Now, while the
V́ . . . V ____ part of (26) does indeed show signs of dephonologization
in the *Vespasian Psalter*—variants such as *micel, micelu* show that it
does not apply regularly, and even applies in what is not its original
environment—no such variation is found in the short environment.
Thus, we find no variant forms like **wīt* or **æld* occurring next to forms
such as *micel, micelu,* and there is no evidence of the rule applying to
new environments, such as after L. But if both parts of the rule are
equally opaque, why is one so much more stable than the other?

An answer can be found in the context of a more abstract theory,
which permits opaque rules if they contribute to the optimal grammar.
It turns out that the morphological classes within which Vowel Deletion
after H appears to be violated are also the classes in which two other
rules are also contradicted. These rules are Breaking, which changes *æ*
to *ea* and *e* to *eo* before *r*C, and Retraction, which retracts *æ* to *a* before
*l*C and *l*V (i.e., before back *l*). Thus *ermðu* and *ældu* are each
        [+back]

doubly exceptional, violating not just Vowel Deletion, but the rules of Breaking and Retraction, respectively: compare *earm* 'wretched' and *ald* 'old.' Now, exactly the same cluster of properties occur in the Weak Class I verbs, which in my analysis have been assigned the underlying structure stem+*i*+suffixes. In the Weak Class I verbs, the apparent lack of Retraction can be accounted for by a rule of umlaut, which refronts *a* to *æ* before *i;* this yields forms like *ældan* 'to delay,' from /æld+i+an/. Similarly, the effects of Breaking are undone by a monophthongization rule that is also conditioned by *i;* from /scærp+i+an/ comes /scearp+i+an/ by Breaking, /scerp+i+an/ by Monophthongization, and, following Vowel Deletion, *scerpan* 'to sharpen' (cf. *scearp* 'sharp,' from /scærp/). Other sample derivations are given in (29):

(29)

Underlying form	/wīti+u/	/æld+i+u/	/ærm+i+ðu/
Retraction	—	ald+i+u	—
Breaking	—	—	earm+i+ðu
i-Mutation	—	æld+i+u	—
i-Monophthongization	—	—	erm+i+ðu
Vowel Deletion	wīt+u	æld+u	erm+ðu
Phonetic form	wītu	ældu	ermðu

Notice that the applications of Vowel Deletion in (29) are all in the environment H ____. By positing an underlying *i* in the forms of (29), I can account for the apparent violations of three different rules with one stroke. At the same time, I can account for the stability of Vowel Deletion in these forms. For although the rule is opaque on the surface, various lines of phonological evidence all converge to indicate to a language learner the presence of an unseen *i* in these forms, enabling the rule to be preserved in a purely phonological form.

If a concrete analysis were correct, on the other hand, none of these considerations should play a role. For the rules of Retraction, Breaking, *i*-Mutation, *i*-Monophthongization, and Vowel Deletion—every rule mentioned in (29)—are all opaque on the surface because *i,* which plays such a central role in this system of rules, never appears at the surface. One would expect that the entire system represented in (29) should collapse, with all the rules becoming morphologized or even eliminated completely. (Note also that alternations within the paradigms of the forms of (29) are lacking.) Yet the system represented in the *Vespasian Psalter* is still extremely regular with respect to all these rules. In an abstract analysis like that of (29), the difference becomes clear: much more phonological evidence bore on the correct analysis of apparent exceptions to the short environment than on the long environment. So, although both were opaque, only the latter succumbed to nonphonological analogical changes.

More Diachronic Evidence

The external evidence just presented is somewhat indirect: the difference in the historical developments of the two parts of Vowel Deletion calls for an explanation, and one is available in terms of my analysis positing underlying *i* in several different morphological paradigms. On the other hand, it is not clear that an equally satisfactory account is available in terms of an analysis that posits underlying representations closer to the surface forms in these paradigms.

These historical developments do not stand in isolation, however, and additional diachronic evidence, of quite another kind, can be brought to bear. Recall that the apparent violation of Retraction in forms like *ældan* 'delay' was taken to be evidence indicating an underlying *i* which conditioned a rule of *i*-Mutation in this form, refronting *a* to *æ* (cf. (29)). This rule of Retraction was made opaque by such derivations, and minimal pairs existed such as *ælde,* the present subjunctive sing. of *ælde,* from /æld+i+e/, vs. *alde,* the dative sing. of *ald* 'old,' from /æld+e/. Retraction can be formulated as in (30):

(30)
Retraction:

$$\begin{bmatrix} +\text{syll} \\ +\text{low} \end{bmatrix} \rightarrow [+\text{back}] \, / \, \underset{[+\text{stress}]}{\rule{1.5em}{0.4pt}} \begin{bmatrix} -\text{syll} \\ +\text{son} \\ +\text{back} \end{bmatrix}$$

Given the opacity of Retraction (30), and the fact that alternations between *æ* and *a* are lacking in most paradigms, the theory that rejects underlying *i* will also disallow deriving *ald* from /æld/. Instead, words with stressed *a* in all surface forms will be derived from underlying /a/. But now both *æ* and *a* are possible underlying phonemes, and their distribution is not predicted by synchronic rules of grammar (although, on this view, the patterns following from an abstract analysis still exist as an artifact of earlier historical periods, though without synchronic significance—that is, without psychological reality—for language learners). It follows, then, that the occurrence of *æ* in *ælde* sheds no light on any underlying *i* that may be hidden in this form. By similar reasoning, neither could any of the rules of (29), for they are all opaque and so would all be ruled out by a theory that disallows such opacity.

Is there any independent evidence, then, that would bear on the choice of the underlying vowel in words like *ald?* There is evidence from change, this time involving a change from the early Mercian of the *Corpus* and *Epinal* glossaries to the later Mercian recorded in the *Vespasian Psalter.* In addition to the rules listed in (29), two other rules of Mercian are relevant: Back Mutation, which diphthongized short front vowels when a back vowel followed, and *a*-Restoration, which backed *æ* to *a* in the same environment. These rules are formulated as (31) and (32).

(31)
Back Mutation:

$$\emptyset \rightarrow \text{ə} / \begin{bmatrix} +\text{syll} \\ -\text{back} \\ -\text{long} \\ +\text{stress} \end{bmatrix} \underline{\hspace{1cm}} [-\text{syll}] \begin{bmatrix} +\text{syll} \\ +\text{back} \end{bmatrix}$$

(32)
a-Restoration:

$$\begin{bmatrix} +\text{syll} \\ +\text{low} \end{bmatrix} \rightarrow [+\text{back}] / \underset{[+\text{stress}]}{\underline{\hspace{1cm}}} [-\text{syll}] \begin{bmatrix} +\text{syll} \\ +\text{back} \end{bmatrix}$$

The *a*-Restoration rule must be ordered before Back Mutation and after Retraction; *a*-Restoration cannot be part of the same rule as Retraction because Breaking must be ordered between them. Sample early Mercian derivations in terms of an abstract analysis are given in (33).

(33)

Underlying	/æld+∅/	/fæt+e/	/fæt+u/	/wer+a/
Retraction	ald	—	—	—
a-Restoration	—	—	fat+u	—
Back Mutation	—	—	—	weər+a
Phonetic form	ald	fæte	fatu	weora

In a concrete analysis, *ald* would be derived from /ald/; the other forms would presumably be derived as in (33), since *æ* alternates with *a* in the paradigm of *fæt* 'vessel,' and *e* and *eo* alternate in the paradigm of *wer* 'man.' The two types of theories would also provide different underlying representations for words like *hafuc* 'hawk': in my analysis it would be derived, like *fatu,* from /hæfuc/ by Back Mutation; in a concrete analysis it would have to be derived from /hafuc/, since all forms of this morpheme have the stressed vowel *a*. In terms of such a theory, the change from earlier *hæfuc* to *hafuc* would still be attributed to *a*-Restoration: but once the change had taken place, the underlying form would have had to be restructured as /hafuc/.

Subsequent to the stage of the language represented by the surface forms of (33), a change occurred whereby *fatu* became *featu* (= [fæətu] or [fæatu]). I have argued elsewhere (see note 7) that this change is the result of the loss of the rule of *a*-Restoration (32) from the grammar. When one looks at the nonalternating *a*'s, one finds that the *a* in words like *ald* remained, while the *a* in words like *hafuc* became *ea*. The difference between the two types of nonalternating *a* emerges clearly in my analysis but is obscured in a concrete analysis. These facts show that the synchronic generalizations about the distribution of stressed *a* and *æ* were not just a historical artifact but were expressed in the grammars of native speakers.

These results support my analysis of hidden *i* in two ways. First, the fact that Retraction (30) remained in the grammar and applied to *ald* indicates that its apparent violation in *ældan* and other such words was indeed a significant fact, which could be used as evidence by the language learner for an analysis in which *ældan* derived from /æld+i+an/. Second, and more generally, these historical data show that opaque rules are allowed when they contribute to a more explanatory analysis; hence the data support the main lines of the theory of phonology, together with assumptions about learnability, which stands behind this particular analysis.

To sum up, synchronic as well as external diachronic evidence supports the abstract analysis of Old English I have proposed. Moreover, a language learner guided by the formal evaluation measure of Chomsky and Halle (1968), supplemented by substantive principles following from the Naturalness condition, would be able to arrive at this grammar—indeed, would choose it—starting from various different bits of data, despite the fact that the acquired representations are quite abstract relative to the heard phonetic forms. Thus, there is no reason to suppose that theories of phonology that allow such grammars impose, as some have claimed, an intolerable burden on the language acquisition device.

Notes

I would like to thank Robert Bley-Vroman, Norbert Hornstein, Patricia Keating, and Jean-Roger Vergnaud for helpful comments.

1. Cf. Braine (1974), Crothers (1971), Derwing (1973), Hooper (1976), and Skousen (1975), among many others.

2. On the abstractness controversy see Kiparsky (1973a), Schane (1974), Sommerstein (1977, ch. 9), and Dresher (1981) for references and discussion.

Reference to abstract (or concrete) grammars or theories is purely for ease of exposition. It is not theories and grammars which are abstract with respect to surface phonetic forms but the rules and representations they allow.

3. The notion "available data" requires some elaboration. I will be making the idealization that all the data considered are available to the language learner at the same time. The actual grammars constructed by speakers will differ from those predicted by this theory if the data taken into account do not contain certain crucial forms, or if there are significant limitations on restructuring of grammars in the course of acquisition. Moreover, forms may be assigned different weightings, depending on factors such as frequency, markedness, or other principles determined by linguistic theory interacting with developmental factors. However, the existence of such real-time effects does not affect the status of principles (7.i)–(7.iii).

4. Cf. Howren (1967), Wagner (1969), Lass and Anderson (1975), Keyser (1975), and Kiparsky and O'Neil (1976).

5. Other relevant phenomena, such as the gemination of the stem-final consonant in *-fremman* and the palatalization of stem-final consonants in other Class I verbs, will not be discussed here, although they can be shown to further support the proposed analysis. See the references cited in note 4 as well as Dresher (1978) for further discussion.

6. Complete paradigms of nouns and verbs are cited for the convenience of the reader. It is not necessary to suppose that the language learner must have access to complete paradigms; scattered representative forms would serve equally well.

7. See Dresher (1980) for further discussion of the language and the texts, as well as for elaboration of the material discussed here in the section on "More Diachronic Evidence."

8. Skousen (1975) concludes that synchronic evidence is not as "substantive" as other types of evidence; see Dresher (1981) for discussion.

9. Keyser and O'Neil (1980) propose a unified formulation in terms of a metrical approach.

Three issues raised, though not always explicitly, by Dresher's discussion are of particular interest. The first is the importance to linguistic argumentation and to the abstractness controversy of what I shall call a learnability demonstration. The second is an interesting logical feature of learnability demonstrations of the type presented by Dresher: the problem of accounting for the learning of morphophonemics seems to differ significantly from the projection problem in syntactic acquisition. Finally, there is in Dresher's historical discussion a kind of "overgeneration" problem: it seems that the learning theory would have the child reach generalizations that are evidently not achieved.

Learnability Demonstrations

Dresher's convincing demonstration that a certain abstract analysis of Old English can be learned is important for two reasons. Not only does it provide an example of what one hopes will become a paradigm argument type for a phonological analysis, but it makes a valuable contribution to the abstractness controversy in current phonology.

Without the context of this controversy, the learnability demonstration may appear pointless, or the assumptions may appear a priori. What evidence is presented, after all, that the learner selects phonologically based generalizations over others; that there is a template for evaluating a particular type of rule; and so on? Dresher correctly emphasizes, however, that he is not trying (at least in this part of the paper) to show that the learning theory presented is correct but only that it is reasonable and that it can lead to certain sorts of abstract analyses. There is apparently a belief among many phonologists—a belief that is thriving, for all one can tell—that only principles of phonology that are obviously true on the surface ("true generalizations" or "rules of pronunciation") can be acquired by the learner. Dresher shows that this belief is not obviously correct; that it is easy to imagine perfectly reasonable alternative views of the acquisition capacity under which analyses could be acquired which embody rules and underlying distinctions that cannot be directly read from the surface in an obvious way. His burden is to show only that the theory of acquisition that leads to such analyses is not obviously absurd and that it is equally as reasonable as the a priori assumptions of "concrete" phonology. In this he succeeds.

If all he achieved was to provide an argument that abstract analyses could conceivably be acquired, then the paper would be of no great interest. After all, one need only look at syntax to be overwhelmed with the ability of the human mind to acquire systems of great intricacy, the underlying principles of which by no means jump out at one when one glances at a sample of data.

More interestingly, Dresher provides in his learnability demonstration an example of what could become a paradigm form of argument in favor of an analysis—a form that can in principle lead both to a tighter view of what constitutes a possible phonology and, in conjunction with other sorts of evidence, to a greater understanding of the principles with which the acquisition capacity operates. From this perspective, the proponent of a given analysis has the triple burden of showing, at least in principle, just how a learner, given certain information, might achieve that analysis; then of making explicit the assumptions of learning theory that are necessary to make that achievement possible; and, finally, of showing that these assumptions are neither obviously unreasonable nor in serious conflict with the learnability requirements of other, well-established analyses.

The requirement for a learnability demonstration must not be confused with the much stronger requirement that linguistic theory must provide a discovery procedure that will lead to uniquely correct analyses. A learnability demonstration shows only that the argued solution could have been arrived at, that a path exists from the data to the analysis—a route that can be traversed by a learner equipped only with abilities he may be supposed to possess. Of course there may be (usually is) more than one route, and, more important, there may be more than one achievable solution. It is in this last point that the requirement for a learnability demonstration is most sharply distinguished from the requirement for a discovery procedure. And it is just because of the non-uniqueness of learnable solutions that an evaluation metric is built into Dresher's sketch of the acquisition process.

To see how the requirement of a learning demonstration rules out analyses, one might pursue a bit further the discussion of Saporta's proposal for South Chilean Spanish. Here a learnability demonstration, although it might be possible, would require assumptions about language acquisition that are unacceptable. One way of arriving at Saporta's analysis is of course by the use of factual knowledge of the history and dialectology of Romance, which the learner cannot be expected to possess. This route must therefore be ruled out, as Dresher points out. Another route, not considered by Dresher, is also available. A learning theory might demand that the learner make the maximum number of distinctions phonological theory allows, whether motivated or not, essentially using distinctions "because they are there"—a sort of reverse of Occam's razor. Thus the learner makes distinctions between some s's that are underlying s, and some that are underlying θ, even though the choice is arbitrary. In this way the learner might at least happen on the analysis proposed.

A slightly less radical proposal might be that once the learner has concluded that a distinction is motivated somewhere in the language, it must be used wherever possible—a sort of strong technological imperative. This theory would require the prerequisite step of showing that a strident/nonstrident distinction in sibilants must be learnable on the basis of some available South Chilean Spanish data, even if not for the data in question. These possibilities are perhaps not completely absurd, but they can surely be ruled out unless very convincing evidence is presented in their favor. (Curiously, the technological imperative seems to be a strong influence on the analyses of beginning students of phonological theory; it is thus at least not unimaginable.)

Dresher's learnability demonstration for hidden *i* is a kind of zeroing in: from various sides, bits of evidence seem to converge inexorably on a particular analysis; each bit of evidence is another clue to the underlying identity of a segment. Convergent arguments are not new in phonology: Brame's (1972) argument for Maltese pharyngeals furnishes a paradigm case; the arguments for the velar fricative in *right* in *The Sound Pattern of English* (Chomsky and Halle, 1968) are also of this type; and there are many others. Although convergent arguments are not always cast in terms of learnability demonstrations, the issues that Dresher raises were often implicit in earlier work. In work that prefigures Dresher's in many respects, Brame clearly suggests that his arguments for abstract pharyngeals show that the analysis is learnable. Brame says, commenting on his own argument, that "great pains were taken to demonstrate that the evidence for underlying ʕ is in the phonetic data. That is, the child coming to the language-learning situation is capable of inducing ʕ on the basis of Maltese phonetics alone" (1972, p. 60). Brame also uses a naturalness condition of the type advocated by Dresher.

One might speculate that any convergent analysis could be converted into a learnability demonstration. Whether analyses not overtly presented in this form can be demonstrated to be learnable in the same way is an interesting question, but one that probably cannot be answered without considerable sharpening of the learnability assumptions of Dresher's theory. It is possible that some analyses would be ruled out. (I have in mind such cases as the arguments for the underlying representation of *spa* in *The Sound Pattern of English*, or cases where an analysis is simply presented, with its own elegance serving as primary argument—for example, the analysis presented by Cathey and Demers (1976). Many of the analyses of Postal, 1968, are also of this sort.)

Given the as yet not fully elaborated learning theory of Dresher, any convergent argument could probably form the basis of a learnability demonstration; nevertheless, a more refined theory could distinguish among them if the evidence should so require. To give just one illustration, the hidden *i* learnability demonstration is compatible with the notion that a distinction must be realized directly on the surface somewhere in the language before it is available to the learner for use in abstract hypotheses. In the case at hand, Old English does have a superficial *i/e* distinction; *i* is not always hidden, only in this particular environment. Thus the case of hidden *i* contrasts with the case of the underlying pharyngeals in Brame's Maltese, which are always hidden. One could imagine a learnability theory under which the Old English case might be learnable whereas the Maltese case might not be.

The Logical Problem of Prerequisite Knowledge

The assumptions underlying Dresher's learnability discussion have a fundamentally different logical character from those frequently made in work on
learnability in syntax. The projection problem in syntax, as often conceived, is
that of determining how—given a fragmentary sample of data and certain
assumptions about the learning capacity, available feedback, and the like—the
learner can arrive at a knowledge of what the sentences of the language as a
whole are. This perspective contrasts sharply with that of Dresher's discussion,
where the learner is not faced with discovering what the facts of the morphophonemics are, based on bits and pieces of paradigms; rather, the learner
apparently is given complete knowledge of the relevant facts and is required to
decide on a systematic representation of them.

The argument for the learnability of hidden *i* is an excellent illustration.
From a projection-problem perspective, one might have asked questions such
as the following: Having heard miscellaneous verb forms, how does the learner
predict in general what the preterite of a given verb might be? How does the
learner come up with a way of telling the difference between verbs of the *hēran*
type and those of the *fremman* type? Supposing he arrives at a classification
system that in fact makes the wrong predictions, what sorts of evidence will
lead the learner to abandon it, and is that information generally available? Will
the learner progress through "incorrect" stages in the acquisition process? In a
discussion of the learnability of morphophonemics such as Dresher's, questions
of this sort cannot arise, because the learner is never faced with actually ascer-
taining what the facts of the morphophonemics are.

Indeed, at the point where the learning demonstration begins, the learner
must apparently be assumed to possess a store of prerequisite knowledge. For
example, he must have noticed—correctly—that the characteristic distinguishing verbs that behave like *fremman* from those that behave like *hēran* is
phonological stem weight, and in this way he predicts the behavior of newly
encountered verbs; he knows that the *hēran* types have no *e* in the imperative
whereas the *fremman* types do; he has seen that the presence and absence of *e*
in the imperative correlates with its presence and absence in the preterite; and
so on. Given this sort of knowledge, the learner has, in one sense, learned the
morphophonemics already. He is presumed to produce all the forms correctly;
his hypotheses run no risk of error. What is there left to "learn"?

In pointing out that discussions of the learnability of morphophonemics like
Dresher's seem logically to require this sort of prerequisite knowledge, it is
important to emphasize that the problem is not that the learner must somehow
be assumed to have access to too much data, to too many or too esoteric forms.
Rather, to put the issue in a slightly different way, the learner is required to
have already succeeded in figuring out the morphophonemics before the construction of an abstract account can begin. How much data he needed to
accomplish that task is not at issue (although it is, in the final analysis, the really
interesting question).

Although within Dresher's framework the learning task is not viewed as that
of figuring out what the correct forms are, one may still ask in what form the

learner may be capable of systematizing that knowledge. Dresher has shown that a certain sort of abstract phonological system is within reach.

Although Dresher does convincingly show that the abstract analysis can be achieved, yet by divorcing the figuring-out problem from the system-building problem and by seeming to make the former a prerequisite to the latter, he may have laid himself open to an interesting sort of antiabstractionist counterattack.

An advocate of concrete phonology might argue in the following way: Given that, in order to achieve the abstract solution, the learner needs to know things like the way to predict conjugation class from stem weight, and so on, let us concede that he has somehow acquired this knowledge. We will not even require that it be shown how that knowledge might have been attained. Let us further suppose that the language capacity can represent the required knowledge in some form. That is, at what may be called stage I, the learner's grammar contains information of the following sort:

1. If a verb has a certain phonological shape, it belongs to a certain paradigmatic class.
2. The inflectional patterns of the different verb (noun) classes are . . .
3. There are certain partial similarities among paradigms (e.g., all the weak verbs have a preterite in -d-).
4. Certain implicational relations hold within a paradigm (e.g., if the imperative ends in e, an e follows the stem in the preterite).

Furthermore, we are willing, for the sake of argument, to accept the notion that the grammar has a way of representing information of this sort, probably in the form of complex lexical entries and general statements about the form of entries, rules of lexical redundancy.

Now, continues the concrete phonologist, having equipped the learner with the prerequisite stage I grammar, we face a sort of bird-in-the-hand problem. The learner has a completely adequate (concrete) grammar, containing a complete and accurate representation of the paradigmatic alternations of his language. Why then should he abandon it to try for a different, "better" account—one that may not even exist? Note, in particular, there are no data that could disconfirm this stage I grammar. Suppose, nevertheless, that the learner did in fact abandon this concrete grammar. There would be no observable change in his behavior: he could still be producing all the correct forms. The abstract phonologist thus finds himself under a very difficult burden of proof.

What is ultimately required, to avoid attacks of this kind, is the explicit adoption of a more realistic picture of the learning process, in which the learner's efforts to discover what the facts of his language are goes hand in hand with his attempt to set up a systematic account of those facts.

The Learnability of High Vowel Deletion

Since the learnability demonstration cannot provide conclusive evidence that an analysis, though learnable, is in fact learned, other sorts of evidence are essential. It is for this reason that Dresher's historical argument is especially important. Dresher attempts to distinguish two cases of a phonological rule by learnability. One case must be shown to be learnable, the other case not. In this way he hopes to explain why one part of the rule is stable through time while the other breaks down. He succeeds only partially; for although the "learnable" case is clearly very easy to acquire given his learnability assumptions, the "unlearnable" one looks only slightly more difficult and it is hard to see what limitation in the proposed theory of the acquisition capacity could prevent the learner from attaining it.

In brief, the argument is as follows. High Vowel Deletion operated at one stage in Old English in two environments: after a heavy syllable (the short environment) and after a sequence of two light syllables (the long environment). It happened that Old English evolved so that the environments for these rules were no longer visible. Moreover, the rules that obscured the operation of the HVD were themselves opaque. Since both subrules—the long and the short environment—were now opaque, concrete phonology could not state them; the phenomena they expressed would be memorized quirks in the paradigms of Old English, like many others. Most important, the two subrules cannot be differentiated by learnability: both are absolutely unlearnable on the assumptions of concrete phonology.

In fact there is evidence, presented convincingly by Dresher, that they are differentiated with respect to learnability. HVD after two syllables began to break down, failing to apply when it should, irregularly applying to new environments where it ought not apply. On the other hand, HVD deletion after a heavy syllable was stable: apparently perfectly learned. Dresher puts the question well: "If both are equally opaque, why is one so much more stable than the other?"

What obscures the environment after a heavy syllable is an abstract underlying i. What obscures the other (now hard to learn) environment is a rule of epenthesis. Dresher's argument is that because there were various converging lines of evidence on the abstract i, which accounts for the apparent irregularity of the heavy syllable case, the abstract i was learnable and hence that case of HVD was also learnable.

The task is now to show that, given the assumptions of the learning theory, the other case of HVD cannot be learned. But it is not clear what will stop the learner from arriving at the unlearnable analysis. All that is required is that the learner figure out that it is the epenthetic vowels that are fouling up the environment for HVD. The epenthesis rule itself is extremely natural and expected; it doubtless corresponds closely to what the evaluation metric would specify as the template for most highly valued epenthesis; it may even be a "true generalization." It is difficult to see how the learner could fail to figure it out, given the assumptions of the learning theory presented. Furthermore, the solution that apparently cannot be learned would allow HVD itself to be stated in what is probably its most highly valued "natural" form and, in addition, would allow both cases of HVD to be covered by a single unified rule. Indeed, the fact that one case of HVD is in fact easy to motivate should provide indirect evidence for the other case of HVD, in the same way that u-deletion is said to make i-deletion easier to learn. Finally, the learner must be prevented from arriving at an analysis that in fact accounts in a general way for all the forms and must be made to choose an analysis that leaves a range of forms as unexplained irregularities.

Clearly, in order to account for the breakdown of the long case of HVD either a far more restrictive view of the acquisition capacity must be developed than that presented here or the explanation must somehow be sought elsewhere than in the cognitive difficulty of acquisition of the rule.

Chapter 8

The Role of the
Evaluation Metric
in the Acquisition
of Phonology

John J. McCarthy

The title of this contribution could more properly refer to "an evaluation metric," since two empirical questions are really at issue here: whether linguistic theory should provide a device for evaluating postulated grammars and what the characteristics of that device ought to be. Responses to both these questions are offered: first, that the need for an evaluation metric is demonstrated by the existence of phonological and morphological projection puzzles (Baker, chapter 10), instances of rule learning despite demonstrably inadequate primary data; and second, that the evaluation metric has essentially the form envisioned in Chomsky and Halle (1968, pp. 330–335), though with some adjustments for later modifications of this general phonological framework.

These two theses cannot be separated in practice, however; any evidence that appears to support the general necessity for an evaluation metric can be interpreted only in the light of a particular form of that metric, and conversely. This essay will, therefore, be chiefly structured around examples that illustrate both points. I present four cases, each involving a projection paradox that can be solved by selecting a grammar with simpler rules and representations, in the technical sense. Two general points are discussed before these more detailed studies. The first deals with the overall formal character of the acquisition of phonology and morphology, the second with some earlier investigations of the evaluation metric as well as the specific form of the metric proposed here.

Two problems will not figure significantly in this treatment, although they may be directly relevant to determining the form of the evaluation metric. First, I will make no attempt to discuss incorporation of a theory of phonetic substance into the phonology. This is often known as the problem of rule naturalness, although that term is by no means used consistently. Several interesting proposals for dealing with this problem formally have been discussed in the literature, such as those by Bach (1968) and Chen (1973). It has also motivated substantial revisions of the overall structure of phonological theory, either along the lines of Chomsky and Halle (1968, pp. 400–435) and Kean (1974) or of Stampe (1972) and Hooper (1976). Second, I have nothing to offer to the debate on natural rule ordering, which can be found in a number of articles that have appeared since Kiparsky (1965). If some observations about natural orderings are correct as claims about synchronic grammars, then clearly an account must be made of them in the evaluation metric. One useful suggestion along these lines is implicit in work by Anderson (1974). In any case, these issues, although they may have import for the form of the evaluation metric, are distinguishable from the problems I discuss here. No considerations of phonological naturalness or of natural rule interactions appear to play any significant part in the following examples.

The Basis of Learning Phonology

Consider the familiar diagram in (1), in which the terms for levels of adequacy are used in the sense of Chomsky (1964a):

(1)

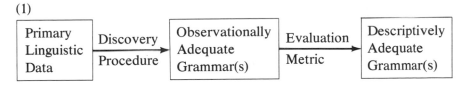

The observationally adequate grammars, which are induced from the primary data by some as yet poorly understood discovery procedure, are all compatible with the primary data. The evaluation metric, or some equivalent device, selects the observationally adequate grammar that most closely models the knowledge actually acquired by speakers. It is possible that more than one descriptively adequate grammar might emerge, but no conceivable linguistic behavior would enable us to distinguish between them. This is, therefore, not an empirical question.

One important characteristic of the problem of the acquisition of phonological and morphological grammars is that, in principle, there could be nothing of interest to learn. One might imagine a model of acquisition in which some set of purely phonetic representations—essentially digitized versions of the corresponding articulatory and acoustic events—is merely memorized by each speaker of a language. A certain amount of computable deviation from this set will be needed to handle the obvious problem of perception despite differences between speakers, but the essential idea remains that something akin to the surface phonetic representation might be the greatest abstraction speakers are capable of. The model of acquisition presupposed by this theory is clearly a simple one: the mapping designated as the discovery procedure in (1) will be the analog to digital function, and the evaluation metric will be a simple isomorphism. In effect, all observationally adequate grammars will be descriptively adequate, so this distinction becomes unnecessary.

It is, of course, well known that the equivalent theory is inadequate to the demands of natural language syntax because recursion in the base leads to potentially infinite sentences. This argument does not carry over to phonology and morphology, though. An upper bound could be placed on the length of the phonological phrase (minimally, there is a physiological limit), which, since the lexicon is apparently finite, would ensure the existence of only a finite number of such phrases.

This does not leave us without recourse, however. There is an alternative, which serves as the basis of much recent work that seeks to validate or falsify the claims of generative phonology on so-called external grounds. Substantial effort in articles too numerous to cite has been directed toward demonstrating the existence or the nature of the generalizations that speakers express in their grammars by adducing evidence not normally available to language learners, although this criterion has rarely been made explicit. The idea is that such evidence reveals aspects of the speaker's linguistic knowledge that could not possibly have been directly memorized, since only the primary linguistic data are input to the discovery procedure. In sum, this method makes it possible to determine which of several observationally adequate grammars is, in fact, descriptively adequate. On the basis of this determination, one can construct a linguistic theory that will more highly value the descriptively adequate grammar or else rule out the other observationally adequate grammars entirely.

What I propose here is a similar sort of investigation. Several observationally adequate grammars, all of which appear to be compatible with the axioms of a plausible phonological theory, will be offered for each body of primary linguistic data. From consideration of data not accessible to language learners it will emerge that only one of these grammars is descriptively adequate, and I will argue that an evaluation metric based on simplicity is able to make this choice. The nonprimary data adduced here are of relatively uncontroversial interpretation, chiefly involving some characteristics of loan words and the like. But in the first example, the process of Expletive Infixation, I will show that there are essentially no primary data at all and so the study focuses entirely on adult speakers' intuitions.

The Evaluation Metric

The fundamental idea behind the phonological evaluation metric is that it should count the linguistically significant stipulations made by different grammars and then select the grammar that makes the smallest number of them, all other things being equal. The definition of a linguistically significant stipulation is provided by the theory; in general, stipulations will be units of the system of formalization for rules and representations. The evaluation metric of a generative phonology is therefore distinct (contra Chen, 1973) from Hjelmslev's (1961) principle of simplicity, which is offered independently of any such theory.

The particular form of the evaluation metric adopted here has the following characteristics. Like the familiar device of Chomsky and Halle (1968), it values competing systems of phonological rules inversely according to the number of phonological features appearing in each system. A few natural elaborations of this procedure are also needed in response to gaps in its applicability.

Recent work on metrical phonology (Liberman and Prince, 1977) suggests that some rules and representations—particularly those referring to stress or syllabification—make use of formal devices, metrical trees, that are rather different from phonological features. Although study in this area is still at a very early stage, certain regularities in the construction of metrical trees and their application to segmental strings can be observed. When these regularities are cast in terms of a formal metrical theory, they can be said to represent a base that can be deviated from only with additional stipulations, although the exact cost of such deviation is unknown. This problem will become somewhat clearer in the discussion of the relevant example from Cairene Arabic.

The mode of evaluating readjustment rules is never described by Chomsky and Halle (1968), although this issue is of some significance. These rules, also known as morpholexical rules (Anderson, 1975) or allomorphy rules (Aronoff, 1976), chiefly account for fairly restricted segmental alternations in morphological terms. But it is possible to give any mildly abstract phonological process such a formulation if only a finite number of morphemes display the alternation. Therefore some procedure is needed to determine when a phonological and when a morphological formulation is appropriate. I will argue that this decision is made by the evaluation metric, based on the following consideration: in a readjustment rule, reference to a single morpheme or a single morphologically defined class of morphemes requires the equivalent of one phonological feature. In other words, an essentially morphological process like a readjustment rule can manipulate a particular morpheme by making a single stipulation. This proposal is in contrast to the occasional descriptive practice of referring to morphemes by mentioning enough segmental information to define them uniquely. The claim is that, all other things being equal, a readjustment rule will be superior to a phonological rule if and only if the process under consideration depends on some single morpheme or natural morphological class.

A final point concerns the extension of the evaluation metric to the lexicon as well as to the rules. Chomsky and Halle (1968) wrestle with this issue inconclusively, dealing primarily with the difficult problem of specious morpheme structure rules. Other questions are involved, however. Suppose, for example, that only rules are evaluated, so the values of the lexicons in competing grammars are not considered by the formal evaluation metric. Under this assumption, regularities not reflected in alternations will never be expressed by phonological rules. If such regularities are left unexpressed, they complicate only the lexicon; but if they are extracted from the lexicon, they complicate the phonological rules. I will make the converse assumption, the one ultimately adopted by Chomsky and Halle (1968): the value of a grammar is inversely related to the number of features in its rules and in its lexicon. This proposal may require considerable elaboration in the light of recent studies in lexical structure (Aronoff, 1976; Lieber, 1980) and of some points raised by Phelps (1979), but it will suffice for the example discussed here.

Expletive Infixation
The first example is quite compelling by virtue of the extreme paucity of the primary data, the clarity of the phenomenon, and the simple mode of application of the evaluation metric. One of the most produc-

tive rules of English morphology, yet the one for which the language learner has by far the least data available, is the process of Expletive Infixation. Any word, subject to some phonological conditions, can have inserted into it an expletive like *fuckin* with a kind of vague emphatic force. A fuller discussion of the phonology of this process can be found in McCarthy (forthcoming); here I will somewhat simplify the problem.

First, let us consider this phenomenon in its sociolinguistic aspect. Until recently it has been, in many social groups, taboo to utter words like *fuckin* in the presence of children at any age when they might be in the process of language acquisition. The significance of this fact should not be underestimated: this is an example in the acquisition of phonology of extremely degenerate primary data, with the environment providing almost no evidence on which to base the formulation of a rule. Casual observation suggests that many (possibly most) speakers learn this process on the basis of the single exemplar *fan-fuckin-tastic*, which may be heard in childhood.

In contrast to this lack of primary data, a process emerges that is extremely productive, usually subject to fluent production and rapid perception. Judgments of well-formedness are normally quite robust for individual speakers and remarkably consistent across speakers. All of these facts are incompatible with any sort of true adult learning or with metalinguistic activities like language games. (Compare English-speakers' control of learned morphology or of pig Latin to Expletive Infixation.) I conclude, then, that Expletive Infixation is a genuine (albeit marginal) part of English morphology and that there is a serious problem in determining how it could possibly be acquired.

I will begin from the assumptions that some trivial initial stimulus, like *fan-fuckin-tastic*, demonstrates to the language learner that expletives can in fact be infixed, and that the entire learning process must be based on this unique form, and perhaps a few others. This example will constitute an extreme test of the evaluation metric and of the concomitant phonological and morphological theory, inasmuch as virtually the whole of the acquisition process for this rule must be a computation by the learner rather than an approximation to grammars of greater observational adequacy.

In fact, phonological theory does provide a partial answer to the question of where an expletive may be infixed. Consider the contrast in the examples in (2):

(2)
a. *fa-fuckin-ntastic
   *fant-fuckin-astic
b. *fanta-fuckin-stic
   *fantas-fuckin-tic
c. fan-fuckin-tastic

The data in (2) represent clearly uncontroversial judgments. The forms in (2a) are ungrammatical because the expletive has failed to lodge at a syllable boundary. The forms in (2b), on the other hand, show that the syllable following the expletive must bear stress. Although the following syllable has primary stress in (2c), this is not essential. Compare (2c) with the equally well-formed *anticipa-fuckin-tory* or *antici-fuckin-pate*, where the following syllable has only secondary stress.

In McCarthy (forthcoming) I demonstrate that these two conditions on Expletive Infixation can be subsumed under a single rubric—an expletive may fall only at the boundary of a metrical foot. The prosodic category foot in English can be defined as the string composed of a stressed syllable and any immediately following unstressed syllables (Liberman and Prince, 1977). Moreover, this condition on the rule of Expletive Infixation need not be stipulated. Rather, it follows from general considerations of the well-formedness of prosodic structures. Since *fuckin* and any other expletive like *bloody* are themselves metrical feet, infixation would involve inserting a foot inside another foot. This would yield an improper bracketing with one foot containing another, distinct foot, a situation that can be ruled out by hypothesis in metrical phonological theory.

The conclusion, then, is that it is a necessary condition for Expletive Infixation at any position in a word that that position be a foot boundary, and this condition follows from universal principles inherently available to the language learner. On the other hand, one must ask whether this is a sufficient condition as well.

The language learner, when presented with the stimulus *fan-fuckin-tastic*, can posit a very large number of possible additional conditions on Expletive Infixation that are consistent with this form. For example, one could hypothesize that only the sequence *nt* may be split by infixation, that the infix may precede only voiceless stops, that only consonant clusters can host the expletive, that only morphologically complex words can have an infix, or that the preceding syllable must be stressed as well. All of these hypotheses are compatible with the given datum, as are many others. Even if the learner were presented with a somewhat richer body of primary data, it would surely be small enough to permit the extraction of some set of similar conditions. In fact, none of these additions is correct, and the universal principle permitting expletives only at a foot boundary is both a necessary and a sufficient condition for Expletive Infixation.

The task, then, is to show why speakers, with great uniformity, do not acquire a version of Expletive Infixation that is restricted to some properties of the lexical item *fantastic* or the like. This observation follows directly from the evaluation metric, since the metric prohibits unjustified complication of this rule. To see how the metric works in detail, let us look in particular at the possible conditions on the stressing of the syllable preceding the expletive.

Two observationally adequate analyses could be proposed that are in agreement with the form *fan-fuckin-tastic*. The first would incorporate into the structural description of the infixation rule a partial environment of the following form: σ ____. That is, the infix appears only
[+stress]

when it has a stressed syllable to its immediate left. The second analysis would be identical except for the lack of this stipulation. Both analyses offer observationally adequate accounts of the primary data.

Since this process is extremely productive, it is not difficult to find nonprimary data to select the descriptively adequate grammar. Many examples show free infixation after unstressed syllables: *Kĕn-fuckin-tucky, Nĕ-fuckin-braska, ĭm-fuckin-portant, air cŏn-bloody-ditioner*. The last two examples are actually attested; the first two reflect strong judgments. The obvious conclusion is that it is incorrect to require that the syllable preceding the infix be stressed.

Application of the evaluation metric to these two fragmentary analyses yields the same conclusion. Since there is no evidence in the primary data showing that the preceding syllable must be stressed, the first analysis is needlessly complicated by virtue of the stipulation
  σ with respect to the second. The second is therefore more highly
[+stress]
valued and consequently is the one incorporated into a descriptively adequate grammar.

Although this is an almost absurdly simple comparison of two competing rules by the evaluation metric, it is nevertheless important. Because of the degeneracy of the primary data, one must take the problem of acquisition very seriously here. There are many inherently plausible, observationally adequate analyses of this tiny corpus of data, yet further evidence of the kind presented shows that nevertheless the data are mapped onto a single process that is remarkably clear and consistent in adult grammars. This phenomenon is, then, a valuable test of the evaluation metric's role in acquisition.

Cairene Arabic Stress
Elsewhere I have presented a metrical theory of the role of syllable weight in stress assignment and an analysis of the accentual phenomena of the Arabic dialect spoken in Cairo (McCarthy, 1979a; 1979b; 1980). What follows is partly abstracted from those treatments, with certain complications suppressed that are not relevant to the argument.

The basis of stress assignment in Cairene Arabic is the division of syllables into two weights. Heavy syllables contain a long vowel (CVV) or a postvocalic consonant (CVC). Light syllables have neither (CV). Heavy syllables will be represented metrically by a branching node, light syllables by a nonbranching node. These geometric characteristics, which correspond to the familiar bimoraic/monomoraic syllable distinction, may be referred to by rules of stress assignment. I will further assume that all final syllables are represented formally as light, with a nonbranching node, though the full story is somewhat more complex.

The role of heavy and light syllables in accentuation can be seen in the data from Cairene Arabic in (3):

(3)
a. Heavy penult:
   maʕáaki   'with you (f. sing.)'
   ʕamálti   'you (f. sing.) did'
b. Heavy antepenult and light penult:
   martába   'mattress'
   šuftáha   'I saw her'
c. Light antepenult and light penult:
   búxala   'misers'
   muxtálifa   'different (f. sing.)'

The forms in (3a) and (3c) represent phenomena that are often paired with one another—compare them with the results of the Romance Stress rule in English *Amánda* or *aróma* versus *América,* or to the related Classical Latin stress rule. What is unusual is the pattern of stress in (3b). For words with syllables of this type the Romance Stress rule gives antepenultimate stress (*ársenal, kínkajou, rádio*), as do many other stress rules, so the Cairene penultimate stress is surprising.

I will present different formal metrical analyses of the data in (3), the differences centering around the treatment of (3b). It will emerge that one of these analyses is clearly preferred by the evaluation metric and that this preference is confirmed by the accentuation of Classical Arabic words according to the Cairene pattern.

In the first putative grammar of Cairene stress, stress assignment is envisaged as a two stage process. First, stress is assigned according to the Romance Stress rule model; then a stress shift rule moves the stress one syllable to the right from a heavy antepenultimate syllable. A metrical formalization of this analysis first maps the basic prosodic unit foot, represented by the label Φ, onto a word from the right boundary toward the left. This foot will maximally be of the form in (4).

(4)
Foot Structure:

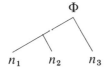

The terminal nodes n_1, n_2, and n_3 are mapped onto the terminal nodes of the branching and nonbranching trees associated with heavy syllables and light syllables respectively. For some representative examples, this mapping yields the result in (5):

(5)
a.   b.   c.

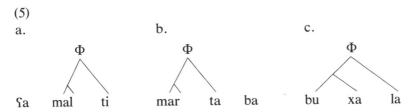

Metrical theory provides another level of tree structure whose terminal nodes are the roots of feet and any syllables not yet incorporated into feet. This word-level tree consolidates all feet and stray syllables in a word into a single metrical structure. I will assume that the word-level structure of Cairene Arabic is represented by a right-branching tree, although this would show up overtly only in forms somewhat longer than those in (5).

Finally, the grammar must specify the labeling of the metrical tree. It indicates a relation of relative prominence defined by complementary *s* (strong) and *w* (weak) labels on nonroot nodes of the tree. In this case, a labeling rule identical to that proposed for English by Liberman and Prince (1977) will operate throughout the tree.

(6)
Labeling Rule:
Label the right node strong (*s*) if and only if it branches.

The final result of foot assignment, construction of a word-level tree, and labeling is the set of representations in (7).

(7)
a.   b.   c.

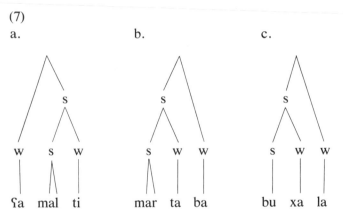

ʕa mal ti   mar ta ba   bu xa la

For (7a) and (7c), the correct stress relations are represented. But (7b) incorrectly shows antepenultimate stress instead of penultimate.

Up to this point the analysis of Cairene Arabic has included all of the characteristics needed to generate stress in Latin or Damascene Arabic, for example. It now must diverge to include a means of assigning the correct stress in forms like *martába,* given the intermediate representation (7b). At least two possible directions can be taken, both at least partly precedented in other fairly well understood metrical systems.

One possibility is to write a relabeling transformation that will move the stress from the antepenult to the penult in (7b). This rule is formulated in (8):

(8)
Relabeling Rule:

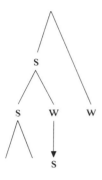

Since the labels *s* and *w* on sister nodes always have complementary values, it suffices to indicate a change in just one sister, as in (8). The application of this relabeling rule to the intermediate structure in (7b) will yield the derived structure in (9), which correctly shows penultimate stress:

(9)

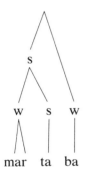

The second possibility is to add a rule of tree formation to the one already formulated in (4). This rule will apply to the tree in (7b) to split it into two feet, as in (10):

(10)
Restructuring Rule:

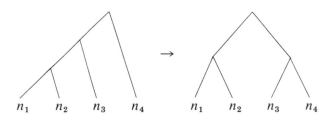

I assume that this rule applies after assignment of word-level structure but before the labeling rule. Its output, therefore, will be subject to the usual labeling, producing the derived structure in (11).

(11)

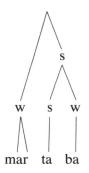

So this alternative also will correctly assign penultimate stress.

This analysis is therefore adequate to handle the facts of Cairene Arabic stress. Moreover, on several counts—Foot Structure (4) and Labeling (6)—it is formally identical to the stress systems of several other languages. It does, however, require the added complication of either the Relabeling rule (8) or the Restructuring rule (10). Both rules are of types that apparently must be countenanced by linguistic theory. Rules of relabeling have been justified in many languages, with some, like the English Rhythm rule, conditioned by stress clashes, but with others, like those of Tiberian Hebrew (McCarthy, 1979a) and Yidiny (Hayes, 1980), conditioned by morphological or syllabic contexts. On the other hand, the Restructuring rule (10) is formally almost identical to an English process applicable in words like *obligatory* (Liberman and Prince, 1977, p. 296). In sum, it seems that metrical theory must provide apparatus that would make either (8) or (10) a possible rule in an analysis of Cairene stress.

An alternative treatment of Cairene stress is based on a very different basic rule of stress assignment. Suppose that stress is assigned by a left-to-right procedure that counts pairs of light syllables. The first syllable in the last such pair will then be the one to bear the main stress. This is somewhat easier to visualize in the metrical formalization.

The foot, assigned from left to right, has the form in (12).

(12)
Foot Structure:

Therefore the foot contains only two moras, taken either from two light syllables or a single heavy syllable. This is actually a reasonably common foot type; one of the clearest cases is in the accentual system of Creek (McCarthy, 1979b). Application of this foot structure to some representative examples yields the results in (13).

(13)
a.   b.   c.

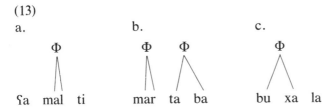

Note that the left-to-right mapping of (12) onto words ensures that the first two and not the last two syllables in (13c) are paired into sisters.

As in the first analysis, provision is made for a right-branching word-level tree and for labeling of structures in accordance with (6). The final output of the stress rules under this proposal will be the set of representations in (14):

(14)

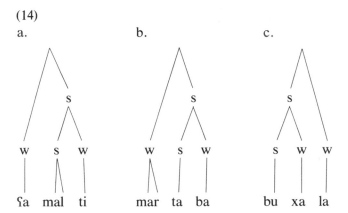

a.   b.   c.

          s   s   s

w   s   w   w   s   w   s   w   w

ʕa mal ti   mar ta ba   bu xa la

These trees, like those derived by the first analysis, indicate the correct accentuation of these forms.

What is interesting about Cairene Arabic is that two such very different grammars are both observationally adequate. A moment's reflection will show that these analyses make different predictions only in words that end in a string of more than three light syllables. Such words are ordinarily impossible in this language for historical reasons. The sole exception, a class of words with four light syllables, belongs to the only major type of morphologically governed stress assignment in Cairene, so it must be discounted. Therefore, no evidence in the primary data would choose between the two analyses purely on grounds of observational adequacy.

The question of which of these observationally adequate analyses is more highly valued is not difficult to answer, even with our current lack of certainty on many details of the metrical formalism. All the rules invoked are possible within the theory and many are even common. But the first proposal, based on the foot structure in (4), involves the added complication of either Relabeling or Restructuring, neither of which is needed under the second proposal. I conclude, then, that the grammar incorporating the foot structure in (12) is formally simpler and therefore more highly valued than the alternative.[1]

It can be shown on the basis of nonprimary data that the second analysis is indeed the one selected by language learners. Such data come from the pronunciation of Classical or Literary Arabic words by native speakers of the Cairene dialect. As no universal standard for the accentuation of Classical Arabic exists, the typical situation is that each dialect area follows its own rule in stressing Classical Arabic words.

This observation is particularly useful because Classical Arabic has words that end in strings of light syllables longer than three. These show the curious pattern of accentuation in (15) when read by a speaker of Cairene Arabic.

(15)
a. Penultimate stress:

šaǰarátu	'tree (nom.)'
šaǰaratuhúmaa	'their (du.) tree (nom.)'
ʔadwiyatúhu	'his drugs (nom.)'

b. Antepenultimate stress:

šaǰarátuhu	'his tree (nom.)'
ʔadwiyatúhumaa	'their (du.) drugs (nom.)'

It is apparent that, under the first analysis, all of the forms in (15) should have antepenultimate stress since they have light penults and light antepenults, like the shorter forms in (3c). But the second analysis, which assigns the foot structure in (12), ultimately yields trees like those in (16):

(16)
a.   b.

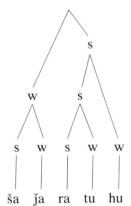

This is, in fact, the desired output, and similar results can be derived for the other forms in (15).

Thus the accentuation of forms from Classical Arabic—essentially the naturalistic equivalent of a psycholinguistic experiment demanding production of nonsense words—demonstrates that only the second alternative provides a descriptively adequate account of Cairene Arabic stress, although both analyses are observationally adequate. The

choice between the two analyses made by the language learner con-
forms to that made by the evaluation metric, so the role of the metric in
this type of learning is confirmed.

Maori Passives and Gerundives

Perhaps the most compelling example of an apparent failure of the
evaluation metric to select the same grammar as that chosen by language learners is Hale's (1973) often cited analysis of the passive and
gerundive formations in Maori. I will review the facts quickly, present
Hale's interpretation of them, and then suggest a rather different understanding of the problem based on the evaluation of systems of readjustment rules.

The basic observation is that there is a consonant/zero alternation in
the active versus passive and gerundive forms of many Maori verbs:

(17)

Active	Passive	Gerundive	
wero	werohia	werohaŋa	'stab'
hopu	hopukia	hopukaŋa	'catch'
aru	arumia	arumaŋa	'follow'
mau	mauria	mauraŋa	'carry'
awhi	awhitia	awhitaŋa	'embrace'

In addition, no Maori word ends in a consonant. In the light of these
simple paradigms and this additional fact, a descriptively elegant and
straightforward analysis presents itself. The grammar of Maori will
be provided with base forms with final consonants like /weroh/ and
/hopuk/, with suffixes /-ia/ and /-aŋa/, and with a rule of final consonant
deletion formulated as in (18).

(18)

$$[-syll] \rightarrow \emptyset / \underline{\quad} \#$$

Although this analysis is cast in generative phonological terms and
notations, it is by no means confined to that tradition. For example,
Bloomfield (1933, p. 219) sets up what he calls "basic forms in theoretical shape" to handle an almost identical set of alternations in Samoan.
Nida (1949, p. 76) accepts this proposal as well, describing the loss of
the final consonant as a phonologically conditioned process.

Yet Hale demonstrates that this phonological analysis of the Maori
data, which is a model of formal simplicity and inherent plausibility, is
actually inadequate and that it is inferior to a basically morphological

analysis along the lines followed by Hohepa (1967, p. 111) or Biggs (1961, pp. 33–34). These authors analyze the consonants preceding -*ia* and -*aŋa* as part of the passive and gerundive suffixes rather than part of the stem. Each verb then idiosyncratically selects one of the suffix alternants without reference to phonological considerations. In effect, Hohepa establishes arbitrary conjugation classes for Maori stems that determine which suffix allomorph is chosen, with -*tia* as the basic alternant from which others are derived by a set of lexically governed transformations.

Before considering Hale's evidence, let me attempt to make this morphological analysis of Maori explicit in terms of a theory of readjustment rules. Passive and gerundive appear in the morpheme list that I assume is part of the lexicon as two sets of morpheme alternants: {-*tia*, -*hia*, -*kia*, -*mia*, -*ria*} and {-*taŋa*, -*haŋa*, -*kaŋa*, -*maŋa*, -*raŋa*}. These sets can be considered partial orderings, with the first alternants -*tia* and -*taŋa* designated as basic or unmarked. The readjustment rules in (19) then apply to these basic alternants to select other members of the set:

(19)
Maori Readjustment Rules:
a. -tia → -hia
   -taŋa → -haŋa
b. -tia → -kia
   -taŋa → -kaŋa
c. -tia → -mia
   -taŋa → -maŋa
d. -tia → -ria
   -taŋa → -raŋa

These readjustment rules are to be understood as operations on morphemes taken from the two sets of suffix alternants, rather than as transformations of the segmental material in the morphemes. Furthermore, they must all be minor rules; that is, they must be unable to apply to any form not explicitly marked to undergo them. Therefore any verb that takes a suffix alternant other than -*tia* or -*taŋa* will necessarily bear a diacritic feature [+rule x], where x indicates one of the rules in (19). As in all conjugation analyses, I will redundantly rule out any stem bearing two such contradictory features.

Of course, other formulations of the morphological analysis of Maori are conceivable, but they all should have the salient characteristics of this one: a list of morpheme alternants in the lexicon, designation of *-tia* and *-taŋa* as somehow basic, and lexically governed choice of other alternants. This choice will involve, as in (19), substituting one morpheme for another.

I turn now to the central problem presented by the Maori data. Hale's evidence shows that speakers fail to internalize the seemingly simple phonological analysis and instead select a morphological analysis along the lines in (19). Quite a mass of data can be brought to bear on this question:

(1) Stems which are basically nominal are often used verbally in spontaneous discourse; when they are so used, in the passive, they regularly take the ending /-tia/. (2) Derived causatives (formed with the prefix /whaka-/ take /-tia/ in the passive even if the basic verb stem takes another alternant when not in the causative. (3) There is a rule whereby certain adverbials are made to agree in voice with the verbs they modify; these adverbials take /-tia/ in the passive regardless of the shape of the passive ending which the verb itself takes. (4) Borrowings from English, including unassimilated consonant-final ones, take the ending /-tia/ in the passive. (5) Compound verbs derived by incorporating a noun from an adverbial phrase regularly form their passives in /-tia/. (6) In general, /-tia/ can be used when the conventional passive termination for a given verb is not remembered. (Hale, 1973, p. 417)

The morphologically based grammar of Maori in (19) can account for these observations with few additional assumptions. Forms derived by extension of passive morphology to categories that are ordinarily nonverbal (1 and 3) will be marked by *-tia* because nonverbs will usually have no reason to acquire diacritics for the minor passive morphology. Use of *-tia* with causatives and compounds despite another passive suffix with the corresponding underived verb stem (2 and 5) can also be readily explained. Kiparsky (1973a, pp. 89–90) has observed that diacritic features (but not segmental material) are often lost under derivation. Therefore *-tia*, which appears on forms that do not bear minor rule diacritics, is correctly predicted for derived verbs. Similarly, loan words (4) will ordinarily fail to have such diacritics. When the diacritic for a particular form is unknown (6), *-tia* should also show up.

The morphological solution, then, will account for the ordinary paradigmatic data and for these additional facts cited by Hale. The phonological solution, although it handles the paradigms, makes no special predictions for any of these additional data. Of course, if the additional data were readily available to language learners, one would expect them to reject the phonological analysis simply as observationally inadequate. Although this argument has not been made explicitly, it appears that the significance of the Maori data lies in the relative inaccessibility to learners of the information outlined by Hale.

The most striking evidence—the treatment of loans and of forgotten desinences—is plainly unavailable for language acquisition since it presupposes knowledge of either the etymology of the word or the mental state of the speaker. Instances of either sort can simply be treated as *t*-final stems in underlying representation in the phonological analysis. Furthermore, learners are likely to perceive the anomaly of surface consonant-final unassimilated loans and not be motivated to restructure their grammars solely on the basis of their selection of the -*tia* allomorph.

A similar analysis is available for the suffixation of -*tia* to spontaneous denominal verbs. The learner cannot judge with confidence that they are spontaneous; that would require a near-perfect knowledge of the Maori dictionary. Therefore such forms can also have underlying representations in final *t*. The passive forms of adverbials can likewise be handled by having all adverbials terminate in *t* in the lexicon. Conceivably this regularity in adverbials would even motivate postulating a suffix morpheme -*t* for this lexical category.

The only remaining fact is the use of -*tia* in derived verbs even when the nonderived stem has another final consonant. This will require a complication of the phonological analysis if that analysis is to be observationally adequate. One can expect that language learners would take note of this fact and express it by a rule taking any stem-final consonant to *t* in a derived verb form. In sum, this is the only fact cited by Hale that is directly available as input to the construction of putative grammars by a discovery procedure.

To complete the argument, we can observe that a serious problem for a theory of phonological acquisition based on the formal evaluation metric is presented by the fact that language learners select the morphological analysis over the phonological one. As an account of all the Maori data cited, the phonological analysis is not only observationally adequate but also more highly valued. The phonological rule system requires reference to a single feature and a boundary in the deletion rule (18) and uncertain but clearly small cost for the rule applied in derived verb forms. On the other hand, the morphological analysis requires the eight readjustment rules in (19), where each will be evaluated at two features, according to the principle I have proposed, since each makes reference to two different morphemes. I know of no likely procedure by which one can evaluate the lexicons demanded under each solution. I will make the not unreasonable assumption that supplying each stem with a final consonant is formally equivalent to a set of rule diacritics and their corresponding list of morpheme alternants, so the two lexicons are equally valued. The conclusion is that the phonological solution has formally simpler rules and consequently is more highly valued than the morphological solution, apparently the wrong result.

Hale's (1973) solution to the problem of Maori passives and gerundives involves an axiomatic exclusion of the phonological analysis. Observing that underlying verb stems have final consonants but no surface forms do, Hale proposes that a universal constraint limits possible grammars to those in which there are no disparities of canonical pattern between underlying and surface representations. This would exclude the phonological solution as a permissible analysis of the Maori data.

Halle (1978), although he rejects this constraint on the basis of work by Kaye (1975), incorporates a similar observation into a proposal for the Maori problem based on a form of the evaluation metric. He points out that the phonological analysis, in return for an account of just two morphemes, requires the deletion rule (18) and the loss of the potential generalization that underlying representations must end in vowels as do surface ones. Against this requirement, the theory weighs the cost of a set of readjustment rules. Although Halle proposes no explicit procedure for evaluating readjustment rules, he suggests that the outcome will favor the morphological solution as more highly valued.

It will emerge that the evaluation metric is in fact the appropriate vehicle for the selection of the morphological analysis; nevertheless, the considerations cited by Halle as militating against the phonological analysis are not persuasive. A number of phonological analyses have appeared in recent work (Halle and Vergnaud, 1978; Kiparsky, 1979a; Lowenstamm, 1978) where surface constraints on canonical form, stated in terms of syllable structure, are apparently violated in underlying representation. Deletion rules like (18) or rules of epenthesis or vocalization bring these underlying representations into conformity with the required canonical pattern in an exact parallel to the phonological solution for Maori.[2] Furthermore, even though I proposed an explicit evaluation procedure for readjustment rules, the phonological solution is apparently still more highly valued. This evaluation procedure could, of course, be simply incorrect, but it already values readjustment rules more highly than many other imaginable procedures do. In other words, readjustment rules are probably already being treated as liberally as possible if any phonological rules at all are to be permitted.

Much additional data of direct relevance to this problem can be found in Hale (1968). Some consideration of the further complications necessary in any observationally adequate grammar shows that the evaluation metric, with its means of treating readjustment rules, does provide the language learner with the correct choice between the two competing solutions.

First, there exist passive verb forms ending in Va with corresponding gerundives in Vηa, instead of the usual Cia and C$a\eta a$ seen in (17): *patu* 'strike,' passive *patua*, gerundive *patu\eta a*. These can be analyzed as underlying vowel-final stems like /patu/ with suffix vowel deletion in hiatus:

(20)

$$V \rightarrow \emptyset \ / \ V + \underline{\hspace{1cm}} \begin{Bmatrix} a \\ \eta a \end{Bmatrix} \#$$

But other verbs do show Via passives and V$a\eta a$ gerundives: *noho* 'sit,' *nohoia, nohoa\eta a*. Hale (1968), observing that there are no passives in *pia* or gerundives in *pa\eta a*, proposes underlying p-final stems like /nohop/, with the p deleted before the suffixes:

(21)

$$p \rightarrow \emptyset \ / \ \underline{\hspace{1cm}} + \begin{Bmatrix} ia \\ a\eta a \end{Bmatrix} \#$$

Rule (21) must crucially follow rule (20), in counterfeeding order.

Second, putative n-final stems undergo several additional phonological processes. Underlying $an+ia$ is realized as *aina*, as in *tua* 'fell,' passive *tuaina*. This alternation can be attributed to a metathesis rule:

(22)
a n + i a #
1 2   3 4   → 132$\emptyset$4

But V$n+ia$, where V is not a, simply loses the vowel i: *hoko* 'buy-sell,' passive *hokona*. This requires another vowel deletion rule ordered after (22).

(23)
$$i \rightarrow \emptyset \ / \ n + \underline{\hspace{1cm}} a \#$$

Third, a slightly different complication emerges in the case of some final-η verbs. One class simply suffixes -*ia* in the passive: *tohu* 'point out,' passive *tohuŋia*. But another, smaller class deletes the *i* of the passive ending: *kai* 'eat,' passive *kaiŋa*. This second class demands still another phonological rule:

(24)

$$i \rightarrow \emptyset \: / \: \eta \: + \underline{\quad\quad} a \: \#$$

Conceivably (23) and (24) could be collapsed, though one would probably wish to exclude this possibility in view of the fact that the former is exceptionless and the latter is under heavy lexical government.

Fourth, a different complication arises in the case of gerundives of *n*- and *ŋ*-final stems. They show up with the termination *ŋa* rather than the expected *naŋa* and *ŋaŋa* (Biggs, 1961, p. 34). This haplology can be formulated as a rather complex deletion process:

(25)

$$\begin{bmatrix} +\text{nas} \\ \left\{ \begin{matrix} +\text{cor} \\ -\text{ant} \end{matrix} \right\} \end{bmatrix} + a \: \eta \: a$$

$$\quad 1 \qquad\qquad 2\;3\;4 \; \rightarrow \; \emptyset\emptyset34$$

A fully articulated phonological solution for Maori passives and gerundives is rather more complex than originally suspected. On the other hand, these additional facts do not excessively complicate the morphological solution. They will require five new conjugation types for the passive form and two new types for the gerundive. The full morphological solution demands the morpheme sets {-*tia*, -*hia*, -*kia*, -*mia*, -*ria*, -*a*, -*ia*, -*ina*, -*na*, -*ŋa*} and {-*taŋa*, -*haŋa*, -*kaŋa*, -*maŋa*, -*raŋa*, -*aŋa*, -*ŋa*} in the lexicon, the readjustment rules in (19), and the new readjustment rules in (26):

(26)
a. -tia → -a
b. -tia → -ia
   -taŋa → -aŋa
c. -tia → -ina
d. -tia → -na
e. -tia → -ŋa
f. -taŋa → -ŋa

The basic distinction between the two solutions that emerges is that whereas the phonological treatment deals with the complex suffix allomorphy by the various phonological rules in (20) through (25), the morphological one simply adds further readjustment rules of exactly the same formal type.[3] The only difference between the readjustment rules in (19) and (26) is that the latter do not show the parallel allomorphy of passive and gerundive observed in the former. This is actually expected under the conception of readjustment rules followed here, an idea I will return to.

It is possible at this point, though not very revealing, to pursue the result the evaluation metric will reach when confronted with the choice between observationally adequate phonological and morphological solutions along the lines I have sketched. The translation of the informal rules (20) through (25) into conventional formalism by the familiar canons of generative phonology yields a total of approximately 49 feature specifications, to which must be added the cost of the deletion rule (18) and the unformulated rule to handle the occurrence of *-tia* passives in derived verb forms. Evaluating the morphological rule system by counting a stipulation of a morpheme as the equivalent of a single feature yields a total of 30 feature specifications. Consideration of the data cited in note 3 will serve only to widen this disparity between the two analyses. The more highly valued solution under the assumptions made here is, consequently, the morphological one, a result that concurs with the one drawn by Hale (1973) from the nonprimary data.[4]

We should not, however, take away with us from Maori the moral merely that such a choice can be made by a rather sterile numerology based on arguable claims about the form of the evaluation metric. This example is of far greater value for what it illustrates about the system of tradeoffs between a morphological and a phonological treatment of some observed set of alternations. Two readily apparent characteristics of the primary data will immediately tend to favor a morphological solution. First, if, as Halle (1978) observed for Maori, only a small number of morphemes participate in the same alternation, then readjustment rules will be the appropriate means of expressing the generalization. Readjustment rules are disfavored to the extent that they need to mention explicitly many different morphemes that could alternatively be collapsed into a single phonological environment. Second, readjustment rules will be preferred in systems where there is relatively greater allomorphy, greater divergence in form between different occurrences of the same morpheme. One need not refer this preference to underlying representations; it suffices to observe that the same morphological category is marked in several widely disparate ways on the surface.

The point, then, of the elaboration of the evaluation metric and its mode of application to readjustment rules proposed here is to provide a formal means of considering these two properties, where the properties and their inverses may be seen as tendencies toward the selection of a morphological or phonological analysis. This proposal correctly reflects the facts of Maori and, I believe, a widely held descriptive practice in generative phonology.

Spanish Epenthesis
It is well known that Spanish does not tolerate word-initial sC clusters, but the proper mode of incorporating this generalization into the grammar is not entirely clear. One view is that there exist underlying representations with initial sC clusters which are subject to an exceptionless rule of vowel epenthesis, yielding surface esC (Harris, 1969, 1979). Thus, *escala* might have the underlying representation /skala/, and the grammar of Spanish would contain something like the rule in (27).

(27)
$$\emptyset \rightarrow e \;/\; \# \underline{\quad} s \; [+\text{cons}]$$

Very likely, rule (27) should be recast in terms of a theory of the interaction of syllable structure and segmental processes like that mentioned in connection with the constraints on canonical form in Maori. This move, however, would not affect the argument advanced here, since it would still be necessary to stipulate that the particular vowel e is inserted, perhaps by mapping it onto a slot in a syllabic template (Harris, 1980).

Another possible analysis holds that sC clusters are ruled out entirely by a constraint on well-formed underlying representations, stated crudely as (28):

(28)
*#sC

Under this analysis *escala* has the underlying representation /eskala/, and a hypothetical underlying representation like /skala/ is blocked by (28).

Although these two analyses are based on rather different conceptions of the problem, both are possible within the generative phonological theory followed here. I take it as given that rules of vowel epenthesis, responsive to certain types of consonant clusters or syllable configurations, must be recognized by linguistic theory. Constraints on well-formed morphemes or syllables appear to be needed as well. Thus these are two of the possible analyses given by phonological theory, and both so far appear to be adequate accounts of the familiar data.

Ordinarily, primary linguistic data in the form of morphophonemic regularities are sufficient to decide between a rule-based and a constraint-based phonological analysis solely on grounds of observational adequacy. Some morphophonemic evidence from Spanish supports the epenthesis rule in (27) over the constraint in (28).

First, there are e/∅ alternations like *escribir/suscribir,* although for morphological reasons such alternations are apparently confined to compounding and derivation and do not appear in more transparent inflectional processes. Second, Harris (1970) notes that the irregular final stress of *estóy, estás,* and *está* can be accounted for if these forms are monosyllables at the point in the derivation when the stress rule applies. In fact, this stress pattern reflects a larger distributional regularity pointed out to me by Harris: with the sole exception of the demonstrative *éste,* no word has stressed *é* in the context # ___ sC, which follows immediately from ordering epenthesis after stress assignment. Finally, Harris (1979) observes that selection of the *-ecit* allomorph of the diminutive suffix, which is restricted to a phonologically defined subset of words with disyllabic nondiminutives, presupposes an underlying disyllabic base word like /studyo/ for forms like *estudio,* diminutive *estudiecito.* So the process of diminutive formation must have access to a level of representation before epenthesis.

It is a matter for careful judgment to determine whether these facts would be available to motivate the language learner's rejection of the constraint analysis as observationally inadequate. On this determination hinges the question of whether we have here an authentic projection puzzle of the sort I described in the introduction. I would claim that the puzzle is authentic, although it is difficult to construct a rigorous argument for this position. The putative learning of epenthesis solely from the data given here must contend with the following difficulties. The evidence of e/∅ alternations and of diminutive formation is relatively obscured to the language learner by the lack of inflectional alternations in the first case and by additional phonological complications of diminutive allomorphy in the second. The apparently irregular final stress, confined as it is to three forms, is not compelling, nor is the distributional gap of #*és*C, since it is not without exception. In the latter case, inference from lexical distribution also raises the problem of the learner's imperfect knowledge of the dictionary, discussed earlier in connection with spontaneous denominal verbs in Maori.

All of these considerations suggest that the choice between a rule and a constraint in Spanish cannot be made solely from the primary data on grounds of observational adequacy. This is not to say that this evidence is without significance. It is of obvious value to the investigator as reflecting the state attained in adult grammars, and it is clear that an account of these regularities confirms for the learner the choice of the epenthesis analysis made, as I will show, by the evaluation metric.

Before pursuing the Spanish case, let us consider the following example from English where the question of a rule or a constraint is completely uncontroversial. English obviously does not permit word-initial *pt* clusters in surface representations. By analogy to Spanish, two different accounts of this observation are possible. The constraint would rule out the sequence #*pt*, probably as a part of a more general set of constraints on possible syllables in English. The phonological rule, on the other hand, would delete word-initial *p* before a nonsonorant consonant. The first grammar would block underlying representations with word-initial *pt;* the second would transform them to surface initial *t*. Clearly the conclusion of any investigator would be that the constraint analysis is the correct one. This conclusion would undoubtedly persist in the face of apparent support for the rule analysis from alternations like *pterodactyl, pterogoid / helicopter, hymenoptera, archeopteryx*. It is unlikely that one could profitably pursue this hypothetical phonological deletion process.

By comparing the parallel cases of Spanish and English, one can see why there might be some doubt as to the correct analysis in the first case but none in the second. Marginal alternations aside, a *p*-deletion rule in English is a needless complication of the grammar, since no underlying representations that have themselves not been needlessly complicated with initial *p*'s before *t* would ever be subject to it. In other words, the choice between these two essentially observationally adequate analyses of English can be made on the basis of a form of the evaluation metric. This choice is possible, however, only if the evaluation metric considers the set of rules in conjunction with its lexicon, as I have proposed and as in Chomsky and Halle (1968).

The evaluation metric will reach the opposite choice for the correct analysis of the Spanish phenomenon, however. Eliminating putative epenthetic *e*'s from underlying representations actually involves a simplification of the whole grammar—a general reduction in the number of phonological feature specifications in the lexicon. The slight complication that comes of having an *e*-epenthesis rule will be more than offset by the removal of all initial *e*'s before *s*C in the list of morphemes. Therefore, since any lexical entry of the form /*es*C . . ./ constitutes a needless complication of the grammar under this analysis, all lexical entries that meet the structural description of (27) must take the free ride with epenthesis. The unique exception to this generalization is *éste*, where there is direct evidence to the contrary from the observed initial stress.

It follows, then, that the application of the evaluation metric to sets of rules with their concomitant lexicons serves two purposes in this case: it selects a rule-based over a constraint-based analysis of Spanish, and it determines that all forms with surface #*es*C have underlying representations without the *e*.

Substantial empirical support can be found for the first claim, both from the evidence of alternations, stress, and diminutive formation already cited and from the treatment of loan words. Loans into Spanish invariably receive *e* if they have initial *s*C clusters in the source language: *esnob, esmoking, esprey*. The constraint analysis predicts in this case only that, say, *snob* is not a possible word of Spanish; it does not indicate how this form can be modified to make it pronounceable and thus fails to anticipate the systematic appearance of *e* before *s*C. A constraint like the one in (28) would allow ad hoc means of dealing with these clusters, either by insertion of some other vowel, by insertion of a vowel after *s*, or by deletion of one of the consonants in the offending cluster. The epenthesis analysis predicts regular insertion of *e* and nothing else; it is therefore confirmed by these observations.[5]

The second result—that all forms with surface #*es*C (except *éste*) will be analyzed as underlying /*s*C . . ./ and so will take the free ride offered by epenthesis—is much more difficult to support, though the question remains in principle an empirical one. It could be partly tested by inspection of the diminutives of all forms that have surface #*es*C followed by two syllables in the base word and that also meet the other phonological conditions for selection of the *-ecit* allomorph. The predicted outcome is that these forms will invariably have *-ecit* diminutives, whereas without the strict free ride demanded by the evaluation metric they would potentially differ arbitrarily in their diminutive allomorphy.

Minimally, what has emerged here is that the learning of phonological and morphological rules and representations is a good deal more complex than envisaged in the trivial analog-to-digital acquisition procedure I described earlier. An adequate phonological theory must clearly contend with an extreme lack of primary data or with apparently crucial evidence that is unavailable to the language learner. More specifically, a particular form of the evaluation metric has been supported as a part of linguistic theory with direct application to the problem of language learning. This metric, like its counterpart in Chomsky and Halle (1968), must evaluate entire grammars on the basis of specific criteria of formal simplicity in the domains of phonological processes, readjustment rules, and the lexicon.

Notes

I am grateful to Lee Baker, James Harris, and Jonathan Kaye for their insights into the problems discussed here. As usual, all errors are my responsibility alone.

1. Another stress shift solution, similar in formal value to the one based on the foot structure in (4), is possible. Briefly, it involves assigning penultimate stress in all forms and then shifting stress, by relabeling or restructuring rules, to a light antepenult off of a light penult. It is apparent that this analysis would encounter the same problems with the data in (15) as the analysis in (4) does.

2. A certain amount of evidence internal to the phonological solution for Maori supports such a syllabic analysis of the final consonant deletion rule. First, Maori lacks syllable-final consonants as well as word-final consonants in surface forms. Second, syllable-final C/Ø alternations are attested in reduplicated forms. Consider the verb *koorero* 'speak,' passive *koorerotia*. Frequentative reduplication, which apparently copies the last two syllables of the stem, yields *koorerorero* 'chatter incessantly,' passive *koorerorerotia*. Application of this reduplication rule to the underlying form /koorerot/ should yield **koorerotrero* after word-final consonant deletion versus the correct *koorerorero*

if all syllable-final consonants are deleted. Of course, complicating the reduplication rule so as to copy up to four segments leftward, starting at the second last one, would avoid the problem. But this sort of internal reduplication seems at best unusual, a property that follows from the theory of morphology presented in McCarthy (1979a). Notice too that reduplicated forms engender no difficulties under the morphological analysis.

3. There are a few additional facts that would require further complications of the phonological solution with relatively little corresponding elaboration of the morphological one. First, two verbs apparently form a passive/gerundive conjugation distinct from all others: *heu* 'separate,' passive *heuea,* gerundive *heueŋa;* and *keu* 'move,' passive *keuea,* gerundive *keueŋa.* Second, Hale has pointed out in class lectures that under some conditions the passive suffix attracts stress anomalously. Under either solution both facts can be dealt with in ways similar to those treated in the text.

4. There is a hidden assumption partly underlying this argument. Here the evaluation metric compares two solutions, each of which treats the passive and gerundive homogeneously by phonological rules or readjustment rules. One could as well imagine a whole family of mixed solutions, where, say, the irregularities in (20) through (25) are spelled out by readjustment rules but the more regular alternations in (17) are dealt with phonologically. It is by no means clear whether such a solution could actually be made to work or, if so, whether it would be more or less highly valued than the alternatives. In any case, I suggest that such a possibility—the differential treatment of morphology of the same general type—should be ruled out in principle. A more precise formulation of this constraint will have to await further study of systems of the Maori type.

5. Hooper (1976) presents an analysis of this Spanish phenomenon based on syllable well-formedness constraints that is claimed to handle the loan word data without recourse to a rule of epenthesis. The position of the inserted vowel, before the *s* rather than after it, is recoverable in this system by a preference for allowing the original order of the consonants to remain the same as in the source language. In fact, the order of the consonants is unchanged if a vowel is inserted in either position; it is rather the arrangement of consonant clusters in the form that is maintained in borrowing. It is clear that such a principle of loan phonology cannot be universal; for example, it is regularly violated in

Japanese and in English. Yet a language learner could discover a language-particular rule specific to loan phonology only by having access to pairs of source language/target language forms displaying the relevant alternation.

The quality of the inserted vowel is deduced in this system from the universal principle that it must be the lowest vowel on a language-particular strength hierarchy. The strength hierarchy can, in general, be discovered by examining synchronic and diachronic vowel reduction rules. The evidence given by Hooper for placing *e* lower on the Spanish strength scale than the other nonround vowels is limited solely to two diachronic reduction rules and no synchronic data.

In sum, Hooper's analysis eschews an epenthesis rule in Spanish only at the cost of two language-particular devices that cannot be discovered except from data that are clearly not available to language learners.

Good articles are all alike; every bad article is bad in its own way. Paraphrasing Tolstoy somewhat, I wish to draw attention to my unhappy task: to comment on a good article, or at least an article with which I agree in all important respects. In such cases one is reduced to quibbling or discussing one's own work. I shall do a bit of both.

McCarthy discusses the role of the evaluation metric in the acquisition of phonology. He outlines the position of this metric in the organization of an acquisition model. This model with its accompanying metric has roughly the form of that proposed in Chomsky and Halle's *Sound Pattern of English* (1968). McCarthy addresses two questions: (1) Is an evaluation metric essential to linguistic theory? (2) If it is, what form should it take? These days, his positive response to the first question is neither unexpected nor controversial. The more interesting question concerns the form of this metric. McCarthy presents the *Sound Pattern of English* model, with some interesting discussion involving readjustment rules and the role of morphological features in evaluating grammars. The remainder of his paper is devoted to the discussion of four sample analyses. In these four cases he shows convincingly that the proposed evaluation metric obliges one to choose a descriptively adequate grammar (or portion thereof) over one that is merely observationally adequate. He shows further that the evidence that leads ultimately to this conclusion—that is, that the grammar selected is indeed the descriptively adequate one—is based on facts that are presumably unavailable to the language learner. The moral of all this is that, yes, there is an evaluation metric and in the form presented by McCarthy it yields the right results in a variety of interesting examples.

With all of this I am in wholehearted agreement, and so I can begin with my quibbles. The model presented by McCarthy distinguishes, on the one hand, a discovery procedure which furnishes a set of observationally adequate grammars and, on the other, an evaluation metric which selects the observationally adequate grammar that most closely models the knowledge acquired by the speaker. I am not convinced that there are two distinct entities here.

Local and Global Uses of the Evaluation Metric

The evaluation metric resolves two sorts of problems. First, it constrains us to seek the most general solution compatible with the available data. I call this the *local* use of the evaluation metric.

Consider the case of a language lacking a labial series of consonants and having a rule of syllable- or word-final devoicing. I assume that the correct representation for such a process in such a language is (1) and not (2).

(1)

$$\begin{bmatrix} -\text{syll} \\ -\text{son} \end{bmatrix} \rightarrow [-\text{voiced}] / \underline{\quad}\#$$

(2)

$$\begin{bmatrix} -\text{syll} \\ -\text{son} \\ \begin{Bmatrix} +\text{cor} \\ -\text{ant} \end{Bmatrix} \end{bmatrix} \rightarrow [-\text{voiced}] / \underline{\quad}\#$$

In (1) it is proposed that any nonsonorant will undergo devoicing. Labials (which do not exist in this hypothetical language) are exempted from undergoing rule (2). Leaving aside the doubtful status of curly brackets, I assume that rule (1) is selected on the basis of having two fewer features, all else being equal in this case. The empirical consequences of such a choice are not immediately obvious. The implications become clearer when it is looked at from a slightly different angle.

A language learner acquiring Polish, a language with a final devoicing rule, is confronted with a form *xlep* 'bread' and a paradigmatically related form *xleba*. Many possible "grammars" are compatible with these data as shown in (3).

(3)

a.

$$\begin{bmatrix} -\text{syll} \\ -\text{son} \\ -\text{cont} \\ +\text{ant} \\ -\text{cor} \end{bmatrix} \rightarrow [-\text{voiced}] / \underline{\quad}\#$$

b.

$$\begin{bmatrix} -\text{syll} \\ -\text{son} \\ -\text{cont} \\ +\text{ant} \end{bmatrix} \rightarrow [-\text{voiced}] / \underline{\quad}\#$$

c.

$$\begin{bmatrix} -\text{syll} \\ -\text{son} \\ -\text{cont} \end{bmatrix} \rightarrow [-\text{voiced}] / \underline{\quad}\#$$

d.

$$\begin{bmatrix} -\text{syll} \\ -\text{son} \end{bmatrix} \rightarrow [-\text{voiced}] / \underline{}\#$$

In (3a) the devoicing rule is limited to labial stops, in (3b) to labial and dental stops, in (3c) to any stop, in (3d) to any obstruent. And of course many other possibilities exist. Given the model presented by McCarthy, the discovery procedure will make available "grammars" (3a–d), along with many others, to the learner. The evaluation metric will then select the most highly valued one, namely (3d), and all is well. In my view the evaluation metric forms part of the discovery procedure in the following sense: potential grammars are entertained in an ascending order of complexity as determined by the evaluation metric. The learner accepts the first grammar compatible with the available data. It follows that this will always be the most highly valued grammar.

McCarthy's discussion of Expletive Infixation in English provides a structurally identical use of the evaluation metric. McCarthy notes that expletives may be infixed at foot boundaries. He proposes two observationally adequate analyses: one contains a partial environment requiring a stressed syllable to immediately precede the infixation site; the second would be identical except for the lack of this stipulation regarding the stressed syllable. With the local application of the evaluation metric, the learner would always adopt the latter solution: the solution without the additional stipulation.

Integrating the evaluation metric into the discovery procedure yields a number of conceptually satisfying results. We see how descriptively adequate grammars may be attained based on ridiculously small and hopelessly skewed bodies of data. It becomes clear how rules that are not "surface true" in the sense of Natural Generative Grammarians may be acquired in the face of apparently contradictory data. The role of positive versus negative data is seen here. A learner having acquired a highly valued grammar, or portion thereof, may be expected to cling tenaciously to it, seeking alternative treatments of recalcitrant facts not involving the abandonment of the original hypothesis. Determining what conditions may force the learner to abandon this first hypothesis constitutes an extremely interesting research problem for acquisition models.

A second role of the evaluation measure as seen in McCarthy's examples involves ranking entire analyses—in other words, comparing two solutions to a given problem, solutions that may involve different rules, different underlying representations, and different lexical constraints. I will call such cases *global* uses of the evaluation metric. I shall argue that all such global uses are illicit and that the selection is made by other means.

McCarthy's discussion of the prothetic *e* in Spanish provides the first example of a global use of the evaluation metric. He notes that there are at least two ways of dealing with the prothetic *e* found in words lke *escala* and *escribir*.

(4)
Rule: $\emptyset \rightarrow e / \# \underline{} s \, [+\text{cons}]$
Underlying forms: /skala/, /skrib+ir/

(5)
Underlying form constraint: *#sC
Underlying forms: /eskala/, /eskrib+ir/

McCarthy argues that solution (4) is favored over solution (5) by the evaluation metric. The small cost of the rule of prothesis is more than made up for by the elimination of all initial *e*'s preceding *s*C clusters in the lexicon. In terms of my suggested model, it is a little difficult to imagine solutions (4) and (5) being part of an ordered list of available solutions. It would seem that if McCarthy's assessment of the situation is correct—that is, if solutions (4) and (5) are indeed available to the learner—the evaluation metric must be considered independent of the discovery procedure. In fact, I suggest that solution (5) is not available to the learner and that solution (4) is incorrect as it stands.

McCarthy's discussion of the Maori case involves a similar use of the evaluation metric. In that case also I will argue that the solution rejected by the evaluation metric is not a possible phonological analysis and hence not available to the learner. Not the evaluation metric but, rather, the theory of generative phonology is at work here. It would be interesting if all such global uses of the evaluation metric could be eliminated by further refinements of the theory.

Given the current direction of research in phonology, in particular the work of Kean (1975; 1979), Kiparsky (1979), Halle and Vergnaud (1978), and Kaye and Lowenstamm (1980; to appear), a richer, more highly constrained theory of phonology is developing. Much of the work once done by the evaluation metric is now accomplished by the reduction in the number of analyses compatible with any reasonably sized data base. Such a consequence is particularly clear in the recent work on markedness, both segmental and syllabic, and in the emergence of the theory of metrical phonology. Such questions are not essential to McCarthy's point. They do, however, have an impact on the role of the evaluation metric within a grammar. To illustrate this point I turn now to a discussion of McCarthy's remaining examples.

Phonological Theory and the Role of the Evaluation Metric

I have suggested that solution (5) for the prothetic *e* in Spanish is not a possible solution within the current theory of generative phonology. If I am correct, what is at work in this example is not the evaluation metric but the refinement of phonological theory. Let us look at the example more closely. What nature of beast is the constraint *#sC in Spanish? It is clearly not a morpheme structure constraint. Morphemes with initial *s*C clusters abound in Spanish: *su+scribir, con+stitucion*. It is for this reason that the # boundary appears in the expression of the constraint. In the light of theoretical developments in phonology, all (or at least most) cases of word structure constraints are seen as constraints on syllable structure. This is true in the case of Spanish. Following this line, the type of constraint in (5) is not available to the learner. Further, all the facts of Spanish prothesis follow as a consequence of the fact that *s*C is not a possible onset in Spanish. The alternative to solution (5) is, as I shall show, without cost.

In a theory of syllable structure along the lines of that proposed by Kaye and Lowenstamm (1980; to appear), syllable constraints and syllable structure are expressed at the level of lexical representation. A morpheme like *scrib* has the following representation:

(6)

 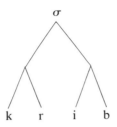

This morpheme consists of two syllables. An initial syllable is of the form CVC, but the onset and nucleus are null elements; only the coda has a segmental representation. The second syllable, *krib*, is a garden variety CCVC. Resyllabification takes place when morphemes are juxtaposed. The guiding principle of this enterprise is to resyllabify, eliminating nulls where this does not violate the syllable constraints of the language.

Consider now the derivation of the forms *escribir, suscribir* (the underlying form of the prefix is of no concern here).

(7)

Resyllabification:

Spelling rule:

     (?)eskribir   ———

In (7) I give the underlying representations of the two forms in question including the syllable structure of their constituent morphemes. After resyllabification, all of the null elements have been eliminated from the representation of *suscribir* and nothing further need be said. As for *escribir*, two null elements remain. All that is needed is to posit a spelling rule to specify how the null elements are to appear in the Spanish surface forms: in the case of the null onset, one may hear a glottal stop; the null nucleus is spelled out as *e*. Spelling rules may be viewed as parameter fixing. The unmarked case appears to be the elimination of nulls from phonological representation. The sole aspect peculiar to Spanish is how the nulls are to be spelled out. There is no rule of prothesis in Spanish. The work is done by a universal process of resyllabification, which constitutes part of phonological theory.

It is quite possible that these facts can be handled by another theory of syllable structure than the one followed here (Kaye and Lowenstamm, 1980; to appear). The key point is that Spanish prothesis should, in any adequate account, follow from the fact that *s*C onsets are illicit in Spanish—a fact that exists independently of the choice of analyses and accordingly has no cost. The Spanish example demonstrates clearly how the enrichment of phonological theory restricts the available options and hence reduces the work of the evaluation metric.

Maori provides an amusing example of theoretical overkill. What started out as a problem for generative phonology—why are Maori children "smarter" than phonologists?—is now an *embarras de richesses* of sound reasons for rejecting an apparently highly valued phonological solution. McCarthy shows that once all the facts are considered, an evaluation metric of the *Sound Pattern of English* type imposes what Hale has shown to be the correct solution. I will not review the facts. They are quite ably presented by McCarthy. I wish only to point out that the fact that the bad solution would be ruled out by the evaluation metric does not mean that the evaluation metric was the hatchet man in this case. In Kaye (1975) I presented another explanation for the Maori case. What is attractive about that proposal is that it unifies the explanation of the facts of Maori with a similar case in French (Kaye and Morin, 1978; Morin and Kaye, to appear). I am not claiming my approach is the correct one, only that the issue is far from settled. If my claim concerning the role of the evaluation metric as an arranger of possible phonologies is correct, it would be another reason not to close the books on the Maori case.

Cairene Arabic stress involves the theory of metrical phonology of which McCarthy is one of the pioneers. The novelty of this theory precludes detailed discussion of the question of evaluating competing analyses. I will assume that everything McCarthy has said on the matter is correct. There are then two analyses, one involving a rule of foot formation plus either a relabeling or a restructuring rule, the other involving a rule of foot formation only. It seems that this is not a case of global evaluation but, rather, is part of the role of the metric in providing the learner with an ordered set of grammars compatible with an array of data. This is what I have called the local use of the evaluation metric. I would assume that phonologies containing only rules of foot formation (such grammars presumably being ranked among themselves by a theory of markedness) would appear before all grammars containing complicating factors such as relabeling and restructuring rules. The Cairene Arabic case then reduces to a purely local use of the evaluation metric. It resembles the expletive infixation and final devoicing examples.

I have shown that the evaluation metric operates in a number of cases at a purely local level. It provides a strategy of selection for the learner. If grammar

A is properly included in grammar B, grammar A will be entertained before grammar B. I use "properly included" in the obvious sense: one grammar wholly includes another, with something to spare. This notion is to be refined to cover such cases as Cairene Arabic where cross-analytic rules of foot formation are assumed to have the same status. It does not preclude an eventual ranking of the foot-formation rules themselves.

Global uses of the evaluation metric, feature-counting of noncommensurate analyses, is thus excluded. What I have in mind is that all decisions involving noncommensurate analyses will be decided by the phonological theory. Put another way, for any array of data, noncommensurate analyses will not be entertained by the learner. Only concentric grammars of increasing complexity will be involved in the decision procedure.

Let me give a possible counterexample: two noncommensurate analyses both of which are possible portions of a phonology. Consider the following forms from Ojibwa:

(8)

a. nima:ca:	'I leave'	ma:ca:	'she leaves'
nitakoššin	'I arrive'	takoššin	'she arrives'
kipakis	'you swim'	pakiso	'she swims'
kiwi:sin	'you eat'	wi:sini	'she eats'
b. nitanokki:	'I work'	anokki:	'she works'
nita:kkos	'I am sick'	a:kkos	'she is sick'
kitaye:kkos	'you are tired'	aye:kkosi	'she is tired'
kitine:ntam	'you think'	ine:ntam	'she thinks'

Analysis of these data quickly reveals two prefixes: *ni~nit* '1st pers,' *ki~kit* '2nd pers' (in nouns one also finds *o~ot* '3rd pers' in the same circumstances); *ni* and *ki* appear before consonant-initial stems, *nit* and *kit* before vowel-initial stems. Two possible analyses can treat these data.

(9)
Underlying prefix forms: /ni/, /ki/, /o/
Rule:

$$\emptyset \rightarrow \begin{bmatrix} -\text{syll} \\ +\text{cons} \\ -\text{cont} \\ -\text{son} \\ +\text{cor} \\ +\text{ant} \end{bmatrix} / \underset{\text{prefix}}{\_\_\_\_]} + [+\text{syll}]$$

(10)
Underlying prefix forms: /nit/, /kit/, /ot/
Rule: $[+\text{seg}] \rightarrow \emptyset / \underset{\text{prefix}}{\_\_\_\_]} + [-\text{syll}]$

In (9) it is assumed that the *t* is epenthetic. Prefixes contain no final consonant in their underlying representation. A rule of epenthesis inserts *t* between a prefix and a following vowel-initial element. Solution (10) posits a series of prefixes all ending in *-t*. A deletion rule will erase the *t* before a consonant.

How is one to choose between the two solutions? Note first that neither rule is otherwise motivated in Ojibwa. Vowel sequences occurring elsewhere are not broken up by *t*. They undergo a truncation rule. The first member of an illicit consonant cluster is not generally deleted. Such a cluster is broken up by an epenthetic *i* or else the first consonant undergoes a dissimilation rule changing it to *h*. Whichever rule is adopted, (9) or (10), it will have to apply in a context limited to prefixes.

Solution (9) is a relatively costly rule of epenthesis. However, the underlying form of the prefixes contains no final consonant. Solution (10) is a simpler rule of consonant deletion, but with the expense of adding a final consonant to the lexical representation of the three prefixes. I can think of no additional evidence, internal or external, that would decide the issue. Counting features might favor solution (9)—the five additional features of the rule are more than offset by the three additional *t*'s in the underlying representations of solution (10). A redundancy rule stipulating that all prefixes end in *t* might narrow the difference between the two. My point is that I believe the Ojibwa case is just the sort of problem that an evaluation metric would not settle. Given the total lack of empirical consequences of such a decision, I can imagine that speakers of Ojibwa might adopt one or another solution in a more or less random manner. Perhaps some improved theory of markedness favoring, say, insertion rules over deletion rules may eventually decide the question. I wish to claim only that an appeal to the evaluation metric seems inappropriate in this case.

I have tried to show that the evaluation metric as discussed by McCarthy does indeed have a place in the theory of phonology. Given the recent advances in phonology that have sharply constrained the number of possible analyses compatible with an array of data, the role of this metric seems to be limited to presenting the learner with an ordered sequence of commensurate analyses. The evaluation metric, operating in concert with a theory of markedness and, of course, the now enriched notion of a possible phonology, constitutes a significant part of the discovery procedure.

Chapter 9
Strict Bounding

Mark R. Baltin

If one attempts to construct a model of language that purports to bear a close (though perhaps not isomorphic) relation to the mental representation of language by actual speaker-hearers, one must give an account of acquisition. As Baker (1979a) points out, however, many linguistic analyses in the literature on generative grammar are motivated by facts not available to ordinary language learners—specifically, the information that certain crucial strings are ungrammatical. Children never utter these ungrammatical strings. Therefore experience itself never gives children the information that would lead them to construct the analysis posited by the linguist.

Given the criterion that a model of language should make available an account of acquisition, one can draw two alternative conclusions about an unlearnable linguistic analysis. One possibility is that the analysis is wrong and the generalizations it captures are spurious. (The notion of a spurious generalization, or coincidence, makes sense only in a model of grammar that claims ontological status; it does not make sense if one simply views a grammar as a fiction or just a way of describing the facts, as does Quine, 1972.)

A second possibility is that a nonlearnable linguistic analysis may be a part of universal grammar and hence a part of the initial assumptions that children bring to bear in deducing the grammatical structure of their language. Linguistic analyses of the second type are those that, for example, posit output constraints or filters (Perlmutter, 1971; Chomsky and Lasnik, 1977) and constraints on the application of various rules (Ross, 1967).

A nonlearnable linguistic analysis that purports to express significant generalizations must, then, be part of universal grammar, under the realist conception of grammar.

I will discuss one such linguistic analysis, a bounding constraint on movement rules. Ross (1967) proposed a constraint on the bounding of rightward movement rules which was subsequently claimed not to hold in certain languages: Navajo (Kaufman, 1974) and German (Kohrt, 1975) are two examples. Because a bounding constraint requires negative evidence for the language learner, it must be innate and hence part of the child's initial assumptions. Therefore, if a given language shows apparent violations of the constraint, a conflict exists between the child's experience and his initial assumptions. Two possibilities exist for the resolution of this conflict.

First, the child may simply, on the basis of the positive evidence available (i.e., sentences that exhibit apparent violation of the bounding constraint) decide that the constraint does not apply at all in his language, contrary to initial assumptions. I shall call this the *total rejection hypothesis*.

A second possibility is that the child reanalyzes the sentences in which the constraint applies so that they are no longer counterexamples to the constraint. I shall call this the *tenacity hypothesis*.

The child may be guided by the total rejection model in some cases and by the tenacity model in other cases. Alternatively, one or the other model may always be the correct one. Obviously, we lack the data necessary to answer these questions. I mention them because future research that demonstrates an awareness of them may lead to an answer, and the answer would yield an interesting insight into the workings of the human mind.

The present study tends to support the tenacity model. I shall propose and justify a new constraint on the bounding of rightward movement rules; this constraint, which is more general than Ross's constraint, is assumed to be universal for the reasons just given. I shall show that apparent violations of the bounding constraint, given in later sections of this paper, are due to the influence of other factors; when those factors are taken into account, the bounding constraint makes its presence felt within the language.

Before proceeding to the analysis, a word about my assumptions is in order. I assume a model of grammar essentially along the lines of Chomsky and Lasnik (1977), in which the grammar can be schematized as in (1):

(1)

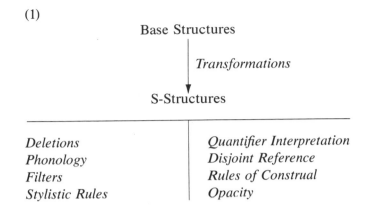

Base Structures

Transformations

S-Structures

Deletions	*Quantifier Interpretation*
Phonology	*Disjoint Reference*
Filters	*Rules of Construal*
Stylistic Rules	*Opacity*

The S-structures level (which is a bit more abstract than what linguists used to consider surface structure) leads to two independent tracks. The rules of logical form (on the right-hand side of the vertical line) apply independently of the rules on the left-hand side. The components of the grammar are assumed to be ordered with respect to each other, but the rules within the components are unordered.

Generalized Subjacency and Its Precursors

Ever since Ross (1967) it has been known that certain seemingly unbounded syntactic processes cannot extract elements out of certain syntactic configurations; in other words, certain syntactic configurations create, in Ross's terms, islands.

For example, *wh*-movement, though seemingly unbounded, has a check on its unboundedness in that it cannot extract elements out of complex noun phrases, as in (2).

(2)
a. Who did Fred pretend that Bob claimed that Mary liked ____?
b. *Who did Fred believe the claim that Mary liked ____?

Looking at other supposedly unbounded movements, such as topicalization, and noticing the same restriction, Ross (1967, p. 127) postulated a constraint.

(3)
Complex Noun Phrase Constraint:
No element contained in a sentence dominated by a noun phrase with a lexical head noun may be moved out of that noun phrase by a transformation.

In (2b), the *wh*-element originates in the noun complement construction, an S dominated by NP which has *claim* as its lexical head noun.
Therefore, the Complex NP Constraint prohibits movement out of this
configuration. Ross proposed various other constraints on transformations which are designed to express restrictions that are not, for various
reasons, most appropriately expressed in the formulations of the rules
themselves.

Another such constraint noticed by Ross, the Right Roof Constraint,
states that rightward movement rules are upward bounded, in the sense
that an element cannot be moved rightward more than one S node past
the point of origin. Thus, from an underlying structure such as (4), $\bar{S}_2$
can be extraposed to the end of $\bar{S}_1$, yielding (5) as a variant.

(4)

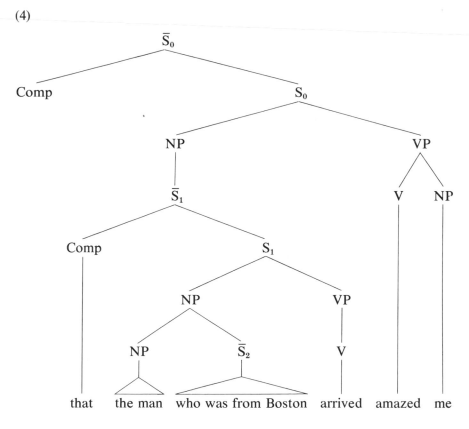

(5)
That the man arrived who was from Boston amazed me.

However, $\bar{S}_2$ cannot be extraposed to the end of $\bar{S}_0$, as in (6).

(6)
*That the man arrived amazed me who was from Boston.

The ungrammaticality of (6) is accounted for by the Right Roof Constraint, since (6) could be derived only by moving $\bar{S}_2$ more than one S node past its point of origin.

In recent years, various investigators (Chomsky, 1973, 1977; Bresnan, 1977; Bresnan and Grimshaw, 1978) have proposed a more general conception of bounding in order to unify Ross's constraints. Chomsky (1973) proposed a bounding constraint known as subjacency, which states that syntactic rules cannot relate elements over nonadjacent cycles, with NP and S being cyclic nodes. Thus, schematically, neither A and B nor A′ and B can be related in the following configuration, where α and β are both cyclic nodes.

(7)
A . . . [$_\alpha$ . . . [$_\beta$ . . . B . . .] . . .] . . . A′

Furthermore, within this theory, cases of seemingly unbounded movements, as in (2a), actually result from successive cyclic movement into Comp (see Bresnan, 1970, 1972, for justification of this category). In this way, Chomsky attempts to capture both the Complex NP Constraint and the Right Roof Constraint. He argues that if we formulate *wh*-movement and topicalization as Comp substitutions, we can account for the Complex NP Constraint. Since NPs lack Comps, the element moved by *wh*-movement or topicalization would have to cross the NP containing the *wh*-word and the matrix S, two cyclic nodes; hence the extraction would violate subjacency.

Similarly, extraposition of the relative $\bar{S}_2$ in (4) would violate subjacency, by crossing the S_1 and the NP of which it was originally a part, if (6) were derived.

Chomsky has thus managed to formulate one bounding constraint that limits both rightward and leftward movements. I shall show, however, that rightward movements are fundamentally different from leftward movements and that uniting rightward bounding with the cases that motivate subjacency based on leftward movement results in a spurious generalization. In particular, I shall argue for the following formulation of subjacency:

(8)

Generalized Subjacency:

In the configuration A . . . [$_\alpha$ . . . [$_\beta$ . . . B . . .] . . .] . . . A′,

i. A′ cannot be related to B where α and β are maximal projections of any major categories;

ii. A cannot be related to B where α and β are drawn from the following list of phrasal categories: (a) PP; (b) NP; (c) S or $\bar{\text{S}}$ or both, depending on the specific language.

Thus, I claim that all major category nodes act as bounding nodes for rightward movement but not for leftward movement; in particular, VP and AP must be bounding nodes for rightward movement, but they could not possibly be bounding nodes for leftward movement.

For the formulation of subjacency, I shall assume that the notion of L-Containment (Chomsky, 1973) is relevant. A node A is said to L-contain a node B if and only if A dominates B and other lexical material. Furthermore, if A and B are both given as bounding nodes by the metatheory, and if A dominates B but does not L-contain B, A is not counted in the counting of bounding nodes in that phrase-marker for the purposes of subjacency.

Detachment

It seems to be the case that sentences in English that contain $\bar{\text{S}}$s and PPs in non-clause-final position have alternative variants in which the $\bar{\text{S}}$s and PPs are in clause-final position. The following sentence pairs illustrate this.

(9)

a. How certain that the Mets will win are you?

b. How certain are you that the Mets will win?

(10)

a. How fond of Sally are you?

b. How fond are you of Sally?

To capture the relation between the (a) and (b) forms in these sentences, it seems natural to posit the following rightward movement rule:

(11)
Detachment:

$$\left\{\begin{matrix} \overline{S} \\ PP \end{matrix}\right\} - X$$

$$1 \qquad 2 \rightarrow 2\ 1$$

This rule is quite general. It moves $\overline{S}$s and PPs rightward, not only out of adjective phrases, but out of other constituents as well; for example, it also moves these constituents out of verb phrases.

(12)
a. Suspect that Fred killed his mother though I may, I'll never be able to prove it.
b. Suspect though I may that Fred killed his mother, I'll never be able to prove it.

(13)
a. Talk to Fred about Sally though I may, he is still blind about her.
b. Talk to Fred though I may about Sally, he is still blind about her.

Given that the grammar must express in some fashion the alternation between these (a) and (b) sentences, let us inquire more closely into the nature of this alternation. I am assuming a model of grammar in which certain movement rules (stylistic rules) do not affect sentence-level interpretation, so they do not crucially feed rules of logical form. If a movement rule does crucially feed rules of logical form, it is assumed to be syntactic. Therefore, in order to determine whether a given movement rule is syntactic or stylistic, one must note the deformation of structure that it yields and examine its interaction with a rule of logical form that crucially depends upon syntactic structure. If the rule of logical form applies in such a way as to act as if the movement rule had not applied, the movement rule is assumed to be stylistic. If the rule of logical form is sensitive to the deformation of structure induced by the movement rule, the rule is syntactic.

With this distinction in mind, let us consider a rule of logical form that has been shown to be dependent upon syntactic structure. Reinhart (1976) argues that the following constraint exists on the establishment of pronoun–antecedent relations:

(14)
A pronoun cannot c-command its antecedent.

A node A is said to c-command a node B if A does not dominate B and the first branching node that dominates A also dominates B. Therefore, in diagram (15), B and C c-command each other but nothing else; the same state of affairs holds for E and F as well as for K and M; G, A, and D, however, c-command each other, as well as the material under the other nodes.

(15)

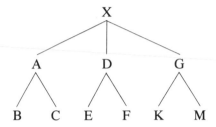

Chomsky (1980a) shows that Reinhart's constraint holds at the level of logical form.

    With the status of (14) in mind, let us consider the following base rule:

(16)
VP → V NP $\bar{\text{S}}$

Rule (16) is responsible for the generation of such sentences as (17), which would have the underlying phrase-marker in (18).

(17)
I convinced him that Fred would lose.

The direct object of *convince* is dominated by the branching node VP, which also dominates $\bar{\text{S}}_1$. Therefore, the pronoun *him* c-commands all of the elements in $\bar{\text{S}}_1$, including *Fred,* and (14) correctly blocks coreference between *him* and *Fred* in sentence (17).

(18)

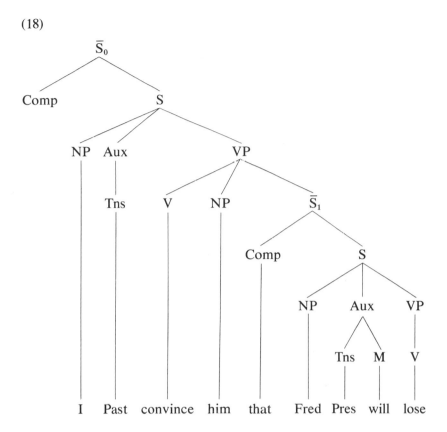

However, it seems that coreference between *him* and *Fred* is also blocked in certain sentences in which the first branching node that dominates the pronoun does not dominate the full NP, as in (19).

(19)
Convince *him* though I may that *Fred* will lose, I'll never convince his manager.

The sequence *convince him* has been moved to the front of the subordinate clause by the rule of *though*-preposing, which fronts VPs (Ross, 1967) and APs in subordinate clauses introduced by *though*. Rule (11), Detachment, may have applied before *though*-preposing; if it did not, $\overline{S}_1$ will be fronted along with the rest of the VP and then moved back to the end of the subordinate clause by Detachment. In other words, Detachment may have applied either before or after *though*-preposing to yield (19); the ordering of these two rules is irrelevant to present concerns. Crucially, however, the pronoun *him* is dominated by the node VP, which does not dominate the material in $\bar{S}_1$. Therefore, the constraint (14) should allow coreference between *him* and *Fred*. Since the two NPs here are not coreferential, it is necessary, if Reinhart's constraint is to be salvaged as a constraint on logical form, to posit Detachment as a stylistic rule.

I have shown the rule of Detachment (11) operating out of APs and VPs. It will also extract PPs and $\bar{S}$s from NPs. This phenomenon has been referred to as Extraposition from NP (Ross, 1967) and Extraposition of PP (Guéron, 1980).

(20)
a. A man who came from Boston appeared.
b. A man appeared who came from Boston.

(21)
a. A review of Chomsky's latest work has just appeared.
b. A review has just appeared of Chomsky's latest work.

The rule of Detachment, stated as in (11), is so general that it will automatically operate to extract PPs and $\bar{S}$s out of NPs; therefore, Detachment subsumes Extraposition from NP and of PP and renders those rules, separately formulated, superfluous. I shall henceforth refer to the process that extracts relative clauses and prepositional phrases as Detachment.

Detachment and VP as a Bounding Node

Although I have established that a rule of Detachment exists, I have not established the position to which the detached constituent moves. In this section I shall show that a constituent that detaches from subject position moves to a position outside of the verb phrase, whereas a constituent that detaches from a noun phrase within the verb phrase ends up at the end of the verb phrase. This fact is anomalous unless VP is regarded as a bounding node for rightward movements. I shall also show that Ross's Right Roof Constraint cannot be made to follow from subjacency unless VP is posited as a bounding node for rightward movements.

Detachment from Subject Position

I assume, following Akmajian, Steele, and Wasow (1979), among others, that VP deletion is a test for verb phrase constituency. Given this assumption, it is possible to establish the derived constituent structure of sentences in which a relative clause or PP has been detached from subject position. One need only examine the interaction of VP deletion and detachment from subject position. If both rules apply, the detached constituent is left behind, indicating that the detached constituent is not part of the VP.

(22)

Although nobody would ride with Fred who knew just him, people would ____ who knew his brother.[1]

(23)

Although not many reviews appeared of Lucretia's performance, one very scathing review did ____ of Max's performance.

Detachment from Positions within VP

Constituents can detach from NPs located within the VP. Thus, direct objects can also launch detached relative clauses and PPs, as in (24) and (25).

(24)

a. John calls people whom he has never met before up.

b. John calls people up whom he has never met before.

(25)

a. John calls people from Boston up.

b. John calls people up from Boston.[2]

The particle *up* intervenes between the head noun phrase and the relative clause in (24b), and between the head noun phrase and the PP in (25b), showing a non-string-vacuous application of detachment from direct object position.

Given that relative clauses and PPs that detach from subject position land at the end of S, as I have shown, the null hypothesis would be that a constituent that detaches from an NP within the VP would again be a daughter to S in derived structure. That is, the correct derived constituent structure for (24b) would be (26).

(26)

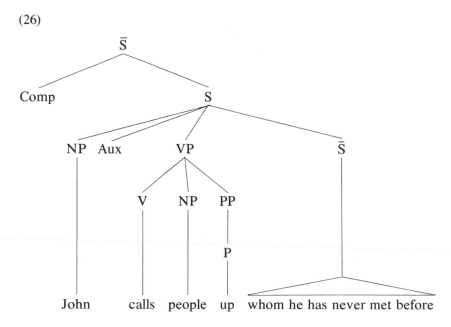

However, there exists evidence that (26) is incorrect. Unfortunately, VP deletion cannot provide independent evidence bearing on the accuracy of (26),[3] but there is independent evidence that constituents that detach from an NP within the VP do not escape from the VP. Therefore, the correct derived constituent structure for (24b) is (27).

(27)

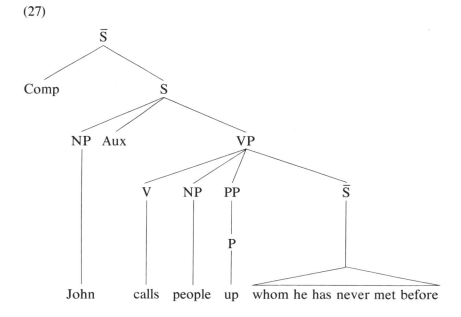

In the application of preposing rules that front VPs, a relative clause or PP that detaches from direct object position not only can but must be carried along with the fronted VP:[4,5]

(28)
a. John said that he would call people up who are from Boston, and call people up who are from Boston he will.
b. *John said that he would call people up who are from Boston, and call people up he will who are from Boston.

(29)
a. Call people up who are from Boston though he may, he's generally pretty cheap about long-distance calls.
b. *Call people up though he may who are from Boston, he's generally pretty cheap about long-distance calls.

(30)
a. John said that he would call people up from Boston, and call people up from Boston he will.
b. *John said that he would call people up from Boston, and call people up he will from Boston.

(31)
a. Call people up from Boston though he may, he's generally pretty cheap about long-distance calls.
b. *Call people up though he may from Boston, he's generally pretty cheap about long-distance calls.

Both (30b) and (31b) are grammatical strings, but not on the intended reading; the PP *from Boston* is interpreted as a sentence adverbial and not as a modifier of *people*.

Since these fronting rules are diagnostics for VP constituency, it seems that constituents that detach from object position move to the end of the VP and no further. In contrast, constituents that detach from subject position end up outside the VP. This situation is anomalous under current theories of grammar. However, the following two conclusions can make sense out of the array of data presented thus far:

(32)
i. VP acts as a bounding node for rightward movement.
ii. Certain movement rules simply move elements as far as they can go, subject to the appropriate notion of bounding.

By these two conventions, detachment of relatives and PPs out of NPs originating in the VP would be violating subjacency if these elements moved out of the NP and the VP.

Notice, however, that VP could not possibly be a bounding node for leftward movement, for if it were, *wh*-movement of direct objects, as in (33), would be impossible.

(33)
Who does Fred like?

Sentence (33) has the underlying structure in (34):

(34)

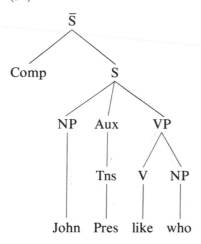

Given the arguments in Chomsky (1977) for S as a bounding node in English, movement of the *wh*-phrase into Comp would be crossing VP and S and hence, if VP were a bounding node for leftward movement, should be impossible because subjacency would be impossible.

This is the first empirical argument in favor of Generalized Subjacency. In the next section I shall show that although detachment obeys the Right Roof Constraint, its inability to apply out of an infinitival complement does not follow from subjacency unless VP is counted as a bounding node for rightward subjacency.

Detachment and the Right Roof Constraint
As noted in Baltin (1978b), Detachment cannot normally apply in such a way as to move a constituent rightward out of an embedded infiniti-

val. Therefore, although (35a) is acceptable, (35b), in which detachment out of the finite complement has occurred, is not.

(35)
a.   Joe was believed to have proven that Fred killed her by everyone in the room.
b.   *Joe was believed to have proven by everyone in the room that Fred killed her.

I shall now examine more closely the reasons for the unacceptability of (35b). I shall assume that (35a) has a phrase-marker along the lines of (36). It is natural to assume that the agent *by*-phrase occurs in the same clause as the passive verb that subcategorizes for it (Chomsky, 1965). Because the *by*-phrase is in the matrix S, the laws of geometry demand that the finite complement be in the matrix clause as well in (35b).

The Specified Subject condition could not be operative here (the trace of *Joe* would function as the specified subject), because, as I have shown, Detachment is a stylistic rule. Chomsky (1980a) has shown that the Specified Subject condition is a condition on logical form and in the model that I am assuming, stylistic rules apply independently of logical form. Standard formulations of subjacency (e.g., Chomsky, 1973, 1977b) would not rule out (35b) either, because the only bounding node separating $\bar{S}_2$ from the matrix S would be $\bar{S}_1$. If detachment of $\bar{S}_2$ were to apply, $\bar{S}_2$ would be crossing only one bounding node, and hence (35b) would be predicted to be grammatical.

If Detachment obeys Generalized Subjacency, however, (35b) would be correctly ruled out. The candidate for detachment, $\bar{S}_2$, would have to cross $\bar{S}_1$ and VP, both bounding nodes in the Generalized Subjacency formulation, and this movement would violate subjacency if it were to apply in such a fashion. Thus, the ungrammaticality of (35b) furnishes support for Generalized Subjacency.[6] Needless to say, detachment of PPs out of infinitival complements is also impossible:

(37)
a.   Joe was believed to have talked to Mary about that by everyone in the room.
b.   *Joe was believed to have talked to Mary by everyone in the room about that.

(36)

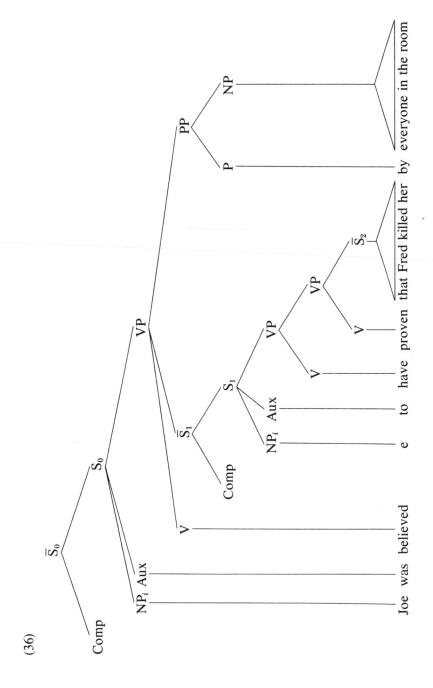

To recapitulate, I have presented two pieces of evidence that VP functions as a bounding node for rightward movements. First, constituents that detach from subject NPs end up at the end of S whereas constituents that detach from an NP within the VP can move no further than to the end of the VP. Second, the stylistic rule of Detachment cannot apply in such a way as to move a constituent out of an infinitival S into a matrix S. Both of these facts are explained in the same way if Generalized Subjacency, (7), is posited as the appropriate notion of bounding.

Detachment and AP as a Bounding Node

Detachment moves a PP or $\overline{S}$ out of an adjective phrase, as in the alternation between (9a) and (9b) and between (10a) and (10b). It also moves a PP or $\overline{S}$ rightward out of a VP, as in (12) and (13). If AP is a bounding node, one would expect that detachment out of an AP L-contained by a VP should be impossible, since the candidate for detachment would be crossing two bounding nodes under the formulation of Generalized Subjacency (7).

The grammar of English must contain base structures in which an AP is nonexhaustively dominated by a VP. That is to say, the grammar of English contains the following phrase structure rule:

(38)
VP → V NP AP

This rule is used in the following sentences:

(39)
I consider him envious of Sally.

(40)
I called him vindictive toward me.

(41)
I found him rude to people.

Sentence (39), for example, would have the underlying phrase-marker in (42).

(42)

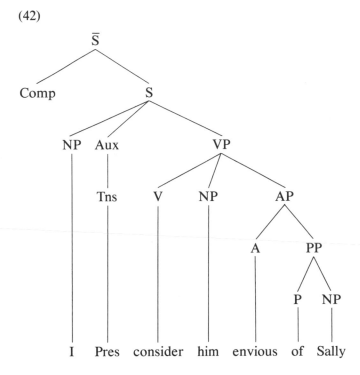

Let us now examine the interaction of *though*-preposing and Detachment. If a VP expanded by rule (38) is *though*-preposed, the adjectival complement cannot be detached to the end of the subordinate clause. Thus, the (a) versions of the following sentences are more acceptable than the (b) versions.

(43)
a. Consider him envious of Sally though I may, it doesn't matter.
b. *Consider him envious though I may of Sally, it doesn't matter.

(44)
a. Call him vindictive toward me though I may, it doesn't matter.
b. *Call him vindictive though I may toward me, it doesn't matter.

(45)
a. Find him rude to people though I may, it doesn't matter.
b. *Find him rude though I may to people, it doesn't matter.

(46)

a. ?Consider myself certain that the Mets will win though I may, it doesn't matter.

b. *Consider myself certain though I may that the Mets will win, it doesn't matter.

(47)

a. ?Find him angry that he wasn't consulted though I may, it doesn't matter.

b. *Find him angry though I may that he wasn't consulted, it doesn't matter.[7]

Again, the unacceptability of the (b) versions of these sentences is anomalous given standard formulations of subjacency, but it follows from the formulation of Generalized Subjacency, with VP and AP as bounding nodes for rightward movement.

The unacceptability of the (b) versions furnishes another bit of support for the postulation of VP as a bounding node for rightward movement.

A Typological Difference

In this section, I shall demonstrate a way in which Generalized Subjacency can solve a problem first raised by Kohrt (1975), who noticed that detachment in German can violate Ross's Right Roof Constraint. Considering a sentence such as (48), Kohrt posits the underlying structure in (49).

(48)

Paul hörte, wie Peter den Mann zwang, zu gestehen,
Paul heard how Peter the man forced   to confess
                              dass er den Wagen gestohlen hatte.
                              that he the car   stolen had.

'Paul heard how Peter forced the man to confess that he had stolen the car.'

Sentence (48) would result from detachment of S_3 to the end of S_2 and detachment of S_2 to the end of S_1. However, it is possible to detach S_3 to the end of S_1 directly, past *zwang*, resulting in (50).

(50)

Paul hörte, wie Peter den Mann zu gestehen zwang, dass er den Wagen gestohlen hatte.

(49)

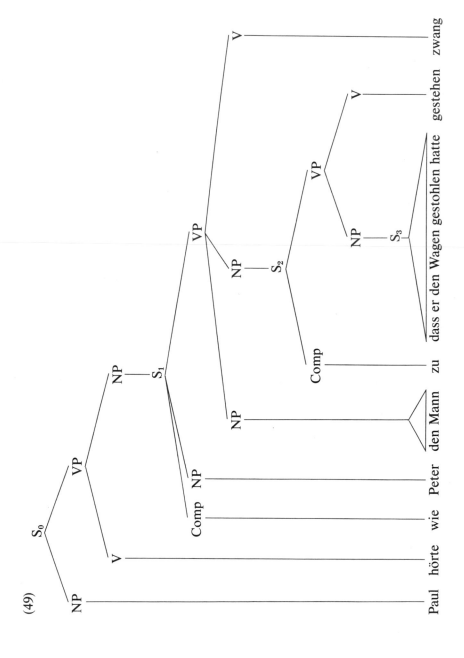

In order to derive (50), S_3 would have to be detached out of S_2. It would therefore appear that detachment in German can violate the Right Roof Constraint, since we have a case of a rightward movement rule that moves an element out of the clause in which it originates. However, detachment cannot apply in such a fashion in English, as is evidenced by the ungrammaticality of (35b) and (37b).

Two possible conclusions can be drawn about this difference between German and English. Under the first alternative, the one taken by Kohrt, the Right Roof Constraint would be language-particular. Under the second alternative, one would say that the Right Roof Constraint is not the appropriate generalization but, rather, is derivable from a more general theory of bounding, which is itself universal. I am proposing, then, that the Right Roof Constraint is not a primitive in universal grammar, and that the phenomena that motivated it are consequences of Generalized Subjacency, which is universal.

German, however, has a property that will cause detachment out of an infinitive not to violate subjacency. Specifically, Schwartz (1973, 1975) has argued, on the basis of facts concerning placement of adverbials and the absence of rules in SOV languages which crucially affect a VP constituent, that SOV languages lack a VP constituent but that VO languages do have a VP node. Therefore, under Schwartz's account, the underlying structure of (48) would not be (49); instead, it would be (51).

Given that German has the basic order SOV (Thiersch, 1978, applying to German some arguments that Koster, 1975, gave for Dutch), Schwartz's claim would prohibit the positing of a VP node for German. Since I used VP as a bounding node for rightward movements to block detachment out of an infinitive in English, I would predict the possibility of non-clause-bound detachment in German. Because German lacks a VP node, the only bounding node over S_3 that would L-contain it would be S_2, and so detachment of S_3 would be possible out of S_2; after all, S_3 would be crossing only one bounding node. In English, which does have a VP, detachment would be clause-bounded, since it could not cross the VP and the S.

The account proposed here makes two predictions that Kohrt's account does not. Generalized Subjacency predicts that if a complex NP, (NP plus a relative clause) were present in the same position as S_3, detachment of the relative should be unacceptable; the relative clause would have to cross the NP that immediately dominates it and S_2.

(51)

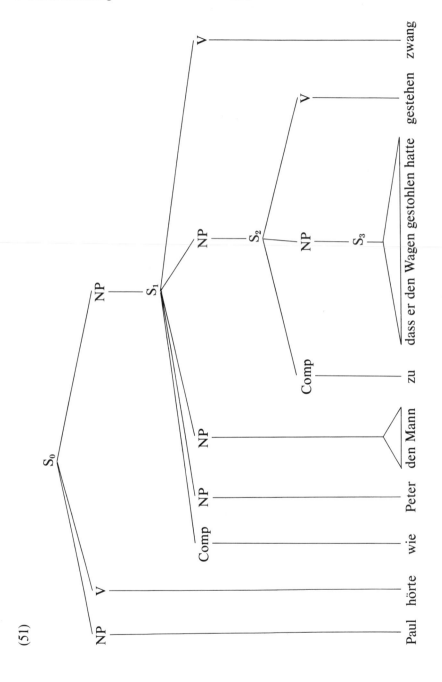

According to my informant, Susanne Wolff, this prediction is realized.
Thus, from a sentence such as (52) it is impossible to derive (53).

(52)
Paul hörte, wie Peter den Mann das Buch, das auf dem Tisch lag,
Paul heard how Peter the man the book   that on the table was
                                              zu lesen zwang.
                                              to read forced.
'Paul heard how Peter forced the man to read the book that was on
the table.'

(53)
*Paul hörte, wie Peter das Buch zu lesen zwang, das auf dem Tisch lag.

Second, if the *dass*-clause that is to be detached is embedded under
one more infinitive, detachment is impossible. A sentence in which the
relevant state of affairs exists is the following:

(54)
Paul hörte, wie ich Brigitte zu versprechen versuchte, anzukündigen,
Paul heard how I Brigitte   to promise tried   to announce
                              dass Peter die Schule verlassen hatte.
                              that Peter the school left had.
'Paul heard how I tried to promise Brigitte to announce that Peter had
left school.'

Sentence (54) has the underlying structure in (55). Generalized Subja-
cency would prohibit detaching $\overline{S}_4$ to the end of $\overline{S}_1$, since it would be
crossing both $\overline{S}_3$ and $\overline{S}_2$, two bounding nodes. Kohrt's account, which
simply says that German lacks the Right Roof Constraint, would again
predict grammaticality. And again the predictions made by Generalized
Subjacency seem to be realized; (56) is unacceptable.

(56)
*Paul hörte, wie ich Brigitte anzukündigen zu versprechen versuchte,
 Paul heard how I Brigitte   to announce to promise tried
                              dass Peter die Schule verlassen hatte.
                              that Peter the school left had.

Generalized Subjacency, then, is to be preferred to Kohrt's account
because it enables one to deduce the distinction between German and
English and allows one to predict further facts about German not noticed by Kohrt. Indeed, the account here may explain a generalization
first made by David Perlmutter (personal communication, 1974). Perl-

(55)

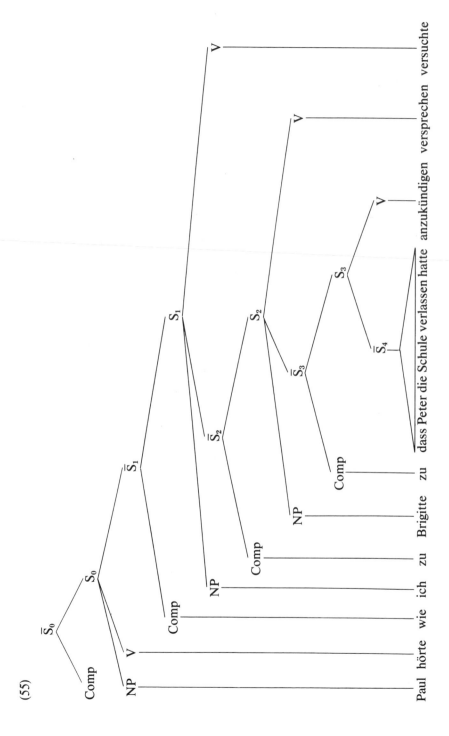

mutter has noticed that all of the languages of which he is aware that violate Ross's Right Roof Constraint are SOV languages (Navajo is another example, as noted by Kaufman, 1974). If the correlation noted by Perlmutter holds up upon continued investigation, and under the same conditions, this fact would furnish additional support for the theory of bounding presented here.

Alternative Accounts

Other investigators have proposed alternative accounts of the phenomena described here by Detachment. These accounts have the effect of leaving unexplained the bounded dependencies that I have described. I shall show that in each case the alternative account fails to account for a sufficiently wide range of phenomena.

Koster

The account I have proposed assumes that Generalized Subjacency is a constraint on the application of movement rules and that the rules that detach relative clauses and PPs out of NPs are movement rules. However, Koster (1978a) has challenged the latter assumption. Koster has suggested that Extraposition of PPs and relative clauses is not a movement rule but rather a rule of discourse grammar which links complements with their heads (the rule is originally Gueron's; see Gueron, to appear). Because rules of discourse grammar do not normally obey constraints on sentence grammar (as shown in Williams, 1977), the bounded dependencies between relative clauses and PPs and their NP heads would fail to be explained if Generalized Subjacency is a constraint on the application of movement rules.

I have shown that there exists independent motivation for a rule of Detachment, stated as in (11). If the sentences paired in this paper by Detachment were individually base-generated, one would not be able to predict the facts concerning the inability of the two italicized NPs in (19) to corefer.

Again, as I have shown, the rule of Detachment, in its optimal form, automatically subsumes the rules that extrapose relative clauses and PPs out of NPs; therefore, the rule of Detachment will automatically move relative clauses and PPs out of NPs.

Therefore, a closer look at Koster's argumentation is in order, since a grammar containing both a rule of Detachment and his discourse rule of linking to focus would always allow two derivations for sentences that have PPs and S̄s separated from the NP heads that they modify. The starred sentences in this paper, in particular, would be predicted to be grammatical under such an account. After all, the rule of linking to focus, being a rule of discourse grammar, should be able to violate the bounding condition, a rule of sentence grammar.

In fact, Koster gives only one argument that the rule of linking to focus is a rule of discourse grammar. He notes that a complement may be linked to a focus in another speaker's discourse, as in the following dialogue:

(57)
A: A book appeared!
B: About relational grammar?
A: No, about Raising again.

However, when a PP cannot be extraposed, it also cannot be linked across speaker boundaries:

(58)
*This book is out of print about relational grammar.

(59)
A: This book is out of print.
B: *About relational grammar?

There is a problem with Koster's argument. His diagnostic would force us to put into discourse grammar things that we know are not part of discourse grammar. For example, reciprocal interpretation is a part of sentence grammar—it obeys the specified subject and propositional island conditions and cannot apply across sentence boundaries in a single speaker's discourse (Chomsky, 1977b); yet a reciprocal phrase can have antecedents in another speaker's sentence in exactly the same way that Koster's examples show that an extraposed complement can:

(60)
A: Joe and Mary were talking for quite a while yesterday.
B: About each other?

Thus, Koster's diagnostic would force us to place reciprocal interpretation into discourse grammar. In fact, I know of no phenomenon that would be excluded by this diagnostic. For that reason I conclude that it should be rejected as irrelevant. However, I feel that it is incumbent upon me to at least try to be explicit about the alternative accounts of the phenomena noted by Koster which would render his arguments moot.

The pretheoretic phenomenon seems to be the following: One can question a sentence uttered by another speaker by continuing that speaker's sentence with an optional final constituent uttered with a rising intonation. There are at least two ways to account for this. One way would be to posit a discourse rule of deletion, which deletes over a variable (for arguments for the necessity of such rules, see Sag, 1976). Thus, detachment of relatives and PPs could precede the deletion rule. The second alternative, if one wished to eschew such deletion rules, would be to say that the strings uttered by speaker B are not generated by the grammar at all. Because there seem to be no restrictions on this type of conversational interchange beyond the one mentioned (that the constituent mentioned by B must be a possible *final* constituent of A's sentence), the second tack does not seem implausible to me.

Koster raises a point about the movement analysis of extraposition of PPs which is quite substantive, however. In discussing an argument by Akmajian (1975) for the status of NP as a bounding node, he notes that Akmajian does not explain why it is impossible to violate subjacency superficially by iterated extraposition of the PP, in successive cyclic fashion. Akmajian had noted that a PP that originates within an NP dominated by a higher NP cannot extrapose out of the higher NP.

It seems to me, however, that the question raised by Koster (and an anonymous reviewer for Akmajian's paper) presupposes that the normal case would be the postulation of rules that can reapply to their own output. However, if one assumes a distinction between cyclic and postcyclic rules, and if one identifies stylistic movements with postcyclic rules and syntactic movements with cyclic rules, then the question receives the straightforward answer that stylistic rules do not apply in cyclic fashion because they are not cyclic.[8]

Williams and Marantz
Williams (1980a), citing Marantz (1979), has observed that such sentences as (61) and (62), which they believe are structurally parallel to (35b) and (37b), are acceptable.

(61)
Although he promised every visitor a demonstration of his great strength, Joe was forced to admit by each one that he couldn't lift the entire encyclopedia with one finger.

(62)

Although the men all wanted to hear about the native beauties, Joe was asked to speak by the women about his exciting adventures canoeing through the rapids of Pago Pago.

Williams concludes that Detachment is not clause-bound, arguing against an analysis by Baltin (1978b) in which the ungrammaticality of such sentences as (35b) was first noted. However, Williams provides no account of the unacceptability of (35b) and (37b).

To resolve this stalemate, I would claim that the sequences *forced to admit* in (61) and *asked to speak* in (62) have been optionally restructured into a single verb, along the lines of Rizzi's (1978) analysis for Italian. As in Rizzi's analysis, restructuring forms a sequence of verbs and infinitive markers into a unit, and transforms an underlyingly complex sentence into a superficially simple one, when the verbs and infinitive markers are contiguous.

As evidence for this restructuring rule, I would like to examine the operation of an ellipsis rule that has been much neglected in the literature. I propose that the rule be formulated as in (63).

(63)

Verb-Plus:

$$\text{Aux-V-}\overline{\overline{X}}\text{-Y-Z-Aux-V-}\overline{\overline{X}}\text{-Y-Z}$$

$$\begin{array}{ccccccccccc} 1 & 2 & 3 & 4 & 5 & 6 & 7 & 8 & 9 & 10 & \rightarrow \\ 1 & 2 & 3 & 4 & 5 & 6 & \emptyset & 8 & \emptyset & 10 \end{array}$$

This rule operates to delete a verb plus a variable when they are separated by an $\overline{\overline{X}}$ constituent. The following sentence pairs are related by this rule:

(64)

a. Although John doesn't like steak, he does like pizza.

b. Although John doesn't like steak, he does ____ pizza. (Term 9 is null.)

(65)

a. Although John didn't put the book on the table, he did put the magazine on the table.

b. Although John didn't put the book on the table, he did ____ the magazine ____. (Term 9 is a PP.)

It seems at first glance that rule (63), which I have dubbed Verb-Plus, is too restrictive, since sequences larger than a single verb can delete in the position of term 7. Examples are the following:

(66)

a. Although Joe wasn't forced to kiss Sally, he was forced to kiss Maxine.

b. Although Joe wasn't forced to kiss Sally, he was ____ Maxine.

(67)

a. Although I didn't try to persuade Max, I did try to persuade Tom.

b. Although I didn't try to persuade Max, I did ____ Tom.

Therefore, one might be tempted to revise the formulation of rule (63) in such a way that term 7 is a variable. This rule would be formulated as (68):

(68)

$$\text{Aux-W-}\overline{\overline{\text{X}}}\text{-Y-Z-Aux-W-}\overline{\overline{\text{X}}}\text{-Y-Z}$$
$$\begin{array}{ccccccccc} 1 & 2 & 3 & 4 & 5 & 6 & 7 & 8 & 9 & 10 \rightarrow \\ 1 & 2 & 3 & 4 & 5 & 6 & \emptyset & 8 & \emptyset & 10 \end{array}$$

Rule (68) is too weak, however. Not all sequences of verbs plus infinitive markers can undergo the rule. For example, most speakers allow this type of deletion when the matrix verb is *force,* but not when it is *believe.* Thus, the following contrast emerges:

(69)

a. Although John isn't believed to like steak, he is believed to like pizza.

b. *Although John isn't believed to like steak, he is ____ pizza.

(70)

a. Although John isn't forced to eat steak, he is forced to eat pizza.

b. Although John isn't forced to eat steak, he is ____ pizza.

I know of no other ellipsis rule that is lexically restricted in this fashion, in which the deleted item must be lexically marked. Gapping, VP deletion, sluicing, and so on, are all lexically ungoverned operations. Assuming then that the property of being lexically unrestricted is a general property of ellipsis rules, I would propose to retain the formulation of Verb-Plus given in (63). When it appears that a sequence longer than a single verb has been deleted, I claim that the sequence has actually been restructured into a single verb, simplifying an underlyingly complex structure into a superficially simple one, along the lines of Rizzi (1978) and Aissen and Perlmutter (1976).

The net result of the proposed restructuring rule in English is that (61) and (62) cease to be counterexamples to the bounding hypothesis presented here, since *force* and *ask* induce restructuring. Thus, the complements of the infinitive verbs embedded underneath them are in the matrix clause after the application of restructuring. Since *believe* does not induce restructuring, the complex structure for the sentence is retained and detachment out of the infinitival complement is impossible, as predicted by the bounding hypothesis presented here.

I assume that the restructuring rule for English is formulated along the lines that Rizzi proposes for Italian; the verbs and infinitive markers that undergo the process must be contiguous. Therefore, the account proposed here makes a prediction that differs from the Williams-Marantz account, even for *force;* when the infinitival complement of *force* is separated from the verb *force* by a nonverbal element (such as an NP), detachment out of the infinitival complement should become impossible. The verb in the infinitive would no longer be next to *force* and therefore could not restructure with it. In a sentence such as (71), therefore, detachment of the complement of *admit* into the matrix clause should be impossible.

(71)
I forced Fred to admit that he was a liar myself.

Since it can be demonstrated that the separated emphatic *myself* is in the matrix clause, modifying the matrix subject, I predict that a variant of (71) in which the embedded clause follows this separated emphatic should be ungrammatical, as it is:

(72)
*I forced Fred to admit myself that he was a liar.

To conclude: According to Williams and Marantz, detachment out of an infinitive is possible. But I have shown their account to be untenable because it does not explain the ungrammaticality of (35b), (37b), or (72). Their examples which purport to demonstrate the possibility of non-clause-bound detachment are explained here as resulting from the application of a rule of restructuring, independently motivated by a consideration of the optimal formulation of an ellipsis rule.

Hendrick

Hendrick (1978) proposes that the (a) and (b) forms of examples (9) and (10) are syntactically related, but he proposes that the derivation proceeds in the opposite direction from the one I consider. Under Hendrick's account, adjectives lack complements underlyingly; therefore, the underlying structure common to (10a) and (10b) would be (73).

(73)

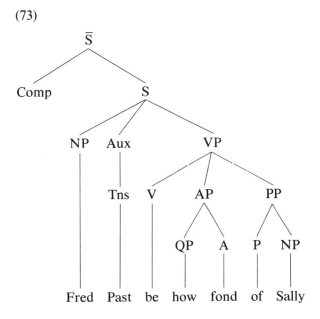

And prior to *wh*-movement an optional rule of complement formation would apply, formulated as in (74)—Hendrick's (51).

(74)
Complement Formation (optional):

$$U_1\text{-}U_2\text{-}A \quad -\left\{\begin{matrix}PP\\ \overline{S}\end{matrix}\right\}\text{-}U_3\text{-}U_4$$

1	2	3		4	5	6	$\rightarrow$
1	2	3+4			5	6	

Therefore, (10a) would result from the application of Complement Formation and (10b) from its nonapplication.

Under the account proposed in this paper, the underlying structure common to (10a) and (10b) would be (75).

(75)

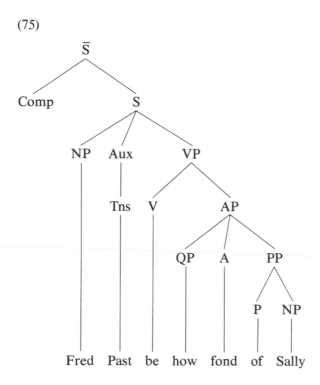

The stylistic rule of Detachment, an optional rightward movement rule, would be responsible for the alternation between (10a) and (10b).

In order to compare the two accounts, recall that a stylistic rule of detachment is required in Hendrick's system, in any event, in order to capture the relations between sentences in which PPs and S̄s are within their VPs and sentences in which they are not—for example, the (a) and (b) forms of (12) and (13). Similarly, Hendrick needs a rule of detachment to capture the case of PPs and S̄s moving out of NPs, as in (20a,b) and (21a,b). Therefore, Hendrick's account will still need the rule of Detachment as formulated in (11). The rule, stated in its optimally general form, will automatically extract PPs and S̄s out of adjective phrases and will therefore, even in Hendrick's system, be a possible derivation for the related structures for (10a,b) and (9a,b).

The rule of Complement Formation, then, will cause two derivations for the same alternation. Given that Detachment is needed in the grammar of English for independent reasons, the null hypothesis would be that this rule alone is responsible for the alternation between (9a) and (9b) and between (10a) and (10b).

Moreover, Hendrick's account furnishes no explanation for the unacceptability of (43b), (44b), (45b), (46b), and (47b). Because Complement Formation is optional, Hendrick's account would posit (76) as a possible predetachment structure for (43b), for example.

(76)[9]

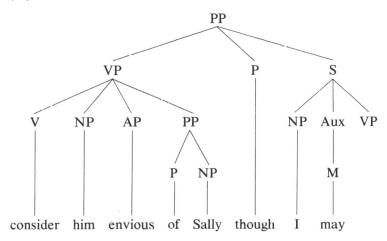

Given that Hendrick's grammar needs a rule of detachment to move out of VPs, nothing would stop the PP *of Sally* from failing to undergo Complement Formation and subsequently undergoing Detachment to the end of the subordinate clause. Hendrick's grammar, then, incorrectly predicts grammaticality for (43b)–(47b).

The account I propose, however, correctly predicts ungrammaticality for these examples. I reject the rule of Complement Formation and assume that the PPs and S̄s in the (a) examples in (43)–(47) are deep-structure sisters to their adjective heads under an AP constituent. This assumption, together with the postulation of AP and VP as bounding nodes for rightward movement, successfully blocks (43b)–(47b).

Therefore, the account proposed in this paper, in which adjectives possess deep-structure complements and all major category nodes are bounding nodes for rightward movement, covers a wider class of facts than does the rule of Complement Formation, and is hence to be preferred.

Conclusions and Implications

I have demonstrated the need for positing VP and AP as bounding nodes for rightward movement, but not for leftward. Akmajian (1975) has shown the need for positing NP as a bounding node for rightward movement (and Chomsky, 1973, has shown the need for positing NP as a bounding node for leftward movement). Baltin (1978a,b) and van Riemsdijk (1978) have demonstrated the need for positing PP as a bounding node for rightward and leftward movements. The resulting conception of subjacency, then, is as Generalized Subjacency (7), in which all major category nodes are bounding nodes for rightward movement, but only a proper subset of these nodes are bounding nodes for leftward movement.

One consequence of the bounding constraint proposed here is the existence of a movement rule, Detachment, which does not move an element to a defined structural position within the sentence but, rather, moves the element rightward as far as it can go without violating the bounding constraint. However, there are movement rules that must specifically mention the structural position—the "landing site"—to which the moved element moves, as shown in Baltin (1978b, 1979). Among such rules are Quantifier-Float, Topicalization, and Extraposition of sentential complements. Therefore, it seems necessary to posit two classes of movement rules: those that have defined landing sites, and those that do not.

It is preferable to try to explain this distinction, rather than simply mark each rule for whether or not it has a defined landing site. One possible correlation might be based on the fact that Q-Float (Baltin, 1978b,c), Extraposition of sentential complements (Reinhart, 1976), and Topicalization all affect logical form,[10] whereas Detachment does not. Therefore, it may be possible to define the rules that must mention the landing site as syntactic movement rules and those that simply move the element rightward (or leftward: see Baltin, 1979) as stylistic movements. If this correlation proves valid, it may provide the basis for a formal distinction between syntactic movement rules and stylistic movement rules.

Another interesting implication of this study is the demonstration that Generalized Subjacency must be defined over stylistic movements and hence cannot be defined on logical form. In a forthcoming study, and in Baltin (1978b), I show that one should in fact view subjacency as a condition on analyzability rather than a condition on binding. This paper is entirely consonant with such a conception of subjacency.

Notes

An earlier version of this paper was presented at the NYU Symposium on Syntactic Categories, McGill University, the University of Pennsylvania, the New York Linguistics Workshop, and the University of Texas, Austin. I would like to thank those audiences and all those who have discussed previous versions of this work with me—in particular Lee Baker, Noam Chomsky, Jim Higginbotham, Terry Langendoen, Bob May, John McCarthy, Marie-Thérèse Vinet, Ellen Woolford, and Annie Zaenen. A special debt goes to Debbie Nanni for her extremely insightful help on matters both stylistic and substantive.

1. It might appear that at times a relative clause detached from subject position can be deleted by VP deletion, contrary to the claims in the text. Such sentences as (i), for instance, are grammatical, with an implicit relative clause on the subject.

(i)
Although few people would ride with Fred who knew just him, some did.

This appearance is strictly illusory; the phenomenon of the implicit relative has nothing to do with VP deletion. Consider such sentences as (ii):

(ii)
Although not many people would ride with Fred who knew just him, some would be willing to take the chance.

Again, we get an implicit relative clause reading on the subject, such that the subject is understood as *some who knew just him*. Thus, there is no argument that a relative clause detached from subject position is deleted by VP deletion.

2. Sentence (25b) is ambiguous. On the first reading, the PP *from Boston* is interpreted as a complement of *people;* on the second reading, it is interpreted as an adverbial. I am concerned here with only the first reading.

3. It is true that a relative clause that detaches from direct object position cannot be stranded by VP deletion, unlike relative clauses that detach from subject position. Therefore, (i) is ungrammatical:

(i)

*John calls people up whom he has never met before, and Bill does
_____ whom he has met only briefly.

(ii)

John calls people up whom he has never met before, and Bill does _____,
too.

One cannot take the unacceptability of (i) as evidence for the correctness of (26), however, because there seems to be an independent constraint that prohibits deletion rules from deleting the head of a phrase
while retaining the modifiers of that phrase (as has been suggested). For
example, Gapping, which deletes proper parts of VPs, is also blocked
when the head of a relative clause detached from object position would
be deleted and the relative clause itself retained, as in (iv):

(iii)

John calls people up who want to be athletes, and Bill calls people up
who want to go into business.

(iv)

*John calls people up who want to be athletes, and Bill _____ who want
to go into business.

Therefore, the existence of some such constraint renders irrelevant the
impossibility of stranding a relative launched from object position for
VP constituency.

   Asakawa (1979) has independently come to the conclusion that relative clauses that detach from subject position end up at the end of S,
whereas relatives detached from object position end up at the end of
the VP. However, since Asakawa's sole argument is based on such
examples as (i), his argument is vitiated. Similarly, Asakawa's argument for relative clauses (and PPs) detached within NP as ending up
under $\overline{N}$ is vitiated by the observations in note 1 of this paper.

4. Unfortunately, it is impossible to test the derived constituent structure that I have suggested for (22) and (23) by using the same fronting
rules, since there seems to be some sort of constraint that the subjects
of sentences exhibiting preposed VPs must be pronominal.

(i)

*Mary said that the guy would arrive late, and arrive late the guy did.

(ii)

Mary said that the guy would arrive late, and arrive late he did.

(iii)

*Love her though the guy may, he'll remain objective.

(iv)

Love her though he may, he'll remain objective.

Given the extremely stylistic nature of these VP fronting rules, it seems plausible to attribute the restriction on the subject NP to some discourse or pragmatic constraint. If the subject must be pronominal, it will never be able to support restrictive relative clauses or PPs, and so no takeoff site will exist for relatives and PPs that modify the subject.

5. One can construct examples that might look as though a PP that detaches from within a direct object *can* be stranded when the entire VP is preposed, contrary to the claims made in the text:

(i)

John promised to help people in need no matter how poor, and help people from all walks of life he did.

(ii)

John promised to help people in need no matter how poor, and help people he did from all walks of life.

However, there seem to be some rather crucial differences between these examples and the examples in the text. Notice that the PP in (ii) is grammatical only with a dash-type level intonation contour (in written English, a dash would be placed before the final PP). It may be plausible, therefore, to say that (ii) is not directly generated by the grammar at all but, rather, consists of a sentence uttered by the speaker together with a PP appended as an afterthought, to clarify the main sentence. As support for this contention, I note the monoguity of (30b) and (31b) and the fact that when the *though*-preposing test is applied to a string like the final conjunct in (ii), as in (iii), the result, according to my informants, is unacceptable.

(iii)

*Help people though he may from all walks of life, he's still a jerk.

Therefore, taking such strings as (ii) as the normal case would seem to be generalizing on the exception.

6. In a later section I consider an apparent counterexample to this claim which has been put forth by Marantz (1979) and Williams (1980a).

7. Some speakers find the contrast between the (a) and (b) forms of (46) and (47) unclear and reject all four sentences. It is plausible to attribute the deviance of (46a) and (47a) for such speakers to some version of an internality constraint (Ross, 1967; Kuno, 1973; Grosu and Thompson, 1977). The unacceptability of sentences containing clauses flanked by lexical material has long been noted, although the exact formulation of this constraint is unresolved and is beyond the scope of this paper. However, any account would have to explain the deviance of (46b) and (47b), and internality is of no help; the sentential complement is not in an internal position. It seems plausible to attribute the deviance of (46b) and (47b) to a factor separate from the factor responsible for the deviance of (46a) and (47a)—namely, a requirement that relative clauses that originate within the VP must end up at the end of the VP.

8. In Reinhart (1976) and Baltin (1978b, 1979), it is argued that Extraposition of sentential complements, the rule that relates (i) and (ii), is syntactic.

(i)
That John is a fool is obvious.

(ii)
It is obvious that John is a fool.

Therefore, one may ask why it cannot iterate, assuming the correctness of the claims made in the text. For example, in the basic form (iii), one can extrapose the sequence *that John was a fool* to the end of the sentential subject, as in (iv), but it cannot be moved to the end of the main clause, as in (v).

(iii)
?That that John was a fool surprised me was obvious.

(iv)
That it surprised me that John was a fool was obvious.

(v)
*That it surprised me was obvious that John was a fool.

This is not a problem for the claims made in the text, however. In Baltin (1979), the rule that extraposes sentential complements applies optionally to an $\bar{S}$ that is exhaustively dominated by NP. The effect of the structural change is to shift the $\overline{\text{S}}$ out of the NP (leaving *it* in its place) and reattach it to the righthand side of the VP. The requirement of domination by NP in the structural description of the rule prevents unwanted iteration, since an already extraposed $\overline{\text{S}}$ will no longer be dominated by NP.

9. I assume Emond's (1976, ch. 5) analysis of subordinate clauses, in which they are PPs consisting of a preposition taking a sentential complement.

10. Topicalization can be shown to crucially affect quantifier scope, which is sensitive to derived structure (Chomsky, 1972b; Jackendoff, 1972). For example, (i) is contradictory but (ii) is not:

(i)
*I haven't read many books, but many books I have.

(ii)
Many books I haven't read, but many books I have.

This difference is explicable if Topicalization of the direct object in (ii) allows *many* to take wide scope. Assuming that quantifier scope is determined at logical form, Topicalization must precede logical form and is thus a syntactic, rather than a stylistic, movement rule.

Chapter 10

Learnability and the English Auxiliary System

C. L. Baker

The system of English auxiliary verbs is an area of English syntax that despite its narrowness raises a number of issues of interest to anyone who wishes to solve the logical problem of language acquisition as it applies to the learning of English. There are many discussions of the English auxiliary system in the generative syntactic literature. These works as a group contain a wealth of information about what can and cannot be done within the English verbal system, and the accompanying analyses contain many interesting suggestions as to what the rules might be that dictate the acceptability judgments that mature speakers of English are able to make.

I will pay particular attention to a number of what can be referred to as projection puzzles or learnability puzzles. Each puzzle takes the form of the question asked in (1).

(1)
Given a representative set of primary data from English and some rules that are descriptively adequate in their projection from this finite sample, what in the general theory within which these rules were framed would have dictated these rules rather than a descriptively inadequate alternative set of rules?

As in two other papers of mine,[1] I will assume that the primary data provided to an English-speaking child will normally yield very little reliable information about what sentences lie outside the set of acceptable sentences. I am assuming that most of the useful information provided to children takes the form of utterances that the child is to regard as exemplifying grammatical sentences of the language. A representative set of primary data relevant for the acquisition of the rules for the English verbal system might thus include examples of the following sorts, all taken to be well-formed.

(2)

a. John stayed at home.

b. Bill has taken the beer.

c. Martha will open the meeting.

d. Fred is writing a letter.

e. Fred is hungry.

(3)

a. Did John stay at home?

b. Has Bill taken the beer?

c. Will Martha open the meeting?

d. Is Fred writing a letter?

e. Is Fred hungry?

(4)

a. John did not (didn't) stay at home.

b. Bill has not (hasn't) taken the beer.

c. Martha will not (won't) open the meeting.

d. Fred is not (isn't) writing a letter.

e. Fred is not (isn't) hungry.

(5)

a. John **did** stay at home.

b. Bill **has** taken the beer.

c. Martha **will** open the meeting.

d. Fred **is** writing a letter.

e. Fred **is** hungry.

There would of course also be examples that gave evidence of subject-verb agreement on the basis of number and person and that showed the various inflectional forms that this agreement dictated.[2]

Some Projection Puzzles

With this as background, let me offer some concrete projection puzzles. In each instance, the puzzle involves some specific set of ungrammatical sentences. Various transformational theories allow grammars that avoid the generation of these sentences, and a number of specific grammars have actually been proposed. The problem in every case is that the theories also allow grammars that do generate these ungrammatical sentences in addition to the primary set of well-formed sentences. These descriptively inadequate grammars are often at least as simple as the adequate grammars. The general form of these problems can be represented graphically as in (6).

(6)

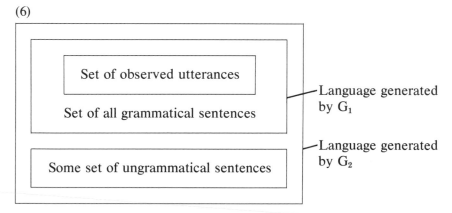

Relative simplicity: G_2 as simple as or simpler than G_1

The general nature of this type of problem has been remarked on frequently: within familiar generative theories, maximally simple grammars tend to suffer from overgeneration, and the data about the language that would motivate corrective complications, data consisting of information to the effect that certain sentences are ill-formed, are nonprimary rather than primary in character.

Do with Other Auxiliary Verbs

As a first puzzle, let us consider the following set of ungrammatical sentences:

(7)
a. *John does have been working.
b. *Fred does not be tall.
c. *Smith **does** have finished.

In Chomsky (1957) these sentences are excluded by postulating that *do* is inserted only in the case where some rule has placed Tense alone (rather than Tense + modal, Tense + *have*, or Tense + *be*) in a position not contiguous to a following verbal element. In several later treatments,[3] these sentences are avoided by making *do* an element of every finite deep structure except those containing modals, with an obligatory rule of *Do* Replacement (or Verb Raising) that replaces *do* with *have* or *be* in any structure in which one of these latter verbs immediately follows *do*. For each of these analyses, it is possible to devise alternative descriptions of equal or greater simplicity which have the bad consequence of generating the ungrammatical sentences in (7) in addition to the grammatical sentences in (2)–(5).

One possibility would be to make two modifications in the analysis in Chomsky (1957). The first would be to revise the basic phrase structure rule for the auxiliary constituent so as to allow *do* as an optional first member.[4]

(8)
Aux → Tns (*do*) (M) (*have en*) (*be ing*)

The slight complication in this one phrase structure rule would be more than offset by simplifications in the transformational component, where all of the rules that referred to Tense alone or Tense plus M, *have*, or *be* could be reformulated simply with Tns + v as the characterization of the affected factor. Under this reformulation, for instance, the rule inverting subject and auxiliary would be stated as in (9b) rather than as in (9a):[5]

(9)

a. NP - Tns ($\left\{ \begin{array}{l} M \\ have \\ be \end{array} \right\}$) - Y

   1   2   3 ⇒ 2 + 1, ∅, 3

b. NP - Tns v - Y
   1   2   3 ⇒ 2 + 1, ∅, 3

This alternative description would yield all of the grammatical examples in (2)–(5), but would in addition give the ungrammatical examples in (7).[6]

Other incorrect descriptions can be derived quite easily by minor modifications of other analyses. For example, suppose that we start with the analysis of Akmajian, Steele, and Wasow (1979), in which *do* is an underlying element of the Aux constituent. An analysis that differed from theirs only in making *Do* Replacement optional instead of obligatory would generate all of the ungrammatical sentences in (7), since it would no longer be required that *be* and perfect *have* replace *do*.[7]

Unstressed *Do*

A second puzzle is provided by the oddness of unstressed *do* in examples such as the following:

(10)
a. *John does raise pigeons.
b. *No one does know the answer.
c. *Who does live here?

In Chomsky (1957) such sentences are avoided by making Affix Hopping obligatory; *do* is inserted only when something prevents Affix Hopping from applying. In a grammar that is the same except for assigning optional status to Affix Hopping, the sentences in (10) would be generated straightforwardly. Similarly, the treatment of Akmajian, Steele, and Wasow (1979) would give these sentences if their rule of *Do* Deletion were made optional instead of obligatory. In Lasnik (1981), where a theory is assumed in which all transformations are optional and where the analysis proposed involves a rule of Verb Raising (having essentially the same ultimate effect as the *Do* Replacement rule of Akmajian, Steele, and Wasow), it is specifically noted (note 10) that sentences with *do* + V sequences are generated.[8]

Modals in Nonfinite Phrases

A third puzzle concerns the modals, which are not allowed in nonfinite structures in English:

(11)
a. *John seems to can do it.
   (Cf. John seems to be able to do it.)
b. *I believe Fred to should pay for the damage.
   (Cf. I believe Fred should pay for the damage.)
c. *John appears to will win.
   (Cf. It appears that John will win.)
d. *Canning go is very important to Julia.
   (Cf. Being able to go is very important to Julia.)

Various means have been suggested for excluding such sentences. Langendoen (1970) suggests a surface structure constraint barring modals from nonfinite constructions; Jackendoff (1972) suggests having modals under an Aux node (along with Tense) and stipulating that nonfinite clauses, unlike matrix Ss, do not contain Aux nodes. Both suggestions involve descriptive complications. Pullum and Wilson (1977) and Gazdar, Pullum, and Sag (1979) propose that the inflectional paradigms for modals are defective, in that they lack infinitival and participial forms. Some variant of this approach seems to me the most promising of the three; I will return to a discussion of what theoretical hypotheses might guarantee an analysis of this sort, even in the absence of direct evidence that sentences like those in (11) are ungrammatical.

Unacceptable Sequences of Auxiliary Verbs

A fourth projection puzzle is provided by sentences showing ungrammatical sequences of auxiliaries:[9]

(12)
a. *John might have had left the day before.
b. *Fred isn't being paying attention.
c. *Martha is having gotten out of bed today.
d. *Arthur must can whistle Dixie.

Three chief descriptive approaches have been employed to solve the problem posed by sentences like these. The first, which goes back to Chomsky (1957), is to specify acceptable sequences by means of some variant of the following phrase structure rule:

(13)
Aux → Tense (M) (*have en*) (*be ing*)

The second, adopted by Emonds (1969), is to deduce the impossibility of certain verbal sequences from general constraints or conditions required for nonauxiliary as well as auxiliary verbs. The third approach, set forth in Akmajian, Steele, and Wasow (1979) and adopted in modified form by other writers since then,[10] is to postulate a series of distinct phrase types based on V. The type of structure Akmajian, Steele, and Wasow envisage is shown in the following trees:

(14)

a.

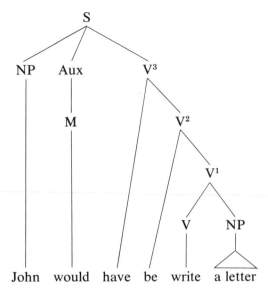

b.

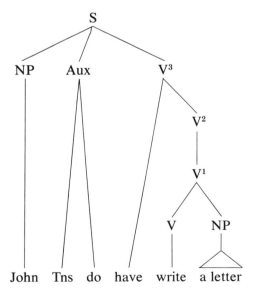

c.

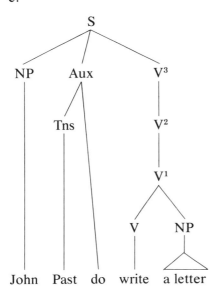

Here, as in previous examples, the analysis in question, although achieving a high degree of descriptive adequacy, suffers from being relatively complicated—more complicated, for instance, than a description in which *have*, *be*, and ordinary verbs headed phrases of the same level. This simpler alternative analysis would give the trees in (15) in place of those in (14):[11]

(15)

a.

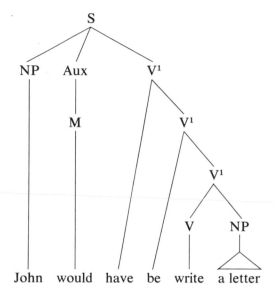

b.

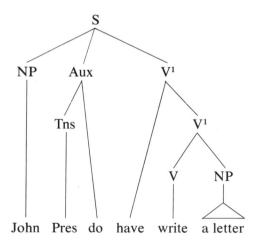

c.

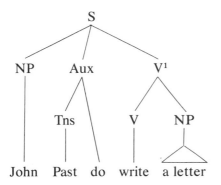

John Past do write a letter

Again, although this analysis overgenerates rather seriously, nothing in the primary data, or in the sort of transformational theories commonly assumed, would exclude it as a possible analysis for English.

A Simple but Descriptively Inadequate Transformational Grammar

To put the point of these puzzles even more sharply, I would like to outline a descriptively inadequate analysis that appears to me to be as highly valued as any other that is consistent with the primary data in (2)–(5) and falls within the framework of the syntactic theories that have been implicit in most generative discussions of English verbal structure. The basic phrase structure rules are those of the so-called main verb analysis:[12]

(16)
a. $V^1 \rightarrow V\ V^1$
b. $V^1 \rightarrow$ *not* V^1

The lexical entries for the auxiliaries are provided with the following feature specifications:

(17)
a. *might:* $\langle V \rangle$ $\langle$ _____ $V^1 \rangle$
b. *have:* $\langle V \rangle$ $\langle$ _____ $V^1 \rangle$
c. *be:* $\langle V \rangle$ $\langle$ _____ $V^1 \rangle$
d. *be:* $\langle V \rangle$ $\langle$ _____ AP $\rangle$
e. *do:* $\langle V \rangle$ $\langle$ _____ $V^1 \rangle$

The transformational rules are the following:[13]

(18)
Subject-Verb Inversion:
X - NP - V - Y
1   2   3   4 $\Rightarrow$ 1, 3 + 2, $\emptyset$, 4

(19)
Not-Verb Inversion
X - *not* - V - Y
1   2   3   4 $\Rightarrow$ 1, 3 + 2, $\emptyset$, 4

With rules like these, we get all of the ungrammatical sentences discussed thus far, as well as the grammatical ones in (2)–(5). The problem now is to try to find a theory that, given the sentences in (2)–(5), would give a set of rules that is not only simple, but descriptively adequate as well.

An Alternative Treatment for English Verbal Structure

I shall propose a set of rules for English verbal structure somewhat different from those that have been proposed to date, and then try to sketch a theory that would make it a relatively simple matter to arrive at this set of rules on the basis of primary data alone. In developing this set of rules and the related hypotheses about universal grammar, I have followed the heuristic of trying to guess what would be the absolute minimum one could say about English verbal structure that would predict its peculiar properties, given a suitable theory of universal grammar as background.

Phrase Structure
The basic phrase structure rules are close to those of the main verb analysis, except that the treatment of modals is slightly different. Modals, *have*, and *be* are heads of phrases, although in the case of the modals, the phrases are not verb phrases.[14] Moreover, in all cases these phrases are phrases of level one in the $\overline{X}$ system. Thus, the trees for (20a) and (20b) are (21a) and (21b) respectively:

(20)
a. John would have been writing a letter.
b. John has written a letter.

(21)

a.

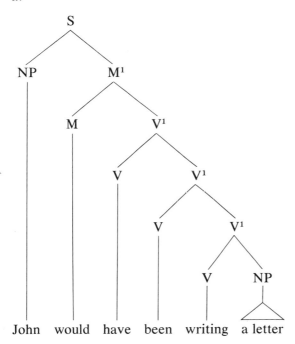

John   would   have   been   writing   a letter

b.

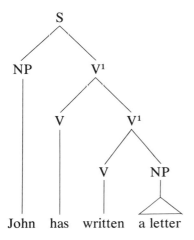

John   has   written   a letter

Subcategorization

The lexical entries for the auxiliaries (as for ordinary verbs) are provided with subcategory features that specify the types of following phrases allowed. In the case of subcategorized V^1 phrases, they must include an indication of a particular inflectional form for the head. For instance, the entry for *have* contains the feature $\langle \underline{\qquad} V^1_{\langle en \rangle} \rangle$, which indicates that the following V^1 must be headed by a past participle. A fuller set of subcategorization specifications might look like (22).[15]

(22)

a. *be:* $\quad \langle \underline{\qquad} V^1_{\langle ing \rangle} \rangle$

b. *have:* $\quad \langle \underline{\qquad} V^1_{\langle en \rangle} \rangle$

c. *might:* $\quad \langle \underline{\qquad} V^1_{\langle Stem \rangle} \rangle$

Another word that belongs on this list, for one quite common colloquial variety of American English, is the word *better,* as used in (23):

(23)

You better watch out; you better not cry.

This use of *better* would have a subcategory specification exactly like that for the more standard modals:

(24)

better: $\quad \langle \underline{\qquad} V^1_{\langle Stem \rangle} \rangle$

For the modal idiom *would rather,* two subcategorization options would be listed. The first would be like that for the other modals, in which a following stem-form V^1 is required. The second would be a feature dictating a following S; this is the feature required for the generation of sentences like (25), pointed out in Huddleston (1978).

(25)

John would rather we stayed here.

On the analysis I am suggesting, sentence (25) would have roughly the following structure:[16]

(26)

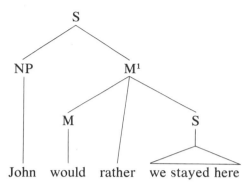

John   would   rather   we stayed here

Paradigm Deficiencies

In the analysis that I am proposing, as in Pullum and Wilson (1977), certain idiosyncrasies in the behavior of the English auxiliary verbs are attributed to deficiencies in the paradigms for the items in question. Perfect *have,* for instance, would have a paradigm in which the past participial slot is unfilled. This feature of the grammar would account for the unacceptability of sentence (12a), **John might have had left the day before*.

The modals are also defective, so defective, in fact, that it is questionable whether they qualify for any verbal paradigm at all, even an incomplete one. I assume that the only syntactic property stipulated for modals in the lexicon (apart from their subcategorization properties) is that the phrases they head are finite, by which I mean that these phrases may go together with a subject NP to form a main clause declarative. Using F to designate this property, the syntactically relevant portion of the lexical entry for a typical modal is as in (27):

(27)

might: $\langle +F \rangle \langle$ _____ $\underset{\langle Stem \rangle}{V^1} \rangle$

Under this analysis, modals will have no *Stem* forms, no *en* forms, and no *ing* forms, so all of the following sentences would be excluded:

(28)
a. *John seems to can do it.   (= 11a)
b. *John will must do it.
c. *We might have could do it.
d. *Canning go is very important to Julia.   (= 11d)

Worth noting in this connection is how finite phrases headed by modals might be related to finite phrases headed by ordinary verbs. A natural suggestion would be that what are commonly referred to as the tensed forms of other verbs are assigned +F status by a redundancy rule of English. The most basic phrase structure rule for English could then be stated as follows:

(29)
$$S \rightarrow NP \; \langle +F \rangle^1$$

Treatment of *Do*
The other item in the English verbal system that clearly requires special stipulations is the auxiliary *do*. The proposal that I will suggest is somewhat different in spirit from those that have been suggested previously in the generative literature; it is more like what might be found in a traditional handbook on English syntax. The basic idea is that there are two types of verbal structures in English, which, for ease of reference, I will call type A and type B. Type A is found in ordinary finite nonemphatic affirmative declarative sentences and in all nonfinite structures (in American English); it consists of a phrase headed either by M, *have, be* or by an ordinary verb. The following would thus count as type A finite structures:

(30)
a. will be working on it
b. have been studying
c. are happy
d. takes Fred to the cleaners
e. disappeared
f. try to stay cool

Type B structures, on the other hand, are typically headed by a form of *do,* with a following complement consisting of a stem-form V^1. For instance, the following are the type B finite structures that correspond to the type A finite structures in (30d–f):[17]

(31)
d. does take Fred to the cleaners
e. did disappear
f. do try to stay cool

These structures arise by the operation of the following rule:

(32)
Given a type A phrase of the form $V^1_{\langle \alpha\text{form}\rangle}$, where α varies over the forms that an English verb may have, the corresponding type B phrase will take the form $do_{\langle \alpha\text{form}\rangle} \ V^1_{\langle Stem\rangle}$.

Certain verbs, however, are "irregular" or "defective," in that their type A structures serve double duty as their type B structures. Thus, the type B structures corresponding to the A structures in (30a–c) are just the following:

(31)
a. will be working on it
b. have been studying
c. are happy

In addition to stipulating the existence of this extra verbal structure type and describing its formation, the grammar of English also stipulates the constructions in which it is employed. Such a list might include the following items:

(33)
a. Inverted finite verb construction[18]
b. Finite verb plus *not* construction
c. Emphatic construction

The constructions mentioned in (33) revolve around what in standard treatments have been described by particular transformational rules, which, given what I have proposed, might be restated informally as follows:

(34)
a. *Subject-Finite Inversion:*
   Move finite head to the left of the subject.
b. *Not-*Finite Inversion:
   Move finite head to the left of the word *not*.
c. *Emphatic:*
   Put emphatic stress on finite head.

The type B structure must somehow be identified as the more marked of the two structures so that the uses of the type A construction can be interpreted by some sort of Elsewhere condition.

This analysis avoids the generation of the ill-formed sentences with *do* given in (7) and (10). In the case of (7), the relevant stipulation is that *have* and *be* have irregular type B structures, idiosyncratically identical to their type A structures rather than being formed with *do*. As with rules for inflectional morphology, I take the existence of an irregular form for a certain item as dictating that the item does not undergo the regular rule. Thus, the ungrammaticality of **doesn't be tall* follows from the existence of the irregular type B finite *is tall* (giving *isn't tall*), just as the ungrammaticality of **choosed* should follow from the existence of the irregular *chose*.

The sentences in (10) are ruled out by listing the uses of the type B constructions. This listing has the effect of excluding the marked variety except in those environments in which it is attested in a language learner's primary data. The fact that sentences like those in (10) are even marginally acceptable may be explained by the circumstance that this use of *do* finites is not altogether missing from the experience of speakers of modern English, being quite common in poetic and legal diction.[19]

A Descriptive Advantage of this Treatment of *Do*

The treatment of *do* just sketched differs markedly from that found in other generative treatments of English. Under most other analyses, beginning with Chomsky (1957) and continuing to the present, nonadjacency of an abstract Tense element with V has been the major criterion for inserting *do;* alternatively, nonadjacency of an underlying *do* to V has been the major criterion for retaining *do*.[20] In Chomsky (1957), for instance, the appearances of *do* in (35) are accounted for by assuming that at a preceding stage of the transformational derivation, given in (36), something intervenes between the abstract Tense element and the following verb.

(35)
a. Did John swim?
b. John did not swim.
c. John **did** swim.

(36)
a. Past John swim
b. John Past not swim
c. John Past E swim

One problem for all of these analyses has been to give a reasonable account of the inversion of the finite auxiliaries with adverbs like *probably, always,* and *never.* When one looks only at sentences containing M, *have,* or *be,* these adverbs seem to call for the same kind of treatment as that given for *not:*

(37)

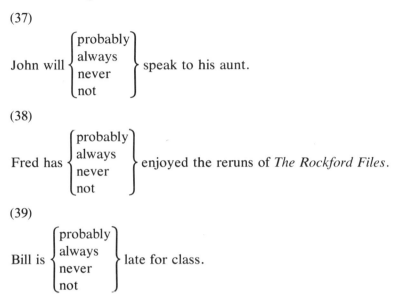

John will { probably / always / never / not } speak to his aunt.

(38)

Fred has { probably / always / never / not } enjoyed the reruns of *The Rockford Files.*

(39)

Bill is { probably / always / never / not } late for class.

To take just one analysis, that of Akmajian, Steele, and Wasow (1979), sentences like (36)–(38) would naturally suggest an analysis in which these adverbs occurred VP-initially, with the preceding Aux constituent serving as the eventual home for *will, has,* and *is,* as depicted in (40).

(40)

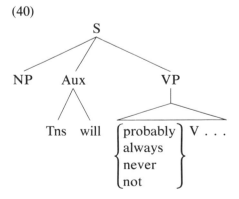

Such a structure, however, would give rise automatically to sentences in which unstressed *do* appeared before these adverbs, as it does before *not:*

(41)

$$\text{John dŏes} \begin{Bmatrix} \text{*probably} \\ \text{*always} \\ \text{*never} \\ \text{not} \end{Bmatrix} \text{go to bed at nine o'clock.}$$

In certain other analyses, notably that of Klima (1964), it is necessary to impose an extrinsic ordering on the rule for switching a finite auxiliary to the left of sentence adverbs and the rule of Affix Hopping.

In the analysis proposed here, by contrast, nothing at all needs to be stipulated to avoid the generation of the starred sentences in (40), since there is never any primary evidence to suggest that these adverbs call for a type B finite phrase. As a result, whatever rules account for the relative position of adverbs and finite auxiliaries will not mention type B structures, and no sentences with illegitimate *do* plus adverb sequences can possibly arise.[21]

Accompanying Hypotheses about Universal Grammar

The treatment of the English verbal system just outlined was constructed with a particular end in view, namely, to have an analysis that would be dictated by some plausible theory of universal grammar, given only primary data about English as evidence about the character of the language. It remains now to say what a theory might look like that would give this description on the basis of exposure to grammatical English sentences.

Main Verb Phrase Structure, Government, and Subcategorization

One area requiring some constraining hypotheses is phrase structure. Specifically, if the proposed phrase structure is correct, then we need constraints that would eliminate from consideration rules like the traditional one expanding an Aux or the initial part of a VP as a linear sequence of auxiliaries. One plausible hypothesis is that the privilege of government as traditionally understood is restricted to phrasal heads. The relevant type of government here concerns the inflectional form that one verbal element dictates for the head verb of a following verb phrase. Given data to suggest that *may* (unlike *probably* or *possibly*) requires a following stem-form verb, it follows easily that *may* must be a phrasal head. Similar evidence would be available for assigning phrasal head status to perfect *have* and also to *be*.

As a further hypothesis, we need to require that subcategorization features involving subcategorized verb phrases make specific mention of the inflectional type or types allowed. That is, of the subcategorization features in (42), only the second should be available.

(42)
a. *have:* $\langle$ _____ $V^1 \rangle$
b. *have:* $\langle$ _____ $V^1_{\langle en \rangle} \rangle$

Paradigm Deficiencies

Let me now turn to the question of what hypotheses about universal grammar might dictate a grammar for English in which are found the defective paradigms I have proposed for the modals and for perfect *have*. That this is a genuine problem can be seen by considering what would happen if regular lexical rules for ordinary verbs were allowed to apply in filling out modal paradigms. In general, the stem form of any English verb can be deduced from the plural present-tense form, since, apart from the paradigm for *be,* these two forms are identical. Likewise, the present participle can be deduced from the stem form. In concrete terms, then, one must ask how a theory might prevent a language learner from deducing a paradigm for *can* in which *can* was listed as a stem form as well as a present plural form, and in which *canning* was listed as the present participle. This incorrect paradigm would be that in (43), allowing the generation of sentences like (11a) and (11d).

(43)

Present sing.	Present pl.	*Stem*	*ing*
can	can	can	canning

The theoretical possibility I am suggesting is that partially filled paradigms in which the attested forms show a high degree of irregularity are exempted from the effects of general morphological redundancy rules that would otherwise fill in unattested forms in individual paradigms. In the case of the modals, the irregularity shown by the attested forms is the absence of the person/number distinction in the present. This irregularity would then have the effect of making these paradigms immune to the usual rule that could fill in the bare stem form on the basis of the present-tense plural form.[22] This suggestion receives independent support from its consequences for another defective verb in English, one that happens not to be an auxiliary. As noted in Pullum and Wilson (1977), the verb *stride* is defective for many speakers of English in not having a past participle. For such speakers the paradigm for this verb is apparently as follows:

(44)

Present pl.	Present sing.	Past	*Stem*	*en*	*ing*
stride	strides	strode	stride	—	striding

Half of an explanation for this gap is that the experience of most speakers does not contain an example of a past participle for this verb. The other half of the explanation, which would explain why the blank in the paradigm is not simply filled in with *strided* by the regular rule for English past participles, is provided by the exemption principle I have suggested. Given that the existing forms suffice to identify this verb as irregular, the paradigm is immune to being completed by the regular rule.

We might consider whether the same idea will afford an explanation for the absence of a past participial form for perfect *have*. The problem that we have to confront in this case is that all speakers of English know that there is a past participle for other uses of *have*. What, then, would prevent a child learning English from borrowing the past participle *had* from the paradigm(s) for nonperfect *have* and using it to fill in the past participial slot in the paradigm for perfect *have?*

One possible answer is provided by the hypothesis that paradigms for radically different senses of the same word (possibly radically different subcategorizations) must be stated independently of one another. If a theory allowed perfect *have* and other uses of *have* to share a common inflectional paradigm, then the most economical representation would be one in which perfect *have* shared the past participial form actually exemplified in sentences containing the other uses of *have*. By contrast, if such paradigm sharing were not permitted, then the paradigms for the two *have*s would have to be arrived at separately, with the result that the absence from primary data of any past participial form for perfect *have* would lead to a corresponding gap in the paradigm.[23]

This prohibition against borrowing or sharing between paradigms of unrelated senses of the same word may also help to explain the ungrammaticality of sentences containing nonfinite forms of the auxiliary *do:*

(45)

a. *Fred might do write a book.[25]

b. *You should be doing take some medicine.

c. *The governor hasn't done keep his promises.

If paradigms were allowed to be shared, the forms *do* (bare stem), *doing*, and *done* could be borrowed from the paradigm of the non-auxiliary *do* to fill the gaps in the paradigm of the auxiliary *do*. In the case of (45), unlike the case of (11) and (12a), there may be an independent reason for the ungrammaticality, namely, the absence from American English of any specific uses to which nonfinite forms of auxiliary *do* are put.

Alternative Structures

I suggested earlier that two major sets of stipulations are needed for describing the behavior of auxiliary *do* in English. The first is a specification of the formation of an alternative type B verbal construction, headed by *do* and filled out with a stem-form verb phrase, together with a list of verbal elements (the modals, perfect *have*, and *be*) whose type B forms are identical with their type A forms. The second set of stipulations concerns the uses to which the type B forms are put, together with a stipulation (to be made unnecessary as a part of English grammar, it is hoped) to the effect that the type A structures are unmarked; that is, they are the appropriate structures to use in all cases where type B structures are not specifically stipulated. The major theoretical problem that arises here is that none of the principles that I have suggested thus far would exclude the possibility of simply assigning auxiliary *do* the same kind of lexical entry that any other verb would get, without saying anything at all about an alternative verbal construction. Under this alternative description, which is identical in relevant respects to the simple but unsatisfactory description discussed earlier, the ungrammatical sentences in (7) and (10) would again be generated.

Although I have not worked out a specific hypothesis that would force the selection of the analysis I am proposing as against the inadequate analysis just described, it seems likely to me that the solution to this problem will involve the fact that auxiliary *do* is semantically empty, in contradistinction to normal verbs. What one might look for would be a principle that would make the first choice among analyses of a semantically empty lexical item like *do* an analysis in which it formed the basis for some kind of alternative structure. Of course we also need a theory of universal grammar that permits such an analysis in the first place—specifically, one that allows grammars to include rules for the formation and use of alternative structures.

As one final matter, it might be worthwhile to have some restrictive hypotheses in hand that would have the effect of excluding both the *do*-insertion analysis and the *do*-deletion analysis. The *do*-deletion analysis would be impossible given the restriction proposed in Baker (1979a, p. 552) to the effect that no rule may involve the deletion of a specified sequence (as opposed to a deletion under identity). The *do*-insertion analysis would also be excluded if this restriction were generalized to exclude insertions of specified sequences as well as deletions. Another possibility for excluding these two analyses would be to require some sort of morphological integrity throughout syntactic derivations, so that it would not be possible to insert an abstract Tense element into a base phrase-marker either in isolation or in company with a word different from the one on which it eventually showed up.[25]

As matters stand, I have given some very rough outlines for an analysis of English verbal structure and for an accompanying theory of universal grammar that would select this analysis on the basis of primary data from English. The proposed analysis is somewhat different, especially in its treatment of *do,* from any of the more or less standard generative analyses. In fairness to these competing treatments, I should note that it is conceivable that alternative hypotheses of universal grammar could be devised that would select them on the basis of primary data alone. My reason for not pursuing these alternative theoretical possibilities in the present paper is simply that in each case in which one of the standard analyses differs from the one offered here, it is difficult for me to see a way of devising the necessary supporting theoretical hypotheses for the relevant aspect of the standard analysis in question.

For any who are still convinced of the correctness of some one of the more standard analyses, I hope that this paper will have given some indication of the theoretical problems that arise in connection with them. For any who accept the broad outlines of what I have proposed here, there is clearly a great deal left to be done. Besides the possibility of improving on individual aspects of this account, either by refining particular proposals or replacing them,[26] several phenomena bearing on English verbal structure have not been touched on at all. Two major topics deserving systematic attention are contraction and ellipsis. Although I have not yet investigated these topics in anything like a thorough fashion, preliminary work leads me to believe that the description I have proposed here can provide the basis for a satisfactory treatment of these additional areas.

Notes

Work on the final version of this paper was supported by the National Science Foundation under Grant BNS-7924672 to the University of Texas at Austin. I would like to thank Gerald Gazdar for detailed criticisms of the preliminary version.

1. Baker (1979a,b).

2. Many other constructions would be exemplified in a representative set of primary data: elliptical constructions, tag questions, *so* and *neither* constructions, etc.

3. Including Pullum and Wilson (1977) and Akmajian, Steele, and Wasow (1979). Similar in its consequences is the analysis presented in Lasnik (1981), where an empty-verb position may appear in Aux, to be filled either by a rule of Verb Raising or by a rule of *Do* Insertion. Lasnik avoids the sentences in (7) by means of a general convention to the effect that less general rules take precedence over more general rules. This proposal has the advantage of not requiring any language-specific stipulation.

4. Many other simple but unsatisfactory possibilities arise, given the abbreviatory conventions employed in Chomsky (1957). To name just two: a grammar could treat *do* as an optional first element in any verb phrase or as a modal. Both proposals, each unsatisfactory in its own way, would be fully consistent with the primary data in (2)–(5).

5. The rule given in Chomsky (1957) is slightly more complicated than (9a), the difference being irrelevant for the present discussion. The rule in (9b) takes seriously the remarks made in Chomsky (1972a), to the effect that v is to be taken as denoting a natural syntactic class consisting of ordinary verbs and auxiliaries.

6. This description obviously gives another set of ill-formed examples, in which an ordinary verb is inverted with the subject:

(i)
*Read you a book on modern music?

(ii)
*Tried John to leave?

7. I have seen the suggestion somewhere (I think it was attributed to Edwin Williams) that obligatory status should be unmarked for transformational rules. This principle would dictate obligatory status for *Do* Replacement in the absence of any examples indicating that it could apply optionally. Given this principle, then, this incorrect alternative to the Akmajian, Steele, and Wasow analysis could not be selected on the basis of English primary data.

8. Lasnik's characterization of this consequence as "completely unobjectionable" seems dubious to me. There is no doubt that sentences with emphasized *do* before an ordinary verb are completely acceptable, but acceptability seems to me to drop drastically when the *do* does not receive emphatic stress. Virtually every generative analysis except Lasnik's contains some rule or stipulation whose express purpose is to exclude such sentences.

9. The grouping of the four sentences in (12) is merely a rough a priori classification; I am not suggesting that all four should be dealt with in the same way. In the analysis I shall propose, (12d) will be grouped implicitly with the sentences in (11) rather than with the other sentences in (12).

10. See, e.g., Baltin (1979) and Lapointe (1980a).

11. It would also be a simple matter to devise an analysis in which there was no separate Aux constituent as a daughter of S.

12. In several such analyses, beginning with Ross (1969), the base rules yield structures in which each auxiliary verb is the head of a VP in its own underlying S, with the rules of Equi-NP Deletion and Subject Raising playing essential roles in deriving the relevant surface structures. The phrase structure rules that I am proposing give something close to the surface structures of these other treatments.

13. The rules as stated are oversimplified slightly. Within a standard theory of transformational rules, as opposed to that proposed in Lasnik and Kupin (1977), it would be necessary to have some term between terms 2 and 3 in each of these rules to allow for intervening sentence adverbs. This is seen immediately in sentences like (i):

(i)

John is not always on time.

A similar point holds for (ii), which I assume is to be derived from (iii) rather than (iv). (See Baker, 1971, for a justification of this position.)

(ii)

Is John always on time?

(iii)

John always is on time.

(iv)

John is always on time.

14. As will be made clear in the next few pages, I am taking the defining properties of the traditional class of modals to be the following: (a) they are not inflectionally recognizable as verbs; (b) they are idiosyncratically allowed as phrasal heads of finite predicate phrases.

15. Perhaps the subcategory features $\langle$ ____ $\langle ing \rangle^1 \rangle$, $\langle$ ____ $\langle en \rangle^1 \rangle$, and $\langle$ ____ $\langle Stem \rangle^1 \rangle$ would be sufficient, without any mention of V as such.

16. This tree represents little more than a guess on the constituent structure of *would rather* constructions.

17. For American English, only finite forms occur, whereas in British English one often encounters nonfinite forms in elliptical constructions:

(i)

I'm not sure that John knew the answer, but he might have done.

(ii)

We're not sure that John lives here, but he may do.

For discussion of the dialectal possibilities in this area, see Huddleston (1978).

The initially attractive view that *done* in (i) and *do* in (ii) are British variants of the American English *done so* and *do so* is rendered implausible by the observation that *do so* does not substitute well for stative verbs, whereas the British construction, like finite *do,* is in no way incompatible with statives, as is made clear by (i) and (ii).

18. This structure enters into the formation of several possibly distinct larger constructions, including at least the following:

(i)

Did he stay at the hotel?   (*Yes-no* questions)

(ii)

Where did he stay?   (Direct *wh*-questions)

(iii)

He stayed at the hotel, didn't he.   (Tag questions)

(iv)

John loves Martha, and so does Fred.   (Preposed *so* and *neither*)

(v)

Not one penny did he spend on frivolity.   (Preposed negatives)

(vi)

John drank more milk than did his brother.   (Inverted comparatives)

19. According to Engblom (1938), the use of unemphatic *do* in ordinary affirmative declaratives peaked during the sixteenth century. His discussion suggests that this temporary failure of complementarity was relatively short-lived.

20. In addition, a requirement that *do* not be emphasized is frequently stipulated.

21. For one treatment, see Baker (1971).

22. As noted in Pullum and Wilson (1977), there is a use of finite *be* for which no corresponding nonfinite forms are found. This is the use that they refer to as modal *be:*

(i)

You are to leave by midnight.   (= P & W (35a))

(ii)

*I want you to be to leave by midnight.   (= P & W (35c))

(iii)

*We expect Cinderella to be to leave by midnight.   (= P & W (35e))

The explanation that I am proposing for the absence of nonfinite forms in the modal paradigm clearly does not extend to this use of *be*. At present, I do not have an explanation for the unacceptability of (ii) and (iii), unless the prohibition against paradigm sharing proposed later in this section turns out to be viable.

23. This explanation has at least one rather dubious hypothetical consequence, namely, that if perfect *have* exhibited regular present-singular and past-tense forms, one would expect the following revised version of (12a) to be grammatical:

(i)
John might have haved left the day before.

Although I have no concrete evidence that such an expectation would be incorrect in this situation, it seems quite conceivable to me that it would be.

24. I have heard a sentence parallel to (44a) in the speech of my four-year-old daughter, where the *do* is used as the bearer of emphasis:

(i)
It might **do** rain.

The intended interpretation was clearly "Maybe it really **will** rain."

25. The theory of inflectional morphology proposed in Lapointe (1980a) would have this effect, as would the theory in Lieber (1980).

26. Given the considerations in note 23, a prime topic for further investigation is the impossibility of iterated perfect auxiliaries.

As usual, Baker has produced an exceptionally stimulating and well-argued paper. However, I have a number of reservations about his analysis of the English auxiliary system. I will organize my discussion by proceeding from my most general comments to my most specific nitpickings.

This paper is part of a larger project that Baker has been carrying out in a series of papers over the past few years. The central feature of this project is the use of learnability as a desideratum in the construction of syntactic analyses. More specifically, Baker argues convincingly that the fact that languages are learned, apparently in the absence of any data about ungrammaticality, provides a powerful criterion of adequacy by which to judge grammars and theories of grammar. On this basis he has argued against a number of widely accepted analyses of aspects of English grammar and has proposed plausible alternatives.

In general, I am enthusiastic about this approach—or indeed about any approach that takes seriously the psychological issues that are commonly cited as the primary motivation behind research in generative grammar. My only reservation stems from the heavy reliance in Baker's argumentation on the assumption of a high degree of psychological reality—that is, a close correspondence between linguists' grammars and (portions of) the mental representations speakers have of their languages. Attempts to find evidence for such a correspondence have been notoriously unsuccessful. The significance of this fact is a matter of considerable controversy, which I do not intend to get involved in here (for my views, see Osherson and Wasow, 1976; Wasow, 1978a,b). I think it is possible to make use of Baker's learnability criterion irrespective of one's opinion of the existing evidence regarding psychological reality, for it is clear that any psychologically real grammar must satisfy the criterion (though not conversely). Since even a skeptic about the importance of psychological reality (e.g., myself) must admit that, all else being equal, a psychologically real grammar is preferable to a psychologically unreal one, it follows that a grammar that satisfies Baker's criterion is to be preferred over one that doesn't. Thus, my reservations about the psychological reality question can be viewed simply as doubts about whether all else is ever really equal. I will put these doubts aside for the remainder of this paper.

In the papers based on this desideratum, Baker has argued for very simple and general rule systems in grammars, with correspondingly richer lexical entries. Much other recent research points in the same direction, and I have no quarrel with this tendency. There is a temptation, however, to regard moving something out of the transformational component into the lexicon as a solution to the projection problem: if we don't need to learn exceptions to rules, then the projection problem disappears. Although this may be the case in certain instances, I don't think it is true in general. Specifically, wherever there is evidence of "the creative aspect of language use"—that is, the use of words in constructions that the speaker has never heard those words used in before—it is necessary to posit some sort of productive rule. However we formulate such rules—as transformations, lexical redundancy rules, context-free metarules, or what have you—if they have lexical exceptions, then the projection problem arises. More succinctly, if there is generalization beyond the input data, then we must account for why overgeneralization does not occur.

Taking a concrete example, suppose we try to account for the well-known exceptions to passivization by saying that these are verbs whose lexical entries don't list passive participles. Then we are stuck with the problem of accounting for how speakers learn that they don't have passive participles. It is not enough to say simply that speakers list passive participles only for verbs they have encountered in the passive, for it is clear that both adults and children do passivize creatively. My favorite example is my four-year-old daughter's exclamation to a friend who had just tripped and fallen on her: *I don't like being falled down on!* It seems to me that similar projection problems might arise regarding the dative construction, even if we eliminate the Dative Movement transformation. Suppose I were to coin a new verb, *to satellite,* meaning 'to transmit information via satellite,' by saying to a friend, *I will satellite my answer to you next week;* it seems to me that it would be perfectly appropriate for my friend to report this remark by saying, *Wasow says he will satellite me his answer next week.* If my intuition on this is correct (I emphasize that I do not have any other data to confirm my feelings), then even a lexical analysis of datives will require some general principles distinguishing between occurring and nonoccurring generalizations beyond the input data.

In short, wherever linguistic creativity is manifest, the existence of lexical exceptions creates a projection puzzle. The key in all such cases is to find general principles that will permit the learning of both the rule and its exceptions without requiring any negative input. In the present paper, Baker has, in fact, proposed several such principles, which are intended to solve some of the projection problems connected with the English auxiliary system.

Baker's Principles

Baker's proposed principles are, for the most part, formal rather than substantive, in the sense that they are concerned with the structure of possible grammars, rather than with their content. Put another way, Baker concerns himself almost entirely with capturing distributional regularities in the language in terms of the organization of the lexicon and the geometry of phrase-markers.

Later, I will argue for an alternative that relies more on substantive universals. That is, I will argue that categorial labels play a crucial role in the acquisition process and that the categorial labels are in part a function of meanings.

It seems to me that there are good grounds for trying to formulate principles that are substantive, in this sense. The difficulty of the task of accounting for the possibility of language acquisition can only be increased if we ignore the fact that children have as input not only strings from the language but also information about what those strings mean, provided by the context of use. Indeed, unless our acquisition principles make use of nondistributional information, we are, in effect, assuming *text presentation* (in the sense of Gold, 1967); that is, we are assuming that the child has only positive syntactic evidence to work with. Gold, and then Wexler and Hamburger (1973), showed that learnability is far more difficult to achieve on the basis of text presentation than with a richer data base. In fact, Gold proved that virtually all familiar classes of formal languages are text unlearnable, a result that provided the primary motivation for assuming a richer input in subsequent work on learnability. Bringing aspects of meaning into the acquisition process is the obvious move to make in this direction.

Having expressed this general reservation, let me turn to a few of Baker's specific proposals.

1. The proposed principle that "as with rules for inflectional morphology, I take the existence of an irregular form for a certain item as dictating that the item does not undergo the regular rule", incorrectly rules out the alternation between *Have you the time?* and *Do you have the time?* (Incidentally, this principle also makes some wrong predictions in the case of morphology, e.g., by ruling out pairs like *leaped/leapt, dived/dove, (has) proved/proven,* and *cacti/ cactuses*). However, this is a minor problem, for the principle in question can be made part of the evaluation metric rather than an absolute.

2. Along similar lines, I question the claim "that partially filled paradigms in which the attested forms show a high degree of irregularity are exempted from the effects of general morphological redundancy rules that would otherwise fill in unattested forms in individual paradigms." Well-known facts of child language argue against this claim, since children use correct irregular forms (e.g., *went*) before they begin to overregularize (*goed*). The fact that irregular stative verbs can appear in the progressive in appropriate contexts also seems to be a counterexample: *More and more students are knowing the answer to this question every year. Know* is irregular, and, being stative, it is used in the progressive only in highly unusual contexts. Nevertheless, I doubt that it is necessary to have heard it in the progressive in order to accept this example.

3. More centrally, I take issue with what Baker calls the prohibition against paradigm sharing. He needs this, e.g., to account for the failure of modal *need* to appear in ⟨−F⟩ contexts: **I don't expect John to need study.* It seems to me implausible to suggest that speakers actually encounter all elements in the paradigms of all irregular verbs and auxiliaries, especially such relatively rare forms as the modal *need* or the *is to* construction. A case in point is the following from my local newspaper: *Through the years I have read many letters in the* Times Tribune *that have upset me. And many times **I have been going to***

send in a response (emphasis added). I sincerely doubt that most people have ever encountered *be going to* in the perfect before, yet its use here is unquestionably grammatical. I believe that paradigm sharing does, in fact, take place, and that its failure to occur in some cases demands a different explanation. In the case of *need,* I would attribute it to a categorial difference between verbs and modals. (Note that paradigm sharing never takes place between items of different grammatical categories, e.g., between the verb and the noun *need*).

An Alternative

I would like to defend an alternative to Baker's analysis of the English auxiliary system, namely, the analysis presented in Akmajian, Steele, and Wasow (1979).[1] More specifically, I will argue that our analysis fares at least as well as Baker's in terms of his learnability criterion, and that this is the case because our analysis incorporates rather strong claims about substantive universals.

A crucial feature of our analysis is that it includes a category Aux containing tense, modals, and (under some circumstances) aspectual verbs. We argued that Aux is part of universal grammar. This means that we can use it as a label for identifying certain elements across languages as being embodiments of the same thing. It also means that it is something that children learning languages would expect to find. That is, the universal properties we attribute to auxiliaries can be used by the language learner in the construction of a grammar. We believe that these properties can serve as vital clues to the learner.

The main characteristics we attribute to the Aux are the following.[2,3]

1.
It contains elements expressing tense and/or modality, i.e., temporal and/or alethic operators.
2.
It is also often involved in the expression of other sentence or discourse level notions, e.g., deontic operators, negation, questioning, commanding, and subject agreement.
3.
It consists of a small, fixed set of lexical items or affixes; it is never a productive phrasal category.
4.
Its elements exhibit syntactic properties distinguishing them from everything else in the language. Among these properties is a relatively restricted range of positional possibilities, including a strong tendency to appear at the periphery of a clause (i.e., in sentential first, second, or final position).
5.
Its elements tend to be reduced phonologically, through contraction or cliticization, or simply by virtue of being inflections.

Let us assume that the child learning a language will be looking for elements exhibiting these properties. Let us assume further that linguistic and nonlinguistic context provide enough evidence about the meanings of utterances for the child to make use of the first two characteristics listed. A number of properties of the English auxiliary system will then come as no surprise to the child;

though they are not strictly deducible from the general properties of Aux, they are among the first hypotheses a learner would entertain.[4]

First, the fact that Aux (and hence modals and auxiliary *do*) are restricted to finite environments follows almost by definition. Since Tense is one of the possible expansions of Aux in our grammar, any environment permitting Aux is an environment permitting Tense. Since modals and auxiliary *do* can be introduced only under Aux, they will be impossible where Tense is impossible. Notice, crucially, that Tense and modality are the primary notional categories one expects to find in Aux.

Second, the fact that it is the modals, *have,* and *be* which, in Baker's terminology, have "irregular type B structures" is a function of the fact that they express the meanings that, across languages, are expressed by elements of Aux. The learner does not have to master the syntactic "irregularity" of this particular set of "verbs" as an arbitrary fact about English; rather, the set of elements involved is just what one would expect on universal grounds.

Similarly, the fact that just these elements are involved in questioning, negation, and contraction comes as no surprise, given that they are elements of Aux.

One problem Baker addresses which is not handled so neatly in terms of a universal category Aux is the sequencing of modals, *have,* and *be.* Akmajian, Steele, and Wasow (1979) dealt with it by distinguishing three levels of verb phrase, V^1, V^2, and V^3, and subcategorizing auxiliary elements (and some main verbs) for different types of V^n complements. Gazdar, Pullum, and Sag (1980) present a descriptively more satisfactory system, which also handles the ordering restrictions in terms of subcategorization. How are such subcategorizations to be learned? I have no real answer to this question at present, but I do have some rather sketchy ideas. It seems to me that this is another case in which meanings might be useful. It has frequently been suggested (e.g., McCawley, 1971; Pullum and Wilson, 1977; Gazdar, Pullum, and Sag, 1980) that at least some of the cooccurrence restrictions in question were actually semantic restrictions. For example, McCawley suggested that the ordering of the perfect *have* and the progressive *be* was a function of the purported fact that statives couldn't appear in the progressive, and *have* is stative. As the example of the progressive stative *knowing* showed (and as we argued in Akmajian, Steele, and Wasow, 1979), this account is untenable. However, it seems to me that the relative rarity of progressive statives might be used in an account of the acquisition of the ordering restrictions constructed along the lines suggested by Grimshaw in chapter 6. Specifically, suppose that the child's first hypothesis is that there is a one-to-one match between syntactic categories and semantic categories. The child therefore assigns to V^1 (the category of complements to progressive *be*) the semantic feature of nonstativity. On the basis of this assignment, together with the stativity of the perfect *have,* the child is forced to exclude *have* from V^1 and hence puts it in V^2. Later, when progressive statives are encountered, the syntactic category V^2 with its various properties is already well established, so the ordering restriction between *have* and *be* is absolute.

Summarizing, if one assumes substantive principles of the sort proposed by Akmajian, Steele, and Wasow (1979) or Steele et al. (forthcoming), then the meanings expressed by the elements in question provide extremely useful evidence to the learner about how they should be analyzed syntactically. Given the tremendous difficulty of the projection problem, I see no reason to exclude this sort of approach to its solution.

Although I don't claim that all the projection puzzles about the auxiliary system are accounted for under the approach advocated here, it seems to me to be no worse off than the system Baker proposes. Hence, in this case, Baker's learnability criterion does not provide a decisive choice between analyses.

Notes

1. Akmajian, Steele, and Wasow (1979) has been the object of a number of criticisms, of varying degrees of soundness. In my opinion, by far the most serious of these are put forward by Gazdar, Pullum, and Sag (1980). However, I have argued (Wasow, 1980) that our most important universal claims are in general supported, not undermined, by Gazdar, Pullum, and Sag's alternative analysis, and these are the claims on which the following discussion is based.

2. See Steele et al. (forthcoming) for a more careful discussion of these and other characteristics, in which a proper subset of the characteristics is distinguished as definitional.

3. At the conference at which these comments were presented, Edwin Williams pointed out that the English complementizer system also satisfies the characterization of Aux given here. This is especially interesting in light of the close relation between auxiliaries and complementizers that has often been noted (see, e.g., Pullum and Wilson, 1977). Unfortunately, I cannot at present offer any modifications of the list given here that would exclude complementizers.

4. See Lapointe (1980b) for a far more explicit treatment of the logical problem of language acquisition with respect to the category Aux.

Bibliography

Aissen, J., and D. Perlmutter (1976). Clause Reduction in Spanish. In H. Thompson, K. Whistler, et al., eds., *Proceedings of the Second Annual Meeting of the Berkeley Linguistics Society*. Berkeley Linguistics Society, Berkeley, Calif.

Akmajian, A. (1975). More Evidence for an NP Cycle. *Linguistic Inquiry* 6, 115–130.

Akmajian, A. (1977). The Complement Structure of Perception Verbs in an Autonomous Syntax Framework. In Culicover, Wasow, and Akmajian.

Akmajian, A., S. Steele, and T. Wasow (1979). The Category AUX in Universal Grammar. *Linguistic Inquiry* 10, 1–64.

Allen, C. (1977). *Topics in Diachronic English Syntax*. Doctoral dissertation, University of Massachusetts, Amherst, Mass.

Allen, C. (1980). Movement and Deletion in Old English. *Linguistic Inquiry* 11, 261–323.

Anderson, J. M. (1971). *The Grammar of Case: Towards a Localist Theory*. Cambridge, England: Cambridge University Press.

Anderson, J. R. (1975). Computer Simulation of a Language Acquisition System: A First Report. In R. Solso, ed., *Information Processing and Cognition: The Loyola Symposium*. Washington: Erlbaum.

Anderson, S. (1974). *The Organization of Phonology*. New York: Academic Press.

Anderson, S. (1975). On the Interaction of Phonological Rules of Various Types. *Journal of Linguistics* 11, 39–62.

Aronoff, M. (1976). *Word Formation in Generative Grammar*. Cambridge, Mass.: The MIT Press.

Asakawa, T. (1979). Where does the Extraposed Element Move to? *Linguistic Inquiry* 10, 505–508.

Bach, E. (1968). Two Proposals Concerning the Simplicity Metric in Phonology. *Glossa* 2, 128–149.

Bach, E. (1979). Control in Montague Grammar. *Linguistic Inquiry* 10, 515–532.

Baker, C. L. (1971). Stress Level and Auxiliary Behavior in English. *Linguistic Inquiry* 2, 167–181.

Baker, C. L. (1979a). Syntactic Theory and the Projection Problem. *Linguistic Inquiry* 10, 533–581.

Baker, C. L. (1979b). Remarks on Complementizers, Filters, and Learnability. Unpublished paper, University of Texas at Austin.

Baltin, M. (1978a). PP as a Bounding Node. In M. Stein, ed., *Proceedings of the Eighth Annual Meeting of the North Eastern Linguistic Society,* University of Massachusetts, Amherst.

Baltin, M. (1978b). *Toward a Theory of Movement Rules.* Doctoral dissertation, MIT, Cambridge, Mass.

Baltin, M. (1978c). The Semantics of Quantifier-float. Paper presented at the Ninth Annual Meeting of the North Eastern Linguistic Society, City University of New York.

Baltin, M. (1979). A Landing Site Theory of Movement Rules. Unpublished paper, New York University.

Belletti, A., L. Brandi, G. Nencioni, and L. Rizzi, eds. (1980). *Theory of Markedness in Generative Grammar: Proceedings of III Glow Conference.* Scuola Normale Superiore, Pisa.

Berwick, R. (1980). Learning Structural Descriptions of Grammatical Rules from Examples. *Artificial Intelligence Memo* TR–578, Laboratory of Computer Science, MIT, Cambridge, Mass.

Berwick, R., and K. Church (1979). Unpublished talk, Cognitive Science Seminar, October 1979, MIT, Cambridge, Mass.

den Besten, H. (1980). A Case Filter for Passives. In Belletti et al.

Biermann, A., and J. Feldman (1972). A Survey of Results in Grammatical Inference. In S. Watanabe, ed., *Frontiers in Pattern Recognition.* New York: Academic Press.

Biggs, B. (1961). The Structure of New Zealand Maaori. *Anthropological Linguistics* 3, 1–54.

Bing, J. (1979). *Aspects of English Prosody.* Doctoral dissertation, University of Massachusetts, Amherst.

Bloomfield, L. (1933). *Language.* New York: Holt, Rinehart & Winston.

Bolinger, D. (1971). *The Phrasal Verb in English.* Cambridge, Mass.: Harvard University Press.

Bowerman, M. (1980). An Evaluation of Reorganizational Processes in Lexical and Semantic Development. For *State of the Art Workshop,* University of Pennsylvania, Philadelphia.

Braine, M. (1971a). On Two Models of the Internalization of Grammars. In D. Slobin, ed., *The Ontogenesis of Grammar*. New York: Academic Press.

Braine, M. (1971b). The Acquisition of Language in Infant and Child. In C. E. Reed, ed., *The Learning of Language*. New York: Appleton.

Braine, M. (1974). On What Might Constitute Learnable Phonology. *Language* 50, 270–299.

Brame, M. (1972). On the Abstractness of Phonology: Maltese ʕ. In M. Brame, ed., *Contributions to Generative Phonology*. Austin: University of Texas Press.

Bresnan, J. (1970). On Complementizers: Toward a Syntactic Theory of Complement Types. *Foundations of Language* 6, 297–321.

Bresnan, J. (1972). *The Theory of Complementation in English Syntax*. Doctoral dissertation, MIT, Cambridge, Mass.

Bresnan, J. (1976). Evidence for a Theory of Unbounded Transformations. *Linguistic Analysis* 2, 353–393.

Bresnan, J. (1978). A Realistic Model of Transformational Grammar. In M. Halle, J. Bresnan, and G. Miller, eds., *Linguistic Theory and Psychological Reality*. Cambridge, Mass.: The MIT Press.

Bresnan, J. (1979). Unpublished lecture notes, MIT.

Bresnan, J. (1980). Polyadicity: Part I of a Theory of Lexical Rules and Representations. In Hoekstra, Hulst, and Moortgat.

Bresnan, J., and J. Grimshaw (1978). The Syntax of Free Relatives in English. *Linguistic Inquiry* 9, 331–391.

Brown, R. (1957). Linguistic Determinism and the Part of Speech. *Journal of Abnormal and Social Psychology* 55, 1–5.

Brown, R. (1973). *A First Language: The Early Stages*. Cambridge, Mass.: Harvard University Press.

Brown, R., C. B. Cazden, and U. Bellugi (1969). The Child's Grammar from I to III. In J. P. Hill, ed., *Minnesota Symposium on Child Psychology,* vol. 2. Minneapolis: University of Minnesota Press.

Brown, R., and C. Hanlon (1970). Derivational Complexity and Order of Acquisition in Child Speech. In J. Hayes, ed., *Cognition and the Development of Language*. New York: Wiley.

Butler, M. C. (1977). Reanalysis of Object as Subject in Middle English Impersonal Constructions. *Glossa* 11, 155–170.

Campbell, A. (1959). *Old English Grammar*. Oxford: Clarendon Press.

Carlson, G., and T. Roeper (1980). Morphology and Subcategorization: Case and the Unmarked Verb Complex. In Hoekstra, Hulst, and Moortgat.

Cathey, J., and R. Demers (1976). On Establishing Linguistic Universals. *Language* 52, 611–630.

Chen, M. (1973). On the Formal Expression of Natural Rules in Phonology. *Journal of Linguistics* 9, 223–249.

Chomsky, N. (1957). *Syntactic Structures*. The Hague: Mouton.

Chomsky, N. (1962). Explanatory Models in Linguistics. In E. Nagel, P. Suppes, and A. Tarski, eds., *Logic, Methodology, and Philosophy of Science*. Stanford: Stanford University Press.

Chomsky, N. (1964a). The Logical Basis of Linguistic Theory. In H. Lunt, ed., *Proceedings of the Ninth International Congress of Linguists*. The Hague: Mouton.

Chomsky, N. (1964b). *Current Issues in Linguistic Theory*. The Hague: Mouton.

Chomsky, N. (1965). *Aspects of the Theory of Syntax*. Cambridge, Mass.: The MIT Press.

Chomsky, N. (1970a). Remarks on Nominalization. In R. Jacobs and P. Rosenbaum, eds., *Readings in English Transformational Grammar*. Waltham, Mass.: Ginn.

Chomsky, N. (1970b). *Current Issues in Linguistic Theory*. The Hague: Mouton.

Chomsky, N. (1972a). Some Empirical Issues in the Theory of Transformational Grammar. In Peters, ed.

Chomsky, N. (1972b). Deep Structure, Surface Structure, and Semantic Interpretation. In N. Chomsky, *Studies on Semantics in Generative Grammar*. The Hague: Mouton.

Chomsky, N. (1973). Conditions on Transformations. In S. Anderson and P. Kiparsky, eds., *A Festschrift for Morris Halle*. New York: Holt, Rinehart & Winston.

Chomsky, N. (1975). Questions of Form and Interpretation. *Linguistic Analysis* 1, 75–109.

Chomsky, N. (1976). *Reflections on Language*. New York: Pantheon.

Chomsky, N. (1977a). On WH-Movement. In Culicover, Wasow, and Akmajian.

Chomsky, N. (1977b). Conditions on Rules of Grammar. *Linguistic Analysis* 2, 303–351.

Chomsky, N. (1980a). On Binding. *Linguistic Inquiry* 11, 1–46.

Chomsky, N. (1980b). On Markedness and Core Grammar. In Belletti et al.

Chomsky, N. (1980c). *Rules and Representations*. New York: Columbia University Press.

Chomsky, N. (1981). Principles and Parameters in Syntactic Theory. In Hornstein and Lightfoot.

Chomsky, N. (forthcoming). *Lectures on Binding and Government*. Dordrecht: Foris.

Chomsky, N., and M. Halle (1968). *The Sound Pattern of English*. New York: Harper & Row.

Chomsky, N., and H. Lasnik (1977). Filters and Control. *Linguistic Inquiry* 8, 425–504.

Crothers, J. (1971). On the Abstractness Controversy. *Project on Linguistic Analysis Reports* Series 2, No. 12, University of California, Berkeley.

Culicover, P., T. Wasow, and A. Akmajian, eds. (1977). *Formal Syntax*. New York: Academic Press.

Culicover, P., and K. Wexler (1977). Some Syntactic Implications of a Theory of Language Learnability. In Culicover, Wasow, and Akmajian.

Derwing, B. (1973). *Transformational Grammar as a Theory of Language Acquisition*. Cambridge, England: Cambridge University Press.

Dowty, D. (1978). Governed Transformations in Montague Grammar. *Linguistic Inquiry* 9, 393–426.

Dresher, B. E. (1978). *Old English and the Theory of Phonology*. Doctoral dissertation, University of Massachusetts, Amherst. (Reproduced by the Graduate Linguistic Student Association, University of Massachusetts at Amherst.)

Dresher, B. E. (1980). The Mercian Second Fronting: A Case of Rule Loss in Old English. *Linguistic Inquiry* 11, 47–73.

Dresher, B. E. (1981). Abstractness and Explanation in Phonology. In Hornstein and Lightfoot.

Dresher, B. E., and N. Hornstein (1979). Trace Theory and NP Movement Rules. *Linguistic Inquiry* 10, 65–82.

Emonds, J. (1969). A Structure-Preserving Constraint on NP Movement Transformations. In R. Binnick, A. Davison, G. Green, and J. Morgan, eds., *Papers from the Fifth Regional Meeting of the Chicago Linguistic Society*, University of Chicago, Chicago.

Emonds, J. (1976). *A Transformational Approach to English Syntax*. New York: Academic Press.

Engblom, V. (1938). *On the Origin and Early Development of the Auxiliary Do*. Lund, Sweden: C. W. K. Gleerup.

Ferreiro, E. (1971). *Les relations temporelles dans le langage de l'enfant*. Geneva: Droz.

Flores d'Arcais, G. (1978). The Acquisition of the Subordinating Constructions in Children's Language. In R. Campbell and P. Smith, eds., *Recent Advances in the Psychology of Language*. New York: Plenum Press.

Foley, J. (1977). *Foundations of Theoretical Phonology*. Cambridge, England: Cambridge University Press.

Fraser, B. (1976). *The Verb-Particle Combination in English.* New York: Academic Press.

Frazier, L. (1978). *On Comprehending Sentences — Syntactic Parsing Strategies.* Doctoral dissertation, University of Connecticut, Storrs.

Freidin, R. (1978). Cyclicity and the Theory of Grammar. *Linguistic Inquiry* 9, 519–550.

Fu, K. S., and T. Booth (1975). Grammatical Inference: Introduction and Survey I. *IEEE Transactions on Systems, Man, and Cybernetics* SMC 5, 95–111.

Fudge, E. C. (1967). The Nature of Phonological Primes. *Journal of Linguistics* 3, 1–36.

Gazdar, G. (1979). Unbounded Dependencies and Coordinate Structures. Unpublished paper, University of Sussex.

Gazdar, G., G. Pullum, and I. Sag (1979). The Phrase Structure of the English Auxiliary System. Unpublished handout, University of Sussex.

Gazdar, G., G. Pullum, and I. Sag (1980). A Phrase Structure Grammar for the English Auxiliary System. Paper presented at the Fourth Groningen Round Table, July 1980.

Gold, E. M. (1967). Language Identification in the Limit. *Information and Control* 16, 447–474.

Green, G. (1974). *Semantics and Syntactic Regularity.* Reproduced by the Indiana University Linguistics Club, Bloomington.

Grimshaw, J. (1975). Evidence for Relativization by Deletion in Chaucerian Middle English. In E. Kaisse and J. Hankamer, eds., *Proceedings of the Fifth Annual Meeting of the North Eastern Linguistic Society,* Harvard University, Cambridge, Mass.

Grimshaw, J. (1977). *English Wh Constructions and the Theory of Grammar.* Doctoral dissertation, University of Massachusetts, Amherst.

Grimshaw, J. (1979). Complement Selection and the Lexicon. *Linguistic Inquiry* 10, 279–326.

Grosu, A., and S. Thompson (1977). Constraints on the Distribution of NP Clauses. *Language* 53, 104–151.

Guéron, J. (1980). On the Syntax and Semantics of PP Extraposition. *Linguistic Inquiry* 11, 637–678.

Hale, K. (1968). Review of P. Hohepa (1967). *Journal of the Polynesian Society* 77, 83–99.

Hale, K. (1973). Deep-surface Canonical Disparities in Relation to Analysis and Change: An Australian Example. In T. Sebeok, ed., *Current Trends in Linguistics* 11, The Hague: Mouton.

Halle, M. (1978). Formal vs. Functional Considerations in Phonology. *Studies in the Linguistic Sciences* 8, 123–134.

Halle, M., and J.-R. Vergnaud (1978). Metrical Structures in Phonology. Unpublished paper, MIT.

Halvorsen, P.-K. (1977). *The Syntax and Semantics of Cleft Constructions.* Doctoral dissertation, University of Texas, Austin. (Available as *Texas Linguistic Forum* 12.)

Hamburger, H., and K. Wexler (1973). Identifiability of a Class of Transformational Grammars. In H. J. J. Hintikka, J. Moravcsik, and P. Suppes, eds., *Approaches to Natural Language.* Dordrecht: Reidel.

Hamburger, H., and Wexler, K. (1975). A Mathematical Theory of Learning Transformational Grammar. *Journal of Mathematical Psychology* 12, 137–177.

Harris, J. (1969). *Spanish Phonology.* Cambridge, Mass.: The MIT Press.

Harris, J. (1970). A Note on Spanish Plural Formation. *Language* 46, 928–930.

Harris, J. (1979). Some Observations on "Substantive Principles in Natural Phonology." In D. Dinnsen, ed., *Current Approaches to Phonological Theory.* Bloomington: Indiana University Press.

Harris, J. (1980). Nonconcatenative Morphology and Spanish Plurals. *Journal of Linguistic Research* 1, 15–31.

Hayes, B. (1980). *A Metrical Theory of Stress Rules.* Doctoral dissertation, MIT, Cambridge, Mass.

Hendrick, R. (1978). The Phrase-structure of Adjectives and Comparatives. *Linguistic Analysis* 4, 255–299.

Higgins, R. (1973). *The Pseudocleft Construction in English.* Doctoral dissertation, MIT, Cambridge, Mass.

Hjelmslev, L. (1961). *Prolegomena to a Theory of Language.* Translated by F. Whitfield. Madison: University of Wisconsin Press.

Hoekstra, T., H. Hulst, and M. Moortgat, eds. (1980). *Lexical Grammar.* Dordrecht: Foris.

Hohepa, P. (1967). *A Profile Generative Grammar of Maori.* Indiana University Publications in Anthropology and Linguistics, *International Journal of American Linguistics* Memoir 20.

Hooper, J. (1976). *An Introduction to Natural Generative Phonology.* New York: Academic Press.

Hornstein, N., and A. Weinberg (1978). On Preposition Stranding. Unpublished paper, MIT.

Hornstein, N., and A. Weinberg (1980). Extraction, Government, and Parameters of Grammar. Unpublished paper, Columbia University.

Hornstein, N., and D. Lightfoot, eds. (1981). *Explanation in Linguistics*. London: Longmans.

Horst, J. (1980). Preposition Stranding in Dutch. *Cornucopia* 2, 85–97.

Howren, R. (1967). The Generation of Old English Weak Verbs. *Language* 43, 674–685.

Huddleston, R. (1978). On the Constituent Structure of VP and Aux. *Linguistic Analysis* 4, 31–59.

Jack, G. (1978). *Rome's destruction* and the History of English. *Journal of Linguistics* 14, 311–312.

Jackendoff, R. (1972). *Semantic Interpretation in Generative Grammar*. Cambridge, Mass.: The MIT Press.

Jackendoff, R. (1977). $\bar{X}$ *Syntax: A Study of Phrase Structure*. Cambridge, Mass.: The MIT Press.

Janssen, R., G. Kok, and L. Meertens (1977). On Restrictions on Transformational Grammars Reducing the Generative Power. *Linguistics and Philosophy* 1, 111–118.

Kageyama, T. (1975). Relational Grammar and the History of Subject Raising. *Glossa* 9, 165–181.

Kaplan, R., and Bresnan, J. (in press). A Formal System for Grammatical Representation. In J. Bresnan, ed., *The Mental Representation of Grammatical Relations*. Cambridge, Mass.: The MIT Press.

Katz, N., E. Baker, and J. MacNamara (1974). What's in a Name? A Study of how Children Learn Common and Proper Names. *Child Development* 45, 469–473.

Kaufman, E. (1974). Navajo Spatial Enclitics: A Case for Unbounded Rightward Movement. *Linguistic Inquiry* 5, 507–534.

Kaye, J. (1975). A Functional Explanation for Rule Ordering in Phonology. In R. Grossman, L. San, and T. Vance, eds., *Papers from the Parasession on Functionalism*, Chicago Linguistic Society, Chicago.

Kaye, J., and J. Lowenstamm (1980). Markedness and Syllable Structure. *Proceedings of the Fourth G. L. O. W. Conference*, Pisa.

Kaye, J., and J. Lowenstamm (to appear). Son of Markedness and Syllable Structure. Unpublished paper, University of Quebec at Montreal and Tel Aviv University.

Kaye, J., and Y.-C. Morin (1978). Il n'y a pas de Règles de Troncation, Voyons! *Proceedings of the Twelfth International Congress of Linguists*, Vienna.

Kayne, R. (1979). Case-marking and Logical Form. Unpublished paper, University of Paris VII.

Kayne, R. (1980). On Certain Differences between English and French. Unpublished paper, University of Paris VII.

Kean, M.-L. (1974). *The Theory of Markedness in Generative Grammar*. Doctoral dissertation, MIT, Cambridge, Mass.

Kean, M.-L. (1979). *On a Theory of Markedness*. Social Sciences Research Report 41, University of California at Irvine.

Keyser, S. J. (1975). Metathesis and Old English Phonology. *Linguistic Inquiry* 6, 377–411.

Keyser, S. J., and W. O'Neil (1980). A Metrical Rule in Early English. Unpublished paper, MIT.

Kiparsky, P. (1965). *Phonological Change*. Doctoral dissertation, MIT, Cambridge, Mass.

Kiparsky, P. (1973a). Phonological Representations. In O. Fujimura, ed., *Three Dimensions of Linguistic Theory*. Tokyo: TEC Co.

Kiparsky, P. (1973b). Elsewhere in Phonology. In S. Anderson and P. Kiparsky, eds., *A Festschrift for Morris Halle*. New York: Holt, Rinehart & Winston.

Kiparsky, P. (1979a). Metrical Structure Assignment is Cyclic. *Linguistic Inquiry* 10, 421–442.

Kiparsky, P. (1979b). On Analogy. Unpublished paper, MIT.

Kiparsky, P., and W. O'Neil (1976). The Phonology of Old English Inflections. *Linguistic Inquiry* 7, 527–557.

Klima, E. (1964). Negation in English. In J. Fodor and J. Katz, eds., *The Structure of Language: Readings in the Philosophy of Language*. Englewood Cliffs, N.J.: Prentice-Hall.

Knobe, B., and K. Knobe (1977). A Method for Inferring Context-free Grammars. *Information and Control* 31, 129–146.

Kohrt, M. (1975). A Note on Bounding. *Linguistic Inquiry* 6, 161–171.

Koster, J. (1975). Dutch as an SOV Language. *Linguistic Analysis* 1, 111–136.

Koster, J. (1978a). Conditions, Empty Nodes, and Markedness. *Linguistic Inquiry* 9, 551–593.

Koster, J. (1978b). *Locality Principles in Syntax*. Dordrecht: Foris.

Kuno, S. (1973). Constraints on Internal Clauses. *Linguistic Inquiry* 4, 363–386.

Langendoen, D. T. (1970). The "Can't Seem To" Construction. *Linguistic Inquiry* 1, 25–35.

Lamb, S. (1966). Prolegomena to a Theory of Phonology. *Language* 42, 536–573.

Lapointe, S. (1980a). A Lexical Analysis of the English Auxiliary Verb System. In Hoekstra, Hulst, and Moortgat.

Lapointe, S. (1980b). The Nonnecessity and Acquisition of the Category AUX. Paper presented at the Fourth Groningen Round Table, July 1980.

Lasnik, H. (1981). Restricting the Theory of Transformations: A Case Study. In Hornstein and Lightfoot.

Lasnik, H., and J. Kupin (1977). A Restrictive Theory of Transformational Grammar. *Theoretical Linguistics* 4, 173–196.

Lass, R., and J. M. Anderson (1975). *Old English Phonology*. Cambridge, England: Cambridge University Press.

Levelt, W. J. M. (1974). *Formal Grammars in Linguistics and Psycholinguistics*. The Hague: Mouton.

Liberman, M., and A. Prince (1977). On Stress and Linguistic Rhythm. *Linguistic Inquiry* 8, 249–336.

Lieber, R. (1979). The English Passive: An Argument for Historical Rule Stability. *Linguistic Inquiry* 10, 667–688.

Lieber, R. (1980). *On the Organization of the Lexicon*. Doctoral dissertation, MIT, Cambridge, Mass.

Lightfoot, D. (1977). Syntactic Change and the Autonomy Thesis. *Journal of Linguistics* 13, 191–216.

Lightfoot, D. (1979a). Rule Classes and Syntactic Change. *Linguistic Inquiry* 10, 83–106.

Lightfoot, D. (1979b). *Principles of Diachronic Syntax*. Cambridge, England: Cambridge University Press.

Lightfoot, D. (1981). Explaining Syntactic Change. In Hornstein and Lightfoot.

Lowenstamm, J. (1978). Remarks on Syllable Structure. *University of Massachusetts Occasional Papers in Linguistics*, University of Massachusetts, Amherst.

MacNamara, J. (forthcoming). *Names for Things: A Study of Human Learning*. Cambridge, Mass.: Harvard University Press.

Maling, J. (1978). An Asymmetry with Respect to *Wh*-islands. *Linguistic Inquiry* 9, 75–89.

Marantz, A. (1979). Assessing the X-bar Convention. Unpublished paper, MIT.

Maratsos, M., and M. Chalkey (forthcoming). The Internal Language of Children's Syntax: The Ontogenesis and Representation of Syntactic Categories. In K. Nelson, ed., *Children's Language* II. New York: Gardner Press.

Matthei, E. (1978). On the Acquisition of Reciprocal Expressions. In H. Goodluck and L. Solan, eds., *Papers in the Structure and Development of Child Language*. University of Massachusetts, Amherst.

McCarthy, J. (1979a). *Formal Problems in Semitic Phonology and Morphology*. Doctoral dissertation, MIT, Cambridge, Mass.

McCarthy, J. (1979b). On Stress and Syllabification. *Linguistic Inquiry* 10, 443–466.

McCarthy, J. (1980). A Note on the Accentuation of Damascene Arabic. *Studies in the Linguistic Sciences* 10, 77–98.

McCarthy, J. (forthcoming). Expletive Infixation and Prosodic Structure.

McCawley, J. (1971). Tense and Time Reference in English. In C. Fillmore and D. T. Langendoen, eds., *Studies in Linguistic Semantics*, New York: Holt, Rinehart & Winston.

Morin, Y.-C., and J. Kaye (to appear). The Syntactic Bases of French Liaison. *Journal of Linguistics*.

Newport, E., H. Gleitman, and L. Gleitman (1977). Mother, I'd Rather Do it Myself: Some Effects and Non-effects of Maternal Speech Style. In C. Snow and C. Ferguson, eds., *Talking to Children: Language Input and Acquisition*. Cambridge, England: Cambridge University Press.

Nida, E. (1949). *Morphology: The Descriptive Analysis of Words*. Ann Arbor: University of Michigan Press.

Oehrle, R., and Ross, J. R. (n.d.). Brevity is the Soul of Everything. Unpublished paper, MIT.

Osherson, D., and T. Wasow (1976). Task-specificity and Species-specificity in the Study of Language: A Methodological Note. *Cognition* 4, 203–214.

Otsu, Y. (forthcoming). *The Subjacency Condition and Syntactic Development in Children*. Doctoral dissertation, MIT.

Peters, P. S. (1972). The Projection Problem: How is a Grammar to be Selected? In P. S. Peters, ed.

Peters, P. S., ed. (1972). *Goals of Linguistic Theory*. Englewood Cliffs, N.J.: Prentice-Hall.

Peters, P. S., and R. Ritchie (1971). On Restricting the Base Component of Transformational Grammars. *Information and Control* 18, 483–501.

Peters, P. S., and R. Ritchie (1973). On the Generative Power of Transformational Grammars. *Information Sciences* 6, 49–83.

Phelps, E. (1979). Abstractness and Rule Ordering in Kasem: A Refutation of Halle's Maximizing Principle. *Linguistic Analysis* 5, 29–71.

Phinney, M. (1979). Acquisition and the *NP to VP Filter. Paper presented at the Winter Meeting, Linguistic Society of America, Los Angeles.

Phinney, M. (in preparation). *On the Acquisition of Filters and Related Topics*. Doctoral dissertation, University of Massachusetts, Amherst.

Pinker, S. (1978). Mind and Brain Revisited: Forestalling the Doom of Cognitivism. *The Behavioral and Brain Sciences* 2, 244–245.

Pinker, S. (1979). Formal Models of Language Learning. *Cognition* 7, 217–283.

Pinker, S. (1981). A Theory of the Acquisition of Lexical-interpretive Grammars. In J. Bresnan, ed., *The Mental Representation of Grammatical Relations*. Cambridge, Mass.: The MIT Press.

Postal, P. (1968). *Aspects of Phonological Theory*. New York: Harper & Row.

Pullum, G., and D. Wilson (1977). Autonomous Syntax and the Analysis of Auxiliaries. *Language* 53, 741–788.

Putnam, H. (1961). Some Issues in the Theory of Grammar. In R. Jakobson, ed., *The Structure of Language and its Mathematical Aspect*. Providence, R.I.: American Mathematical Society.

Quine, W. V. O. (1972). Methodological Reflections on Current Linguistic Theory. In D. Davidson and G. Harman, eds., *Semantics of Natural Language*. Dordrecht: Reidel.

Randall, J. (1979). Productivity in the Acquisition of Causatives. Paper read at the October 1979 meeting of the New England Child Language Association, Amherst, Mass.

Ransom, E. (n.d.). A Constraint on the Advancement and Demotion of Noun Phrases. Unpublished paper.

Reinhart, T. (1976). *The Syntactic Domain of Anaphora*. Doctoral dissertation, MIT, Cambridge, Mass.

van Riemsdijk, H. (1978). *A Case Study in Syntactic Markedness*. Dordrecht: Foris.

van Riemsdijk, H. (1980). Marking Conventions for Syntax. In Belletti et al.

Rizzi, L. (1977). Violations of the WH Island Condition in Italian. (To appear in *Italian Linguistics*.)

Rizzi, L. (1978). A Rule of Restructuring in Italian Syntax. In S. J. Keyser, ed., *Recent Transformational Studies in European Languages*. Cambridge, Mass.: The MIT Press.

Roeper, T. (1981). On the Importance of Syntax and the Logical Use of Evidence. In S. Kuczaj, ed., *Language Development*. Washington: Erlbaum.

Roeper, T., J. Bing, S. Lapointe, and S. Tavakolian (to appear). A Lexical Approach to Language Acquisition. In S. Tavakolian, ed., *Language Acquisition and Linguistic Theory*, Cambridge, Mass.: The MIT Press.

Roeper, T., and M. E. A. Siegel (1978). A Lexical Transformation for Verbal Compounds. *Linguistic Inquiry* 9, 199–260.

Roeper, T., B. Stack, and G. Carlson (1979). The Acquisition of Stress and the Role of Homogeneous Rules. In F. Eckman and A. Hastings, eds., *Studies in First and Second Language Acquisition*. Rowley, Mass.: Newbury.

Rogers, H. (1965). *Theory of Recursive Functions and Effective Computability*. New York: McGraw-Hill.

Ross, J. R. (1967). *Constraints on Variables in Syntax*. Doctoral dissertation, MIT, Cambridge, Mass.

Ross, J. R. (1969). Auxiliaries as Main Verbs. In W. Todd, ed., *Studies in Philosophical Linguistics* 1, Evanston, Ill.: Great Expectations Press.

Ross, J. R. (n.d.). What's in a Name? A Rose by any other Name would Smell as Sweet. Unpublished paper, MIT.

Rouveret, A., and J.-R. Vergnaud (1980). Specifying Reference to the Subject: French Causatives and Conditions on Representations. *Linguistic Inquiry* 11, 97–202.

Sag, I. A. (1976). *Deletion and Logical Form*. Doctoral dissertation, MIT, Cambridge, Mass.

Saporta, S. (1965). Ordered Rules, Dialect Differences, and Historical Processes. *Language* 41, 218–224.

Schane, S. (1974). How Abstract is Abstract? In A. Bruck, R. A. Fox, and M. W. Lagaly, eds., *Papers from the Parasession on Natural Phonology*. Chicago Linguistics Society, Chicago.

Schwartz, A. (1973). The VP-constituent of SVO Languages. In J. Kimball, ed., *Syntax and Semantics* 1. New York: Academic Press.

Schwartz, A. (1975). Verb-anchoring and Verb-movement. In C. Li, ed., *Word Order and Word Order Change*. Austin: University of Texas Press.

Skousen, R. (1975). *Substantive Evidence in Phonology*. The Hague: Mouton.

Smith, C. (1979). The Acquisition of Complex Sentences: Evidence from Temporal Reference. Paper read at the October 1979 meeting of the New England Child Language Association, Amherst, Mass.

Smith, C. (1980). States and Dynamics. Unpublished paper, University of Texas, Austin.

Sommerstein, A. H. (1977). *Modern Phonology*. Baltimore: University Park Press.

Stampe, D. (1972). *How I Spent My Summer Vacation*. Doctoral dissertation, University of Chicago, Chicago.

Steele, S., A. Akmajian, R. Demers, E. Jelinek, C. Kitagawa, R. Oehrle, and T. Wasow (forthcoming). *An Encyclopedia of AUX: A Study in Cross-linguistic Evidence*. Cambridge, Mass.: The MIT Press.

Strunk, W., and White, E. B. (1972). *The Elements of Style,* 2nd ed. New York: Macmillan.

Tavakolian, S. (1978). The Conjoined Clause Analysis of Relative Clauses and other Structures. In H. Goodluck and L. Solan, eds., *Papers in the Structure and Development of Child Language.* University of Massachusetts, Amherst.

Thiersch, C. (1978). *Topics in German Syntax.* Doctoral dissertation, MIT, Cambridge, Mass.

Traugott, E. (1972). *The History of English Syntax.* New York: Holt, Rinehart & Winston.

Vat, J. (1978). On Footnote 2: Evidence for the Pronominal Status of *þær* in Old English. *Linguistic Inquiry* 9, 695–715.

Vergnaud, J.-R., and T. Roeper (forthcoming). On Complex Verbs in English.

Visser, F. Th. (1963–1973). *An Historical Syntax of the English Language,* 3 vols. Leiden: Brill.

Wagner, K. H. (1969). *Generative Grammatical Studies in the Old English Language.* Heidelberg: Julius Groos.

Wasow, T. (1977). Transformations and the Lexicon. In Culicover, Wasow, and Akmajian.

Wasow, T. (1978a). On Constraining the Class of Transformational Languages. *Synthese* 39, 81–104.

Wasow, T. (1978b). Remarks on Processing, Constraints and the Lexicon. In D. Waltz, ed., *Theoretical Issues in Natural Language Processing* 2. Department of Computer Science, University of Illinois, Urbana.

Wasow, T. (1980). Some Remarks on the ASW-GPS Controversy. Comments prepared for the Fourth Groningen Round Table, July 1980.

Weinberg, A. (1980). Evidence From Grammar and Processing: A Critical Discussion of Aspects of the Lexical-interpretive Theory. Paper presented at the GLOW meeting, Nijmegen.

Weinberg, A., and N. Hornstein (1981). Case Theory and Preposition Stranding. *Linguistic Inquiry* 12, 55–92.

Weiner, E., and Labov, W. (n.d.). Constraints on the Agentless Passive. Unpublished paper, University of Pennsylvania.

Wexler, K. (1980). Learnability Constraints. In U. Bellugi and M. Studdert-Kennedy, eds., *Signed and Spoken Language: Biological Constraints on Linguistic Form.* Weinheim, Germany; Deerfield Beach, Florida; and Basel: Verlag Chemie.

Wexler, K., and P. Culicover (1974). The Semantic Basis for Language Acquisition. *Social Sciences Working Paper* 50, University of California at Irvine.

Wexler, K., and P. Culicover (1980). *Formal Principles of Language Acquisition.* Cambridge, Mass.: The MIT Press.

Wexler, K., and H. Hamburger (1973). On the Insufficiency of Surface Data for the Learning of Transformational Languages. In K. J. J. Hintikka, J. Moravcsik, and P. Suppes, eds., *Approaches to Natural Language,* Dordrecht: Reidel.

Wharton, R. (1977). Grammar Enumeration and Inference. *Information and Control* 33, 253–272.

Williams, E. (1977). Discourse and Logical Form. *Linguistic Inquiry* 8, 101–140.

Williams, E. (1980a). Predication. *Linguistic Inquiry* 11, 203–238.

Williams, E. (1980b). Abstract Triggers. *Journal of Linguistic Research* 1, 71–82.

Williams, E. (forthcoming a). X-bar and the Analysis of Categories. In S. Tavakolian, ed., *Language Acquisition and Linguistic Theory.* Cambridge, Mass.: The MIT Press.

Williams, E. (forthcoming b). Pseudoclefts.

Williams, G. (1972). *Networks of Coreference.* Doctoral dissertation, MIT, Cambridge, Mass.

Zwicky, A. (1971). In a Manner of Speaking. *Linguistic Inquiry* 2, 223–232.

Index